GOOD FOOD ON A BUDGET

GOOD FOOD ON A BUDGET

GEORGINA HORLEY

Drawings by Tony Odell

ANDRE DEUTSCH

First published by Penguin Books Ltd, 1969
This edition published 1970 reprinted 1971 by
André Deutsch Limited
105 Great Russell Street, London WC1
Copyright © 1969 by Georgina Horley

233 96164 x

PRINTED AND BOUND IN ENGLAND BY
HAZELL WATSON AND VINEY LTD
AYLESBURY, BUCKS

Four people have taught me most of what I know about cooking and to them this book is dedicated:

MY MOTHER

MURIEL DOWNES

ROSEMARY HUME

AND

X. M. BOULESTIN

CONTENTS

'How inestimably important in its moral results – and therefore how praiseworthy in itself – is the act of eating and drinking! The social virtues centre in the stomach. A man who is not a better husband, father and brother, after dinner than before is, digestively speaking, an incurably vicious man. What hidden charms of character disclose themselves, what dormant amiabilities awaken when our common humanity gathers together to pour out the gastric juices! ... And there are men in this world who, seeing virtues such as these developed at the Table, as they are developed nowhere else, can, nevertheless, rank the glorious privilege of dining, with the smallest diurnal personal worries which necessity imposes on mankind – with buttoning your waistcoat, for example, or lacing your stays! Trust no such monster as this with your tender secrets, your loves and hatreds, your hopes and fears. His heart is uncorrected by his stomach, and the social virtues are not in him.'

WILKIE COLLINS, *Armadale*, 1866. (Portway reprint from Smith Elder's Ed., 1877)

INTRODUCTION

Coyness veils a need to balance the household budget in the affluent Britain of our day. While advice on sex may now be bought as easily as the groceries in the supermarket, advice on cutting costs in the home is rather harder to come by. The object of this book is to help even the score.

Economy recipes run the risk of ending up like war-ration cooking instructions – explaining how to make lemon meringue pie without actually using lemons or meringue – culinary triumphs of ingenuity in place of ingredients. But there is no need for a well-balanced kitchen budget to be synonymous with an ill-balanced, cheeseparing diet. Because they made just this point, two books that tackled the problem for housekeepers in the first quarter of this century were best-sellers in their day. They were the inspiration for the present book. Since Mrs C. S. Peel, in 1899, and Marcel Boulestin, in 1925, published their books domestic life has undergone a revolution. Conditions for both these writers, despite the world war between their dates of publication, were not so very different, as the following passages show. They also show the need for a fresh approach although, amid the smiles I hope they will provoke, there may be a nod or two in agreement.

First Mrs Peel, introducing *Ten Shillings A Head Per Week for Housebooks* :

It may now be asked, what is a fair housekeeping allowance? Roughly speaking, for a family of six or more persons, an average of £1 per head a week allows of luxurious living; 15s. per head for good living; 10s. for nice catering of a simple description; and 8s. 6d. per head for a sufficiency of wholesome food.

In the year 1898 I wrote a series of articles for *Hearth and* on the subject of catering at 10s. a week, which called forth siderable correspondence. . . . Some writers declared that to manner suggested was impossible under an expenditure of Others held that it could be done on 10s. a week, or ev ladies were good enough to send me a week's menus a ing week's bills; and one or two earnest housekee year's household accounts for inspection. . . . I remained firm in the opinion, formed from personal experience, that it is possible to provide menus . . . for an average cost of 10s. a week per head. . . . If the cook is incorrigibly careless and wasteful; if the mistress is ignorant; if the master is exacting, not to say greedy; if a freshly-cooked joint is expected each day; if the family contains delicate children or invalids; if meat or other provisions cannot be procured at reasonable prices – then it will be impossible to carry out the menus on an average of less than 11s. or 12s. per head a week.

In London or other large towns the mistress should make test purchases at the surrounding shops, and obtain price-lists from the various butchers and fishmongers. These should be compared and the tradesmen selected. A few weeks later the prices charged in the weekly books should be compared with those given in the price list, as it is not uncommon to find that ½d. a lb. is added here and there as soon as the tradesman considers he is secure of patronage.

Then Boulestin, writing in *The Conduct of the Kitchen*:

It is a great mistake to believe that it is indispensable to spend lots of money if you want to live well . . .

By spending 'lots of money' I mean spending something like thirty shillings a head a week. Yet I understand from many people that they spend quite that and sometimes even more, though they have many meals out, and, when they are in, their fare is of the plainest – which must be due to bad ordering, careless management, indifference, and ⸻fore waste.

⸻⸻ easily reduce your bills to sixteen shillings a week. ⸻ an example out of some ideal home, but a fact, ⸻ averaging my own weekly bills for six ⸻ shillings a week a head, in a ⸻le, and this figure includes ⸻ party) and no meals out. ⸻ does not include a real ⸻ of tea, toast and jam ⸻e other hand, all the ⸻ is ever allowed in, the ⸻tton Welsh. Needless to ⸻ *gras* or caviare and things ⸻nu, representative of what ⸻, simple, varied, economical

To price ingredients nowadays, as turn-of-the-century editions of Mrs Beeton did, or to give exact budgets like those quoted, would make this book out of date before it was printed. However, in addition to using less expensive ingredients, this book aims, as do the other two, to help you avoid waste. Emphasis is also placed on saving fuel and time.

If you have a limited income, but want to eat well, you must face the fact that, for the most part, time has to replace money. Cheap meals are rarely quickly prepared meals, while economical cooking yields weekly, rather than daily variations in the main ingredients – the more so where time also is to be saved – though few complain of a second chance in a week to eat a tasty dish.

The plan of the book is based on the seasons. It is true that deep and dry freezing provide many foods out of season, but these are seldom bargain buys. Foods in their seasons are still usually at their cheapest, and always at their best. The first section consists of calendars showing month-by-month home-produced and some imported foods as they come into the shops and kitchen-garden.

Consulting the calendars before planning menus will help you to get ideas for dishes and to shop speedily. By planning a week's menus at a time you save both time and money, since you can shop for and cook some dishes to cover several days. (Storing raw and cooked foods has its special section on pp. 39–42.)

I have tried to keep in mind the variation of raw materials available to different households. While many town greengrocers, for instance, keep garlic, pimentos and avocados, unobtainable in a village, the country-dweller often has sportsmen in the family who bring home brown trout, game, shellfish – impossible luxuries for budget cooks in town.

Your table will gain immeasurably if you are able to grow anything at all, from a few pots of herbs on a town windowsill, to the full round of crops in kitchen-garden or allotment (ask your Town Hall about the latter). Vegetables and fruit, often among high-priced items, are nutritionally vital as well as being gastronomic stars. For this reason the chapter 'Growing Your Own' has been included.

Economy in food does not involve living meanly, and whilst the recipes are intended for day-to-day meals, many would do you credit at dinner parties, when grander ways to serve them are suggested and there are hints on garnishing, dishing and finishing dishes, in particular for cold food.

Although basic methods and foundation recipes are given, this book was not written chiefly for beginners. Particularly if you are a novice cook, study these preliminaries. Choose simple dishes at first, plan menus to avoid more than one hot course, and more than one sauce per course (a useful mnemonic!). By trying out a few new recipes each month you will soon acquire skill and a sound repertoire.

NOTE: Quantities are for four unless otherwise stated, but most of the dishes are suitable for two- or single-person households, provided the quantities are halved or quartered. Because mistakes are easily made when one is in the middle of preparations, I do urge the *writing out* of revised amounts, since faulty proportions can spoil the whole dish, wasting both the food and your labour.

ACKNOWLEDGEMENTS

Everything in the modern world changes quickly, the craft of cookery not excepted. To produce a useful general cookery book would be impossible without help and advice on many matters. To take only a single instance: when I trained, puréeing was still most commonly done by wooden spoon and sieve; today's cook has almost arrived at laughing at such antique implements as she sets up her electric blender. But even the blender changes from year to year. Thanks to many firms, or their expert public relations officers, I have been able to inspect, have demonstrated and often used the latest equipment and raw materials – for the latter also is subject to change – and have had my many questions patiently answered. But I must emphasize that no manufacturer or public relations officer approached me at any time. I applied to them, and always with the warning that they could expect nothing in return! My thanks and appreciation to all the following:

Atlas Lighting (British Light Industries Ltd); Messrs Clarbat Ltd; Corfield Sigg Ltd; Miss Pauline Viola and Danish Agricultural Producers Information Service; Miss Betty Jakens and The Flour Advisory Bureau, who gave permission for the use of their tables for Christmas cooking and ready-mix recipes (with only very slight modifications of my own); F.M.S. (Farm Products) Ltd and their Chief Chemist, Mr D. A. Boswall; Fowler Ltd; Miss Dilys Wells and the Herring Industry Board; Peter Rendall Associates, and Judge International Ltd; Miss Vivien Jones and Kenwood Ltd; Mrs Isobel Richardson and Midland Metal Spinning Ltd; Andrews Houseware Manufacturers Ltd; New Zealand Lamb Information Bureau; C. J. Lytle Ltd; Mr R. Drewell of William Page Ltd; Miss Joan Peters and The Pig Industry Development Authority; Mr D. W. Ravenhill of T. J. Poupart Ltd; Mr Leonard Moss of The London Meat Traders' Association; Messrs A. C. Wheeler (Fish Section, British Museum of Natural History), R. W. Blacker, B.Sc. (Fisheries Laboratory, Lowestoft), G. R. Watkin (The Fish Inspector, Fishmongers' Company, Billingsgate) and R. D. Portch (J. Portch and Sons Ltd) for help with the Fish Calendar; Mrs Diana Short and Mr P. M. Codd and Van Den Berghs Ltd; Mrs Mary Law of Taylor Law and Co Ltd; Vent-Axia Ltd; Waterford Ironfounders Ltd.

ACKNOWLEDGEMENTS

Thanks of a particularly personal kind to Mr Ronald Kinton, Head of the School and Mr V. J. Regnaud, Lecturer, and Chef in charge of the Larder at Ealing Technical College's Catering School, who arranged a most instructive morning for me on the subject of veal escalopes; to Miss Helen Hornsey for editorial help; and to Timothy Mansfield for research on the subject of game fishing.

GLOSSARY

The list comprises standard culinary terms and usages peculiar to this book not explained in the text.

ARROSER: To sprinkle or moisten; to baste.

BEURRE MANIÉ: A liaison of equal amounts of fat and flour worked together uncooked, to be added to hot food to thicken it.

BLANCH: A preliminary cooking process in which the food is put into cold water and brought to the boil, the boiling being continued for a specified number of minutes. See also SCALD.

CHAMBRER: To bring red wine to room temperature, i.e. around 60°F; a useful term employed by me for food as well as wine.

COCOTTE: That which the English call a casserole. A casserole in France is any kind of saucepan.

CONCASSER: Used chiefly to cover the operation of skinning, pipping and chopping tomatoes. Can also mean chopping or pounding.

DARIOLE MOULD OR TIN: Sometimes called castle-pudding tin, a one-helping mould, tall, narrow, tapering at top.

DEGLAZE: Add liquid to coagulated juices in cooking vessel to make sauce.

EN BRANCHE: Vegetable (usually spinach) cooked with leaves left whole.

FAMILY: Large family – 6 or more persons (mixed ages) in residence. Average family – 4 persons. Small family – 3 persons. Single person household – one person (quantities here usually allow two good helpings).

FARCE: Stuffing, forcemeat.

GLAZE: A thin, transparent or shiny finish applied to food, hot or cold, sweet or savoury, by means of various substances such as jam, aspic, etc.

JULIENNE: Food, usually vegetables, cut in thin strips.

LIAISON: Thickening or binding.

MAÎTRE-D'HÔTEL: Best known in British Isles as butter creamed together with seasoning, parsley and lemon juice, but usually indicates that butter and parsley are involved. e.g. *maître-d'hôtel* potatoes.

MARINADE (TE): To soak article of food in pickle-like sauce, usually spiced mixture of oil with wine or vinegar, to improve taste and texture. The pickle or sauce itself.

MASKING: Coating with sauces or glazes.

MIREPOIX: Mixed vegetables used as bed for meat to be braised, or for flavouring sauce or stew.

PASTE, PÂTÉ: pastry or dough.

POACH: To cook food in liquid that is just below simmering point so that surface merely quivers.

QUENELLES: Small, delicately composed fish or meat dumplings.

RAVIGOTE: A mixture of chopped herbs which may include onion or garlic.

RÉCHAUFFER: To reheat, applied to dishes made from already cooked ingredients.

ROUX (ALSO PANADA): Combination of flour and fat, usually cooked, to thicken liquids.

SCALD: Pour boiling water over food, or put food in cold water, bring just to boil, plunge in cold water.

SEAR (OR SEAL): To scorch surface of food, (usually meat) in order to contain juices.

SIMMER: To cook just at boiling point with few bubbles appearing.

SLAKE: To mix dry substances with liquid.

STOCK, LIGHT: Stock pale in colour, or of a thin or delicate character.

SWEAT: Food simmered in fat until tender but not coloured.

MEASURES AND TEMPERATURES

TEMPERATURE EQUIVALENTS ON THERMOSTATS

General indication	°F (most electric ovens)	Numbers (most gas ovens)
Very low or cool	240–250	¼–½
Low or slow	275–325	1–3
Moderate	350–375	4–5
Hot or Quick	400–425	6–7
Very hot or bread	450–500	8–10

EQUIVALENT MEASURES

English	Metric	U.S.
1 lb.	½ kilo (approx.)	1 lb.
8 oz.	227 grams	8 oz.
4 oz.	113 grams	4 oz.
1 oz.	28 grams	1 oz.
1 tbs.	20 ml.	2 tbs.
1 dessertsp.	10 ml.	1 tbs.
1 teasp.	5 ml.	1 teasp.
1 pint (20 fl. oz.)	6 dl. (approx.)	2½ cups
½ pint (10 fl. oz.)	3 dl. (approx.)	1¼ cups
¼ pint or 1 gill (5 fl. oz.)	1.5 dl. (approx)	⅓ (scant) cup

FOOD CALENDARS

These four calendars indicate, by symbols, when the principal raw materials of cookery are available in the best condition and/or at the cheapest prices. The blank indicating 'off season' is used also to indicate when some foods are so poor in condition or expensive that they are not worth buying even if in the shops. A few foods are always dear unless you grow them yourself or live near the source of supply; others are not marketed. This is why such items as sea-trout and wortleberries feature in the lists and recipes. Other points are made in notes on the charts themselves.

Make allowances for a variation of a week or so in the indicated seasons, for climate and other irregularities.

	January	February	March	April	May	June
	The price of home-killed meats depends upon quantity. A glut of, say, Argentine beef, could bring home-killed prices to below that of pork at certain times of the year. Weather, also, affects prices of, for example, stewing meat, which is usually cheapest in summer. This particular calendar, therefore, indicates quality for money spent rather than straightforward cheapness.					
BEEF English	Available throughout the year. Scarcer and dearer in early months of Spring. Stewing cuts cheapest, grills dearest in Summer. Plentiful and top quality in Winter. (Scotch variations indicated below.)					
Scotch	◆	◆	◆	◆	○ ○ ○ ○	○ ○ ○ ○
LAMB English and Welsh				◆	◆ ◆	◆ ◆
Scotch					◆	◆ ○
New Zealand	◆	◆	●	●	●	●
New Zealand grading	Clear grading aids purchaser. Most good butchers leave labels on. Best are Down lambs: green label marked D or 2; next, Primes blue label D or 2; then Primes blue label 8, 4, T in that order; then F.A.Q. (fair average quality) red label YL, YM, YH. N.Z. lamb carcases stamped 'New Zealand *Lamb*'. Available all year, top quality begin arriving early months of year when home-killed out of season, which raises N.Z. prices above year's steady average.					
MUTTON	Available, usually to order, all year. Not necessarily tough, often of excellent flavour, esp. Welsh. Whole joints weigh 5 lb. upwards. New Zealand carefully graded into: 1. Hoggets, 2. Wethers, 3. Ewes.					
PORK and BACON	Supplies all year. Pies, sausages, etc. reflect price changes. Untrue pork should not be eaten in summer.					
VEAL	English veal not reliable. Farmers slaughter only to weed out unwanted calves. Few now rearing veal calves, but as expensive as Dutch – the best. Buy only from butcher you trust, or specialist (see pp. 78–80).					
GAME	→					

20

MEAT

	July	August	September	October	November	December
BEEF English						
Scotch	O	O	◆	●	●	◆
LAMB English and Welsh	O	●	O	●	●	●
Scotch	O	●	●	●	O	O
New Zealand	O	O	O	O	O	O
New Zealand grading						
MUTTON						
PORK and BACON						
VEAL						
GAME						

BEEF — English: Available throughout the year. Scarcer and dearer in early months of spring. Stewing cuts cheapest; grills dearest in summer. Plentiful and top quality in autumn and winter. (Scotch variations indicated below.) Dearest at Christmas.

New Zealand grading: Clear grading aids purchaser. Most good butchers leave labels on. Best are Down lambs: green label marked D or 2; next, Primes blue label D or 2; then Primes blue label 8, 4, T in that order; then F.A.Q. (fair average quality) red label YL, YM, YH. N.Z. lamb carcases stamped 'New Zealand *Lamb*'. Available all year, top quality of year when home-killed out of season, which raises N.Z. prices above year's steady average. Blank in the case of lamb indicates lamb is at its least good, although excellent treated as mutton.

MUTTON: Available, usually to order, all year. Not necessarily tough, often of excellent flavour, esp. Welsh. Whole joints weigh 5 lb. upwards. N.Z. carefully graded into: 1. Hoggets, 2. Wethers, 3. Ewes.

PORK and BACON: Supplies all year, prices fluctuate with quantity, including pies, sausages etc. Untrue that pork should not be eaten in summer. Dearest (and special qualities) at Christmas.

VEAL: English veal not reliable. Farmers slaughter only to weed out unwanted calves. Few now rearing veal calves, but as expensive as Dutch – the best. Buy only from butcher you trust, or specialist in veal (and see pp. 78–80.)

GAME: Plentiful from now on but dearer until November ——>

O *average season.* ● *best season and sometimes cheap.* ★ *cheapest and sometimes best.* ◆ *dear.* Blank indicates *off season.*

FISH

FISH	January	February	March	April	May	June
FRESH						
Bream	○ ○	○ ○ ○			○ ○ ○ ○	○ ○ ○ ○
Brill	○ ○ ○	○ ○ ○ ○	● ● ● ●	○ ○ ○ ○	◆ ◆ ◆ ◆	○ ○ ○ ○
Cod	● ● ● ●	○ ○ ○ ○	◆ ◆ ◆ ◆	◆ ◆ ● ●	★ ★ ★ ★	★ ★ ★ ★
Dabs	◆ ◆ ◆ ◆	◆ ◆ ◆ ◆	○ ○ ○ ○	◆ ◆ ○ ○	● ● ● ●	◆ ◆ ◆ ◆
Eels	◆ ◆ ◆ ◆	◆ ◆ ◆ ◆	○ ○ ○ ○	○ ○ ○ ●	● ● ● ●	● ● ● ●
Eels (Conger)	● ● ● ●	● ● ● ●	○ ○ ○ ○	●	○ ○ ○	● ● ● ●
Gurnard			◆ ◆ ◆ ◆	○ ○ ○	○ ○ ○ ○	○ ○ ○ ○
Haddock			○ ○ ○ ○	◆ ◆ ◆	◆ ◆ ◆ ◆	◆ ◆ ◆ ◆
Hake				○ ○ ○	○ ○ ○	◆ ◆ ◆ ◆
Halibut						○
Herring	See note at end of calendar*					
Lemon Sole	● ● ● ●	● ● ● ●	● ● ● ●	◆ ◆ ◆ ◆	○ ○ ○ ○	○ ○ ○ ○
Mackerel	● ● ● ●	● ● ● ●	● ● ● ●	○ ○ ○	○ ○ ○ ○	◆ ◆ ● ●
Mullet (Grey)	○ ○ ○	○ ○ ○ ○	○ ○ ○ ○	◆ ◆ ◆	● ● ● ●	● ● ● ●
Mullet (Red)	←——— Some frozen fish sometimes ———→					
Plaice	○ ○ ○ ○	○ ○ ○	○ ○ ○ ○	◆ ◆ ◆	○ ○ ○ ○	● ● ● ●
Saithe (Coley)	◆ ◆ ◆	◆ ◆ ◆ ◆	○ ○ ○ ○	○ ○ ○	★ ★ ★ ◆	★ ★ ★ ○
Salmon	Irish – very dear				● ● ● ●	● ● ● ●

22

FISH

FRESH	July	August	September	October	November	December
Bream	● ● ● ●	★ ★ ★ ★	★ ★ ★ ★	★	O O O O	O O O O
Brill	O O O O	O O O O	O O O O	O O O O	O O O O	O O O O
Cod	O O O O	O O O O	O O O O	O O O O	★ ★ ★ ★	● ● ★ ★
Dabs	★ ★ ★ ★	★ ★ ★ ★	O O O O	O O O O	O O ● ●	◆ ◆ ◆ ◆
Eels	O O O O	O O O O	O O O O	O O ● ●	O ○ ● ●	◆ ◆ ◆ ◆
Eels (Conger)	● ● ● ●	● ● ● ●	● ● ● ●	● ● ● ●	◆ ◆ ● ●	◆ ◆ ◆ ◆
Gurnard	O O O O	O O O O	O O O O	O O O O	● ● ● ●	● ● ● ●
Haddock	O ◆ O O	O O O O	● ● ● ●	● ● ● ●	● ● ● ●	★ ★ ★ ★
Hake	O O O O	O O O O	O O O O	O O O O	★ ★ ★ ★	● ● ● ●
Halibut	O O O O	O O O O	● ● ● ●	O O O O	O O O O	O O O O
Herring	See note at end of calendar*					
Lemon Sole	O O O O	O O O O	O O O O	O O O O	O O O O	● ● ● ●
Mackerel	◆ ◆ ◆ ◆	O O O O	O O O O	O O ● ●	● ● ● ●	● ● ● ●
Mullet (Grey)	O O O O	O O ● ●	● ● ● ●	● ● ● ●	● ● ● ●	● ● ● ●
Mullet (Red)	O O O O	O O O O	O O O O	O O ★ ★	★ ★ ★ ★	★ ★ ★ ★
Plaice	O O O O	O O O O	O O O O	O O O O	O O O O	● ● ● ●
Saithe (Coley)	★ ★ ★ ★	★ ★ ★ ★	O O O O	O O O ★	O O ★ ★	● ● ● ★
Salmon	● ● ● ●	● ● ● ●	● ● ● ●	● ● ● ●	● ● ● ●	● ● ● ●

O average season. ● best season and sometimes cheap. ★ cheapest and sometimes best. ◆ dear. Blank indicates off season.

23

FISH

	January	February	March	April	May	June
Skate (Raie)	● ● ● ●	○ ○ ○	◆ ◆ ◆ ◆	◆ ◆ ◆ ◆	○ ○ ○ ○	○ ○ ○ ○
Smelt	● ● ●	● ● ●	○ ○ ○ ○	○ ○ ○		◆
Sole (Dover)	★ ○	◆ ○ ○	◆ ◆ ◆ ◆	◆ ◆ ◆	◆ ◆	◆ ◆
Sprats	● ●	● ● ●	○ ○	○		
Trout (River)		———— All the year. ————				
Trout (Sea)				◆ ◆ ◆ ◆	○ ◆ ◆ ●	● ◆ ● ○
Turbot	● ● ●	○ ○ ○	● ● ● ●	○ ● ● ●	● ● ● ●	● ◆ ● ●
Whitebait	○ ○ ○	○ ○ ○	● ● ● ○	○ ○ ○ ○	● ● ● ●	● ◆ ● ●
Whiting	★ ★ ★ ★	★ ★ ★	○ ○ ○	○ ○ ○ ○	○ ○ ○ ○	● ● ● ●
Witch Sole	● ● ● ●	● ● ●	○ ○ ○ ○	○ ○ ○ ○	○ ○ ○ ○	○ ○ ○ ○

SHELLFISH

Cockles — Sold salted or pickled all year. Some localities specialize, when they may be had fresh, mostly in summer.

Crab — Obtainable all year, best and often cheapest in Summer.

Crawfish — Obtainable rest of year. Most plentiful late summer. Prices vary with locality and supplies.

Lobster — Obtainable all year. Best and most plentiful throughout summer, but never cheap.

Mussels — ○ ○ ○ ○ ● ● ●

Prawns — Obtainable all year. English seasonable through summer, but mostly only in local shops. ● ● ●

FISH

	July	August	September	October	November	December
Skate	○	○	○	○	●	●
Smelt	○	○	○	○	●	●
Sole (Dover)	○	○	○	○	★	★
Sprats		○	○	○	★	★
Trout (River)			○	○	●	●
Trout (Sea)				── All the year. ──→		
Turbot	●	●	○	○	●	●
Whitebait	◆	◆	○	○	○	○
Whiting	○	○	○	○	★	★
Witch Sole	○	○	○	○	●	●

25

SHELLFISH

Cockles — Sold salted or pickled all year. Some localities specialize, when they may be had fresh, mostly in summer.

Crab — Obtainable all year, best and often cheapest in Summer.

Crawfish — Most plentiful late summer to end of year. Prices vary with locality and supplies. ──→

Lobster — Obtainable all year. Best and most plentiful throughout summer, but never cheap.

Mussels — ● ● ● ● ○ ○ ○

Prawns — Obtainable all year. English seasonable through summer, but mostly only in local shops.

○ *average season.* ● *best season and sometimes cheap.* ★ *cheapest and sometimes best.* ◆ *dear.* Blank indicates *off season.*

FISH	January	February	March	April	May	June
Scallops	o o o o	o o o o	o o o o	o	—— if in shops probably frozen ——>	
Shrimps	As prawns, except that English shrimps are obtainable in shops all over the country.					
Whelks	<—— In season from spring to early autumn ——>					
Winkles	o o o o	o o o o	o o o o o	o o o o o	o	

SMOKED FISH	January	February	March	April	May	June
	Obtainable all year, but sometimes particularly good – or rather poor – as indicated.					
Bloaters						● ● ●
Buckling			<—————— Less good ———————			
Haddock						
Kippers						● ●
Sprats	● ● ●	● ● ●				

FISH

FISH	July	August	September	October	November	December
Scallops	—If in shops probably frozen→		◆	◆ ◆ ◆	◆ ○ ○ ○	○ ○ ○ ○
Shrimps	As prawns, except that English shrimps are obtainable in shops all over the country.					
Whelks	—In season from spring to early autumn→					
Winkles			○ ○ ○ ○	○ ○ ○ ○	○ ○ ○ ○	○ ○ ○

SMOKED FISH

Obtainable all year, but sometimes particularly good – or rather poor – as indicated.

	July	August	September	October	November	December
Bloaters	● ●	● ●	● ●			
Buckling						
Haddock						
Kippers	● ●	● ●	● ●			
Sprats			Best but rarely on ←sale→	○ ○ ○ ○	● ● ● ●	● ● ● ●

*Herring Are available all the year, frozen fish being almost as good as the best fresh; much better than small fish of late winter, early spring catches. Some connoisseurs consider early spring Loch Fyne herring the best. Not easily found. Soft Roes. Now very difficult to find fresh. Ludicrously expensive. Roes from bloaters better than most frozen roes, which are often badly broken and almost liquid; frequently tasteless.

○ average season. ● best season and sometimes cheap. ★ cheapest and sometimes best. ◆ dear. Blank indicates off season.

VEGETABLES

	January	February	March	April	May	June
Artichoke (Globe)					◆	○ ○ ○
Artichoke (Jerusalem)	○ ○ ○ ○	○ ○ ○ ○	○ ○ ○			
Asparagus					◆ ◆ ◆	○ ○ ○
Beans (Broad)					◆ ◆	◆ ◆ ◆
Beans (French)					◆ ◆ ◆	○ ○ ○
Beetroot	All the year, but sometimes in Spring, small young beets obtainable which are delicious served hot.					
Broccoli (cauliflower type)	● ● ● ●	● ●	○ ○ ○	○ ○ ○ ○	○ ○ ○	
Broccoli (White and Purple Sprouting, mostly in gardens and Scotland)	●	● ●	● ●	○ ○ ○		
Brussels Sprouts	● ●	● ●	◆			
Cabbage	Available all year in many varieties which include savoys, salad cabbages (especially in winter), summer cabbage, spring greens.					
Carrots	⟵ Scarce, poor ⟶		All the year. Homegrown new carrots delicious, but expensive if bought in Spring. ⟶			
Cauliflower	⟵ All the year. Homegrown best from July to November. ⟶					
Celery	○ ○ ○	◆ ⟵ Scarce, poor	○ ○ ○	○ ○ ○	● ● ●	✳ ✳ ✳ ✳
Cucumber	◆	◆	○ ○	○ ○	✳ ✳	✳ ✳ ✳
Endive (Belgian)	○ ○ ○	○ ○	○	○ ○		
Endive (or Chicory)	○ ○	○	○	○ ○		
Kale (Scotch)	● ● ●	● ●	○ ○	○ ○		
Leeks	● ● ●	● ●	○ ○	○ ○ ⟵ Scarce, poor ⟶		

VEGETABLES

Vegetable	July	August	September	October	November	December
Artichoke (Globe)	O	O	O	◆	O	O
Artichoke (Jerusalem)				◆	●	●
Asparagus	O	O				
Beans (Broad)	★	★	O			
Beans (French)	★	★	★	◆	◆	
Beans (Runner)		★	★	★	O	O
Beetroot	All the year, but sometimes in spring small young beets obtainable which are delicious served hot.					
Broccoli (cauliflower type)			O	O	O	O
Brussels Sprouts			O	◆	●	●
Cabbage	Available all year in many varieties which include savoys, salad cabbages (esp. in winter) summer cabbage, spring greens.					
Carrots	All the year. Homegrown new carrots delicious, but expensive if bought in spring. →					
Cauliflower	All the year. Homegrown best from July to November. →					
Celery			◆	◆	◆	◆
Cucumber	●	●	●	O	O	O
Endive (Belgian)			◆	◆	◆	◆
Endive (or Chicory)			O	O	O	O
Kale (Scotch)	★	★		O	●	●
Leeks			← Scarce →		O	●

O *average season.* ● *best season and sometimes cheap.* ★ *cheapest and sometimes best.* ◆ *dear.* Blank indicates *off season*

VEGETABLES

	January	February	March	April	May	June
Lettuce			◆	◆	○ ○ ○ ○ ◆	● ● ● ○ ○ ◆
Marrow (inc. Courgette, Zucchini)					◆	○ ○ ◆
Mushrooms	——— All the year. Stalks cheapest, when obtainable, for flavouring. ———→					←Shallots→
Onions		——— All the year. ———→				
Parsnips	★ ★ ★ ★	★ ★ ★	◆	◆	◆ ●	● ●
Peas	See notes on frozen peas, p. 468.		◆	◆	◆ ○ ○ ○ ○	● ○ ○ ○
Potatoes (Old)	○ ○ ○ ○	○ ○ ○ ○	←— Poor quality —→			○ ○
Potatoes (New)					◆	○ ○
Radishes	——— All the year. Homegrown best in Spring. ———→					
Spinach	——— All the year – various varieties. ———→					
Swedes	} All the year, if both are taken together. Turnips best in Spring and early Summer. Swedes in Winter.					
Turnips	○ ○ ○ ○	○ ○ ○ ○	○ ○ ○ ○			
Turnip tops	○ ○ ○ ○	○ ○ ○ ○	○ ○ ○ ○			

FRUITS TREATED AS VEGETABLES

	January	February	March	April	May	June
Aubergine		◆	◆	◆	◆	◆ ● ●
Avocado	○ ○ ○ ○	○ ○	——— Obtainable all year, slightly cheaper late summer/autumn ———→		○ ○ ○	● ● ○ ○
Pimentos			◆	◆	◆	◆
Tomatoes (Dutch and English)					◆	○ ○ ○ ○

30

VEGETABLES

	July	August	September	October	November	December
Lettuce	● ●	● ● ●	● ○ ○ ○	○ ○		● ● ● ● ★
Marrow (inc. Courgette, Zucchini)	○ ○	★ ★ ★	★ ★ ○	○ ○ ○	◆	○ ○
Mushrooms	All the year. Stalks cheapest, when obtainable, for flavouring. In some country towns in Autumn field mushrooms on sale.					
Onions	←Shallots→		——— Pickling onions ———→			
Parsnips						
Peas	★ ★ ★	★ ★ ★ ○	●	◆ ◆ See notes on frozen peas p. 468.	● ● ●	● ● ★
Potatoes (Old)	★ ★ ★	★ ★ ★ ○	○ ○	○ ○	○ ○	○ ○
Potatoes (New)	● ● ●	★ ★ ★	★			
Radishes	All the year. Homegrown best in Spring. ———→					
Spinach	All the year – various varieties. ———→					
Swedes	All the year, if both are taken together. Turnips best in Spring and early Summer. Swedes in Autumn					
Turnips	and Winter.					
Turnip tops	———→					
FRUITS TREATED AS VEGETABLES						
Aubergine	◆ ◆	○ ○	○ ○ ○	○ ○ ○	○ ○	○
Avocado	◆ ● ●	● ●	● ●	○ ○ ○	○ ○ ○	◆ ◆
Pimentos	● ●	● ●	○ ○ ○	○ ○ ○	○ ○	◆ ◆
Tomatoes (Dutch and English)	○ ○	● ●	○ ○ ○ ○	◆		◆ ◆

Obtainable all year, slightly cheaper late summer/autumn ———→

○ average season.   ● best season and sometimes cheap.   ★ cheapest and sometimes best.   ◆ dear.   Blank indicates off season.

31

FRUIT

FRUIT	January	February	March	April	May	June
Apples (English)	● ● ●	● ● ●	○ ○ ○	○ ○ ○		
Apples (Imported)					○ ○ ○ ○	○ ○ ○ ○
Apricots	◆	◆ ◆	◆		○	○
Bananas						
Cherries					○	●
Currants					○	●
Gooseberries					○	●
Grapes						
Grapefruit	◆	○ ○ ○ ○	○ ○ ○	○ ○ ○	○ ○ ○ ○	★
Lemons	◆ ◆ ◆	○ ○ ○ ○	○ ○ ○	○ ○ ○	○ ○ ○ ★	★ ★ ★ ★
Limes						
Mandarins (inc. tangerines, satsumas, etc.)	○ ○ ○ ○	○ ○ ○ ○				
Melons	◆	◆	◆	○ ○ ○ ○	○ ○ ○ ★	★ ★ ★ ★

Apples (English): Chiefly Cox and Bramley

Apples (Imported): Mostly from South Africa and Australia. — European

Apricots: South African Dessert →. Available all year. Canaries best flavour but difficult to find as mass market prefers size to flavour.

Currants: Never cheap in shops. (Order of ripening: White, Red, Black)

Gooseberries: Imported varieties all the year. Special kinds only noted.

Grapes: English hothouse end June

Grapefruit: ← Trinidad →. Several varieties all year, prices average, except as noted, when all, including the favoured Trinidad, are in short supply.

Lemons: and with thick skins.

Limes: — Jamaican. Specialist shops mostly —

FRUIT

	July	August	September	October	November	December
Apples (English)	← Beauty of Bath →	○ ○	○ ○ ○ ○ ← Cookers →	● ● ●	● ● ●	● ● ●
Apples (Imported)	Grannie Smith and Sturmer now – will cook, though dear for this purpose. →					◆ ◆ ◆ S. African ◆
Apricots	← European → ○	◆				◆
Bananas	Available all year, including Canaries – best flavour – but these difficult to find as mass market prefers size to flavour. Look out for: ——— Jamaican ———					
Cherries	● ● ●					
Currants (Order of ripening White, Red, Black)	○ ● ●	○ ○ ○ ○	○ ○			
Damsons		○ ○ ○ ○	○ ○ ○ ○	○ ○ ○		
Figs (Green)		◆	◆ ◆	(English) ◆	(Imported) ◆	◆ ◆
Gooseberries	● ● ●	○ ○	○ ○ ○ ○			
Grapes	← English Hot-house →	← Seedless White →	All year. Special kinds noted.			← Colmar →
Grapefruit	Several varieties all year, prices average, except as noted, when all, including the ← Trinidad → favoured Trinidad, are in short supply.				◆	◆
Lemons	★ ★ ★ ★	★ ★ ★ ★	★ ★ ★ ★	○ ○ ○ ○	○ ○ ○	○ ○ ◆
Mandarins (inc. Satsumas, Tangerines etc.)				○ ○ ○ ○	○ ○ ○ and with thick skins.	○ ● ◆
Melons	★ ★ ★	★ ★ ★ ★	★ ★ ★ ★	○ ○ ○ ○	○ ○ ○	○ ○ ◆ ◆

○ average season. ● best season and sometimes cheap. ★ cheapest and sometimes best. ◆ dear. Blank indicates off season.

33

FRUIT	January	February	March	April	May	June
Oranges	Sevilles ←——→ Available all year. Spanish best winter and spring. South African: May to mid-November, Jamaican: December to March.					
Peaches	◆	◆	◆		◆◆ ○ ○ ○	★ ★ ★ ★
Pears	←——— Comice types – imported ———→ Other varieties throughout year					
Pineapples	←——— Available all the year ———→					
Plums (English and Imported)	◆	◆ ◆	◆			
Rhubarb	◆	◆	◆	○ ○ ○ ○ ○	★ ★ ★ ★ ★	★ ★ ★ ★
BERRIES	Never cheap in shops					
Cranberries	○ ○ ○ ○	○ ○ ○				
Logan and Raspberries						◆ ◆ ◆ ◆ ○ ○ ○
Strawberries					◆	◆ ◆ ◆ ◆ ○ ○

FRUIT

	July	August	September	October	November	December
Oranges	Available all year. Spanish best, winter and spring. South African: May to mid-November. Jamaican: December to March.					
Peaches	★ ★ ★	★ ○ ○ ○	○ ◆			◆ ◆
Pears	Other varieties throughout year. — Comice – (some English, but dear) → English in autumn. Available all year →					
Pineapples	★ ★	★ ★	★			
Plums (inc. greengages)	★ ◆	◆ ○ ○	● ●	●		◆
Rhubarb	★ ★ ○	○ ○	Available all year			◆
BERRIES						
Blackberries or Brambles	Never cheap in shops.	○	○ ○ ○ ○	○ ○ ○ ○		
Blue, bil-, or Wortleberries	In shops only in North. Grow wild in west country. ○	○ ○ ○ ○	○ ○ ○ ○			
Cranberries					○ ○ ○	○ ○ ○ ○
Logan and Raspberries	○ ○ ○ ○	○ ○ ○	○			
Rowan or Mountain Ash	Do not appear in shops.	○ ○ ○ ○	○			
Strawberries	○ ○ ○ ○	○ ○ ○				

NOTE: A great deal of imported fruit is sold slightly under-ripe in the shops. Do not put it either in the refrigerator (which can kill tropical fruits), or near direct heat while waiting for it to ripen. Simply keep in warm room. Some fruit may be put in airing cupboard, but not directly over tank.

○ *average season.* ● *best season and sometimes cheap.* ★ *cheapest and sometimes best.* ◆ *dear.* Blank indicates *off season.*

35

The Economics of the Kitchen

Shopping

Eating well means shopping well. To shop well, even with un-
limited money, needs intelligence, experience and time. Bad shopping wastes time, exhausts the shopper and fails to bring home
the bacon.

To shop well you must:

get to know the range and quality of goods and services in
your local shops;

find out (pp. 20-35) what is in season and so may be available;

decide what you want and how much of it;

shop from a list, however good your memory; it speeds
things by concentrating your attention, and also keeps 'impulse
buying' at bay.

Menu Planning

A meal that is gastronomically good will automatically be
nutritionally well balanced. The reverse is not necessarily true.
The nutrition expert is concerned with colour, texture and flavour
only where these affect poor or faddy appetites. Provided the meal
contains its quota of protein, fat, carbohydrate, minerals, vitamins
and so on the nutritionist does not mind which foods provide
them, whereas the gastronome insists that the food at each meal
must be as varied as possible.

Here are some pointers to menu making:

Any course, not just the main course, may be the starting
point from which the rest of the meal flows.

A starchy pudding should be preceded by a light, fresh or crisp main course.

Fried fish should not be followed by pancakes.

Beware tomato soup! It can limit your choice of accompaniments, since anything made with tomatoes is out.

If chips with everything is a bore from day to day, likewise cream or wine with everything is boring from course to course. Flavours should positively contrast sometimes, as well as merely varying from course to course. Try to vary colours as well (for example, avoid following a paprika dish with an apricot mousse). This matters least in the family, and most at a cold meal, when everything is on the table together.

Textures should contrast from course to course, though not necessarily within a course. For example fish, in one of the many white sauces, may be accompanied by one of the *pommes purée* variations, but should not be preceded by a white soup or followed by a soft, pallid pudding. Fruitarians or dentists might enjoy a menu composed of carrot salad followed by nut cutlet and Waldorf salad, and ending with dessert pears; gastronomes would deplore it.

The above are some of the niceties of menu-making. It is not possible to adhere strictly to them in day-to-day cooking but, borne in mind as a general guide, they become your habitual thinking about food, helping you to provide a healthy family diet and, for special occasions, some memorable meals.

Meal Planning

Both shopping and cooking time, as well as money, are saved by planning meals by the week. It is hard to persuade people of this, but here is an illustration of only part of a week's meals to make the point more clearly.

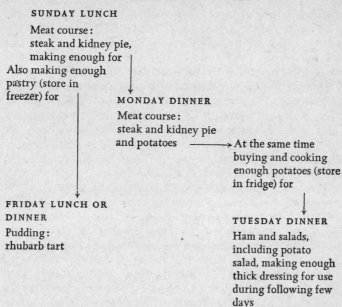

SUNDAY LUNCH

Meat course:
steak and kidney pie,
making enough for
Also making enough
pastry (store in
freezer) for

MONDAY DINNER

Meat course:
steak and kidney pie
and potatoes ———→ At the same time
buying and cooking
enough potatoes (store
in fridge) for

FRIDAY LUNCH OR
DINNER

Pudding:
rhubarb tart

TUESDAY DINNER

Ham and salads,
including potato
salad, making enough
thick dressing for use
during following few
days

In this connexion see also the mass production ideas on pp. 68–9.

Storing Food

Refrigerators, so far, are one of the few unmixed blessings of modern engineering. They deserve top place on any list of kitchen equipment, and the bigger the better. This is not to decry the equally important and useful larder. To get the best performance from either you must know the rules of the game. These rules also apply to the bed-sitter ventilated food-safe (or unventilated cupboard, alas).

Unless attacked by insects, bacteria, fungi or viruses, most foods would simply dry to dust if kept long enough. Preservation of foods is directed to sterilizing them (usually by heat through cooking) and keeping them in a sterile atmosphere (canning, or vacuum-packing in other materials); keeping them in an atmosphere too cold for organisms to develop (refrigeration of all sorts); keeping them in a sterile medium (salting, pickling).

Raw meat needs, firstly, protection from flies, but also the maximum possible fresh cold air. When meat is hung, air can flow not only over all its surfaces, but also between the stretched fibres. Meat hung in a flyproof, cold larder has the best storage outside the butcher's cold-room. (The amount of air, as well as the hanging of the carcase and joints, possibly accounts for the better flavour of meat kept by the butcher, over meat kept on a plate in the restricted air space of a domestic refrigerator.) A hook screwed to the underside of an upper shelf in the larder, plus the smallest-size butcher's hook is all the equipment you need for this. Next best, stand meat on a grid over a plate.

The best flyproofing is provided by a large sheet of clean newspaper, or kitchen paper, or a big paper bag. Enclose the meat completely in this as in a paper balloon, twisting the edges to seal, but without the surface of the paper touching the meat at any point. The texture of the paper ensures that flies cannot penetrate it but allows air to circulate. However, if moisture from meat should touch and soak through the paper, this provides enough nourishment for fly eggs to develop, when they can penetrate the moist paper, continue feeding on the meat beneath it, and develop into maggots. (Those interested in the details can look them up in Fabre at their local library.)

Flies can drop eggs downwards from a little distance, but cannot shoot them sideways. An all-gauze meat-cover or food-safe with ventilation holes in its roof is therefore no protection. A solid-topped meat-cover or safe is better, provided that the side ventilation holes are very small. Ventilation for all food storage units should always be through very fine-gauge mesh.

Cooked meat, on the other hand, keeps better in an airtight wrapping such as polythene or foil.

All cooked or raw meat to be put in the freezing compartment should be wrapped, and the wrapping given time to thaw slightly before being removed.

Fish, raw or cooked, keeps best in airtight wrappings. Smoked fish should be wrapped for a refrigerator, hung in the air in a larder. Re-use foil or polythene that has covered fish only for fish, as fishy smells are difficult to wash out.

Cooked vegetables and fruit are best covered for storing.

NOTE: It is assumed that readers know that all the above foods should be cooked or used in a matter of days; or hours if there is no properly ventilated storage available, or in hot weather. The exception here is storage in the refrigerator freezing compartment, where time of storage may be slightly longer. Some indications of these longer times are given throughout the book.

It is often a good plan to wrap cooked foods complete with their dishes.

Raw vegetables and fruit keep best in the cool, although the refrigerator can be too cold. Cucumbers, for example, get frosted and rot; the best way is to stand them with the cut end in half an inch of water in a larder or cool corner.

Refrigerator salad boxes are not airtight, and the dry cold can wilt some vegetables. It is best to put most of them in a polythene bag in the box.

Salad greens, except watercress (which should be eaten on the day of purchase), keep equally well, unwashed, in the refrigerator in polythene, or in a closely-covered saucepan on a cool floor.

Cabbage, sprouts, cauliflower and leeks are poor keepers. They discolour, wilt, rot and smell very quickly. Coldness and moisture-proof wrapping are important, even overnight.

Spinach should be kept unwashed in polythene and used quickly.

Onions need coldness and light, although in spring they will start sprouting whatever you do.

Potatoes need coolness, but not frost, and dark, especially when new, as they turn green and bitter. Old potatoes sprout in the spring or in warmth.

Cooked vegetables and fruit should be kept cold, and covered. But eat them up quickly to avoid losing vitamins.

Eggs are usually stored point downwards in the rack, in order to keep the yolk in the centre, so they say; but yolks in my eggs always turn out to be at one end or one side! If they are kept in a refrigerator let them warm to room temperature before boiling them. Once they have been shelled, store them well covered, as they breed bacteria. Cover unbroken yolks with a little cold water.

Dairy produce. The colder this is kept the better. Pottery milk and butter coolers, and the dodges with cloth with ends dipped in water, help only marginally. To keep milk overnight in hot weather scald it, pour into a jug and cover with foil at once, when the rising cream will not set into a skin, but may be whisked back into the milk next day. Store cheese in foil or polythene. If refrigerated, chambrez at least one hour before eating. To ripen Camembert 'naturally', store in cool, and turn over every so often.

Bread, flour, cereals. Unless in polythene in a refrigerator, bread needs a properly ventilated bin (plastic or metal) or porous pottery crock. Biscuits and cake need airtight storage. Polythene bags are excellent and save more space than tins. Plastic boxes are fine, but dearer, and also need space. Flour needs a bin in a dry place. Cereals of all sorts need dry sealed storage. Don't buy more cereal than you can use quickly, as it may contain insect eggs that will develop in the warmth.

Stocks, soups, gravies. Keep in refrigerator or boil each day. Large amounts of stock or soup need simmering for about 10 minutes. Onion ferments quickly and should not be used in stocks that are to be kept. Strain them and remove all the 'bits' as soon as they are made.

The foregoing is intended as a rough guide only and concentrates on methods and apparatus for storing everyday foods. It is in general as true now as ever it was that the fresher food is eaten the better.

Kitchen Planning

The desirable features in a kitchen are:

nearness of sink, stove and saucepans;

nearness of utensils and ingredients (especially where these are numerous as in cake and pudding making) to each other, to the work surface, and to stove and sink;

adequate dry storage space for equipment and foodstuffs, which may include space on walls for fixing racks, etc.; the storage space must be within easy reach;

cold, ventilated food storage;

hot water;

warmth, including means of drying cloths, and ventilation to remove steam and cooking smells.

This is asking a lot of one room in a domestic dwelling, and the truth is that the kitchen is primarily a workshop, and only incidentally or perforce a domestic room. A much better kitchen will always result from thinking of it in its workshop character.

Dream kitchens are, however, rarely the lot of budget cooks, who may have nothing more elaborate than a ring and the shelf of a cupboard in a corner. In hundreds of houses the kitchen must do duty as homework room, sewing room, hobbies room and carpentry shop. In cities, even above-budget cooks may be landed with the partitioned-off segment of some once-grand room on the upper floors of a *ci-devant* town mansion; while others, like me when I married, may take over a custom-built twenties kitchen with stove, sink, larder and dry-goods cupboard one in each of its very far-flung corners. Kitchens such as these may be impossible or exorbitant to alter radically, but I offer a few modest suggestions for their improvement.

Landlord's kitchen

First you must realize that you may need his permission even to plug walls for putting up a shelf, and that if you install a posh sink unit you'll probably be making him a present of it when you leave. Try, therefore, to make portable improvements.

A second draining-board could be one of the clip-on aluminium type, on which you could stand a plastic-covered basket-type plate-rack. Firms of do-it-yourself white-wood furniture-makers, such as Liden, have a vast assortment of kitchen unit pieces of differing heights with backs, so that you could use them singly now, fitting them later on into a larger scheme. One of the most versatile of these is a small cabinet with cutlery drawer, second, deeper storage drawer and shelved cupboard below. Topped with Formica, such a piece not only holds a lot of equipment, but can do duty as work-surface and pastry-board, being placed near stove or sink as required. A food safe could stand on the top, bringing together ingredients, sink and equipment; or ingredients, stove and equipment, so saving a lot of foot-work.

Central tables may be frowned on by modern kitchen planners, yet in a badly designed kitchen a big centre table is a blessing. You can do all the running at once, assembling ingredients, tools, bowl for veg., basin of washing-up water and pots and pans at one point. Certainly in a kitchen used by all the family a central, large table may be a necessity and, luckily, the best are second-hand. (Cautionary note: If you find a good thick-topped, plain-legged old-fashioned table, think well before covering with Formica or similar. Plastic surfaces are slippery. Carving on them is difficult. Plates tend to slither if, for example, learner-eaters are trying to use their first spoon and fork. To remove the stuff if you tire of the colour is a major operation.) On benches or dressers, however, Formica is excellent.

Very small purchases that may improve your lot: a saucepan stand; a couple of suction dishcloth holders put near a source of heat for drying; a lidded, pedal waste-bin; a heavy stoneware type of jar to hold kitchen tools.

If you are allowed to plug the walls, a hanging food-safe, a shelf or two, a cook's rack and tools, or a set of storage jars are only the more obvious smaller buys that, well placed, may make a big difference to the convenience of a too small or awkward kitchen.

Owned kitchen

A conveniently arranged kitchen is a selling point in any house, so that even if you know you will not stay forever in your present house anything you do to improve the kitchen will add to its value.

Positions of flues and drains determine to a great extent the positions of boilers and sinks, and alterations to either can be dear. However, it is sometimes possible to move a sink along a wall a foot or so, or to move it from one angle to the other of the same corner, to provide better light or to bring, say, stove and sink nearer together.

Stoves also can often be moved a few feet by the addition of gas piping or an additional power-point. True, these items are not negligible but they must be considered in relation to the cost of other things, to say nothing of the cook's health. It is far more important to have an easy-to-run kitchen than an elaborate gadgety cooking stove.

Plan your kitchen improvements also with the rest of your circumstances in mind. In a country house with a good kitchen garden and a family to feed, it would be more useful to build a good larder than to buy an expensive refrigerator, since fresh and preserved fruit, vegetables and preserving equipment take the sort of space possible only in a country larder.

In an older town flat converted from other rooms, however, any spare money would be better spent on installing extra electric points for labour-saving equipment; or fitting up a good sink unit in which to stow unsightly pails and awkward saucepans; or putting up a line of wall-cupboards (Liden again have several do-it-yourself types) to keep restricted work-surfaces free of clutter. Some older kitchens in converted flats have a built-in cupboard. If this is against an outer wall it can be made into a larder by putting in a small, fly-screened window and screened vent-holes in the door, and flyproofing the door frame. These last two jobs you can do yourself without much skill. Foam rubber draught-proofing strip make an efficient fly barrier round doors.

Making a hatch between kitchen and living-room is another smallish structural change that often saves much trouble in any sort of dwelling.

These are only some of the points, but they may help you to look at your own kitchen with a fresh eye.

Lighting the kitchen

This applies to both rented and owned accommodation and deserves a more central place in most thinking about kitchen improvement. Quite simple changes make big differences, and luckily most light fittings can be installed without structural damage.

Are your lamps powerful enough? The old-fashioned tungsten

'bulb' should be no weaker than 75 watts even in a 6 foot by 6 foot kitchen. There should be good light over both sink and stove, for nothing is more tiring, or productive of tension, than peering for hours on end. Lighting men frown, but the cheap and easy way to achieve this is by using an adapter with the second lamp on a long flex. You must obviously make such adaptations neat and safe, helped by an up-to-date do-it-yourself book from the library. Light switches should be the pull-type, or be placed so that it is impossible to touch them with wet hands.

In your own kitchen make permanent lighting improvements. Fluorescent lighting is good to work by. The trouble is that it distorts colours, and the 'mix' thought generally acceptable stems from the sales techniques of supermarkets, where even wilted vegetables are made to look viridian, tomatoes Post Office red, and oranges bright as the Eternal Bonfire.

However, firms like Atlas, Philips and Merchant Adventurers have produced some better 'shades' (diffusers to the trade), one being a round fluorescent light with a quite agreeable cover, and lighting men recommend a mixture of fluorescent lighting with tungsten to make the colour more acceptable. A good division in a family kitchen would be fluorescent light for the sink/stove section of the kitchen and tungsten over the table.

My own pet form of kitchen-table lighting is a gadget known as a rise-and-fall fitting, by means of which you can push the light up high or pull it down to table-lamp height. Older people will remember early versions, and such fittings solve the multi-purpose kitchen problem: pulled down, they make a pretty light for dining and a sensible light for sewing or homework, and, pushed up, a good general room light. Atlas make an up-to-date version.

For more daylight in your own kitchen: where possible, omit curtains, replacing plain glass by reeded glass for privacy; find out the cost of enlarging existing window(s); find out the cost of making an additional window where walls permit (a handy husband might manage the work if advised how and where). An extra window may also help ventilation.

Smells

Extractor fans, if good, are the answer for most kitchens. X-pel-air is one of the popular and good makes, while Vent-Axia will not only arrange to send their man-in-the-area to cottage or castle to advise on size, positioning and supplier, but will actually advise you against having a fan if they think it won't work. (In some rooms they won't.)

Provided you have the glass in the window replaced, you can take an extractor fan with you from rented premises. As a rule you need a special point installed.

Equipment

In this section I mention some manufacturers of kitchen equipment. I have made no attempt to produce a *Which?* report, a Design Centre guide, or a British Standards Institute appraisal. My aim has been rather to name a few names of long-established firms whose goods are likely to be found all over the country. There are dozens more makers of equal merit, but a section of this sort must have limits and if you have a pet brand stick to it. Obviously, also, you could find cheaper and dearer things than those I mention. I have tried to strike a middle price-range with good quality and agreeable design.

Boulestin is reported to have said that all a cook really needs is one sharp knife, one bowl, one saucepan – or something of this order. In her witty, excellent *Cooking in a Bedsitter* (Penguin) Katharine Whitehorn lists a round dozen essential cooking tools. She makes out a good case for this, and those who prefer a slight struggle now and again to multiplying possessions should read and consider her list. My minimal list will not be quite so Spartan, but my average list will be less lavish than many I have read.

Tools for the job

In deciding on equipment, however, it is important to weigh up your special needs.

A family woman who enjoys icing and decorative work would get more use from a full set of good icing equipment than from the cast-iron omelette pan which is the joy of her business-woman neighbour. If you don't like pastry, why give house-room to a rolling-pin? A bottle will do for the few times you're obliged to make pastry.

So, you see, above a basic minimum it is impossible to advise other cooks on what they *should* have, except to say buy little and good until you find out what your special needs are. This is very important when considering bigger items such as preserving pans, electric gadgets and pressure cookers. Nothing is worse than having to house large unused hardware. Apart from wasting space, it provides a continual reproach, a reminder of inadequacy and folly.

KNIVES. One really sharp knife serves many kitchen purposes. With an entire battery of blunt knives merely passable cooking is impossible. Yes: impossible. Ask any chef, read any cookery book; you will find this sharp knife theme dominating any advice they have to offer.

It is now quite difficult to get an ordinary stainable steel cook's knife. Much fashionable nonsense was generated just after the war about the inferiority of Sheffield knives. In London several shops stock French makes, but you may have to go to a cutler's – a rare shop these days – to find a Sheffield knife. (See Address Book, p. 556.) When found, Sheffield cook's knives are equal to the best. You should have:

> 1 cook's knife, 7-inch blade, stainable preferred
> 1 vegetable knife
> 1 peeler (avoid the 'swing-wing' type unless used to them, or left-handed).

Because stainable knives are not universally obtainable the following list ends with two good makes of stainless knives: Ventura (Sheffield); Wostenholm (Sheffield); Victorinox (Swiss); Gustav Emil Ern (German); Sabatier (France's Sheffield); Friar (Sheffield); Granton (Sheffield).

SHARPENING KNIVES. Whatever sharpener you use, it is vital to sharpen along the whole length of the blade and the tip, otherwise you will have a concave knife useless for half your jobs. Best for beginners is flat, fine-grain carborundum. This is what you do when sharpening a knife:

Section through new
knife (much enlarged)

edge

Knife after use
edge worn down

Object in sharpening to
remove fraction of
steel from either side of
blade until edge is remade

Wrong angle. Blade raised

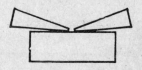

Correct angle.
Blade almost flat on carborundum
(turn and do other side)

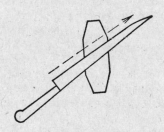

Push knife lightly and almost flat
over surface of carborundum
from point to hilt

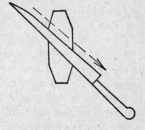

Turn blade over, draw almost
flat, lightly over surface from
hilt to point

49

Use all sharpeners lightly. Never press on the blade. Don't go on and on. If the knife is not sharp in a few strokes you are handling wrongly, or the knife needs re-grinding. N.B. Most fancy-edged knives should be sharpened only on the flat side.

Once familiar with this way of knife-sharpening you will find it easy to use a steel.

Beware patent sharpeners. Wrongly used, some rip steel out of knives, leaving them bowed and blunt. A cheap, good easy sharpener, if it is used exactly as directed, is made by Tala. It is a 'wheel' of carborundum set in a roller. There are table and wall models – I prefer table, as it is more adaptable. For a long knife you may have to stop and move along the blade.

Make a dirt-cheap, very efficient do-it-yourself sharpener from a flat piece of wood cut at one end into a 'handle', and covered with fine emery cloth (NOT emery paper). Fasten the emery cloth very taut with tiny tacks at the corners, or glue on. Renew the emery about once a year.

'Cricket bat' – home-made sharpener. Emery cloth, on both sides, must come exactly to the edges. About 7 to 8 inch blade, 2½ to 3 inch handle.

CHOPPING BOARD. A really thick wooden one – about 1 inch. Thin boards can't take the washing-up, plastic is too slippery. If your local ironmonger has only the two latter try a timber merchant – stating your purpose, as not all wood will do; or a catering supplier in the nearest large town.

MIXING BOWL. Tala have an enamelled one, I have an aluminium one. These can be very useful as they will go over direct heat or in the oven. Otherwise pottery is fine. All will do duty as salad bowls and for vegetable peeling.

COLANDER. Some have long handles.

BOWL-STRAINER/SIEVE. Wire mesh or nylon. Single-person households could probably dispense with colander if largest size is bought.

WOODEN SPOONS. Many varieties for different purposes. Best if chosen from caterer's supply department where variety is displayed. Advisable to have two.

PALETTE KNIVES, SLICES. Avoid the thin, too flexible type that come with 'sets'. They can back-lash, flipping the fried egg to the ceiling. Best for multi-purpose use is a broad, long-bladed affair with an angled handle, called by some makers a fish trowel as opposed to a fish slice. Otherwise, stainable chef's palette knife, 7 to 8 inch blade, together with fish slice.

COOK'S FORK AND SPOON. Confusion is apt to arise about cooks' forks. There is the carving type; then there is the blunt, wooden-handled kind you cook with, and that is what I refer to here; thirdly there are sharp-pronged kinds for several operations. The sort that come in 'sets' are easy to find and well made, with metal parts chromed or stainless; prices vary. There are matching spoons with bowls plain, marked for measuring, or perforated for draining. You can baste with the first two. You should have this sort of fork and spoon for safety. Cooking with dinner forks and pudding spoons can result in nasty burns, as well as doing no good to tableware. Tala and Skyline are both good makes.

RUBBER BOWL-SCRAPER. Called by the awful name of Lastlik, they get every bit from pans and bowls, saving waste. They also fold in, scrape down electric-mixer bowls and marble cream on the tops of purées.

FLOUR DREDGER. Even – or specially – in a bedsitter, a real labour-saver for coating, as well as the obvious pastry-board sprinkling. You can tip out flour and use for sugar at a pinch. Plastic slightly dearer than tin, but no risk of rusting.

MEASURING AND WEIGHING. You need a measure marked with fluid ounces and, for preference, not the sort that marks them off in 2, 4, 6, etc. but 1, 2, 3. This can be a ½-pint but a pint is more useful, and must have gill (¼ pint) marked. Pint measures should also have ¾ pint marks. Tala have an aluminium ¾-pint measure printed with English and U.S. pint and cup measures and with levels equal to weights in flour, sugar, rice and so on, giving many single-person households all the measuring equipment necessary.

The best scales are still the old-fashioned sort with weights.

H. Fereday & Sons' Weylux series are reliable and big enough for most households. Use pound packets of sugar, etc. for additional weights in a crisis. If you have room only for a spring balance get a good make like Salter's. Avoid gimmicky models with fancy little scale pans – the sugar will cascade everywhere.

WHISKS. One of the earliest numbers of *Which?* included their choice of hand whisk, still unbeaten: Skyline spiral whisk – a spoon-shaped piece of heavy wire with thin, spiral-wire spring round, fixed in wooden handle. Light to use, marvellous for egg-whites, vinaigrettes, mayonnaise, de-lumping sauces, frothing drinking chocolate, batters. Imitations not as good. Very cheap.

Rotary whisk by Prestige, Tala and others. Cheap two-beater tinned rotaries may not last, but are better than nothing.

OVEN-CLOTH (usually called glove). O.K. item from Woolworth's – and cheapest there. Asbestos is essential for safety.

GRATER. The old-fashioned 'three-panel' grater is most useful as it does spices, citrus peel, cheese and vegetables. Tinned and stainless steel. Some have chip cutter.

The above, apart from pots and pans (see below), would allow you to cook a range of dishes, not including pastry and cakes. The following items include pastry and cake equipment, and are things you will soon want if you enjoy cooking or must cook.

Pastry equipment

· BOARD. Necessary if table or bench is not suitable.

ROLLING-PIN. Usually wood, can be china or glass (which you can fill with ice if you think it helps).

CUTTERS. Most-used sizes are five graduated in ¼-inches from 2 to 3 inches. Those with edges and no handle much cheaper than fluted ones with handles.

BAKING-SHEET. Measure oven shelf before shopping. Sheet must not touch sides or overhang back. One edge only turned up is best. Tala and Tower have non-stick versions.

FLAN-RING. Plain 7-inch. Fluted, for pastry cooks, dearer. 8-inch plain for family or entertaining.

COOLING-RACK. One 16 by 10 inches should do for most family needs.

CAKE TINS. 7-inch round. 2-lb. loaf. Two 7-inch plain sandwich.

BUN (OR PATTY) TRAY. One 12-cup tray, plain rounded cups.

NON-STICK TINS. Save time and trouble. Marvellous for meringues and other egg-white mixtures. Hide bound cooks object to resulting smooth surface of cakes, mistaking this for a change in texture. Not so; merely that non-treated tins (and paper) pull away little bits of cake to give the familiar rough appearance. 'Bakewell' (silicone treated) paper makes good substitute for those already fully kitted with older tins. Wipes clean for repeated use. Not always easy to buy. Try Smith's and department stores.

Special items

A short list of more expensive items, not essential, but of immense benefit for the needs indicated.

ELECTRIC MIXERS AND BLENDERS. For cake and pudding-makers. For baby-foods, and many diet items. For keen and ambitious cooks. For coffee-snobs. For vegetarians.

The Kenwood Chefette is a mixer and blender combined. Bowl and stand available and desirable. Excellent. Blender on big side for some things. Coffee, spices ground at owner's risk. 3 speeds. Cost (*at time of writing only*, and given for indication) around £16 including bowl and stand.

In the Moulinex (French) range, there are all sorts of prices to suit many purses. At *time of writing*, for example, small grinder, to do coffee, nuts, spices, breadcrumbs, about 51s. Small liquidizer/grinder to do all foregoing and purées, liquidizing fruit and vegetables, making mayonnaise and other jobs, £5 3s. There are also hand beaters and bowl-and-stand outfits. Well-documented list.

NOTE: Electric-blender makers' mayonnaise instructions tend to optimism. Use only enough oil at first to cover *bottom* blade. Small blenders will *not* mince dry meat.

MINCERS (these are on the borderline of essential equipment). Spong is almost synonymous in Britain with the word mincer.

Get a small mincer only if you're single, mean to stay so and never entertain. Suction models for plastic-topped work surfaces.

Mouli (French) make many sorts, from herb-chopping mill (Parsmint) to the big Moulin-Légumes referred to throughout this book, and which will do all purées. There is also a (sort of) mincer which is said to do meat as well, but I have no experience of it. Cheese and nut mill (Mouli Grater) is their best-known item in Britain.

CAN-OPENERS. Skyline Miracle wheel opener won the *Which?* stakes for hand model. Rudman Darlington wall opener has Design Centre award.

MOULDS, PIE DISHES. A small and a No. 2 size china soufflé case could be made to treble up as cake tins, jelly moulds and pie dishes, but for family use this would be too limiting, when you really need 1 ½-pint and 1 1½- or 2-pint mould; 1 1-pint and 1 2-pint pie-dishes.

Equipment for top-of-stove/gas-ring cooking

A large number of people will never have an oven. Many others may be in situations where it is inconvenient or expensive to use the oven all the time. Increasingly we shall be on North Sea gas in Britain. Natural gas, at present, can be difficult to burn low. To all these problems here are a few solutions by way of special equipment.

ASBESTOS MATS. Cheap, easily destroyed. Provided heat is not too intense, even oven-glass utensils can be used on them (use one mat on top of another if necessary). But if flame or element is allowed beyond mat, glass (or pottery) may crack or explode. Put asbestos mats under metal saucepans for burners or elements that will not turn low enough for simmering. One asbestos mat is almost essential.

MIJOSKA. A patent simmering device from France, where simmering is properly valued as a cooking method, and experience with natural gas advanced. This is a long-term item, solidly made and, of course, much dearer than an asbestos mat. It is a circle of a fire-clay nature fixed into a vitreous enamelled plate which, firebrick side down on the burners, heats through evenly, and maintains low, steady heat. Very valuable for all-day cooking while you are at work or whatever. Keeps sauces, coffee at ready-to-serve heat without risk. Heat stays under pans for 30 minutes after gas is turned off. Combined with a pottery or oven-glass cocotte makes perfect oven-to-table substitute; with covered roaster, better than average pot-roast.

TOASTERS AND GRILLS. There are some cheap, flat, tinned metal squares with grids and handles, on which digs-girls can, with practice, make toast and frizzle bacon over burners and radiant rings. Cast-iron French version, made for example by Le Creuset, works on the principle of charcoal grill – i.e. intense bottom heat, food just raised enough not to catch fire. A serious piece of equipment, not intended as a substitute for the radiant top-heat type of grill. The smaller of these grills will do 4 ¼-lb. steaks at once. Also makes toast and there's no reason why it shouldn't do drop scones (even if slightly wavy !). Amount of fuel used is far less than for radiant grills, so the (not too high) cost is soon made up.

Colorcast, Le Creuset (and innumerable other makes, of course), cast-iron lidded vessels of many sorts and sizes should particularly be considered by permanent top-of-stove cooks. Many things can be managed in cast-iron that even the heaviest of other metals cannot do. Cakes have been baked on top of the stove (not by me) in cast iron. Once hot, cast iron retains heat, saving fuel bills.

PRESSURE COOKERS. Difficult to say who would and who would not find them useful. Good for last-minute cooks, bottling, holidays – especially in caravans and rented houses; or for tough ingredients. They cut cooking time by, on average, two thirds. Makers' times tend to optimism, but the following are average times established after long use: beef stew, ½ hour; potatoes, 7–10 minutes according to age and size; young chicken, 15 minutes; very old whole carrots, 20–30 minutes.

Miscellaneous

Egg slicer.

12–15 inch nylon forcing bag, with ½-inch plain and star vegetable pipes. (See also Icing, p. 535.)

Potato masher (unless you have Moulin-Légumes, sieve, etc.). These come in the matching cooks' tools ranges already noted.

Grapefruit knife, or (better) Tala patent grapefruit cutter.

Steamer – either to fit on top of or inside saucepan. Former for cooking two things at once.

Vegetable rack (almost an essential). Painted sort always rust eventually. Plastic-covered wire good. Office stacking trays for small space. Tala (once again) rack of 3 baskets for gardeners.

Pots and pans

This is the moment to say: no one should scorn Woolworth's. Woolworth's produce a huge range of fantastically cheap, often more-than-adequate kitchen hardware, without which hundreds of thousands would have to spend harder and longer hours in the kitchen. However, a good workman will always prefer the best tools because he knows that without them he cannot produce his best work, and that that work takes more time than it should. I say this who have used a Woolworth rotary whisk all my cooking life – just to prove the rule! But you cannot expect advanced design (as opposed to 'styling'), durability, finish and performance from cheap mass-market goods, and there are aesthetic and psychological benefits to be got from handling good things.

NON-STICK SAUCEPANS. Just as it is practice, not a fancy knife, that will improve your vegetable slicing, so it is practice (chiefly at turning down the heat controls), not a non-stick pan, that will improve your frying and simmering. There seems to be some idea abroad that non-stick pans prevent food burning. This is not so. Only you can do that. Food can burn in non-stick pans, and when it does is likely to spoil the non-stick coating at the same time. This is made clear on the instructions coming with most non-stick pans. The best case for non-stick is to be made at the sink rather than the stove, for it is ease of washing-up that is the joy of these utensils – for instance, roasting tins.

Non-stick has advantages in egg cookery and for cake tins because it saves the tedious chore of greasing and lining; and milk pans, for those who don't believe they wash best in cold water. (So do non-stick : try it !)

Since I have warned about too-cheap pans, what sort of level do I mean? The pots and pans I suggest are only a few of dozens of good makes, a standard of comparison. They are examples of the main types of material used for pans, and have national distribution. Some makers produce the same basic design in several qualities and price-ranges; others have a particularly wide range of sizes.

It is useless to cook with 'gas-weight' pans, of whatever material, on electric hotplates. The manner in which heat is conducted and distributed by electric hotplates makes it essential that the base of the pan shall be flat against the heating surface. Thin or lightweight pans soon distort on electric plates. If you can afford them, electric, or machine-based, pans, as they are called, cook better on gas also, for it is a general rule that the thicker the cooking vessel the better. In the matter of sizes I have a general criticism of most 'matched' sets (not that I'm an enthusiast for too much matchery – different materials and shapes do different jobs) : the largest saucepans of matched sets are apt to be 8 inches in diameter; not big enough to take the average 3–3½-lb. chicken, or a moderate leg of mutton. On the other hand, one of the best additions to today's pans is the lidded skillet – sold under several names, and often in the guise of a poacher – a good way to buy one. In this you can fry, stew, make omelettes and poach fish. You can often order a poacher top (sometimes with slightly different size of lid) for your skillet as an 'extra'.

Aluminium needs good cleaning, will dent if roughly handled, and pit if food is left in it. It is light to handle, responds quickly to raising and lowering of heat, can stand high temperatures and cannot chip, or crack, or rust. Its liability to staining can sometimes be reduced if, when new, pans are first boiled for 15 minutes with 1 tbs. borax or alum per pint of water.

In plain aluminium excellent specially easy-to-clean pans are made by Crown Merton, who have three price ranges in matched sets. Handles and knobs – all of sensible size and shape – vary in material and colour; so do lids. Each pan is stamped clearly with its diameter size and capacity in pints. The ranges include poacher skillets, colanders and deep frying-pans. In the middle price-range there are also large-sized saucepans.

Tower is another maker of good aluminium in several price-ranges, with up to a 10-inch-diameter saucepan in one matched range. They specialize in non-stick and have more items in this, at the time of writing, than most manufacturers, including roasting tins and a poacher skillet with all parts non-stick coated.

Vitreous enamel is glass fused to steel or cast iron at intense heat. It is one of the best surfaces to clean, can be produced in a wide range of colours (note some of the Italian ware), is very resistant to scratching and staining, and does not bend or dent. The drawbacks are weight, liability for the enamel to chip off the metal if knocked, and for food to stick.

Among the best-known British vitreous-enamel pans are Judge. They have several matched ranges varying in colour, shape and price, all suitable for either gas or electric stoves. The larger sizes are in the cheaper range, which ends at 8-inch diameter, 6-pint capacity – small for some households. Judge also do enamel gas and electric kettles, and a non-stick range including a large covered roaster, which would double as fish kettle. This range is dearer.

Tala make a limited but good-quality range of gas-weight saucepans and covered roasters in enamel.

Three other materials for pots and pans are *stainless steel, cast iron* and *copper*. The latter is sometimes combined with stainless steel, as is aluminium. Solid copper is very heavy and very expensive, and must be kept coated with tin. And polished. Copper pans, if really good, are wonderful for experienced cooks, but are a luxury beyond the scope of budget cooks. Stainless steel is not tricky to use, as copper is, but belongs to wedding-present lists for most of us, or for anniversary presents by request. (I disapprove of women being given, unasked, kitchen utensils for presents. No one dreams of giving men luxury filing-cabinets or gift-wrapped in-trays for birthdays !) Crown Merton and Tala both have fine stainless-steel ranges combined, by different processes, with aluminium.

The Eire firm Waterford Ironfounders have their widely distributed Colorcast range of cast-iron vitreous non-stick ware in black and white. Doyen of enamelled cast iron is the French Le Creuset ware, which has a quite undeserved reputation for high cost. These ranges include some of the most aesthetically satisfactory cooking ware, all of which can be used for top heat and in the oven.

As far as drawbacks go for the cook, vitreous cast iron has only two: weight – women with weak wrists or backs might find it difficult to handle and lift; secondly, food tends to stick when pans are used on top of the stove. Otherwise, even heat, thickness, response to temperature changes, easily cleaned surfaces and lifetime durability (I've heard of a Le Creuset pot that cooks perfectly without leaking though cracked through) must make the possession of at least one piece the ambition of every cook.

In buying pans apply the same rules as for other equipment: does it fit your life and tastes? Before buying anything, look well in a big ironmonger's or the kitchen department of a big store. Pick up the pans, lift the lids. Remind yourself that you will have to handle things when hot through the thickness of an oven glove; that *all* your equipment has to be housed somewhere; that it has to be cleaned.

Saving Money and Time

•••

Although economy is not a polite name for cheeseparing, it does mean that the cook and her family must exercise restraint. The odd idea dominates these days that restraint is bad for you, and the younger you are the worse the psychological damage. To the mother who is determined that her children must have exactly what they want to eat – even if it means a sort of starvation for herself, and dental problems for her children later – this chapter has very little to say. When, for example, cream is suggested as an accompaniment to a pudding, children should be restricted to their share with everyone else.

Readers who may be astonished to find cream and eggs looming large in puddings, wine appearing now and then in meat and fish dishes, can keep an absolutely detailed account for a month of what they spend on the sort of eating suggested here. It will cost no more than the average diet of British families with its mountains of packets of biscuits, breakfast cereals, potato crisps, 'luncheon sausage', sausage rolls and pies, shop cakes, tinned fruit with packet custard, sweets, ice-cream and chips with everything.

To save on the cost of food without it showing, you need to have your wits about you. For the family woman with money-earning capabilities there is also the question of saving time in the preparation of food, so this section ends with some guidelines on mass production.

Substitutes

Apply the following list throughout the book. Even where I say 'no substitutes', if you must you must, but at your own risk.

Butter and margarine

Margarine. Where I consider margarine is perfectly adequate the word appears alone, and only spendthrifts will use butter. For instance, to use butter for the sauce for broad beans is absurd, for their marked flavour, with that of the parsley or savory, drowns the taste of so small an amount of butter.

Margarine/butter means that margarine alone will do; a proportion of butter, including that in the 10 per cent margarine-with-butter at the grocer's, is nice if you can manage it; or butter alone may be used if preferred.

½ margarine/½ butter means that this is to be preferred, or the nearest to it that you can manage; or butter alone if you like.

Butter/margarine means use all, or as much butter as possible.

Butter alone means that you really should use butter for a satisfactory result. Fish cooked *à la meunière*, for instance, really isn't what it ought to be when margarine is used.

Other fats

Lard and dripping are animal fats. Lard may always be used in place of dripping; dripping in place of lard where the taste does not matter, or where the dripping has been clarified (see below). The most useful drippings are beef, pork or bacon. Among the most delicious, though too soft for some purposes, is the dripping from poultry. Mutton dripping is seldom usable owing to its strong taste.

White shortenings are chiefly vegetable fats, and may often be used in place of margarine, dripping, or lard. They are also often dearer than margarines, depending on the quality of the fat, whether it is pre-creamed, and so on.

Cooking oils are vegetable fats. The best is olive oil, but it is far dearer than any other. Next best in flavour are corn and sunflower oils, then groundnut and lastly cottonseed. Boots' olive, sunflower and corn oils are cheaper than most, but almost all the taste seems to be refined out of them, which will suit some palates, disappoint others. One of the best-flavoured corn oils I've struck (marvellous for mayonnaise) is Sainsbury's. Some oils, often sold in fish shops and particularly recommended for frying, have a taste that is not agreeable for salads.

Oils are the best frying medium, as they give a crisp finish. For fried foods that are to be eaten cold, oil is essential, as the coating or surface of the food does not become soggy on cooling.

Clarify butter by 'oiling' it over a low heat until the milky sediment separates out, then pouring off the clear part for use. Dripping is best cleared by being boiled with water, left to get cold when the fat on top is removed, scraped, and heated until smoking; the clear part is then poured off for use. Watch for sputtering.

Cream

Too much cream 'softens' flavours too much. To accompany a pudding about one dessertspoonful is enough. There are roughly 4 dessertspoonsful per fluid oz., so that a ¼ pint (5 fluid oz.) carton of cream gives about 20 helpings used in this way. Cream and fruit are nutritionally sounder and cost less than an ice-cream apiece. When ice-cream is used with fruit use less of it than you do when eating ice-cream alone. For your health's sake as well as your palate's, add no sugar to cream, and no extra sugar to fruit when serving with ice-cream.

Double or thick fresh cream is necessary for whipping, although a proportion of thin cream, up to 50 per cent during spring calving when cream is extra rich and thick, may be added. If double cream has become very thick or is on the point of turning, thin cream or milk – *added by teaspoonfuls and stirred between additions* – improves it.

Thin fresh cream is perfectly adequate for most purposes where whipping is not necessary.

Tinned and bottled cream can be difficult to detect from fresh cream especially when mixed into foods, and is cheaper. It is, in fact, fresh cream that has been 'boiled'. It will whip.

Evaporated unsweetened milk will stand in for cream in some mixtures. It will whip if the (unopened) tin is boiled for 20 minutes, then cooled. But it has a marked taste and a 'powdery' texture which can usually be detected. This also applies to its close relation, tinned top milk. Both spoil the flavour of fresh fruits.

Yoghurt is good for most purposes. Does not whip, but goes into mousses as it is. As a salad dressing ingredient is worthy of consideration in its own right. Better than cream with apricots.

Sour and soured cream, cream (not curd) cheese, have many uses, but take care while stirring them or they may turn into butter. Thin with fresh top milk, or thin cream, by spoonfuls. Add sugar if liked.

Top milk can be used for thinning over-thick creams as above, for liaisons for soups and sauces, and to enrich mixtures. On the thin side for fruit except *en famille.*

Milk powder. Use double strength as a cream substitute in salad-dressing or mousses. Tastes slightly of evaporated milk.

Imitation creams – liquids and powders. A matter of personal taste. Children seldom mind them, so useful for children's parties, and in cakes and puddings as an occasional economy.

Wine and liqueur

Cider may often be substituted for wine, although it is inclined to thinness and acidity by comparison.

Sweet white wine is a reasonable substitute for sherry, Marsala or Madeira, which are all interchangeable. Red wine instead of sherry is better than nothing at all.

Rum is the best substitute for brandy and liqueurs. Whisky often does also, especially if you add a little sugar to it. Sherry can often do the work of brandy.

Light ale can sometimes stand in for cider. Brown or strong ale or milk stout does quite well instead of sherry in cakes and puddings – though perhaps not in the sauces that go with them !

Suspect any recipe that tells you to boil something in half a bottle of claret. ¼ pint wine is the maximum needed in all but the rarest instances (not included here), while 1 to 2 tbs. is enough to give a fillip to most dishes. Too much wine can make food taste foul.

Cheap Spanish, Algerian and French wines are excellent for

cooking, so is South African sherry. British wines and sherries are not successful in my experience, Merrydown wines being the exception (Merrydown are best known for their vintage cider, called apple wine these days). Wine keeps, for cooking purposes, far longer than many cookery and wine writers say. Pamela Vandyke Price, most sensible of wine experts, advises transferring cooking wine to a smaller bottle as it is used, for it is mainly air that causes wine to deteriorate. Bottles should always be well corked, and stored in a cool dark place. Sherry, however, keeps almost indefinitely if well stored.

Sugar

Which? did a piece on sugar and emphasized that white sugar is sugar whether it comes in lumps, grains or powder, and recommended using granulated sugar for almost everything for the sake of economy. In general terms this is good advice, and granulated sugar should always be used where the sugar is to be dissolved in water or another liquid – for example in jam-making or for stewed fruit. It is not necessarily so good in cakes or on fresh fruits, or for other recipes needing fine texture or rapid melting, where castor sugar is better. Nor will it give the flavour or texture of demerara or soft brown sugar. Sugar in 2-lb. bags costs less per lb.

Jams or honey can, in an emergency, stand in for sugar in some puddings, sauces, cakes, etc.

Marmalade, especially home-made, can often replace oranges or candied peel in sweet dishes, sauces and cakes. (Reduce the quantity of sugar slightly.)

Miscellaneous

Mushrooms. In many instances mushrooms stalks can be used instead.

Celery seed or the dried leaves of celery are excellent for flavouring out of the celery season, and better than the tasteless and expensive American celery now offered out of season.

Vinegar or cold tea used in the proportion of 1 tbs. vinegar or ¼ pint cold tea plus 1 level tsp. bicarbonate of soda to each ½ lb. self-raising flour can be used for cake mixtures in place of eggs in an emergency. Add 1 level tsp. baking powder to plain flour.

Bacon rinds will do in place of bacon, ham or bacon bones for flavouring soups and stews. They help 'jelly' the gravy when added to the meat for cold pies. Remove at end of cooking.

Egg-white can replace a second yolk for mayonnaise, when made with a whisk as suggested on p. 249. The resulting mayonnaise is very light and thick, and usually needs thinning.

Whipped white, folded into cream or butter cream, adds bulk and lightness, and softens and lightens thick 'boiled' egg custard, and cold white sauces. An extra white expands mousses and soufflés.

Cheddar cheese when used instead of Parmesan is best dried either before or after grating. Parmesan in the piece is cheaper and fresher than grated packets. Regginito (for those with an Italian grocer nearby, or who can get to the Fratelli Camisa in Soho) is shillings cheaper than Parmesan.

Rabbit used to be used as a substitute for chicken. Very often nowadays rabbit is the dearer, but has more flavour. Use whichever your purse will run to.

Pig's kidney is excellent for steak and kidney pie or pudding, pig or ox liver for braising and flavouring.

Making More of Scraps, Leftovers, Small Amounts

Stock. Use for cooking vegetables.

Soup. This is very important to budget cooks, as is emphasized throughout. Good home-made soup can be made from odds and ends. With cheese, it makes a first-class luncheon for everyone, with minimum time for preparing, eating and clearing up.

Outside leaves, peelings, etc. if merely coarse or unwanted, but not blemished, should be cooked, chopped up and mixed with a little gravy, milk or margarine for pet food. Keeping a pet can be a sacrifice for many old people, but no one need fear this suggestion is depriving a pet. On the contrary, the outer parts of vegetables often contain more and better nutrients than the better-looking bits.

Cheese. Grate, dry and store stale ends of cheese for cooking. See also mock duck, p. 446.

Mixed uncooked or cooked odds and ends of, say, mushroom stalks, bacon rashers, peas combine perfectly (with an onion – cooked first if the scraps are cooked) for omelettes, risotti and pasta.

Cold fish or meat. Mix with white or brown sauces and vegetable leftovers for luncheon patties. See also meat moulds and jellies, p. 138, kedgeree, pp. 305–6, risotti, pp. 335, 392–3.

Liver. Use uncooked for risotto, savouries, stuffings; add to stews or pies. When cooked use for stuffings, 'family' snacks, sauces.

Puddings. Steamed puddings (including steak and kidney) can be covered down and reheated. Or cut unfilled sweet puddings in thick slices, fry in margarine or butter, dust well with sugar, and serve with jam sauce, treacle or more sugar. (N.B. My home help, whose family has lived in Mortlake for over sixty years, recommends frying leftover steak and kidney pudding with the breakfast bacon – perhaps an old-established Londoner's breakfast dish.) Transfer milk puddings to smaller dish (or individual oven dishes), reheat and serve with fruit; or serve cold with ice-cream (plain choc-ice in particular), or grated plain chocolate; whisk an egg-white, and fold in with a spoonful of cream.

Also transfer leftover fruit pies to a smaller dish, cut the crust in portions, rearrange on top, serve hot, scattered with castor sugar, or cold, dusted with icing sugar. Cut jam or fruit flans in portions when finishing up – they look more attractive than half a flan on a sticky dish.

Add syrup from canned fruits to jellies in place of some of the water.

Expand luxury foods such as salmon, sole, soft fruits, asparagus by : making savoury or sweet flans of them; adding hard-boiled eggs and plenty of good salads; setting them in jelly.

All these methods are described in the recipes.

Bread. Elderly bread can be quickly rejuvenated. Preheat the oven at 450° F, gas 8, for 15 minutes. Hold loaf, crumb side down, and pass once, rapidly, under the cold tap. Stand crumb side down on bars of oven shelf just above centre, and bake 4 minutes. Invert and bake further 4 minutes. Cool on a rack. Excellent eaten hot. This treatment can be used to give 'home-made' crisp crust to steam-baked factory loaves.

Cut wafer-thin and toasted, rusk-like melba toast will keep well in a tin. Crisp up before use with soups, etc.

MELBA TOAST

Cut ¼ inch slice of bread and toast in the usual way, split through to give two ⅛ inch slices, and toast the raw side. Care – so thin a slice burns quickly.

Breadcrumbs

Kind	How to make	Uses and storing
Fresh (brown or white bread)	Sieve. Plastic grater. Electric blender	Suet crust in equal quantity with flour. Stuffings. Charlottes. Bread sauce. Fried for game. Thickening stews, etc. Store 2 to 3 days in polythene in cold
Dried white	(1) Make fresh crumbs and dry in airing cupboard or *very low* oven – door open (2) De-crust stale bread, dry out as above and crush (between thick paper) with rolling-pin until *very fine*; or put through mincer; or in electric mixer if suitable (see manufacturer's instructions)	Mixed with cheese for gratin dishes. Coating for frying. Crumble topping. Charlottes. Stuffings. In suet crust in emergency (but less good than fresh). Store in airtight container

Kind	How to make	Uses and storing
Browned (white or brown bread)	(1) Make fresh crumbs and brown in moderate oven (2) Brown stale ends of loaves as above and crush in the same way	Coatings for frying – but less good than dried white as the frying darkens them. Topping for gratin dishes. Store in airtight container

Short Cuts

Baking

Older cooks are familiar with 'bake days' – a method of mass production necessitated by wood- or coal-fired brick ovens and ranges in the past. To arrive at bread heat took a lot of fuel, skilled stoking and manipulation of the dampers controlling draughts in chimney and hearth. As much baking as possible was done at one time to take advantage of the fire. However, a bake day for making batches of cakes and tarts is still a sensible plan. Work out how you will fill the oven: small items such as fairy cakes or tartlets at the top, medium sizes – flan cases, sponge, sandwiches – in the centre, large cakes or cocottes of meat or fruit below.

Mass production

If you have a very cold larder (especially in winter), or refrigerator, make large quantities of pastry, white sauce, salad dressing or mayonnaise, butter cream. (Add grated parsley, cheese, softened mushroom or onion, anchovy, etc. to the ready-made sauce as needed.)

Keep about half a dozen hard-boiled eggs on the go for snacks, additions, sauces, lighter dishes.

Cake and pudding makers should keep going a supply of red and yellow jam glazes, butter cream, stock syrup (canned fruit syrup may also be used for this), fondant icing, almond paste, toasted nuts (chopped and otherwise) and the mixes below.

Pastry will keep 2 to 3 days in a larder according to the weather; longer, obviously, during an icy spell in winter in a north-facing larder (or food-safe on an outside wall). Some kinds keep about 7 days in the main chamber of a refrigerator, and about 10 to 14 days in the freezer.

Potatoes. Always do extra boiled potatoes ready for sautéeing, purées, salads. Bedsitter cooks should use them up next day; in a larder they will keep 1 to 2 days, or in winter, 2 to 3 days; about 5 days maximum in refrigerator.

Ready mixes

To cut out the job of rubbing fat into flour each time for pastry, scones or plain cakes, prepare some mixes and store in closed polythene bags, polythene containers with airtight lids or screwtop jars. They will keep for up to 3 months in a refrigerator or 2 to 3 weeks in a cool dark place – it must be below 60° F. Date the mixes.

Use half quantities for smaller families, one third for single-person households.

PASTRY MIX

3 lb. plain flour, 3 level tsp. salt, 12–15 oz. fat.
Sift flour and salt. Rub in fat and store.
Use to make:
Shortcrust pastry: To 12 oz. mix add about 2–3 tbs. cold water.
Rich shortcrust: To 12 oz. mix add 1 tbs. castor sugar, 1 beaten egg and about 1 tbs. cold water.
Cheese pastry: To 12 oz. mix add ½ tsp. dry mustard, pinch cayenne pepper, 4 oz. finely grated hard cheese, 1 beaten egg and about 1 tbs- cold water.
Mix to dough. Use as usual.

SCONE MIX

3 lb. plain flour, 3 level tsp. salt, 1 lb. margarine. Sift flour and salt. Rub in margarine. Store.

Use to make:

Sweet scones: To 12 oz. mix add 1 oz. castor sugar, 1 level tsp. bicarbonate of soda, 2 level tsp. cream of tartar. Stir well, and add about ¼ pint milk. Bake at 425°F, gas 7, for about 10 minutes.

Herb scones: To 12 oz. mix add 1 tsp. mixed herbs, bicarbonate of soda and cream of tartar as above and about ¼ pint milk. Bake at 425°F, gas 7, for about 10 minutes.

CAKE MIX

(see also pp. 489, 494ff.)

3 lb. self-raising flour, 3 level tsp. salt, 1½ lb. margarine. Sift flour and salt. Rub in margarine. Store.

Use to make:

Fruit cake: To 12 oz. mix add 4 oz. castor sugar, 4 oz. mixed fruit, 1–2 beaten eggs and 2–3 tbs. milk. Mix to a stiff dropping consistency. Bake in a lined and greased 7-inch cake tin at 325° F, gas 3, for 1½ hours.

Crumble topping: To 6 oz. mix add 2 oz. castor sugar. Use to cover fruit in a 1½–2 pint pie dish.

And other cakes made by the rubbed-in method.

How much mix to use:

The pastry and cake mixes have half as much fat as flour. In a recipe calling for 8 oz. flour and 4 oz. fat use 12 oz. mix.

For pastry allow about 1 tsp. of water for every 1½ oz. mix. Use 4 oz. pastry mix to cover 1½-pint pie dish or line 7-inch flan-ring, with the pastry ⅛-inch thick.

Use 6–8 oz. pastry mix to cover 2½-pint pie dish, or line-and-cover a 7-inch flan-ring or pie plate; or make 12 to 16 tarts, cut with 2½-inch cutter; pastry rolled ⅛-inch thick. The mixes can be used straight from the refrigerator.

Grow It Yourself

The budget cook with a vegetable plot is very nearly no longer a budget cook. Quite apart from money saved on many run-of-the-mill vegetables, she (or her family on her behalf) can grow choice varieties of everyday vegetables or fruit, and a selection of less familiar plants. It is with these last two categories that this chapter deals. You will need a fully fledged gardening handbook for general advice*.

It is surprising what you can pack into the smallest plot. What you must always do is feed your ground. A mixture of compost, dug in a foot or so down, with a dusting of chemical fertilizer on top and, in towns during high summer, a watering or two with liquid fertilizer will get surprisingly good crops, even from a London back garden. Compost is kitchen and garden waste sandwiched between layers of earth.

Raspberry canes can be trained along the side of the garden shed or on a section of fence. Do this by stretching plastic-covered wires between galvanized, large-headed nails at 9-inch intervals up the shed or fence (wall nails or vine-eyes for brickwork). Plant the canes about 9 to 12 inches apart, tying each to the wires as it grows. Each year the plants send up new shoots; cut back ruthlessly all but 2 to 3 of these per plant, leaving the strongest only. Raspberries are a woodland plant in nature, so do well in semi-shade if necessary. Water roots frequently as soon as the flowers begin to fall. Grow Himalaya Giant Blackberry on trellis in town gardens. Prune ruthlessly each autumn, leaving 2 or 3 of the strongest new shoots only.

Use radishes as an edging to the vegetable plot. If long enough, even a single bed can be divided up to take a succession. For the winter put in some Black Spanish radishes. These are large and

---

*See New Vegetable Grower's Handbook, A. J. Simons, Penguin.

spicy, and are used cut in slices. Other edgings include parsley and spring onions, and you will have enough of the former to make soup (pp. 363, 412).

Train courgettes, small marrows, squashes or ridge cucumbers up a wall or fence, or in an odd corner, or plant in a second unused compost heap if you have one. Small-fruited members of the marrow clan will do in tubs if assiduously 'fed'. Peas and runner beans will grow up fences and trellis work, and I always make a maypole of runners round my clothes-post by putting two beans to a bamboo cane in a circle round the post, then running wires from the canes to the top of the post. Mix a traditional scarlet runner with Blue Coco for added decoration.

Herbs

If you have one of those small squares of garden in front of a south-facing or west-facing suburban terrace house, turn it into a herb garden. Most of the flowers will be too insignificant to merit stealing, the herbs so shrubby and luxuriant that they are hard to damage, while you will have a 'gourmet's cuisine' for the picking, plus a scented, bee-humming garden the whole summer long, taking the minimum of work. Edgings here can be chives and marigolds (petals give a tang to stews), and in the years they consent to bloom together, they make a cheerful splash. In a London herb garden the notorious Russian tarragon is useful as it is hardy enough to withstand polluted air, while the pollution keeps its weedy, rampaging habits in check. If the legends of its tastelessness on the one hand and coarse flavour on the other are true, none of the eaters of my mayonnaises, vinaigrettes or poulets estragon have yet dared complain !

Thyme is very temperamental to grow, but if it 'takes' it goes like a breeze, expanding into fat fragrant cushions, the shelter of woodlice, little jewelled beetles and earwigs, (which don't seem to harm herbs). Golden and silver thyme have pretty, variegated leaves, but the flavour is indistinguishable from black. Grow all three in good air, but black thyme is tougher for town gardens.

Lemon thyme has a gorgeous scent, but the lemon flavour is lost in the kitchen. Lemon balm has no culinary value, spreads itself as the weed it is, yet make room for one plant by the path to pinch at, in passing, for the scent.

Sages (horticultural name Salvia) vary in their flowers, and you may like a Salvia or two to provide decorative colour as well as flavour.

Find, if you can, a geranium grower in your area, and plant rose and peppermint geraniums. The latter is very rare, most attractive and of delicate constitution. If you get one, treasure it, and grow new cuttings each August from it, nurturing these indoors on a sunny windowsill through the winter. The leaves of both 'perfume' custards, puddings, jellies and fruits. The flowers of both are an unremarkable cluster of small lilac 'stars', but the leaves are very decorative. Window boxes and tubs are perfect for them.

Grow mint or Russian tarragon in a pot, to 'contain' them. Basil is not at its best in a pot. Winter savory, marjoram and chervil are all useful and easy. The handsomest everyday herb is bronze-leaved fennel, which grows in tall feather-swathed columns, the capitals being large webbed platters of bright yellow flowers beloved, as are all herb flowers, of every sort of bee.

For full details about herb-growing and a choice array of recipes consult *The Penguin Book of Herbs and Spices* by Rosemary Hemphill.

Britain is lucky in its high standard of seedsmen. Every Woolworth counter is laden with its own-named seeds and those of Bee's and Cuthbert's. Every local garden shop and ironmonger has its stand of Sutton, Carter, Dunn and so on. All these are first-quality seeds in generous amounts for the average garden. Rarer kinds, very special qualities, new introductions and large amounts are a feature of such firms as Dobies of Chester, from whom may be obtained, on request, their own splendid catalogue and the list of famous Bunyard specialities which they have taken over. Many of the things mentioned in the herb paragraphs can be raised from Dobies' seed, and all the vegetables are on Dobies' or Bunyard's lists, though some of the Dobie varieties have been developed under special names. The Herb Farm, Seal, Kent, have a very complete range of herb seeds and plants.

Choice Varieties of Vegetables

RUNNER BEANS Dobies' Yardstick and As Long As Your Arm. In good soil I've grown beans 15 to 16 inches long. Exhibitors manage 18 inches! Beautifully tender and delicious. You should get a few 13 inches in town. Miss Dorothy Brown, one of the thirteen children of a Worthing gardener, taught me a useful piece of country lore on the subject of runners: eight beans of assorted lengths are enough for two people. Runners can't have too much water, including a light spraying over the flowers to set them.

BUNYARD'S CLIMBING BLUE COCO. Purple pods of medium size, fine leaves, and purplish stems. No strings! On cooking, alas, the beans turn green, decoration and food together.

BROAD BEANS. Not easy to grow in towns and they need space. Green-seeded have the flavour, of which Green Windsor is the best known.

FRENCH BEANS. Easy as runners and need no stakes. Canadian Wonder or its descendants are most reliable, and there are some 'stringless' sorts. (None should need stringing if you harvest properly.) Dobies' Golden Butter are a yellow-fleshed kind, and Bunyard's have a true French flageolet, Chevrier Vert, grown for the seeds, like broad beans. Over-blown French beans can also be used up as flageolets (p. 390). Royalty New is a dwarf version of Blue Coco. Water as runners.

PEAS. If you want the earliest, most prolific and delicious old-fashioned pea (especially on chalky or limey soils), and are prepared to stake, try and find a seedsman who still keeps Pilot. (Dobies don't do this one.) Tall peas are still the best, I think, and as dwarf peas really need *some* staking, you might as well get the bigger yield of tall varieties. Alderman or Dobies' Greensleeves are prolific for later crops. For a good early dwarf pea Kelvedon Wonder holds its own, and Little Marvel is earlier still. Second earlies include such established favourites as Early Onward, Kelvedon Monarch and Laxton's Superb. Bunyard's Petits Pois are self-explanatory.

Sugar peas (English for Mange-Tout) are picked when still small and flat. They are cooked complete, having a delicious nutty taste. Prolific, tall. Dobies have them. Bunyard's list includes Asparagus Peas. Like the sugar peas these must be gathered while small. They have very pretty winged pods and an asparagus flavour. Dwarf. You need one long or two short rows of these two sorts, for you must make big pickings as the pods are small in size.

POTATOES. Duke of York is my favourite early potato. Yellow-fleshed, beautiful flavour, medium cropper. Local seedsmen who keep it sell out early. Turns up now and then in branches of Woolworth's. Rude things – such as 'the fish and chip potato' – are said about Majestic, but it does well in Sussex so probably will in other chalk soils. As the name implies, grows large for large families. The Arran varieties are sound and seem to do well in most soils. Pink-skinned potatoes seem to be favoured by the black slugs that prey on potatoes, so take care in heavy soils. Water once or twice in the growing season (as you earth up is as good a time as any) with liquid 'Slugit'.

British potatoes seem to be bred to be floury when mature. If, like me, you like potato dishes of various kinds this is a curse. Floury potatoes break up or are undercooked. They make horrible potato salad or dishes calling for sliced or shaped spuds. Bunyard's specialize in French seed potatoes, so make your own selection from their list – on request from Dobies.

BROCCOLI AND CAULIFLOWER. The first comes earlier, including the sprouting sorts. Dozens of kinds if you have space, fairly heavy soil and big numbers to feed, for they take months to mature and usually turn in all together, so you give away far more than you eat. All this applies to cabbages. Make your own selection.

CELERY. As above, but needs more work.

SPROUTS. Their habits are like those of all the cabbage family, but they seem to 'stand' longer without running to seed, and home-grown crops are seldom heavy enough to be an embarrassment. Firm soil and planting essential.

75

LEEKS. They need trouble and good ground, but if you like them they're worth it since shop leeks seem to get worse each year. Musselburgh and The Lyon still take some beating.

LETTUCE. Webb's Wonderful – no further comment needed.

SHALLOTS AND ONIONS. The first are so obliging, adaptable and trouble-free one can hardly claim to have grown them – they do it themselves. A must in every kitchen garden or plot.

The only onions I've ever bothered with are Dobies' 'sets' – time-saving and splendid. They're show specimens when grown, and it is pleasant to hang them in a prominent spot for the admiration of visitors and adornment of the kitchen.

SPINACH. Many varieties, but the several perpetual types are best for smaller gardens.

TOMATOES. They will grow out of doors in the south of England without much difficulty, though spraying is essential. The blight of tomatoes and potatoes spreads from one to the other rapidly, and round the neighbourhood. It overwinters in soil, composted haulms – everywhere. Many Sussex gardeners I have known cut down potato haulms as soon as they start yellowing at the base of the stem, and prune outdoor tomato leaves to two above each cluster. This, they say, helps reduce risk of blight, but they also spray. Sprayed outdoor tomatoes, picked green in October, tissue wrapped, and stored in a dry place, will go on ripening, and you can have your own tomatoes for Christmas. (This was another tip of Dorothy Brown's.) Tomato plants are a worthwhile buy, but you will have to raise the golden kind from seed (Dobies' Golden Boy or Peach). Do this on a sunny windowsill if you have neither frame nor greenhouse.

AUBERGINE, CUCUMBER AND PIMENTO. All will grow outside with luck and a reasonable summer, but are a surer bet under glass. They do need mothering somewhat though. For special outdoor cucumbers see Bunyard's list.

MARROW FAMILY. Dobies' Little Gem and Zucchini. Bunyard's Courgette and other 'specials'. Some years these plants, and ordinary marrows, produce masses of flowers. You can cook and eat them: fried in batter, stuffed and baked. Not a gourmet's treat, but fun.

See Address Book, p. 557.

Basic Facts and Skills

The Raw Materials

Meat

BUYING MEAT. This comes with experience. To the novice eye all meat has scarlet or purplish-red lean, and cream-coloured or white fat, according to who is looking at it, and in what light it is seen. Such descriptions help little. You can learn to know what good meat should look like, though you may not be able to afford such high quality, by studying the windows and displays of the best butcher in your locality, by buying a little of the best when you can, and by going to as good a family butcher as you *can* afford, talking to him and learning from him. Until you get to know a little about meat avoid buying :

from supermarkets;

from the sort of 'chain' butchers who staff their shops with boys obviously too young to have any more knowledge of meat or butchering than you think you have;

from cheap butchers whose windows are a chequerboard of chopped up bits and pieces;

from butchers where the staff wear dirty aprons (all butchers' clothing gets bloody, but it should not have been there so long that it is in several strata and dark brown);

meat that has an area of dried-looking lean, or dingy yellow fat. It may have 'been in the cold room overnight', but was also in the window too many days.

Suitable cuts of meat are given with recipes, but take it as a general rule that :

cheap home-killed beef will be inferior;
grilling meats are extravagant;

77

forequarters of animals yield the cheaper, hindquarters the dearer cuts;

fatty and bony meats are cheap only for those who can eat some fat, and are good about picking meat from bones;

there is more nourishment in a good stew than a cheap roast.

In buying New Zealand lamb a guide is provided by their excellent grading system (p. 21), about which they have plenty of leaflets (pp. 423-4).

A Note about Veal

Quite experienced cooks and quite knowledgeable local butchers have very hazy notions about escalopes of veal. Continental butchering of veal is a special skill. Home cooks find that escalopes from the local butcher do not end up as the thin, flat, tender slice they have eaten in restaurants, while the price from specialist shops is alarming. When I began writing this book I was resolved to get the escalope question clearly settled, along with others relating to veal, for I knew many people beside me who were puzzled by it.

England is a beef country. Only a handful of farmers rear veal calves 'on purpose'. Most English calves are 'bobby calves', infant animals, mere weeks old, that the dairy farmer does not wish to rear. The total average weight of the whole carcase is around 40 lb., of the legs 5 to 7 lb.; whereas Dutch (the best) and other Continental veal carcases, which *are* reared for butchering, average 100 lb., and the animals may be 9 to 10 months old. They are 'finished' indoors – that is fed on a large percentage of milk, which helps to produce the delicate texture, flavour and colour. And finally, and very importantly, Dutch veal legs often go to 40 lb., or the weight of the entire English carcase. It is from the leg (the leanest part of any animal) that veal fillets are cut for escalopes.

Look at a leg of English veal (or of lamb), and you will see that it is made up of several cushions of meat divided by thin membranes. If you were to pull apart these cushions, the largest might weigh about 8 to 10 oz., while that from a leg of Dutch veal would be about 3 lb. (Note that the equivalent cushion from a leg of beef makes the long roll of topside, from which the butcher gets two or three family joints.) If you were to cut your English veal cushion into ⅜-inch-thick slices, each might measure about 1½ inches across and weigh 1½ oz. But the Dutch veal cushion would slice at about 4 inches across and weigh 4 oz. or over, and these are the slices used for escalopes. Only the biggest three cushions of veal are used for escalopes (or sometimes for a roast of veal), so out of a 100-lb. carcase less than 18 lb. would be suitable for escalopes. This accounts for the price, in a similar way that the price of fillet steak is accounted for – because it is a tiny fraction of the whole beef carcase. Chefs in hotels and restaurants buy a whole leg of Dutch veal from which to cut escalopes. Of the 31 lb. remaining from say, a 40-lb. leg, a chef would use the larger pieces of meat for 'scallopines' (miniature escalopes, of which each portion contains two or three; with a good sauce, delicious, but less in demand than escalopes), the smaller pieces at the knuckle end (equivalent of leg of beef) would be used in pies,

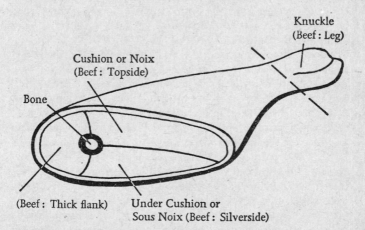

Knuckle
(Beef : Leg)

Cushion or Noix
(Beef : Topside)

Bone

(Beef : Thick flank)   Under Cushion or
Sous Noix (Beef : Silverside)

Leg of veal showing equivalent beef joints
(Diagrammatic main sections only shown)

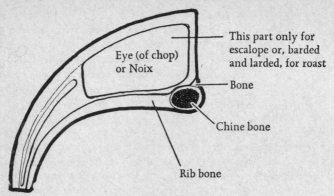

Section through loin of veal for escalope

blanquettes or veal stews, and the bones for stock. A butcher, however, has no guarantee that he will sell the inferior cuts.

The 9 lb. the chef cuts from a leg for escalopes is further trimmed of all membrane so that the thickish 4-inch slices can be 'batted out' without risk of the escalopes buckling and shrinking when cooked (they do shrink slightly in any event). These trimmings go into the stockpot in a big kitchen, but a butcher cannot sell them at all.

Because of the work and the wastage involved, butchers who cater to the 'veal trade' charge apparently high prices for escalopes and veal roasts. But beware! In renowned Leadenhall Market I have seen escalopes cut British fashion, from Dutch veal, and costing the highest Dutch veal prices.

The non-specialist butcher cuts the upper end of the small English veal leg in slices across the cushions of which only the largest circle can make so much as *one* scallopine. The price will still be quite high, and you will have a lot of trimming to do. It is far better and cheaper to make your own escalopes, or a good lean roast. To do this, order a complete loin of English veal from your butcher (this is the joint he usually cuts into chops), making sure he does no chining or chopping of the bones. You then cut out the cushion of lean, trim off all membrane, and cut ⅜-inch slices from that. They might be 2½ inches across and weigh 3 oz.

(maximum), batting out to about 4 inches (use a rolling-pin, beat steadily and quite gently on a board). They will not be as big as restaurant escalopes, but will be very good. Trimmings, bones and small odds and ends will make pie or blanquette, and a medium pot of veal stock. For roasting you would need to bard (p. 85) the fillet and perhaps also lard it (p. 85).

An escalope of pork is an excellent substitute and even cheaper. Cut from a large leg, or loin, as for veal. You will get something between Dutch and English sizes. (Bone, or get the butcher to bone, the leg, take out the largest cushion for your escalopes, stuff, roll and roast the rest.)

Calves' liver. From the foregoing it will be seen that calves are not numerous in England. Nevertheless older people find the modern lack of calves' liver annoying. Liver is among the most perishable articles of fresh meat, so that butchers near slaughterhouses or big markets are likely to get more than others. Since the war, slaughterhouses have much decreased in numbers, especially in big towns, though many have increased in size. Town butchers have less ready access to calves' liver, and what there is tends to go to those districts where customers are willing to pay the higher price scarce commodities always command. When extra liver is about, few average family butchers can get more than two calves' plucks at a time.

If you specially want calves' liver you will do best to order it. Quite often the butcher has a special day for offal, so you may have to make a special visit on the day advised by him.

Butchery

Butchery gets worse all the time as the family businesses vanish. Supermarkets and chain-stores furnish merely the saddest examples of the decline in a highly skilled and important craft.

MAKING A BETTER JOB. Some common faults of clumsy butchering can be improved by:

adding strings where these are too sparsely spaced;
sewing up badly hacked or gashed joints (the gashes are

concealed by supermarket packing) with trussing needle and thin string or thick button thread;

skewering small straggly bits of meat in place with poultry pins;

chopping off excess bone and trimming down thick fat.

To re-shape and re-tie joints needs a little practice, a few medium and longer metal skewers and medium string (not so thin it will cut the meat, not so thick it is difficult to tie). Shape the joint as you want it, remembering that fat on the outside bastes the meat while cooking, and skewer it to hold in place while you tie. Slip-knots work well, secured by a final turn. Tie tightly as meat shrinks in cooking, but don't pull so hard on the knot that you squeeze out the stuffing, or the ragged ends you've just tucked in. Don't stint the string. A tie too many is better than one too few. When re-tying a well-butchered joint that you have untied for stuffing or marinading, of course, follow the original way it was rolled and the original string marks.

BONING MEAT. To bone meat first locate the ends and then the direction of the bones. Do this by prodding through the meat with a thin skewer, if the joint is so huge you can't feel the bones by pressing with your fingers.

Sharpen the knife – a thin flexible knife for poultry and very small-boned joints, such as best-end of lamb; a heavy point-ended knife for larger joints, such as shoulder, or ribs of beef. Do not work on a smooth hard surface, as the meat slips. Wood is best.

In working, keep the knife against the bone, always cutting away from the hand holding the meat, always withdrawing the knife promptly when the meat leaves the bone, to avoid slashing through the lean beyond the knife point. Avoid starting again in a new place if the patch at which you're working becomes difficult, or you will have a messy result, all bits and pieces. As you sever the meat push it back from the knife, noting the shape as you go, so that you can truss it neatly afterwards. Keep a cloth beside you to wipe knife and hands as needed. Re-sharpen the knife as needed.

BIRD. Bone out a bird by slicing first straight down the centre back and working towards leg and wing. Insert the knife point down the side of leg bones, loosen the meat, turn it back, like a glove from a finger, until the first joint is cleared. Cut through the ligament and remove the thigh bone, continuing with the glove technique for the drumstick, taking care not to pierce the skin, and turning the meat right side out finally. Do this for the wing, but discard the wing tip altogether. Do leg and wing on other side. Continue against the carcase until the breast meat is freed, first on one side, then on the other – on a young bird this more or less pushes away from the bone – until carcase and flesh are joined only along the top of the breast-bone. See the knife is sharp, and shave the skin away with a paper-thin sliver of the bone adhering. This prevents a broken skin.

BONING BREAST OF LAMB OR VEAL; BELLY (OR PICKLED) PORK. Schematic diagrams only to show main lie of bones, as sizes and numbers vary with animal, cut and butchering. *Strip papery skin from fatty side of lamb before boning.*

Lamb usually has diaphragm flap attached; sometimes long solid breast-bone down one side. Veal and pork seldom have these. Cut back flap to expose all bones, but do not detach entirely if stuffing meat. Cut away shallow dryish meat from crosswise short bones and lift out, cutting under breast-bone to remove when rest are cleared.

At thin end crosswise bones are attached to one or more thin cartilage strips set at angle. Present in all three meats.

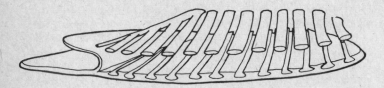

Stuffing goes under flap if one is present. Leave margin round stuffing as it is pressed to edges with rolling. Roll from thicker end, skewer roll for firm hold while tying. Use medium string, pull fairly tight, but not to cut or eject stuffing. Err on generous side with number of ties.

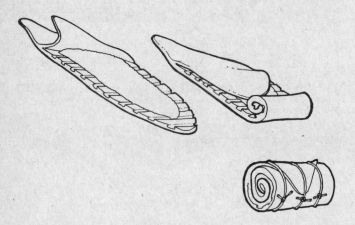

Fat is vital to tender meat. The problem is to have enough of the right kind where it is wanted, both for the breeder and the cook. Hence the rather crazy-seeming process of trimming off fat and then adding it by various means. But do this transposition yourself, rather than paying the higher price for trimmed meat *plus* extra fat to lard it.

Basting is said to be unnecessary in the modern oven. I disagree. If one is roasting a joint of lamb it should be basted, when its leanest side is uppermost, either by placing a piece of fat on top, or by spooning dripping over it from time to time in the traditional way. If fat is placed on top of *any* meat it should be removed before the last 20 minutes of roasting so that the meat can brown and crisp.

On the other hand, where fat naturally covers lean, some may need to be removed if thick. Many people find lumps of fat repulsive. A great deal of fat in a roasting tin spatters all over the oven. (Some newer oven tins have perforated grids to help solve this problem.) Pare down fat on lamb of all kinds where thick; on pork joints (crackling can be tied on again afterwards); and also on topside etc. of beef where the butcher has added this very thickly. The wrapping of fat on lean beef joints is necessary, but over ½ inch is obviously profiteering. Take some, if not all, including the ribbon of gristle that lies below it, from rump steak; and absolutely every scrap from fillet, which should be barded.

LARDING. The very best way of adding fat, in particular to beef, exactly where it will lubricate and tenderize the lean, and in so small an amount that it will repel no one. Larding imparts flavour and is a great improver of cheaper cuts. Can look decorative in cold meats when cut.

You need a larding needle. Chefs now recommend the kind with a toothed, hinged flap (made by Rostfrei, from Jaeggi, p. 556). Chefs buy special pork fat, and this is best, but good beef fat does well, as does bacon fat. Keep good fat trimmings in the freezing compartment of the refrigerator. The important thing is that it should be long and firm in texture, for instance the strip from a rump steak. Chill the fat before starting to work with it (chefs keep it on ice), cut it into strips ⅛ by ⅛ inch. Insert well down into needle, clamping firmly. Lard through the thickness of the meat if a big piece, or 'sew' short pieces into the surface of small cuts.

BARDING. This is the wrapping of meat in thin slices of fat or bacon.

BREASTS OF FOWL. I have evolved a most satisfactory method

of my own for this : insert first two fingers beneath skin at neck end, gently loosening skin all over breast. Take either a piece or two of bacon fat from a rasher, or some of the chicken fat itself. Push under the skin so that it hangs over the breast bone about an inch either side. During cooking the fat melts completely away, giving a beautifully moist result but leaving no sign or residue. It is far superior to barding the breast.

Fish

Which? demonstrated a few years ago that frozen fish is fresher than some of the fresh fish on sale in our shops. This surprised very few established housewives. The White Fish Authority has done something to improve matters, but the standard still falls far short of reliability. There are far too many boxes of defrosted mass-filleted plaice, cod and haddock around; too many exposed, flies' landing-fields, too high prices, unskilled shop assistants, and – ignorant customers.

Fresh fish is : firm fleshed; bright- and convex-eyed; springy if the tail is wiggled; tail and fins soft, slithery and not withered at the edges; well-scaled (herring, coley, mullet); slimy (plaice, soles); bright-coloured (e.g. mackerel, an iridescent shimmer; plaice, clear orange spots; herring, red round eyes and gills). The smell is always fishy, but should be fresh, sea-breezy, iodiney, not an objectionable niff that creeps through the house calling all flies to buzz round larder door and window.

The flesh of fish is not always white – coley is pinky-brown until cooked, for instance. But I can think of no fish round these islands that ought to be yellowish. Reject it if offered.

The methods of filleting are shown in the diagrams. You need a thin, flexible, freshly sharpened knife.

SHELLFISH. See pp. 271–80.

FILLETING FLAT FISHES

Step 1. *All flat fishes.* Trim fins and tail, leaving only a narrow margin for easier handling.

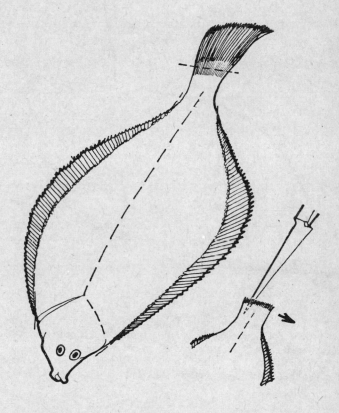

Step 1a. *Skinning of soles and witches* (NOT plaice, dabs flounders). Ease knife-point under skin across tail, as dotted line, to loosen enough skin for inserting thumb. Go to Step 2.

Step 1b. *Plaice etc.* (NOT soles or witches). Cut down centre line to bone, knife held at slight angle to clear ridges of spine. Go to 2a.

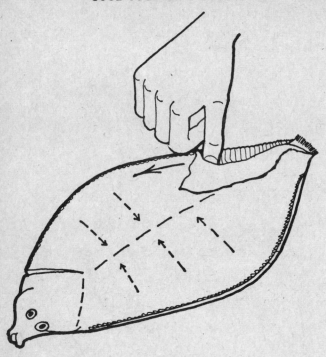

Step 2. *Soles and witches only.* Using thumb in letter-opening action, free skin all round edges from tail to head. Using cloth to grip, pull skin from sides to centre as dotted arrows, working close to fish to avoid tearing skin or pulling up flesh. Finally remove at centre from tail to head. Turn and skin second side. Go to 2a.

Step 2a. *All flat fishes and small brill, turbot.* Cut round or remove head. Cut down centre as 1b. Keeping knife almost flat to bone, cut fillets from bone in sweeping strokes. On 'short' side, where fishmonger cuts to gut, roe is found under fillets, which are pulled gently, not cut from roe. Roe sac rubbed from fillet with damp cloth

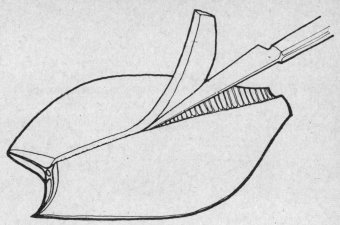

and salt. Fillets removed in any order, but last always most tricky when skeleton no longer held rigid by flesh.

Step 3. *Skinning plaice etc, also cod, coley, haddock fillets.* Lay fillet skin side down on board, push flesh from skin with knife held almost upright, shifting grip (use cloth if necessary) to work close to fillet, moving knife forward yet across skin in sawing action, and keeping skin as flat against board as possible.

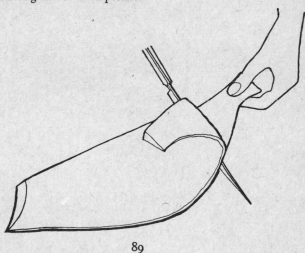

All *fillets*, are folded or rolled, rough or bone side outwards, smooth or skin side inward.

Herring best scaled as well as gutted by fishmonger, otherwise do this from tail to head with knife-back. Remove head, fins, trim tail. Slit down belly, slightly to one side to clear bone, which you should feel with knife. Turn fish over, press down centre to loosen back-

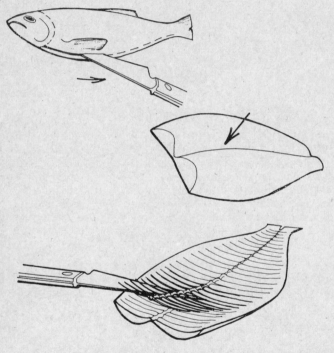

bone. Lift bone from head to tail, bringing away some side bones also.

Mackerel. Behead and trim. Split down centre back, continuing cut just to clear bone across width of fish and from head to tail to produce one fillet. Turn fish and repeat to produce second fillet. Pull out bones which you will feel by running finger-tip lightly down centre of each fillet. Halve very big fillets down centre to make four.

Fruit and vegetables

Quality and freshness here are much easier for the novice to see. All the same, British greengrocers get away with murder. It is a legal offence to palm off (and it is in the palm of his hand that the cunning greengrocer hides the blemishes) bruised apples, withered oranges and wilted greens on the purchaser, as it would be to sell 'over-ripe' meat or fish. This is called unsound food, but it is difficult to prove in a law court. Nor are these blemished portions excluded from the weight of the goods, so the swindled customer suffers a double loss. Again barrows and cheap shops can turn out to be dear. Buying at the end of the season is a risk, as buying at the beginning is dear.

Here are a few points to watch regarding fruit:

Oranges should shine, a greenish tinge is not undesirable.

Suspect wrinkled skin at flower end of oranges; enormous English dessert apples; yellowish Bramleys; withering just where stalk enters pear, particularly if the pear is also very yellow.

Look at the side of bananas hung away from inspection up near the 'handle' of the bunch, and if blackish reject them.

Warm-climate fruits are fragrant when ripe. You can't expect to be allowed to prod expensive fruits with your thumb and bury your nose in them, but you should be able gently to press pineapples and melons and to sniff at them (stem end usually) from about 2 inches' distance. A greenish tinge to peaches does not necessarily signify under-ripeness, nor a rosy blush ripeness. Enormous peaches and strawberries from cheap shops and barrows are probably woollen.

To keep soft fruits for 24 hours, hull or stalk them, spread on a plate, *sprinkle well with castor sugar*, and put in a cool place. If in the refrigerator, slip the plate into a polythene bag and allow to warm to room temperature about an hour before use. All soft fruit to be served fresh is improved if sugared a little time before use, unless from the garden, when it is best of all eaten still warm from the sun.

Tomatoes are best bought when an orangey colour and, in the opinion of many connoisseurs, best eaten then. They will ripen steadily in an unheated room, slowly in a cold larder or refrigerator (in foil or polythene), quickly in a sunny window or the airing cupboard.

Through the winter and spring Spanish and Channel Islands tomatoes are available. They are grown outdoors, and seem to be inadequately sprayed, for they almost invariably 'go off', owing to infection from blight. Blight frequently attacks tomatoes from inside, so that it is difficult to know what state they are in until you use them. In my view they are a bad buy both for this reason and because, again due to blight, the flavour is poor. Canned tomatoes, juice and purée are better value. Never throw blighted bits of tomatoes on the compost heap. The spores, which survive all weathers, are likely to infect your own potato and tomato crops, establishing this dread garden disease for years.

Never buy distorted cucumbers, usually a sign that bees got into the greenhouse – the crop will be very bitter.

'A touch of frost' is good for no green living thing. After a severe frosty period reject greenstuff that has any watery, transparent-looking leaves. It will *not* be 'all right inside, love'. It will most likely be a slimy rotting mess. At such a time the only good buy in frosty vegetables comes out of the deep-freeze cabinet.

In the early spring there is a special greengrocers' breed of new potatoes and carrots. The first won't scrape, the second have wooden middles. Neither tastes of anything. Both cost a lot. Budget cooks can afford something better – to wait.

Management of the Cooker

Making good use of the oven

Present-day ovens are designed to give as even a heat throughout as possible. Nevertheless the laws of convection still apply and the top half of the oven is hotter than the lower half. What is called the 'true heat', that is the heat at which you set the thermostat, is in the centre. This means that in a large oven with eight shelf positions the centre three positions would give true and near true heat, so that you can bake several trayfuls of, say, small cakes at once in the centre. It is a strange piece of economy on the part of cooker manufacturers that they provide only two oven shelves in all the welter of gadgetry that goes with bigger cookers. However, for a trifling sum you can buy an extra shelf.

The same centre-shelf-true-heat applies to small ovens, but the spacing of the shelf positions above and below may give a wider variation of heat in these positions. It is always a good plan, in any event, when baking several batches of similar items together, to move the top batch down and the lower batch up as soon as the top batch has risen and set. Do this with doors and windows shut, without fluster, to avoid draughts, sinkings or spills. Turn up the thermostat while the oven door is open.

Take advantage of the variation in the temperature zones of the oven to cook all or most of a meal in it. For instance:

roast beef in the centre of a moderate oven 375° F, gas 5 (with roast potatoes round or Yorkshire pudding beneath in the same tin);

potatoes or Yorkshire pudding in upper part of oven in separate tin.

fruit crumble added to this shelf 30 to 35 minutes before the meal;

braised celery (blanched first) on lower shelf, with custard or milk pudding, or stewed fruit for another meal.

A very full treatment of this way of using the oven has been a special feature of the Radiation New World Cookery Book for years (it is now in its 54th edition!). It will repay study by anyone who leads a busy life. All ovens can be used in this way, and many of the recipe books belonging to various cookers suggest it; but the Radiation book is particularly inventive and varied on the subject.

But always, when you have to use the oven try to cook more than one item in it, not simply to save fuel, but because having extra dishes ready-cooked is an advantage, and in summer particularly it is pleasanter to keep the oven off.

Oven temperature chart on p. 17.

Using the top of the stove

The importance of simmering is stressed throughout, for few people carry it out accurately. When it is realized that on old coal-fired ranges merely the heat of the iron casing was used to simmer stockpots, some idea of the gentleness of the process is understood. On modern gas rings and electric hotplates the problem is often to lower the heat enough. The newest cookers often have special settings and burners for the purpose, but many readers will not possess such stoves, and for them one of the heat-distributing devices described on p. 54 is a way out of the problem. It is generally true that if a gas flame touches the base of the pan it will soon rise above simmering heat. Therefore, if you need to simmer something for a long spell unattended, look under the pan and see the flame is really low. Also make sure there is no draught that could blow out the flame.

Electric hotplates are fairly easy to use for more than one pan if a lowish heat is needed, provided the pans are of proper electric-cooker type. Gas rings are inclined to burn that section of the pan half on them when used in this way, as the flame laps up the side of the pan. Here again a heat-distributing device is useful, in particular to bedsitter tenants – provided the one-and-only ring is set in a flat hob, that's to say

Fast boiling seldom means that you need the heat at maximum for the whole job. Once boiling point is reached, keep the heat high enough to keep the liquid bubbling and churning, but no more.

Solid electric hotplates can be used as girdles for making girdle or drop scones or blinis. I have known of penniless bedsitter tenants who fried bacon and eggs on them, a process not calculated to endear one to the landlady. It needs practice, too. Still, in desperation . . .

Grilling is dealt with fully on pp. 315–17.

Cleaning the oven after each using is, in my view, a waste of time. Unless a strong substance is used, and much elbow-grease, some particles get left on. These burn on and build up but the eye of the daily-wipe-with-a-damp-cloth brigade gets used to them, doesn't notice them, and in due course, for all the daily labour, the oven looks just as dingy as those of the clean-it-when-I-have-to school. I find that unless it happens to have been used for extra-fatty cooking several times, about once a month is reasonable. The spray cleaners will do for one or two goes, but every so often an overnight soak in Kleenoff is needed, and is then less exhausting for self and oven than scrubbing away with abrasives at the bad bits. Frequent wiping with a damp cloth over the hob pays off, however.

Some Cooking Processes

This book does not aim to cover every basic technique of cookery in detail. My object is to emphasize methods of cooking that either use the minimum of fuel or make the best of lower-priced ingredients.

Roasting

PREPARING THE MEAT. Do any butchering, make stuffing.
Not more than 10 minutes before meat is to go into oven: lightly season the cut surfaces of meat or inside of fowls. Seasoning greatly improves the roast, but salt liquifies blood, so too-early seasoning would leach out the juices and spoil the meat. So do not stuff meat too early as stuffing contains salt.

QUICK METHOD. Set the oven at 425° F, gas 7, put the prepared joint in the centre and cook the whole time at this setting, timing per lb, as shown in the table on p. 99. Good for joints up to 3½ lb., and 'thin' joints such as best-end lamb, loin of pork. Some cooks prefer the quick method for pork, duck and goose.

MEDIUM METHOD A. Set the oven at 425° F, gas 7, put prepared joint in centre of oven, lowering the temperature after 30 minutes to:
(1) 375° F, gas 5, for joints of 2½–3 lb.;
(2) 375° F, gas 5, for 30 minutes, then to 325° F, gas 3, for joints of 4 lb. and over for rest of time.
(3) as (2), but a further reduction to 300° F, gas 2 for exceptionally large items.
Timing per lb. as shown in table on p. 99. Good for joints of 3 lb. and over.

MEDIUM METHOD B. Set oven at 375° F, gas 5. Put joint in

centre. Time as table on pp. 99–100. (This method gives a lighter finish and is useful for unattended cooking.)

For good pork crackling or crisp poultry, by either medium method, it is often necessary to raise the heat to 400–25° F, gas 6–7, for last 20 minutes to ½ hour. Oil crackling.

SLOW METHOD. Set oven at 325° F, gas 3, put prepared joint in centre of oven, unless very big when it should be just above centre, and cook at this heat for whole time, timing per lb. as table below. It is also possible to roast meat like lamb or veal at 300° F, gas 2, for several hours. This is useful for those out all day who wish to come home to a hot roast joint. The prepared joint should be set in the centre of the oven. Joints are less brown and crisp when cooked slowly, and may lose juices somewhat.

SPIT-ROASTING METHODS. Roast meat should be crisp outside *all over*. Hence the spit. A reasonable substitute for spit-roasting is to stand the meat on a rack in the tin. This must not raise the meat completely out of the tin (unless oven cleaning is not objected to !), otherwise, for a very lean joint, frequent basting will be needed. Meat on racks or grids may need the oven shelf positioned slightly below centre. Joints or birds may also be hung from an upper shelf. In this instance the roast may need to be inverted half-way –ʻor more often – through cooking heat being greater at the top. The hanging must be by strings tied round the meat, then looped over a butcher's hook. Take care not to pierce with hook when inverting, or juices will escape from heat-sealed outer crust.

Perhaps it is marginally better to preheat the oven for 10 to 15 minutes before inserting the roast, as this may seal it more quickly. But if in haste no great harm will be done by starting in a cold oven. Allow 15 minutes extra on the time at the end.

Covered roasters do not produce a roast joint. They bake meat, by a combination of dry and steam heat. The surface may be coloured and crisped more at the end by removing the lid of the roaster. The principle is that of pot-roasting, but takes more fuel. Excellent for cheaper joints and tougher birds, but flavour and texture are not equal to true roasting, and juices are drawn out of meat and must be taken as gravy. Popular with cooks who hate oven-cleaning more than they like a first-class roast. A covered roaster may be simulated by enclosing meat and tin in foil. Allow 20 minutes extra roasting time by this method.

Yorkshire pudding needs a hot oven – see below.

Turn the meat during cooking at least once; work out which side you will start to carve or must carve, so that it is uppermost during the latter part of the process.

Resting the meat. Let the meat stand in a low heat after dishing, for 15 minutes before serving. (Make the gravy during this time.) The steam formed between the fibres of the meat in cooking will escape, the meat compacting down to a closer texture for carving, and holding its juices evenly. The last point is demonstrated when a roast is cooked to be carved cold. The jellied juices occur through the meat or bird, and flavour and succulence are often better than in hot meals.

Fats. Basting and larding have already been dealt with. Other points concerning fats are:

brush *oil* on to pork crackling;

do not prick the skins of geese or ducks during cooking, only before dishing if liked;

pour off excessive fat from roasting tins during cooking, leaving only about 1 tbs. in the tin;

baste veal frequently where recipe does not call for larding or barding;

where butter is the only roasting fat mentioned, and where the meat is dry, a proportion of lard, oil or dripping is advisable, as butter is not really suited to high temperatures;

grease the bars of grids or roasting racks;

preheat dripping or roasting fat until sizzling, dip exposed cut surfaces of lean in this, or spoon it over meat;

turn meat fattiest side up to begin cooking, so fat runs over rest of joint.

Cooking round the joint. Potatoes, root vegetables and fruits are often roasted in the meat tin, exchanging flavours with the meat and saving work and fuel. They will tuck in round a grid or rack, but need basting once whatever the cooking vessel.

Root vegetables must be parboiled before adding to the meat

tin. Potatoes are altogether superior if parboiled for 5 minutes, drained (keep water for gravy), and shaken together to roughen their surfaces slightly. They then roast with crisp outsides and fluffy centres.

Yorkshire pudding is at its best cooked below the meat so the juices run on to it. (In this case potatoes must go into a separate tin.) Fat must be 'smoking hot' when batter goes in, whether below meat or in separate tin. Oven must be at 400° F, gas 6, or if at about 325° F, gas 3, raise it to the higher setting, putting meat tin down a shelf, putting Yorkshire pudding high in oven; once the pudding is risen and colouring, heat may be reduced to 350° F, gas 4. (Batter recipe pp. 122–3.)

Gravy is best very simply made in the meat tin when the joint is dished. Water, boiled up until the toasted juices liquefy into it (deglazing), is adequate where the joint has been well flavoured. But if Yorkshire pudding has been cooked below the beef, stock will be necessary.

For thick gravy brown 1 dessertsp. of flour per ½ pint of liquid in the residual fat of the meat tin, adding a slice of onion into it. Add the liquid and boil up, seasoning as necessary.

Excellent thin gravy results from pouring a cupful of water over the roast during the last 15 minutes of cooking; vegetables to be removed before this operation.

Roasting Times
(minutes per pound plus time over at end)

Meat	Quick	Medium	Slow
Beef on bone	15 + 15	20 + 20	20 + 20
Beef, boned	20 + 15	20 + 20	25 + 20
Lamb	20 + 15	25 + 20	25 + 20
Pork*	25 + 15	30 + 20	35 + 20
Veal*	25 + 15	30 + 20	35 + 20

*Pork and veal must not be undercooked. Err on the side of over-cooking rather.

By quick and medium methods, minimum 45 minutes for small joints. By slow method, minimum 1 hour.

Chicken	Quick	Medium	Slow
Unstuffed chicken up to 3 lb.	1 hour	1¼ hours	1 hour 20 minutes
Chicken (3½ lb. and over) according to weight and stuffing	1¼ – 1¾ hours	1 hour 25 mins. to 2 hours	1 hour 25 mins. – 2 hours 10 mins.

For times of Christmas poultry see p. 482.

Boiling

Loosely used to cover stewing and braising. Boiling is rarely used as such, for the fast movement of the water breaks up the food, yet at the same time gives a less tender result. Where fast boiling is necessary the recipe indicates it.

Stewing and Braising

Stewing is carried out in simmering liquid, braising in the steam – or mainly in the steam – of simmering liquid plus the heat given off from the cooking vessel itself. Cooking takes place either on top or in the oven. It is a most economical method of cooking.

MEAT. Meat is usually seared, before either operation, in hot fat. Formerly this was thought to seal in the juices, but such a result must be impossible when meat is cooked for several hours in moist heat until the tissues are broken down enough for the meat to be really tender. But searing gives meat an agreeable flavour and colour, and colours the liquid at the same time, making it more appetizing. (Vegetables should also be browned as a rule.)

Stewing and braising render really tough meat tender, break gristle and bone down to jelly, and make picking meat from bones very easy. This means that cheap meat can be used; that nutrients from gristle and bone are released, as they are not from roasted meat; that nutrients from any vegetables are retained in the gravy; and that waste is kept to a minimum. What is more, stews and braises save time, space and fuel, since meat and vegetables can be cooked in the same pot at the same time, and low heat is essential. This, in turn, also means that stews and braises are very tasty.

Do: cut meat for stews in about 2-inch squares, not in inch pieces, which end by looking like the dog's dinner;

cut vegetables neatly, using small ones whole;

pour off surplus frying fat before adding liquid;

cook the stew or *braise long enough.* 2 hours, often given in recipes, is long enough only if you are using roasting quality meat. Reckon on 3 hours average, 4 hours for joints, ox-tail, shin and leg;

cover the pot really well, putting foil beneath badly fitting lids;

skim off fat at the end, before dishing or thickening, etc.;

arrange dished meat and vegetables attractively, and see they are really hot before serving.

Bacon and ham are exceptions to the above. Bacon needs soaking: 6 hours or overnight for smoked; 2 to 6 hours for unsmoked. Braise bacon only if you can be sure it is not too salt. Stew or boil by just covering in unsalted water, or ½ water, ½ cider, ale, or white wine, and simmer 20 minutes per lb. plus 20 minutes; minimum 1 hour.

Potatoes may be included in the pot; steamed in steamers over pot, peeled or in jackets; wrapped in foil either peeled or otherwise. If cooked whole in these ways, medium to large potatoes will need up to 2 hours.

FISH. The equivalents of stewing and braising for fish are boiling and poaching. For the first a *court bouillon* is often employed. This can be water, or a mixture of water and wine or cider, in which fish bones or trimmings, flavourings such as bay, lemon, carrot, onion, one of the anis-flavoured herbs (tarragon, fennel, dill, chervil) and seasoning are simmered for 20 to 30 minutes, the liquor being strained and sometimes cooled before the fish is put into it. True fast boiling is only rarely used. As a rule simmering is advised – the liquid only just bubbling gently.

For the second the liquid is minimal; on top of the stove it just covers the bottom of the pan; in the oven it may consist merely of a squeeze of lemon, a tablespoon of wine, or water shaken from a wetted hand. A good deal of liquor from the fish is produced during cooking, and is incorporated into any sauce made. The fish is lightly seasoned before it is put into the (covered) cooking vessel, and the liquid is seasoned only lightly. Butter/margarine is sometimes dabbed on top of fish. The cooking times for boiling or poaching are often too short, and the cooking itself too gentle for vegetables to be added. Flat-fish fillets take 7 to 20 minutes according to size and how they are folded; whole fish and thick steaks, and fillets from large fishes such as haddock and coley, take 15 to 30 minutes according to thickness. In poaching the liquid is kept barely moving with only occasional bubbles breaking the surface.

VEGETABLES AND FRUIT. These also may be stewed or braised. Vegetables are particularly good cooked in stock, or water flavoured with lemon juice. Frying first in a little butter or good oil adds flavour and richness. Root vegetables respond well, and rather battered old specimens can be made tasty and presentable by this treatment – a valuable point in hard winters.

Fruit is best cooked in the oven, especially when it is to be served cold or put into flans, as it breaks up less than on top of the stove. Use little or no water. Add sugar only after fruit has begun to soften, as sugar tends to harden fruit skins. Strips of orange or lemon peel or a little citrus juice, elder flowers, herbs, rose petals, a little honey and wines are some of the additions for fruits.

MAKING PIES AND PUDDINGS is only another method of stewing or braising, the crust forming part of the cooking vessel.

BLANQUETTES, FRICASSÉES, GULYASES AND CURRIES are stews that use sauces instead of water or wine.

PRESSURE COOKERS stew or braise quickly by forcing steam through the prepared foods.

Frying

This means boiling in fat – either added fat or fat present in the food itself. Bacon and herrings, for example, may be fried without added fat. Some fats reach very high temperatures, and cooking with them is quick. Butter does not reach a high temperature without burning. It will successfully cook eggs and thin fillets of fish. To give the flavour of butter to fried meats use oil, lard or dripping up to half the quantity of fat needed, and brown or sear the meat in this, afterwards adding the butter. Avoid mutton dripping as the flavour is intrusive.

Shallow frying calls for a shallow wide pan and enough fat to cover the bottom of it to a depth of about ⅛ inch for most purposes, but up to ½ inch for some things, including frozen foods.

Deep fat frying requires a suitable pan to serve as the fat bath and a wire basket to fit the pan. Those who like a lot of fried food ought to buy the purpose-made equipment, but otherwise a good saucepan will often serve well enough. Also there is no quicker way of carrying out the operation than by 'setting up the system' in an orderly manner, otherwise the advantage of the quick cooking is lost. You need about 1½ pints oil, or 1 lb. cooking fat; at least 2 good tbs. dried white crumbs (p. 67); 1–2 tbs. well-seasoned flour; at least 1 egg, beaten with 1–2 tbs. water on a large plate. Working as near the stove as possible, put on to heat enough fat to come half-way up the bath; spread flour on a large sheet of paper, place the egg-plate and a small brush next to it, spread the crumbs on a second sheet of paper next to the plate, and lastly line up the basket. Turn each piece of food to coat lightly in the flour; transfer to egg and brush to cover well, lifting on skewer to allow surplus egg to run back on to plate; lower into crumbs, coating well by lifting paper at corners to roll each portion over until covered. Press crumbs on lightly with palette knife and lift into basket.

It is essential for all frying that the fat be hot enough, but the result of too cool fat is particularly unpleasant with deep-fried food. Unless really boiling, the surface of the food is not sealed, fat soaks in, making food greasy. The result is not crisp, while the appearance is pallid and the centre of thicker items may be lukewarm or raw. When hot enough dripping or lard gives off a faint bluish haze – not smoke – and any sputtering stops. Oil becomes almost still and the surface is free of bubbles. The vapour is virtually invisible unless the oil begins to burn, but there is a hot smell. To test, drop an inch cube of bread in the fat, which should turn golden in one minute. (Chefs use thermometers but I think this excessive for home use. For interest, however, the correct average temperature of boiling fat is 340° F.)

Grilling, see pp. 315–17.

Finishing Techniques

Skin tomatoes, peaches and grapes by plunging in boiling water for no longer than 60 seconds, then immediately in cold, and remove skin thinly. The red flush is transferred to the flesh of the fruit beneath. If only 1 or 2 tomatoes are to be peeled spike on cook's fork and turn in high gas flame until skin pops and scorches. Run under cold tap, remove skin. Take out hard core from stem end of tomatoes.

Skin fish – see pp. 87–90.

Skin and bone fish for fish pies, casseroles, etc. for cold fish dishes.

Skin meat – for example cutlets, roast best-end neck of lamb, liver; always remove skin and fat from meat for réchauffés, except meat for mincing, or ham.

De-crust toast, sandwiches (after making) and fried bread croûtons (before making).

Stone grapes, plums, apricots, cherries, olives for fruit salads, garnishes, hors-d'œuvres, preserves, unless recipe directs otherwise. Black olives will halve like plums for stoning, green olives are cut round their stones spirally and 'put together' again for appearance.

Peel oranges for fruit salad and garnishings with sharp (stainless if possible) knife thickly enough to take off a very fine layer of pulp so that no pith remains and outer membrane of sections is removed.

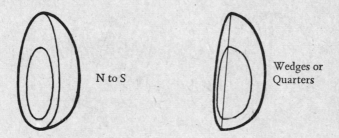

N to S

Wedges or Quarters

CUT: (1) Eggs: *'north to south' for egg salad, in halves or quarters/ wedges. 'Round the Equator' for stuffed eggs* plus a slice from base to stand egg upright.

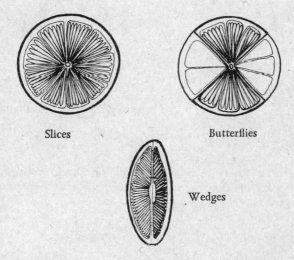

Slices

Butterflies

Wedges

(2) Lemons: *Wedges or Quarters. Slices* (if you expect diners to squeeze lemon don't cut thin. Wedges better). *Butterflies*, cut each slice as the shaded portion. (A wasteful and finicky garnish for most of us. If you must, though, use only when drinks before dinner can use up the leftovers).

(3) Radishes from shops: *Lilies.* Deep cuts across top. *Rose.* Peel in 4 sections almost to stem. Put in water 1 to 2 hours before use, when cuts will open out.

Lilies (a)   Lilies (b)

Rose (a)   Rose (b)

Best of all pull from garden, remove root, leave 'plumage'. Wash well.

Glaze: (1) flans and tartlets with jam (pp. 525–6) or arrowroot glaze in colour to match fruit or filling used. Take glaze over lattice and sides of flan-case.

(2) covered fruit pies and tarts, by brushing top *lightly* with water and sprinkling well with castor sugar. Mince pies may be thickly dusted with icing sugar.

(3) savoury pies with glaze of proportions: (a) 1 egg, pinch salt, 1 tsp. water; (b) 1 egg-white, salt, 1 tsp. water; (c) 1 yolk, salt, 1 tsp. water; (d) 1 tbs. milk, good pinch salt, as these may be available.

(4) buns and some breads, as directed in recipe.

Marbling cream on to fools, purées, soups and so on is less wasteful than and as decorative as piping. Run a spoonful of cream on each individual dish or soup-cup, 3–4 tbs. on a big dish. With knife-point, fork or skewer barely touching the surface, swirl cream, or draw it over the food in regular lines until a pattern is made. Keep to the surface, or you'll merely stir the cream in.

Your food will still be enjoyed if you do none of these things. It will be talked of if you do.

*Quantities in the recipes serve four
unless otherwise stated*

*Plain flour is intended in recipes
unless otherwise stated*

Foundation Recipes

By these are meant those items or methods that form parts of complete dishes, having variations to suit different foodstuffs. They are important to any cuisine, but vital to budget cooks since they allow the use of many low-cost ingredients, making, often, a virtue of necessity. They come over and over again in recipes and, although neither difficult nor lengthy, need accuracy, particularly in measuring and weighing.

Stock

Is a stockpot necessary? No. If you have no room to keep a stockpot, use a ready-made stock of bouillon cube or extracts. Varieties include old friends like Oxo (cubes), Bovril and Marmite (jars), Symington (packets and cubes), and newer names like Knorr, Lemco, Sainsbury, Maggi (cubes).

However, if you have world enough and time, not to say space on stove and in larder, and a large saucepan, you can have stock to hand practically free, and a home-made stock is usually better for stews, gravies and so on.

Brown stock is made from beef or veal bones, meat (if liked), onion and root vegetables browned in fat, covered with cold water, seasoned and flavoured with herbs (as available or liked). Bring to boil and simmer 3 to 5 hours.

White stock is made as above, but omit browning. Also chicken may be used – the carcase from roasting birds, or the water in which a boiling fowl is cooked.

Improvised stocks, however, are more likely to be made in modern households, and for them nothing is bought specially. Odds and ends of bones from joints (not lamb as a rule), vegetable water (take care with cabbage water, it can be too strong), gravy and sauces can all go into the pot.

Care of stock is important : See food storage notes, p. 42. Lift off the fat when cold and clarify if wanted for dripping (p. 62).

Soups

In this book soup plays an important part, and it should do for every household of modest means. One of the most versatile of dishes, soup can be made so that it is 'a meal in itself', a luxury course, and a means of using up material otherwise useless or awkward (see the soups that use odds and ends of garden produce, p. 217). The well-filled feeling soup gives makes it useful for slimming diets, and for a first course where appetites are hearty or where the main course has been planned for quality rather than quantity. In illness soups are often all the patient can digest.

BROTHS. These are almost the same as stock, although some broths are much more elaborate (e.g. Scotch Broth). Those made only from bones are not a complete food even though, when cold, they set to a thick nourishing-looking jelly. For proper nourishment complete protein, which is made up of a number of amino acids, is necessary, but in bone stock an essential amino acid is missing. If, therefore, broth is to be used as a food it would need, say, minced meat added in the cooking, or toasted cheese and croûtons served with it.

THIN SOUPS. (1) Broths made from good-quality ingredients as well as bones. (Classic clear consommés are an example, hardly met with these days outside the very best restaurants or, oddly, in tins !)

(2) Unthickened purées – usually vegetable.

Thin soups can be very nourishing, and are preferable in summer, and before rich food at all times.

PURÉES. Usually vegetable, made by cooking the main ingredient in stock, milk, water or a combination of these, sieving or pounding the solid ingredients to a paste and recombining with the liquid. Lentil soup is an example. Basic proportion: 1 lb. fresh vegetables to 1 pint water.

THICK SOUPS. These may be basically broth or purée but thickened by the addition of a fat-and-flour roux, or a liaison of egg with milk or cream. The latter thickening is also a means of providing extra nourishment, and should be borne in mind by those living alone, who often 'can't be bothered with a meal'; by slimmers; and by anyone who has faddy appetites to deal with. That it is delicious goes without saying, and so it is preferable when entertaining. Basic proportions: roux – 1 oz. each fat and flour to 1 pint liquid; liaison – 1 egg or 2 yolks to 2–3 tbs. single cream to 1 pint liquid.

When using liaisons, the hot soup is poured slowly on to the liaison, stirring continually, after which it must not be boiled. A little cornflour creamed with the liaison allows reheating without so much risk of curdling.

ACCOMPANIMENTS to soups may be used for extra nourishment. Small fried croûtons are the classic accompaniment for thick soups. They have the virtue of staying crisp for a time after immersion in liquids, and are successfully reheated so may be made in advance. Small 'snippets' of dried bread – rusks – can be used, and larger toasted croûtons sprinkled with cheese. Grated cheese may also be handed round to be sprinkled direct on to the surface of soups. Chives and other chopped herbs are sometimes added to soups in the last few seconds of cooking, or scattered on the top of each helping as it is served.

Sauces

Proportions for thickened sauces

For:	To each ½ pint of liquid add:
Panada or binding sauce	2 oz. each fat and flour
Coating sauce (the most-used consistency)	1 oz. each fat and flour
Flowing sauce (for puddings, pasta, etc.)	¾ oz. each fat and flour
Thickening for gravies, soups, etc.	½ oz. each fat and flour (When combined, fat and flour are called the roux.)

For egg-thickened sauces use 1–2 yolks to each ½ pint liquid.

When a recipe stipulates '½ pint sauce' it is referring to the amount of liquid used.

For most purposes ¼ pint panada is enough. ¼ pint of coating or flowing sauce is usually enough for dishes for 2 people. ¼ pint of sauce is usually enough for combining with other ingredients for savoury moulds, soufflés, flan fillings, etc.

To avoid sauces lumping: if the liquid is hot the roux should be cold; if the liquid is cold the roux should be hot; the liquid should be added at once, but slowly, and above all off the heat, while stirring continually, to disperse the roux evenly; once returned to the heat, stirring continues briskly until the sauce boils; should there be any signs of lumps, remove at once from heat and whisk until lumps disappear, returning to heat to finish cooking.

Some cooks prefer to add liquid a little at a time and bring this to boiling point each time before adding the next lot, as for brown sauces, q.v. The method may be helpful for large amounts of sauce and nervous cooks. For small quantities it does not seem helpful, as sauces can lump just as badly if the cook is careless, and it takes longer. In some instances the sauce seems to thin again.

Brisk stirring and whisking give sauces a good gloss.

Avoid using a metal whisk with an aluminium pan for more than a short burst of whisking, as the reaction of the metals is apt to give a grey tinge. *Use a small wooden spoon.*

A really small, straight-sided pan with a lid helps greatly in sauce-making.

To avoid skin when setting aside cooked sauces, fit a butter or margarine paper, greasy side down, right on the surface of the sauce so that all air is excluded, scraping off any sauce from paper when reheating. Cover pan with its lid. Sauces keep hot for a long time in a *bain marie* (water bath – a meat tin of hot water does) kept just at simmering point. Or a Mijoska if you have one (p. 54). Asbestos mats are not to be trusted. Whisk sauces, hot or cold, before reheating or using them, to restore even smoothness.

Use caution in thinning a too-thick sauce. Add the extra liquid only by tablespoons, heating and stirring well between spoonfuls.

Thicken a too-thin sauce by stirring a teaspoon of flour to a smooth paste with liquid of the same kind as the sauce (if possible), stirring in well, off the heat, and then bringing sauce back to boil for about 1 minute.

Butter adds its fine flavour to sauces, but is not necessary. Even the French use margarine these days *en famille.*

White sauces

In this book I refer variously to 'white sauces', 'Béchamel', 'good white sauce', 'well-flavoured' or 'good Béchamel'. Sometimes I also say 'any good white sauce', referring to masking fish or pepping up an egg dish.

English cooking permits a simple white sauce flavoured only by pepper and salt. Make this if you must when merely 'white sauce' is mentioned. However, it seems to me that most households, even single-person households, usually have onions and a packet of dried herbs to hand, and to add a sliver of the one and a pinch of the other is little trouble. It is true the dried herbs should be tied in muslin or strained out at the end, but their appearance is not offensive, and rather have speckled sauce with flavour than plain tasteless sauce. Béchamel sauce is made by a slightly different method, and should be flavoured with seasoning and a bouquet garni (parsley, thyme, bayleaf), a slice or so of carrot, onion, celery, and either a pinch of nutmeg or blade of mace. Good Béchamel means that as much of all these as possible should be in, but a muted Béchamel can be claimed, I think, if the onion, bayleaf and nutmeg or mace are present. Good white sauce, made by the Béchamel method, would have the herbs and onion and something from the Béchamel list as well. 'Any good white sauce' as I use the phrase includes Béchamel but could be mushroom, parsley, egg, anchovy, prawn and so on.

SIMPLE WHITE SAUCE

½ pint milk
1 oz. each margarine and
    flour
small slice of onion

Sprig of parsley etc. (or pinch
    of dried herbs)
seasoning
½ bay leaf

Melt margarine and, *off the heat*, stir in flour. Add milk, stirring smooth, add flavourings, and season well. Return to heat and bring slowly to the boil. Stir rapidly all the time, scraping wooden spoon firmly across bottom of pan. Cook 2 to 3 minutes until thick. If possible cover and leave aside, keeping hot, for 10 to 20 minutes for flavour to develop. Remove flavouring agents before using.

GOOD WHITE SAUCE

½ pint milk
bouquet garni
celery flavouring via either
    a slice of stalk, leaves,
    salt or seed

bayleaf
1 oz. each margarine and flour
seasoning
slice of onion

Put all the flavouring in the milk. Bring just to boiling point, cover and leave to cool as long as possible. If not cold when used, take care not to make the sauce lumpy. Melt margarine, and *off heat* blend in flour. Add liquid through a strainer, or lift out herbs, onion, etc. Return to heat and bring slowly to boil, stirring smooth. Cook 2 to 3 minutes, stirring all the time.

ALL-AT-ONCE WHITE SAUCE

Here the principle of mixing fat, flour and liquid all in one go is applied to sauce-making. It saves time at the final cooking stage of Good White Sauce and Béchamel, and altogether for Simple White Sauce. Proportions and ingredients are the same, and the milk is infused before use as for the traditional methods.

Put milk, fat, flour and seasonings into small pan over low heat, and bring to boil, stirring very briskly all the time, and clearing the base of the pan well as soon as the sauce starts to thicken. Cook 2 to 3 minutes.

Herbs, grated cheese, tomato or anchovy paste and powdered spices may be included successfully in the mix. Mushrooms or onion, etc. must be first sweated in the fat, as for the traditional method, but then the rest of the ingredients may be put in all together for the final stage.

Provided the stirring is thorough so that the mixing is even and no lumps or (with mustard, tomato, etc.) streaks form, I doubt if even quite expert cooks would be able to say which method you had used.

BÉCHAMEL SAUCE

Ingredients and method as for Good White Sauce (above), but add slice of carrot, pinch of nutmeg or blade of mace, and leave the milk to infuse for ½ hour.

For a special dish add 1 to 2 tbs. cream (or substitute; see p. 62).

Additions for sauces

These three sauces are suitable as the base for the various white sauces used in this book. Most additions, chopped parsley for example, are stirred in about 1 minute before the sauce is finished.

Other methods include adding the ingredient to the flour (mustard sauce can be made in this way); cooking it in the fat (prawn, mushroom), when extra fat may be given in the recipe; replacing some of the milk with it (fish liquor, stock, wines). Quantities are as given in recipes.

Proportions for ½ pint sauce

FRESH HERBS: minimum 1 level tbs. after finely chopping.

DRIED HERBS: 1 level dessertsp. Scald if liked in 1 tbs. boiling water, squeeze out surplus moisture before using.

Example: Parsley Sauce.

ANCHOVY: about 1 level tsp. but strength and quality of essences, pastes etc. vary.

MUSTARD: 1–2 level tsp. dry mustard (according to taste) mixed with 1 tsp. wine vinegar or lemon juice and added to roux.

CHEESE: 1–2 oz. grated cheese *added after cooking*, according to type of cheese. The drier the cheese the less you need. ½ tsp. mustard added to roux with or without dash vinegar and cayenne. If cheese is boiled up in a sauce it turns to rubbery strings.

MUSHROOM: not less than 2 medium whole mushrooms, or 6–8 stalks, chopped down very finely indeed with 1 tsp. (chopped) onion or 6–8 chive blades. Soften in the fat for the roux, then proceed with rest of method. A little chopped mint is a good addition. Season well.

ONION (Soubise): 1 medium onion, chopped fine and softened in the fat. Add ¼ oz. fat if liked.

EGG: add 1 finely chopped hard-boiled egg, returning sauce to gentle heat for a few seconds. If suitable a heaped tsp. of a chopped fresh herb may also be added.

LIAISONS are sometimes used to thicken or enrich a white sauce: 1 yolk, 1 tbs. cream per ½ pint is a good proportion. For method see p. 113.

BROWN SAUCE OR SIMPLE SAUCE ESPAGNOLE

½ pint brown stock (vegetable water, etc.)
1 oz. each dripping (or other fat) and flour
½ each small carrot and onion
1 tbs. sherry or other wine
1 clove crushed garlic
2-inch piece of celery
1 rounded tbs. tomato purée (or 1 to 2 fresh or canned tomatoes, or 2 tbs. tomato juice)

{ when suitable, making sauce into a simple Espagnole

Slice vegetables and fry in fat in small saucepan. When just turning colour add flour *off heat* and blend well. Return to heat and simmer slowly until flour and vegetables are nut brown.

This process is a cooking commonplace, but beginners tend to carry it out either on too fierce a heat, when it burns, or too gentle a heat, when it takes too long. The secret is a medium heat, constant stirring, and a small pan so the small quantities of ingredients are of even depth over the bottom of the pan. The whole surface of the roux should bubble, the browning taking about 10 minutes.

The stock added to brown roux must be cold, and should be added gradually *off the heat,* each addition being stirred over gentle heat until smooth. The reason for this is that the flour grains burst in the frying, and when liquid is added the flour swells immediately. If all the liquid is put into the very hot pan it heats so quickly that it cooks the swollen flour to lumps. When all the liquid is in, stir in the tomato purée. Simmer the sauce 20 minutes, rub through strainer. Where sherry is used, add, and reheat sauce.

N.B. Where whole tomatoes are used, they must be skinned and added with the last lot of liquid.

SAUCE BÉARNAISE

Put 3 tbs. tarragon (or good) vinegar into a very small pan with 1 tsp. finely chopped shallot and good shake black pepper. Boil down to about 2 tbs. Cool, 'cream' in 1 to 2 egg-yolks and, over very low heat (or in pan of simmering water), gradually beat in ¼ lb. butter/margarine (some of this *must* be butter). Sauce should be of whipped cream consistency. Rub through fine sieve. Finish with 1 tsp. finely chopped tarragon. Some cooks add the tarragon to the vinegar at the beginning, and strain the reduced vinegar, rather than sieving.

TOMATO SAUCE

See p. 149.

BREAD SAUCE

See p. 182.

N.B. For other hot sauces, see also Œufs Mollets, p. 148ff, and *passim,* where quantities and details are given individually.

Cold sauces

TARTARE SAUCE

See p. 233.

MAYONNAISE

See p. 248.

SALAD DRESSINGS

See pp. 247–51.

FRUIT JUICE SAUCE FOR PUDDINGS

½ pint liquid made up from:
  juice left from stewed,
  canned or syrup-bottled
  fruit; or orange or lemon
  juice with or without the
  grated rind; syrup from
  preserved ginger; and water

1–1½ oz. sugar according to
  sweetening already in juice
1 heaped tsp. cornflour
vanilla, lemon, rum, etc. to
  flavour, if desired

Slake the cornflour in 2 tbs. of the cold liquid. Dissolve sugar in rest of liquid and boil up. Pour on to cornflour, return to pan and stir briskly over heat until cornflour thickens – about 1 minute. Add flavourings.

Wine may be used in place of fruit juice: ½ wine, ½ water. Use only 1 oz. sugar and omit lemon juice.

JAM SAUCE

2 tbs. jam
¼ pint water
1 level tsp. cornflour

juice of ¼ lemon or orange
strip of lemon or orange rind

If jam has large pieces of fruit in it, sieve through a bowl strainer. Heat the water and pour through the strainer to clear it. Otherwise omit sieving. Slake cornflour with 1 tbs. cold water. Bring jam and water to the boil with rind; add juice. Pour on to cornflour, blend, return to pan and boil up, stirring until the mixture thickens – 1 minute.

NOTE: Arrowroot may always be used in place of cornflour, but it is more expensive. It is the most refined flour thickening, and should be used where appearance matters, as it gives a jelly-like transparency. Arrowroot has the property of thinning again if cooked more than about 2 minutes. It is therefore a bad choice for sauces needing reheating or keeping hot, but excellent for busy cooks. If an arrowroot sauce or gravy thins, take another spoonful and repeat the process.

SABAYON SAUCE

2 yolks, or 1 whole egg and 1 yolk	¼ pint mixed fruit juice and sweet wine (sherry,
1 dessertsp. castor sugar	Madeira, Marsala are best)

The hollandaise of the pudding world. With it a steamed canary pudding or castle puddings (recipes not in this book, but a Victoria mixture does the trick) become dinner-party dishes.

Make it at the last minute. Put all ingredients into small basin which fits on to, but does not sit in, a pan of water taken from the boil. Whisk with a light whisk until thick and frothy. Have ready a heated sauceboat. Serve at once.

It is quite *comme il faut* to make the Sabayon at – or at the side of – the table when you are cook-hostess, and to keep the diners waiting for it in any case.

NOTE: Pure wine and 4 eggs turn this recipe into Zabaione (for 3). Serve in wine glasses, with wafers or ratafias.

HARD SAUCE (RUM OR BRANDY BUTTER)

See p. 473.

Batters

When recipe stipulates '½ pint batter' it refers to total amount of liquid.

THIN BATTER

For Yorkshire and sweet puddings, pancakes, thin coatings. Water here is not a meanness – it makes a beautifully light, easy-to-handle batter. This quantity makes about 16 pancakes – when correctly thin and lacy as they should be. For many families half the quantity will be enough for a Yorkshire Pudding (use ½ beaten large egg, or 1 small).

1 gill each milk and water	1 egg
4 oz. plain flour	¼ tsp. salt
½ oz. melted margarine or	pepper if liked, for savoury dishes
1 tsp. salad oil (optional)	

Beat all ingredients very well together until there are no lumps or specks of unmixed flour floating on top. These rise when beating stops, so it is sensible to leave the batter now and then to let them collect. Scrape round bowl also, to release flour that may have stuck. The added fat helps, especially at the start of cooking pancakes, to keep the batter from sticking. Leave the batter to 'rest' if possible, well covered. The odd colour some batters go is harmless, and disappears in cooking. Give a final whisk before cooking. Really good heat is necessary. Lard, white shortenings or oil are the best fats for frying. For pancakes melt about 1½ oz. fat in small jug standing in hot water. Use about 1 tsp. of this per pancake, pouring back any surplus into jug. All that is needed is a mere film of fat over the bottom of the pan. ¾ oz. dripping will do a ½-pint Yorkshire pudding, if not cooked in meat tin. Get it smoking hot (3 to 5 minutes in upper part of oven) before pouring in batter. Oven at 400° F, gas 6; cooking time approximately 35 minutes, depending on the size of the tin.

Tin sizes: about 10 by 7 inches for ½ pint Yorkshire pudding; 6 by 8 inches for 1 gill. These give a thin, light and crisp pudding.

FRITTER BATTER

For fritters and coating foods for deep-fat frying.

3 oz. flour	*For sweet dishes*
1½ tsp. baking powder	add 1 tsp. sugar
2 fl. oz. each milk and water	*For savoury dishes*
1 egg	add pepper, spices, chopped
1 tsp. oil	herbs, etc. to taste
¼ tsp. salt	

Separate egg-white from yolk. Mix all ingredients except egg-white, beating well to a thick cream. Whisk egg-white to stiff snow and fold in. Use at once, as baking powder begins working once wet.

WAFFLES. This batter also makes excellent waffles for those with waffle machines or irons. Add 1 tsp. sugar to the above quantity, and use all milk, or sour milk if available. This quantity will make about 4 waffles.

Pastries

I have given no recipe for puff pastry in this book as I consider it extravagant of both ingredients and time for most households, and not necessary except for party dishes. However, bought puff pastry can be very good. I make perfectly good individual vol-au-vent cases from flaky and rough-puff simply by adding two extra folding and rollings. Hot hands and a warm room are drawbacks for beginners whose lack of practice slows them down. Fat melts very easily and, if you linger over the job, can turn dough into a sticky mass that smears on to pin, board and hands. Therefore work as quickly as you can always, but especially in hot conditions. If you do have hot hands use a pastry blender, or cut the fat down with two knives; run the tap until really cold, getting the water only when ready for it.

Modern margarine is excellent for pastry because, except for pre-creamed margarines, it is rather harder than other pastry fats, and is used in flaky pastry, where too soft a fat gives a less good crust. Therefore avoid 10-per cent butter types for flaky pastry. Lard is considered by many chefs and older cooks to give the best shortcrust. White cooking fats are also excellent, but dearer than lard and, sometimes, than margarine. Both these last named are soft fats, as is dripping. Cleared pork, beef or chicken dripping (or a mixture of any of them) makes delicious light, short pastry, and should be used for savoury dishes whenever possible.

Keep the flour dredger going but – careful! – let your motto be little and often. Thick drifts of flour soon add up to ounces and these, worked in by rolling, upset the proportions you have accurately (for of course you *have* measured accurately?) measured out. Keep the dough moving: turn it often on the rolling surface (marble, board, table-top), lifting and sprinkling lightly beneath with flour. This is of particular importance with richer, softer pastes like flaky and sucrée. Flour the pin or your hands, whichever you are working with.

Use your hands to keep the sheet of dough the shape you want and of even thickness, by gently pulling, or lightly knocking it into shape with the heel of your hand or your knuckles. Roll the paste in a shape to match the dish, where possible: round for flan-rings, oval or oblong for pie dishes. This cannot be done with layered pastes, for in making these it is important to keep the sheet a regular oblong, pulling the corners to good right-angles before each folding, to make layers even.

Kinds of pastry

The three chief kinds of pastry for general use are:

Short crust – (half fat to flour), the most versatile, least rich and most quickly made, with variations of ingredients for sweet and savoury dishes, including shortbread, pâte sucrée (English version usually called rich shortcrust) and dripping pastry.

Hot-water crust – fully described on p. 343. For raised pies.

Layered pastries – varieties include flaky, rough puff (⅔ fat to flour), puff (equal fat to flour) and yeast pastries (the two latter not given here). For savoury and sweet dishes of the more 'elegant' kind – or that's the theory.

The fourth sort, with limited uses, is choux paste, which is really a batter, and is not rolled, but piped or 'spooned' into shape. See p. 133.

COVERING PIES. Except for the glaze and decoration, the method of covering pies is the same for sweet and savoury.

Roll out paste to approximate size and shape of dish. If possible use empty dish as cutting guide, inverting it on sheet of paste and cutting round with pastry wheel or sharp knife. From the trimmings cut strips to fit the flange of the dish. Damp flange and

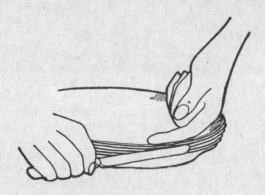

press strips on, joining neatly. Damp pastry lid and cover pie, pressing edges on to lined flange. Press all round edges to seal. Lift pie on left hand and, with a sharp knife held so that point leans outward from flange, cutting edge away from you, slice off overhanging bits and pieces to give a clean edge – fractionally wider than flange to allow for shrinkage in cooking. Stand pie on table, and use knuckle to weight and guide you in 'knocking up' cut edge. Do this by little chops at the edge with the knife, giving it a frilled look.

Savoury pies traditionally have the flange marked with the prongs of a fork; they may have pastry leaves or flowers (see Raised Pies), or any other decoration you choose. Glaze with egg-yolk, water and salt; beaten whole egg; egg-white; milk and salt.

Sweet pies have various finishes to the flange. One is done by cutting the edge of the flan at right-angles or obliquely inwards towards the centre of the pie, at intervals the width of your thumb all the way round, this makes the petal-like edging. Or you could make a pattern with a spoon handle, knife blade or something of the kind. The centre is traditionally left plain, but there is no need to follow tradition. Glaze by brushing with water and thickly sprinkling with castor or fine brown sugar; or dust cold pies with icing sugar.

Baking pastry

Pastry needs temperatures in the upper range as it must be cooked quickly, being thin, and to give it a crisp finish and attractive colour. The rule is: the richer the pastry – that is the more fat, sugar and eggs in it – the hotter the oven. But where pastry is the covering or container of other foods the temperature is often lowered once the pastry is cooked, to allow the rest of the dish to cook.

Many cooks precook meat and fruit for pies, when the only further cooking needed, after the pastry is risen and coloured, is to allow the contents thoroughly to heat through. The method is more successful, in my view, for fruit pies (if one has the time to divide the operation into two). Uncooked fruit shrinks a lot and sinks quickly, so that the pastry often does not absorb the flavour, whereas one can fill the dish with cooked fruit and know that it will keep the level. On the other hand this method hás dangers. Pastry softens in the oven to begin with, and can sink on to the wet fruit and stay there, becoming soggy and heavy. To avoid this put a pie-funnel or inverted egg-cup in the middle in the centre of the filling. With a meat filling shrinkage is slower and less, and the pastry absorbs some of the gravy to gain in flavour and succulence.

The trick of long cooking for pastries is to allow the pastry to cook completely, then remove the dish from the oven and twist lightly but completely over the pastry a 'hat' of tissue paper, returning the pie to a lower heat to finish cooking. It must be tissue paper: anything thicker can form steam and sog the pastry.

Paradoxically you may, in renewing the tissue towards the end of long cooking, damp it before putting it on. (The heat of the oven soon dries it out.) I use this method successfully for steak and kidney pies that need 3 to 3½ hours (at the lower temperature, of course) to finish cooking the meat.

Blind baking is cooking flan or tartlet cases without fillings. These are usually called pastry shells. Pastry needs fast dry heat to crisp it without hardening, which is why one removes flan-rings and the sheets of beans from blind-baked pastry shells about half-way through cooking. If the centre of blind-baked shells rises, prick the bubble and it will sink.

Choux pastry takes some practice to make with confidence. The variation in ovens makes it less foolproof than the shortcrust and layered groups. Some chefs bake choux pastry cases on a 'rising oven' – that is they raise the heat towards the end of the baking. Give choux plenty of time to allow sides to harden and centres to dry out – much more satisfactory than scooping out uncooked dough.

Pastry tins need no greasing. Damp baking-sheets for puff and choux. Layered pastries tend to exude their fat, which is not incorporated in the dough in making, only sandwiched between layers; so put a drip tray in the bottom of the oven to avoid a big clean-up afterwards.

NOTE: As stated already, plain flour is intended for all recipes in the book, except where stated. As it is particularly important in pastry, I have given it in the ingredients as a reminder.

When a recipe stipulates '¾ lb. pastry' it refers to the amount of flour.

STANDARD SHORTCRUST

8 oz. plain flour	3 tbs. water
4 oz. margarine, lard or dripping; or a mixture of these	large pinch salt

Sieve salt with flour into mixing bowl, add fat and cut into pieces, roughly an inch cube, turning about to coat with flour.

With fingers, and avoiding palms of hands which are warmer, 'pinch' fat smaller. Keeping it constantly mingling with flour, rub it through fingers and thumb smaller and smaller, letting it fall back into bowl, and bringing up flour from bottom of bowl all the time to mix with it. The particles of fat will take up more and more flour, becoming smaller in size but thicker in texture and, gradually, crumb-like. Lift hands slightly above bowl so that air is incorporated. Avoid squashing and hanging on to particles so that they turn to an oily paste. The rubbing should be light and quick, fresh particles and more flour being incorporated the whole time until the appearance is that of fine breadcrumbs. Shake or knock bowl now and again to bring larger pieces to the top. After about 5 minutes rubbing in, these larger pieces will be merely crumb-sized particles that are clinging together. At this stage the rubbing-in is finished.

Make a well in the centre and add measured liquid. With a palette knife stir the mixture until it clings together in large lumps. Lightly flour fingertips of one hand and gently press into a single ball of dough, pulling in any dough on sides of bowl by dabbing at it with the main lump. The bowl should be left quite clean of what the Cornish used to call 'slut's fingers'.

Flour the board or rolling area lightly, and very lightly knead the dough by rocking it, turning it round all the time on the board with a flat, floured hand until it is smooth.

It is now ready to roll and use, but may be kept up to 24 hours in a cool larder well wrapped in polythene or foil; longer in fridge or freezer.

For easier working and superior pastry add an extra ½ oz. fat to up to ¾ lb. quantities; 1 oz. extra fat to over that quantity. Bake at: 375° F, gas 5, centre of oven or just above, 20 to 30 minutes; or 400° F, gas 6, centre of oven or just above 15 to 20 minutes.

STIRRED METHOD. Good shortcrust can be made by using pre-whipped white cooking fat, or pre-creamed margarines. Proportions: 8 oz. flour, 4 oz. fat, 2–3 tbs. water. Salt. Chambré fat in room at 60° F, but on no account oil it. Put all the ingredients together into bowl, and stir with fork or wooden spoon until blended – about 1 minute. Proceed thereafter as for Standard Shortcrust recipe.

RICH SHORTCRUST

8 oz. plain flour	1 egg-yolk mixed with 1 tbs.
4 oz. margarine	water
1 oz. castor sugar	pinch salt

Rub in fat and flour with salt as for Standard Shortcrust. Stir in sugar with palette knife. Mix to dough with egg and water. Roll thinly – ⅛ inch maximum unless recipe states otherwise. Powdered spices and other flavourings may be incorporated with this paste, which is, of course, for sweet dishes. A 4–5 oz. quantity fills a 7-inch flan-ring.

Bake at: 375° F, gas 5, centre of oven or just above, 25 to 30 minutes; or 400° F, gas 6, centre of oven or just above or below, 15 to 20 minutes; or 425° F, gas 7, centre of oven or just below, 10 to 15 minutes, for blind baking, cooked fillings, small pastries, or as recipe directs.

STANDARD PÂTE SUCRÉE (OR SUGAR PASTE)

4 oz. plain flour	3–4 oz. margarine – a proportion
2 oz. castor sugar	of butter is an improvement
2 egg-yolks	3 drops vanilla

Make and use as Rich Shortcrust; but it is a softer and stickier paste, and is easier to handle if cooled for about 30 minutes to 1 hour before being rolled out. Spices may be added instead of vanilla. Bake as Rich Shortcrust. May be used for biscuits.

NOTE: Both the above recipes respond well to the stirred method; ingredients must be the same as recipe.

RICH CHEESE PASTRY

See p. 183.

FLAKY PASTRY

8 oz. plain flour
3 oz. each lard and margarine
  (or good dripping and
  margarine for savoury dishes)

scant ¼ pint very cold water
pinch salt

The two fats are necessary to arrive at the right consistency. They may be creamed together for adding to the dough (as described below), or kept separate when creamed, and added alternately to the dough. Whichever way round, there must be four equal portions of fat: one for the rubbing-in, three for the additions to the dough. At first the dough will be very slack and inclined to be tacky; light and frequent powderings with flour are necessary at the beginning. The layers and lightness of good flaky pastry come from air between the layers. Therefore, although the added fat must be soft enough not to pierce through the thinly rolled dough, it helps aeration if the little blobs of fat stand up rather than being smeared on flat. Work in this order:

(1) Sieve flour and salt into mixing bowl. Cut each kind of fat in half. Put half lard in with flour, leave rest of fat on plate.

(2) Rub lard into flour as usual, add water and stir with palette knife to form dough. Flour hands and rolling area well. Knead dough smooth as for Standard Shortcrust. It is a wetter dough at this stage than shortcrust, but this allows for the stretching that takes place when the pastry is folded over the fat, and for taking up extra dredging flour as well as the fat itself. Pat and gently pull kneaded dough to an oblong block. Flour rolling-pin well and roll to a strip about 4 by 12 inches, of even thickness, and with good straight sides and squared corners – pull these by hand. Note that dough strips for this kind of layered paste must be three times as long as they are wide. Many cooks roll the strip out thinner and larger, but at this stage I find the work goes better if one does not stretch out the dough too much or too thinly. Mark the side of the strip a third of the way up from the short end nearest the worker, by a light dent with a fingertip.

(3) Cream the fats on the plate either together or keeping each kind separate. They must be as soft as the dough to prevent breaking the layers.

(4) From one portion of creamed fat (which, if kept separate, must now be margarine) cut pieces approximately ½ inch in size, and dot them over the top two thirds of the sheet of dough, in even lines about an inch apart each way, and leaving a margin of ½ inch at edges. Lightly flour the blobs of fat.

(5) Turn bottom (blank) third of dough up over lower (fat-dotted) third; turn top (fat-dotted) third down, so that the blank

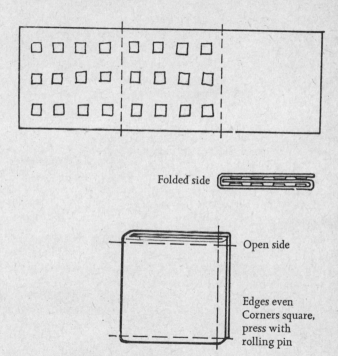

Folded side

Open side

Edges even
Corners square,
press with
rolling pin

third is now sandwiched between two fat-dotted layers. Folding must be exact so layers are even. Press edges of block with rolling-pin to seal. Flour rolling area, and turn block so that the folded side is on left of worker, open side on right. With rolling-pin held level, give a few light thumps up the block, before starting second rolling, to bed down the fat and distribute air. Roll out to strip

5 by 15 inches. Repeat steps (4) and (5) using the third portion of fat, and again using the last portion, increasing size of rolled-out strip each time until it is 18 by 6 inches at the last rolling.

(6) Rest the dough 20 to 30 minutes (or more; the pastry will keep 48 hours in cold larder, up to 1 week in refrigerator) in a cool place wrapped in foil or polythene.

Cut out with sharp knife; some cooks use a heated knife, to prevent layers being spoiled.

Bake at: 400° F, gas 6, just above centre of oven, 20 to 30 minutes; or 425° F, gas 7, centre or just above, 15 to 20 minutes; or 450° F, gas 8, centre or just below, 10 to 15 minutes, for blind baking, cooked fillings, small pastries, or as recipe directs. The higher temperatures help minimize the risk of fat running out, as the starch grains in the flour burst more quickly to absorb the fat.

ROUGH PUFF PASTRY

8 oz. plain flour	scant ¼ pint very cold water
pinch salt	squeeze of lemon juice (for
6 oz. margarine, lard or	easier handling of dough),
mixture of both (dripping	if available
for savoury dishes)	

Work in this order:

(1) Cream fat to an even texture, especially where fats are mixed. Do not make it too soft, however; chill slightly if necessary. Pat into a rough square about ½ inch thick. Cut into ½ inch squares.

(2) Sieve flour and salt into mixing bowl. Tip in squares of fat, adding any scrapings from plate. Add water, and lemon juice if used.

(3) Stir with palette knife until large lumps form. Turn on to well-floured rolling area. *Do not knead* but, with floured finger-tips, draw all together lightly into a single lump of dough and shape into oblong with floured hands.

(4) Flour pin well and roll into strip 18 by 6 inches, seeing that thickness is even, sides straight, corners square. Mark into thirds with a light dent at one of long sides. Fold up bottom third, fold down top third, so there are three layers, with corners square,

edges level. Turn, with fold to left of worker. Press edges with rolling-pin to seal. Thump evenly and lightly up the block to distribute air. Repeat rolling and fold a further 3 times.

(5) Rest, store, bake and use as Flaky Pastry.

NOTE: Although Rough Puff is a little quicker to make, I do not think it gives so good a crust as Flaky, since evenness of rising is less easy to control. To my taste flaky is the pleasantest pastry to make, as to eat.

A few variant pastry recipes are given throughout the book. Quantity of pastes for different sizes of flan p. 171.

CHOUX PASTRY

4¼ oz. plain flour	pinch salt
1¾ oz. margarine/butter	for sweet pastries only:
2 eggs	¼ oz. sugar
4½ fl. oz. water	

Sieve flour on to piece of paper. Bring fat, salt (and sugar when used) to the boil in the water. Tip flour in all at once and stir briskly with wooden spoon until mixture leaves sides of pan and is smooth. Cool slightly and add one beaten egg, beating it in well. Beat second egg, and add enough or all of it to make a smooth glossy paste, soft enough to pipe, but firm enough to hold shape with no spreading. Bake at 400 to 425° F, gas 6 to 7, according to size, until risen, brown and crisp. This may take 15 to 25 minutes. Crispness all round is essential, otherwise the case goes soggy on cooling and collapses. Choux cases are deep-fried for some recipes.

SUET CRUST OR DOUGH
Savoury quantity to line 2-pint pudding basin

5 oz. each plain flour and fresh white breadcrumbs *or* 10 oz. plain flour	5–6 tbs. water
	2 heaped tsp. baking powder *or* 1 level tsp. bicarbonate
3–4 oz. suet	of soda, 1 heaped tsp. cream of
large pinch salt	tartar

Sweet quantity for plain puddings or to line 1½-pint basin

4 oz. each plain flour and fresh
   white breadcrumbs *or*
   ½ lb. plain flour
2–3 oz. suet
pinch salt
1 tbs. castor sugar

4–5 tbs. water
1½ heaped tsp. baking
   powder *or* ½ tsp.
   bicarbonate of soda, 1 level tsp.
   cream of tartar

Sieve flour and raising agents, mix well with suet, crumbs, and for the sweet mixture, the sugar. Lift the mixture through the hands to ensure no unmixed ingredients fall to bottom of bowl. Add water to make a soft and *slightly* tacky dough – it must not be really sticky. If on dry side so that dough does not readily form, add extra water by teaspoonfuls. Knead only very slightly to form a ball of dough. (Some older recipes bake suet dough. For this use less water or the crust will be very hard. Baked suet is anyway hardish.)

For lining basins, cut off one third for lid, roll out to size and use as quickly as possible. Cooking should be brisk for first 20 minutes for all suet doughs.

Various flavours for sweet puddings are added with dry ingredients: for example 1 tsp. powdered ginger; grated rind of lemon or orange; replace 1 oz. flour by 1 level tbs. cocoa; 1 to 2 oz. dried fruit. As for savoury crust, use quickly once dough is mixed, as water causes raising agents to start working.

The savoury mixture is suitable for dumplings. Some people also use it for puddings.

Covering suet puddings

If moisture reaches suet doughs they become unpleasantly slimy. Care in covering down puddings is therefore important. It is also necessary to leave room for doughs to rise or swell. First cover the pudding (or wrap suet rolls loosely) with well-greased greaseproof paper, then with a second piece of damped greaseproof paper or with foil. The second covering may have a tuck across the top of pudding basins, or be well folded but baggy round a roll. In both instances it should be completely sealed by being tied with string or twisted. Getting puddings out of steamers can be difficult, so take the string across the top to form a handle, when the pudding can be lifted out without risk of scalding hands. Only be sure you make secure ties. Never handle puddings while pan is on the heat, and avoid bending over bubbling steamers to inspect the contents.

Cooking suet doughs

Boil water fast for first 20 minutes of cooking time, thereafter keep water just on the boil without galloping. Add boiling water as needed. Exception: small dumplings, which must merely be simmered or they break up.

A Gauge of Thicknesses

Many people have only vague notions of measurements, and few would want to keep a ruler in the kitchen. But to help check your ideas of, for instance, '¼ inch thick' with what it really looks like, and what is intended in these pages, the gauge below may help. In among the pastry seemed as good a place as any, but it

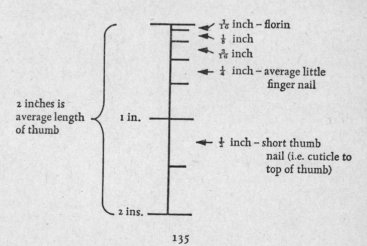

2 inches is average length of thumb

1 in.

2 ins.

$\frac{1}{16}$ inch – florin
$\frac{1}{8}$ inch
$\frac{3}{16}$ inch
$\frac{1}{4}$ inch – average little finger nail

$\frac{1}{2}$ inch – short thumb nail (i.e. cuticle to top of thumb)

should be used for everything else – slicing vegetables, cutting up meat, putting things in layers.

Custards

Custards have great value for budget cooks. They form part of many puddings, rivalling and sometimes surpassing expensive dishes in delicacy and attractiveness. Custard-based puddings have high nutritive value, so can follow cheaper filling, but starchy, main courses. They are also easy to eat and digest, which makes them useful for children, invalids and the elderly.

In his admirable *Où est le garlic* * practical Len Deighton says:

Almost always when people have trouble with it this is because they haven't put the ... cornflour in. They feel it's cheating, that egg custard must never have flour of any kind near it. The sentiment is a noble one, but it makes the job more difficult, for without that cornflour the mixture is far less stable and will react to heat variations of the slightest degree.

With this I agree, although I think less than his 2 tsp. does the trick. When cornflour is present, egg custard may heat enough for bubbles just to start, but if it actually boils it will probably curdle as readily as when, without cornflour, it merely overheats a degree or so. Some people may find it helpful to remember that eggs coagulate completely at a temperature of 160° F, while the scalding point of milk is 186° F, and of water 212° F. Work at first with a bowl of cold water beside you, so if the mixture starts to lump or separate, the pan can be put in, and the mixture stirred quickly to cool it.

Egg-white helps give a firm texture, which is why it is included in custards for trifles and in crèmes caramels. You *can* thicken these with yolks only but, apart from the extra cost, they taste too eggy for my palate.

Where a recipe stipulates '½ pint custard', this refers to the amount of milk.

* Penguin, 1967.

'BOILED' EGG CUSTARDS

SAUCE AND BREAD PUDDING CONSISTENCY

1 large egg	3–4 drops vanilla (or pod
½ pint milk	cooked in the milk)
1 level tbs. sugar	1 level tsp. cornflour
	(optional)

TRIFLE, SET OR STEAMED CONSISTENCY

2 eggs for trifle, whole egg	4–5 drops vanilla (or pod
and 1 yolk for others	cooked in the milk)
½ pint milk	1 level tsp. cornflour
1 rounded tbs. sugar	(optional)

Cream together in a small basin the egg, sugar, cornflour where used, and vanilla. Heat milk to below boiling point and pour slowly on to egg mixture, whisking all the time. Return to pan and cook over low heat, stirring, until when fingertip is quickly drawn through mixture on back of wooden spoon, the mixture does not run together again.

To *steam*, turn the mixture into a greased mould at the stage when milk is poured on to egg mixture. Cover with greased grease-proof paper or foil, and steam as for steamed puddings about 45 minutes. See that water does not come above half-way up mould.

BAKED CUSTARD

For crème caramel or cup custards.

The trifle custard will do, or use 2 small whole eggs and 2 yolks for a creamier result. For a less extravagant dish, if using 1 pint of milk, 2 whole eggs and 1 yolk is a good compromise. Increase the sugar and vanilla a little to taste. Proceed as for steamed custard in last recipe. Bake *au bain-marie* at 300–325° F, gas 2–3, for 25 to 45 minutes (depending on depth of mixture in mould), and with a butter paper lightly twisted over top to prevent brown skin forming.

The addition of cheese, spices or seasoning and the omission of sugar gives savoury custards. (Mayonnaise and hollandaise sauces are the custard sauce of savoury dishes.)

Gelatine

There are three chief points to remember in using gelatine.

(1) Gelatine is used in very small amounts. If you stir vigorously when melting it, you will wash a great deal against the sides of the pan, so losing the amount needed to set the dish; while half-melted gelatine round the pan forms a strong glue, which you will persuade off the pan only with difficulty. It is best to add the small amount of liquid directed in the recipe, gently thump the pan against your hand to spread the gelatine powder evenly, then leave a minute or two to soak. Warm it over a mere whisper of heat or dunk the pan in water just off the boil, tipping it very slightly until the liquid clears and no 'grains' appear on the bottom of the pan. Use care to scrape out every bit for the reason given above. A 'Lastlik' type of rubber bowl-scraper is invaluable here.

(2) Except when making jelly by the full process (pp. 258–61), never allow gelatine to boil. It will turn to rubbery strings, and you will have to start again and have a sticky pan to soak clean.

(3) Over-hard moulds result from using too much gelatine or from over-chilling. Use only the stated amount – ½ oz. or 1 level tablespoon gelatine powder sets 1 pint liquid or purée, including any solid additions such as fruit or vegetable slices, shellfish, pieces of fish or meat. The exception to the rule is in the summer. Unless the recipe instructs otherwise, take moulds out of the refrigerator ½ hour before serving. Do not leave gelatine mixtures in the freezer, or they crystallize and spoil: 5 to 10 minutes at a time in an emergency will not hurt, but as soon as mould shows signs of setting remove to main cabinet of refrigerator.

If a gelatine mixture starts to set too soon, stand the bowl in hot, not boiling, water until it dissolves again. Avoid stirring clear jelly, as bubbles form in it.

WARNING: Fresh pineapple contains an enzyme that prevents gelatine from setting. Use canned pineapple for jellies for preference, or poach fresh pineapple, before using, in a light syrup.

Long-Grain Rice for Savoury Dishes

2 oz. rice per person is enough for most dishes.

Wash rice very well to avoid a sticky finish : put it in a bowl (better still a conical) strainer, and run cold water through it fast, stirring it round with a wooden spoon handle, then swish the strainer in a mixing bowl of cold water, changing the water until the cloudiness diminishes somewhat.

ORDINARY PAN. Boil up 3 pints water for each 4 oz. rice, adding 1 level tsp. salt per 4 oz. Add the washed rice, and stir until water reboils, seeing that no grains stick to bottom of pan. Boil fast, uncovered, for 12 to 15 minutes. Test after 12 minutes, removing pan from heat while you do so. Cool and nibble ½ tsp. grains. There should be no hard core at the centre.

When done, drain at once in a colander, 'rushing through' the rice about 1 pint boiling water to rinse out any remaining starch. Push a wooden spoon handle here and there through the rice to make 'ventilation holes', and leave to dry in colander 5 minutes. Turn it into a serving dish, and stir into it 1 tsp. oil, or scant ½ oz. margarine to each 4 oz. quantity, to keep grains from sticking. Cover dish with butter paper or foil and put into oven, or over hot water, 2 to 3 minutes to ensure serving hot.

PRESSURE COOKER. The best method as far as I am concerned. Wash rice as above. Boil up in the cooker 1 pint water per 4 oz. rice. Add 1 level tsp. salt. Add rice and boil up, stirring and freeing any grains sticking to bottom. Put on lid of cooker and cook under pressure 6 minutes. Strain, rinse with hot water, and finish as above.

Keep cooked rice covered in foil or polythene.

Dried Vegetables (Pulses)

There are now many sorts of dried beans in the shops besides the familiar haricot and butter beans, lentils and peas. The flavours are much the same, but many of them cook better than the poor-quality haricots often sold. There are cow and chick peas, which are still beans, the one being an attractive brown colour, the other an attractive shape. There are the smart black-eyed beans. For all these use the same preparation and procedure as for Boston Baked Beans (pp. 402–3), allowing a minimum of 2 hours' cooking time, (lentils) but an average of 4 hours. Pressure cook according to instructions given in book with cooker. Lentils are washed but not soaked.

Polenta or cornmeal is treated much as lentils, but does not need washing of course. Allow ¾ lb. polenta to a pint of liquid, adding more meal or reducing liquid by boiling as for thicker consistency. Simmer with care as it is a prize sticker, at least 30 minutes. Plenty of seasoning is needed, a good stock being the best liquid. Polenta may be cooled, cut into squares and served with pasta sauces and cheese.

January

‡‡

Soups

First read soup notes on pp. 112–13.

ONION AND POTATO SOUP (POTAGE PARMENTIER)

Whether you make it with leeks, shallots, spring onions, even chives, this is *the* classic soup, and is a perfect combination of flavours and textures – an all-purpose, all person soup which can be based on any stock, even mutton stock, or water. Raise its status by the addition of a liaison, by colouring it a delicate green, by handing round a saucer of little croûtons and by using its French name. Make it more filling still by topping with slightly bigger croûtons, or crisped dice of fat bacon. Be generous with the pepper – ground white in this instance.

BASIC INGREDIENTS	OPTIONAL EXTRAS
1 lb. potatoes	Garnishes :
½ lb. onions or trimmed leeks	Croûtons : frizzled dice of flank bacon rashers
1¼ pints stock	Finishes (or for additional nourishment) :
¼ pint milk	
1½ oz. each margarine and flour	1–2 egg-yolks
salt, white pepper	2–4 fl. oz. single cream
	1 tbs. yoghurt to each plate
	green colouring

Split leeks lengthwise, wash very thoroughly (inspecting by separating the leaves), cut in inch lengths. Slice onions. Peel or scrub potatoes and cut in thick pieces – about the size of small eggs. Melt half the margarine and soften leek or onion, covered, 5 minutes over very low heat. Add potatoes, stock and ½ tsp. salt. Bring to boiling point and simmer ½ hour or until the point of a knife goes very easily through the potato. Lift pieces of

141

potato (removing skins, if cooked in them) about six at a time on to a Moulin-Légumes, or drum sieve, and rub them through. Follow potato with the leek. (If you try to sieve a mixture of both, it will turn slimy and be quite unmanageable. Too much at once of any substance takes longer to purée than a bit at a time.) Finally pour stock through Moulin. Melt rest of fat, stir in flour off the heat, and add soup, stirring well. Bring to boil, stirring all the time, adding the milk last. Simmer 3 to 5 minutes to allow flour to cook and swell thoroughly.

If using liaison, first cool soup for 2 minutes. If liked, add a few drops of green colouring. Send to table with extras as indicated.

This is obviously not a slimmer's soup but, by omitting the flour, and stirring well before each helping to keep the vegetables 'in suspension', slimmers will take less harm than from the full version. When a 2-yolk liaison is used flour may obviously be omitted.

SOUPE AUX CHOUX

Serves 8 to 10.

This is a soup made by the method familiar to many European country people: that is, meat or a fowl is cooked in, but served after the soup, as the main course; or a slice or so of the meat may be served with the soup. Soups of this sort are intended for more than one day, or for a very large number of people. The quantity and the long slow cooking make them useful for lunch or supper during a busy spell – for example when marmalade-making.

1 good firm cabbage (about 1½–2 lb. including outside leaves)	12 peppercorns
	½ bayleaf
	1 clove
1 lb. piece of mild smoked, or green, streaky bacon, or pickled pork (some smoked bacon is very salt; if obliged to have it, soak overnight)	small blade of mace
	1 each medium carrot, onion, stick of celery
	1 heaped tbs. chopped parsley
	2 cloves garlic chopped finely
salt to taste	4 pints water

Into a large saucepan put meat, water, carrot, onion and celery, cutting the vegetables into about 4 pieces. Add spices tied in muslin and attached by a string to pan handle so that you can fish them out easily. Add *no salt* at this stage. Bring to boil and simmer 1½ hours. Meanwhile thoroughly wash cabbage, discarding only the coarsest outer leaves, and shred it finely. Add to pot and cook a further 1½ hours. Have ready the parsley and garlic which, at the final chopping, can be made really fine by being chopped together. Taste the soup and add salt now if needed. Add the parsley and garlic and simmer a further ½ hour. Remove spices and meat, and stir well before serving, as cabbage sinks in the broth. Give a piece of carrot to those who like it.

A very acceptable reduced version may be made from a small cabbage, or half a big one that is being used for another dish, a quart of water and a bacon bone from the grocer, or a few rashers of streaky bacon, even bacon rinds, with half quantities of the other ingredients.

SINGLE PERSON VERSION

1 pint stock made from
bouillon cube, bacon rinds,
bone, or rashers as available

outer leaves of cabbage

MUTTON BROTH WITH HERBS

1½ lb. scrag of mutton
2 pints water
1 each medium carrot, turnip,
outside stick of celery,
onion
1 large clove garlic
thinly pared rind of ½ lemon
(optional)
sprig of rosemary or sage (or
½ tsp. of dried, tied in muslin)

6 good sprigs parsley tied
together
2 level tsp. salt (or to taste)
generous shaking ground
white pepper
1 tbs. tapioca (what used to
be called seed tapioca is
most commonly on sale
nowadays; if your shop has
both avoid the larger sort)

Remove as much fat as possible from the mutton. Very briskly pass under fast-running cold tap any pieces of meat that have

143

splintered bones, and wipe with clean cloth to remove splinters. Crush garlic in 1 tsp. of the salt. Put water and all ingredients except tapioca into pan, boil up and simmer 1½ to 2 hours until meat is easily picked from bones. Pour soup through colander, lift out meat and remove all bones, chopping meat very small before returning to broth. Dice the root vegetables and put back, but remove the herbs. Reheat soup to boiling point, throw in the tapioca and stir well for a few minutes so that it does not stick. Lower heat to simmering for 20 minutes, occasionally scraping across the bottom of pan to prevent tapioca sticking. The tapioca thickens the broth slightly, but as it cooks it clears, giving the soup a slightly jellied look suited to its light character.

There is always fat from mutton stock and the best way to remove it is to leave the pan in a cold place overnight, when the fat sets and can be lifted off. But a little fat enriches broths and may be left.

TWO OLD-FASHIONED INVALID SOUPS

The shifts and strategems of nutrition experts have provided one of the recurring amusements of the past thirty or so years:

We ought to take more vitamins. We're taking too many vitamins. Milk is the aqua vitae. Milk is a killer. Potatoes are good for you. No, they're bad. No, they're good after all. Why bother with food – we can nourish you better and more scientifically (whatever that means) by pills or tonics. Tonics are unnecessary, pills are harmful, what you need is *natural* food.

Well, no claims for beef tea or onion gruel have been made for a long time, but I will risk saying that, when you feel wan and peevish about food, beef tea will go down agreeably. If you are suffering from a feverish cold, a boil in an awkward spot, pink-eye or any other of those minor ailments that together with the awful weather make you wish you were dead, onion gruel will warm, console and affirm your status as a martyr. Neither can harm you.'

BEEF TEA

Serves 2 to 3.

1 lb. topside or buttock steak	½ tsp. salt
1 pint water	pepper if liked

The beef itself must not be boiled; there must be no fat on the tea. The meat fibres are not taken, but the coagulated meat juices are. That is why beef tea is made in a china jug or basin, for even a double boiler, being metal and thin, would probably cause the tea to become too hot; and why it is put through a coarse strainer such as a colander which will collect the fibres while allowing the coagulated particles through.

Remove as much fat and gristle from meat as possible and mince or scrape it into shreds. If the latter, work quickly so that the juices are not lost. Put the meat and cold water into a thick jug or basin, and leave to soak 1 hour. Then stand the jug in a pan of boiling water and cook for 2 to 3 hours. Allow to stand 5 minutes in the hot water after cooking and, if fat is seen on top, blot it off with absorbent paper. Pour through a coarse strainer. Serve with melba toast, if the patient can take it. To reheat beef tea, return in jug to pan of boiling water.

THICK ONION GRUEL

1½ lb. onion	2 tbs. thin cream
1½ pints milk	1 *heavy* oz. flour
1½ oz. margarine	seasoning
1 yolk	

Chop the onions. Melt the butter in a saucepan, and sweat the onions until quite transparent and soft, but without colouring at all. Scatter in the flour off the fire, and mix it well. Add the milk, stirring well as you add, and bring to a full boil, stirring continually to make sure the soup is perfectly smooth and adding salt and pepper to taste. When the soup is fully at the boil, clap on the pan lid, and move off the heat. Leave in the warmth of the kitchen for about ½ hour without removing the lid. This allows the flavour fully to develop without curdling the milk. Reheat without allowing soup to boil, and stirring or whisking to re-incorporate any skin that may have formed. Beat the yolk and cream together, pour a little hot soup on them and pour back into the pan stirring well. Serve with melba toast (p. 67) if liked.

First Courses and Snacks

POTTED BLOATER

2 good-sized bloaters (they will weigh about ¾ lb. after beheading and removing roe; include roe if not wanted for roe on toast)

5 oz. salt butter

1 dessertsp. (minimum) tarragon or similar vinegar

1 tsp. Tabasco (½ tsp. cayenne pepper may be substituted but cayenne packed in this country is apt to be adulterated, and not 'telling' enough)

½ tsp. freshly ground black pepper

anchovy paste to taste (avoid U.K. bottled anchovy sauces, often very salty but weak in anchovy flavour; look for continental tubes of anchovy paste, Burgess's paste in pots; or pound a few fillets from a tin)

salt and lemon juice to taste

The amount of seasoning absorbed is surprising: exact quantities are a matter of taste.

Top and tail fish, lay in shallow baking dish with water to come slightly less than half way up fish. More may leach out the smoky flavour. Cover well with foil. Bake in oven 1 hour at 250° F, gas ½–1. Carefully unseal, turn fish over, tasting a small piece from tail end. If very mild, sprinkle very lightly with salt. Re-seal, return to oven, lowering heat to 225° F, gas ¼, for 2 to 3 hours, until tail of fish will easily mash with a fork. Leave until quite cold. Drain and pound well with 4 oz. of the butter and all flavourings, tasting until paste is sufficiently flavoured to your liking. Long slow cooking 'dissolves' all small bones and completely softens larger ones, so that there is no need to remove them. Pack paste well down into small clean pots (empty plastic yoghurt or cream cartons do very well), filling last ¼ inch with melted butter from the remaining ounce. Will keep about 2 weeks in cold larder, longer in refrigerator. Fills about 3 cartons.

No butter is needed on the hot toast, crumpet, or roll with which the paste is eaten, as there is enough in the mixture. Good spread on celery for cocktail snack (or slimmers), and a spoonful may be added to fish sauces.

MACARONI CHEESE

An old favourite for economy, nourishment and tastiness when well made. When nasty very nasty, so a good recipe is worth giving. As a complete course allow 3–4 oz. macaroni per person; as a first course, 1½ oz. per person. Increase or decrease sauce in proportion. A good dish for preparing the day before, so long as the top is really well covered in sauce and gratin topping, so that the macaroni is not exposed to the drying effect of air. Slip dish into polythene bag to make sure. Reheat gently to avoid spoiling sauce, finishing it under grill.

I use Quaker Quick macaroni, however that may shock food snobs, for it really does cook in the 7 minutes claimed by the makers.

12 oz. macaroni	browned crumbs
1 oz. butter, margarine or oil	
SAUCE: ¾ pint milk	scant level tsp. salt
rounded tsp. made mustard	white pepper
1 tsp. vinegar	1½ oz. each margarine and flour
slice onion	4 oz. grated dry cheddar or
½ bayleaf	2½ oz. grated Parmesan or
1 blade mace	Regginito

Boil up milk with onion, herbs and seasoning. Cover and leave to cool. Cook macaroni (p. 391), meanwhile making sauce as follows:

Melt margarine, add flour and mustard off the heat, and stir till smooth. Add cooled and strained milk, stirring well. Boil, stirring or whisking to avoid lumps. Add vinegar, remove from heat and shoot in all but ½ oz. cheese. Stir well, taste and add a little more salt, pepper, or made mustard if the sauce does not have a good bite to it.

Drain macaroni in a colander, and into the hot pan put the butter to melt. Return macaroni to pan, turn it carefully and thoroughly in the fat. Pour on sauce, off heat, stir once and turn into serving dish. Mix 1 tbs. browned crumbs with rest of cheese, strew over the top of macaroni and put into a hot oven (400° F, gas 6) for 10 minutes, then under grill to brown top. If you have time to spare you may brown top in the oven, but this takes about ½ hour and then does not always give so even a finish as the grill.

The points to note about good macaroni cheese are:

(1) The sauce must be strongly flavoured, for the pasta absorbs flavour very much, and if the sauce is weak to start with it will become insipid when mixed with the pasta.

(2) *On no account boil sauce once cheese is in*, for this makes the cheese turn stringy and glue-like.

(3) See the sauce is of the correct consistency and that there is neither too much nor too little. The finished dish must be succulent, but not swamped.

(4) The top must be really crisp and brown. Browned crumbs are not essential, but they help.

ŒUFS MOLLETS

Not a single recipe, but a method of cooking and serving eggs that lends itself to great variety.

Choose medium-sized eggs, allowing 1 each for a first, 2 each for a main course.

Boil eggs for *exactly* 5 minutes, at once running cold tap on them for a few seconds to stop further cooking. This produces an egg with firm white and soft yolk, and one which can be gently reheated without hardening the yolk. Leave in the shell until you are ready to use, then gently tap the shell all over to crack thoroughly, and roll between your palms so that it peels easily without pulling off white. Absolutely new-laid eggs are best avoided for this dish, as they are very difficult to shell without pieces of white being pulled off.

Then make a good sauce, put the eggs into it as you take the pan from the heat, and either put the whole into a heated serving dish in a low oven for 10 to 15 minutes to heat the eggs through, or put a buttered paper on to the top of the contents of the pan, a lid on the pan, and stand near but not on the heat for the same time, and dish direct on to plates.

Here are several ways of using the eggs. Quantities given for 4–6 eggs.

First consult sauce notes pp. 113–14.

À LA CRÈME. ¼ pint binding good white sauce with a small carton thin cream stirred in when sauce is made. Reheat without boiling; add eggs. A bland dish before a spicy main course. Good for convalescents and delicate palates.

AUX CHAMPIGNONS. Weigh ingredients for ½ pint sauce as for Diable (see below). While milk is infusing flavours from vegetables, sweat 2 oz. mushrooms, or stalks, very finely sliced, in the butter. Scatter in the flour and mix smoothly. Add milk when ready, to complete the mushroom sauce. Add eggs.

DIABLE. Make ½ pint coating good white or Béchamel sauce. Add 1 rounded tsp. made mustard, good shake cayenne and 1 tsp. Worcester sauce. Add eggs.

FLORENTINE. Sauce as Mornay (see below), but a bed of spinach (en branche or purée) goes under the eggs. Rather substantial for a first course for present-day appetites. Better as light main course.

KARI. Make ½ pint curry sauce as on p. 152, or use up leftover curry. Good way to make an extra helping or so if not quite enough curry remains for a second go. Sometimes an ingredient in curry dyes egg-whites odd shades. Not harmful.

MORNAY. White sauce as for Diable (above), but 1 oz. grated Parmesan or 2 oz. grated Cheddar cheese is added. Eggs arranged in gratin dish, masked with sauce, ½ oz. extra cheese and 1 dessertsp. browned crumbs (optional) scattered on top. Brown under grill.

NAPOLITANA. Tomato pulp from ½ lb. tomatoes (skinned, hard core removed, quartered); 1 finely chopped rasher; 1 small onion coarsely sliced; pinch or sprig of thyme or marjoram, ½ bayleaf, 1 blade mace, tied in muslin; 1 clove garlic crushed in salt. Sweat onion, bacon and tomato in ½ oz. margarine. Add tomato, herbs and garlic, and some freshly ground black pepper. Cook over medium heat so that liquid evaporates somewhat to make thickish sauce. Adjust seasoning. Add eggs.

SOUBISE. Soften 1 chopped onion in the butter for ½ pint quantity of coating white sauce, and continue sauce recipe incorporating the onion. Pour over eggs in gratin dish. Border with small, triangular fried or toasted croûtes.

All these dishes may be served with small croûtes round the dish or under the eggs. Another way is to make a flan-case of flaky pastry (p. 130), set the eggs in this and pour the sauce over.

Use what is to hand to invent variations of your own.

BACON, CHEESE AND CHUTNEY TOASTER

For a main luncheon course cut one slice per person of bread from a large loaf (round loaves are attractive for this); for a savoury small or half slices. For each large slice, grate 1 oz. cheese and allow 1 large rasher or 2 streaky rashers, 1 dessertsp. milk, 1 dessertsp. chutney.

Toast bread. Mash cheese with milk. Spread chutney on toast, then cheese mixture, and return to brown under grill. De-crust toast thinly, and keep hot. Grill bacon crisp, arrange on toast. Serve mustard with this.

Reduce quantities for small slices.

Fish

First read fish notes on p. 86.

COD IN CURRY SAUCE

Concerning curries

Curry is no mere dish. It is an entire cuisine. Get one of the curry books by Harvey Day, published by Nicholas Kaye (your public library may have one). They are full of interesting facts as well as recipes for curries and Indian puddings, which bear resemblances to puddings in modern Greece. Speculating on the world distribution of recipes and different sorts of cookery is fascinating. Curries turn up in China, Japan and Africa, to name only a few regions, and all are a little different, all related. Some curries are so peppery the stranger can hardly stand a mere dab on his tongue, others are more like our own devilled dishes. Yet we British had included this exotic cooking in our sober repertoire when other nations, whom we think of as outlandish in their tastes, hardly knew the word. Early editions of Mrs Beeton include several Indian recipes.

But the curries we serve at home are not the numerous dishes produced at a good, average Indian table, although in the last ten years we are tending to do this for dinner parties. So the curry sauce I give claims nothing but adaptability, and has no pretensions to authenticity. It is a blend of several recipes and ideas that have been given me, or that I have had or read, from Indians and Englishwomen, and that I find good to eat, with ingredients easily procurable.

You need not follow it exactly. If you have only a couple of tomatoes, make them up with an apple, some orange juice, a bit of gravy left from a roast, water, stock or a little thin soup. Use plums instead in their season. Yoghurt can be replaced by a sherry-glassful of top milk or a couple of tablespoonfuls of evaporated milk. Condensed milk won't hurt if used sparingly, for the essence of many curries is a mixture of sweetness with pepperiness. Indian cooks – indeed most Asian cooks – cook by taste. They add a bit of this or that until the flavour pleases, and this method suits curry far better than fixed quantities.

The flavour of coconut is most commonly introduced into curry by infusing the coconut in water and making, in this way, a coconut milk. But an excellent Indian restaurant in London uses coconut directly added to some curry dishes. This my mother often did at home in my childhood, and it turns up in Victorian cookbooks. I do it for quickness as well as for the taste and texture – coconut thickens a sauce. And any time you happen to shy a fresh coconut, of course use a spoonful of the real milk for curry.

In districts having an Indian or Pakistani community you will find a greater variety of curry powders and pastes, chutneys, pickles, and curry accompaniments on sale. Where there is a version of a curry powder or pickle labelled *mild* try that to start with, rather than one marked *hot*. Bombay manufacturers mean hot when they say so. In any event use the ingredient sparingly until you have tried it at least once. A make of chutney, by the way, that is popular with Indians and Pakistanis is one to go for. Some of the better-known-to-us brands often use very tough, woody mangoes that an Asian housewife would return to the shop. Follow their lead, also, in the matter of other ingredients, and don't be too shy to ask their advice if you're standing hesitating at the same shelf in the supermarket. Bolsts' curry powder or paste is good, but use about a third the quantity stated in the recipe of the *hot* version of the powder to start with.

CURRY SAUCE

1 large or two medium onions, sliced
¾ lb. tomatoes, skinned
1½ oz. each butter (or bacon dripping) and margarine
1 rounded dessertsp. curry powder mixed to paste with a little stock or milk
juice of ½ lemon
1 clove garlic
salt

1 carton yoghurt (usually 5 fl. oz.)
about 1 gill (maximum) stock or water, heated
1 level dessertsp. desiccated or chopped fresh coconut
sugar, treacle, jam, or similar to taste (a good way to use up syrup from canned fruit)

The curry sauce will dress meats as well as fish, but when currying fish, stock made from the fish trimmings gives a very good flavour.

Brown the onions well in the fat in a heavy pan. Add the curry paste and stir until fat separates, lowering heat right down so that the paste cooks without burning or sticking. Stir now and then. This should be continued 7–10 minutes. If there is any sticking add a spoonful from the heated stock. Add the skinned tomatoes, cutting and breaking them up as they cook, the garlic crushed with salt, the yoghurt and lemon juice. Stir well and bring to simmering point. Add the coconut and cook, stirring for 5 minutes. Add half the gill of stock, cover the pan and simmer very gently for 20 minutes, inspecting occasionally. If the sauce seems to be thickening to a stodgy consistency, add a spoonful or two more stock. Cook a further 10 minutes, then taste and add 1–2 tsp. sugar (any kind), treacle or jam, etc., and salt, until the sauce is to your liking.

All the better if made the day before, when a little extra stock may be needed on reheating.

PREPARATION OF THE COD AND RICE. While the sauce is cooking cut 1½ lb. skinned (see p. 89) cod fillet into 4 portions. Season, lightly flour them, and fry them in hot fat (oil is best) ½ inch deep in a frying-pan. Turn them once only, allowing about 4 minutes each side. Fish easily breaks up, but it will keep together better if a brown crust has formed, quite apart from the crisp finish being the final touch to this dish. In turning use a thin, flat slice, cutting against the bottom of the pan so that you don't pull the fish away from this crust. It is very important that the fat be really hot (p. 103) before you put in the fish. Arrange fish in serving dish and keep warm.

Cook ½–¾ lb. rice (p. 139).

Just before serving pour sauce over fish, and either arrange rice in a border round, or serve in a separate dish. But add sauce to fish at the last moment so as not to soften the crisp surface.

For the single-person household the separately packed frozen cod steaks are a convenient, if less cheap, buy for this dish. And a curry sauce is a good example of something well worth making in a quantity big enough for two meals. It keeps well, so that you need not eat curry 2 days running, and for the second go you can curry eggs or meat.

A selection of curry accompaniments

POPPADUMS. The vowels vary, but it's the same thing. Usually cheaper bought loose from Indian grocers, but a five-bob tin holds a lot. They are wafer-thin, stiff pancakes and, stored with the tin re-sealed each time with Sellotape, last indefinitely as far as my experience goes. Cook in a little very hot fat in a clean frying-pan for about 30 seconds each side, until golden and blistered.

Drain well. 1 per person. Crisp and delicious. Serve, as you do bread, on a side-plate.

YOGHURT. Hand a bowl of this, allowing ½ carton per person. Plain, no additions.

BOMBAY DUCK. A marvellous *Soldiers Three* name for dried bummalo fish fillets. These also seem to last indefinitely. Heat in the oven and crumble over the curry. 1 per person.

LIME PICKLE. Halved limes are pickled in a hottish sauce; flavour marvellous. Bombay Emporium is a good make, modest in price, if you can get it. MacFisheries' supermarkets should have it. Eaten in small bits at a time, the chilli pickle doesn't bite too much. ½ a lime cap per person. Stir small tsp. (or to taste) of the juice into the curry sauce before the end of cooking, to give an extra nip and subtle flavour.

MANGO CHUTNEY. 1 level tablespoon per person.

BANANA. ½ banana per person, fried in butter or margarine, or raw.

ORANGE SALAD. Unauthentic, but a marvellous contrast and palate cooler. Slice up or section (p. 104) about ½ an orange per person, sugar very lightly, and serve as cold as possible. A little saucer each of orange water-ice or sorbet is also good.

CUCUMBER SALAD. Peeled, and either thinly sliced, sugared, salted and chilled; or halved, the halves thickly sliced and mixed with thinly sliced onion, and a vinaigrette dressing with a very small amount of sugar in it.

HADDOCK MEUNIÈRE

The most simple and delicious of all ways of cooking fish in my view.

For each person for a main dish you need a cutlet of haddock about 1½ to 2 inches thick, or a piece of filleted haddock weighing not less than 6 oz. after skinning. For each 2 portions allow 2 oz. butter and ½ lemon. Start the cooking with a scant tbs. oil, and when really hot add half butter. When bubbling but *not* brown, put in the fish, lightly seasoned. Watch fat, and if it begins to brown lower heat a little. Cook cutlets 4 minutes before

154

turning with a slice, 'cutting' against the base of the pan so as to turn fish without breaking it or leaving its browned surface sticking to the pan. Arrange fish on hot serving dish and keep warm. Put rest of butter in pan, heat and add lemon juice, scraping any browned juices from pan to make a syrupy sauce. Spoon a little over each portion. You may add a little finely chopped parsley to the pan at the last minute, but only the last minute as it must not brown.

A carefully made purée of potatoes (p. 194) is the best accompaniment for family meals in winter. But if you are entertaining either go and beg a pound or so of small potatoes from the greengrocer, or cut down large potatoes, rounding them with a peeler to look like small ones. Serve plainly boiled, rolled in melted butter/margarine with a dusting of chopped parsley. Simmer carefully, or steam cut-down large potatoes as they break up easily.

HAKE OR FILLETED WHITING WITH RED POTATOES

Hake and whiting are sometimes said to be the most easily digested fish – whatever that means – and therefore good for children and invalids. Whilst I find hake pleasant enough, if unexciting in flavour and texture, whiting is a fish I avoid like the plague on account of the bones, which I find as trying as some people find herring bones and, having picked my way through the skeletal jungle, I don't find the flesh very rewarding. However, I know many people who like whiting, and this way of serving fish tempts child convalescents ('red potatoes?') to tuck in to some nourishing food.

1½–2 lb. fish (4 medium whole whiting, or piece of hake)	1 lb. each potatoes and carrots seasoning
½ gill tomato juice, or 1 heaped tsp. tomato purée	juice of ½ lemon
2 oz. margarine/butter	1 slice and 1 tsp. finely chopped onion

SAUCE: ¼ pint milk, ¾ oz. margarine and flour.

Put on carrots and potatoes to boil 15 minutes before fish. Arrange fish, cut into 4 helpings if a single, large piece, in a greased baking dish. Shake over them a little water from your hand, season, tuck slice of onion beneath each, squeeze over lemon juice, cover closely and bake in a moderate oven 12 to 20 minutes according to thickness of fish. When cooked, flesh will be opaque, slightly shrunk and firm to the touch. There will be a good deal of whitish liquor in the dish, and this is added to the sauce.

Pass the cooked and drained vegetables through a Moulin-Légumes or sieve – potatoes first, then carrots. Melt the fat in a saucepan with the tomato juice, or tomato purée diluted with 3 tsp. water. When bubbling, add the sieved vegetables, and beat well with a wooden spoon till smooth, adjusting seasoning. Arrange this purée in an oblong mound down the centre of a serving dish, and keep warm, putting the cooked fish on top, and covering with a butter paper to prevent drying, while making the sauce.

SAUCE. Melt the fat, stir in the flour off the heat, add the milk stirring till smoothly mixed, bring just to the boil stirring well, and add the fish liquor, cooking until the sauce just thickens. Spoon over the fish.

TURBOT AND HALIBUT WITH EGG AND PARSLEY SAUCE

Bake the fish as above, using the liquor to make scant ½ pint good coating white sauce (p. 113ff.) making up the quantity with milk. While the fish is cooking, hard-boil and chop small a large egg, and finely chop 1 tbs. parsley. Add these, with a generous shake of pepper, to the finished sauce. Just mask the fish with sauce, handing the rest separately in a sauceboat. Potatoes, as for Haddock Meunière, are the best accompaniment plus, if a second vegetable is insisted on, some nicely done frozen peas.

Meat

BOHEMIAN ROAST PORK

Adapted from the dish that in the Bohemian countryside is equivalent to our roast beef and Yorkshire pudding. But the Czech housewife raises her dumpling with yeast and, instead of carving a big joint, she roasts a very thick pork chop for each person; a good method for the single, who could also bake a small suet dumpling alongside the meat. You may not like caraway seed in seed cake, but in cabbage the flavour is quite transformed.

PORK. For a family, hand of pork – equivalent to shoulder of lamb – is a good buy, for you will certainly want some pork left over for eating cold. For a couple, a small spare-rib or piece of belly is enough. See that the crackling is really well scored by the butcher and that the strips are not cut too wide.

Read the meat and roasting notes (pp. 77, 81, 96), and roast the pork by Quick Method. Baste the crackling from time to time.

DUMPLING. Make suet dough as follows:

¼ lb. fresh white crumbs	2 level tsp. baking powder
¼ lb. plain flour	1 level tsp. salt
about 4 fl. oz. water	½ tsp. pepper
3 oz. suet	½ small onion chopped very finely

Well blend all dry ingredients and the onion. Mix to a soft dough with water, form into thick roll not too long to fit your largest saucepan, allowing room to swell and for wrappings. Wrap in butter paper and then seal in foil. The foil must be well folded, but room must be left for swelling of dough. Drop into boiling water or place in steamer and cook ¾–1 hour.

CABBAGE. Discard outer leaves of cabbage, quarter it, wash thoroughly and cut into fine strips, from top towards stalk, as the stalk holds leaves together for easier handling. Melt 2 oz. margarine in a large pan, and in this soften the other half of the small onion (from the dumpling), also chopped finely. Stir in the cabbage gradually, seeing that it is well mixed with the fat. Add a pinch of caraway seed and a good shake of pepper. Do not add salt at this stage. Stir well, cover pan and put on a low heat for 12 to 20 minutes, stirring occasionally. The cabbage soon cooks down, at which point add salt to taste. When quite tender, press well in a colander and reserve the liquid. Dish.

GRAVY. When the meat is done, dish and keep it warm. Make up the cabbage liquor to ½ pint with water or light stock. Pour off fat from roasting tin, add liquid and boil up, scraping down the sides and bottom of the tin to dissolve the meat juices. Add a teaspoon of lemon juice if liked.

Dish the meat with the thickly sliced dumpling alongside, serving a slice of dumpling with each helping, moistened with a little gravy. Hand the gravy-boat afterwards as usual.

GERTRUDE GOSLIN'S BROWN STEW

Serves 6.

The provenance of this unusual recipe is something of a mystery. I believe that walnuts are pickled only in England, yet my mother assures me the recipe did not come from family sources, and so far I have failed to find anything resembling it in old books, nor inded have I encountered any recipe using pickled walnuts in a hot dish. It is a great favourite with men and with children who like savoury dishes. Good mild ale is the best of all drinks with it – the spicy flavours kill wine.

¾ lb. each Scotch or English shin and skirt
6 pickled walnuts
2 tsp. of the pickle juice
1 tsp. vinegar
½ level tsp. ginger
1 dozen peppercorns
bayleaf
1 clove
salt, if needed, to taste

1–2 tsp. brown sugar (optional)
1 large or 2 medium onions
1 clove garlic
1 pint stock or water
about ½ teacup fresh *brown* breadcrumbs
To *fry*: use beef or bacon dripping for preference, up to 1½ oz., or up to 1½ tbs. oil

Prepare meat as for stewed steak on p. 101. Slice the onions, quarter the walnuts, crush the garlic in salt. Heat the fat and quickly sear the meat, putting it into a cocotte or saucepan, and keeping it warm while frying the onions until brown but not burned. Add to meat. Pour off any surplus fat in pan, add the liquid and bring to boil, scraping juices from pan and blending with the liquid. Add to meat with all other ingredients except the crumbs. Stir once, cover down well, and cook in low oven 300° F, gas 2, for 1 hour, then 250° F, gas 1, for rest of time, that is 3 to 3½ hours; or on top of stove just at simmering point. Half an hour before the end stir in the breadcrumbs. Serve with more walnuts handed separately.

This is a very rich, warming and spicy dish. Accompaniments must be of the simplest : jacket potatoes as suggested in the stewing notes (p. 101); plain boiled with a garnish of chopped parsley – no butter – for entertaining; sprouts, peas or carefully cooked root vegetable, if a second vegetable is liked. But for preference serve a salad after the meat course.

POULET ERIC

Serves 6 to 8.

A dish designed to save time yet still not dear. Originally pressure cooked. There is no preliminary frying, no need for extra vegetables, and no final thickening. 6 to 8 helpings according to the size of the chicken joints and appetites, so will do two days. Good for a busy patch, exotic enough for a dinner party.

6 leg portions of roasting chicken	1½ lb. potatoes
½ lb. sausage meat	5 tbs. white wine
4 button or 1 medium onions	2 slices lemon
2–3 stoned olives (p. 104) (black or green)	2 rashers bacon
	1 clove garlic crushed in salt

PRESSURE COOKER METHOD. Peel onions – quarter medium – and put in cooker with garlic. Add chicken with any juices dissolved out of it. Put lemon slices on top, scatter the olives over. Divide the sausage meat into 8, and roll into 'boulettes' in lightly floured hands; cut the bacon into ½-inch strips and put these on top of chicken. Lastly add wine, pepper and a pinch of salt.

Pressure cook 5 to 10 minutes. Meanwhile peel and cut potatoes into ½-inch dice. Reduce pressure, add potatoes, and re-pressure 5 to 7 minutes. Dish with the various ingredients in bouquets round the chicken. The rich gravy is poured over the meat.

ORDINARY PAN. Fill ingredients into pan as above. Bring liquid just to boil then turn heat down to simmering point and cover pan with greased paper or foil below the lid. Cook 1 hour, add the potatoes, baste them with the pan juices, re-cover and cook 20 minutes more.

The best second vegetable, if needed, is frozen peas.

BRAISED SHEEP'S HEARTS

During the first 3 months of the year excellent tender New Zealand hearts are plentiful and cheap. Allow 1 heart per person.

STUFFING for 4 hearts:

3 tbs. fresh breadcrumbs
1 egg (plus 1–2 tbs. milks as needed)
grated rind of 1 orange
½ small onion finely chopped

1 tbs. fresh herbs (mixed or of one sort) or
1 tsp. dried mixed herbs
1 oz. butter/margarine
seasoning

FOR THE BRAISING POT:

1 medium onion
2 medium carrots
1 stick celery
scant ½ pint stock or water
1 dessertsp. tomato paste

1 turnip
bouquet garni
juice of ½ orange
} or ½ pint canned tomato juice

This quantity is necessary even for 1 heart owing to the long cooking.

FOR BROWNING:
1 oz. good dripping

PREPARATION OF HEART. Most hearts on sale today have been well cleaned; if not, rinse thoroughly to remove any coagulated blood, and rest in lightly salted cold water ½ hour.

Carefully pull away all the string-like fibres and valve divisions inside the heart and, rather a fiddling job, as much as possible of the membrane covering the muscular flesh of the heart walls outside. This is not always done because the heart tears more easily when the membrane is removed. On the other hand it is much more tender and takes less cooking time. The long cooking is vital for heart, which, undercooked, is rubbery. (André Simon notes in the old edition of the Wine and Food Society's *Encyclopedia of Gastronomy*: 'The ingenious Soho restaurateurs have discovered that the texture of suitably cooked Calf's heart is very similar to that of Wild Duck, and the breast of Wild Duck served in Soho with a spicy brown sauce and sliced orange has often been in reality thin slivers of Calf's Heart.' I wonder if it still is?)

STUFFING. Melt fat and soften onion. Stir in crumbs off the heat. Add rest of ingredients and, lastly, well beaten egg. If the stuffing is too dry add milk, by the spoonful, until it holds together but is not too soft.

Fill the hearts with stuffing and firmly twist damped greaseproof paper over the ends to keep stuffing in.

Peel, thickly slice and fry the pot vegetables until well browned, and lay them in the bottom of the cocotte. Finally, and with care so that they stay put together, briskly brown each side of the hearts and put them on the vegetables. Pour in the liquids and cook in a slow oven (250° F, gas 1) for 3 to 4 hours.

Cook jacket potatoes to accompany the meat, and if a second vegetable is wanted, simply prepare extra carrot, turnip or celery and add to the braising pot about 2 hours before the cooking time is ended.

Cooked in this way the meal costs little in raw materials and fuel. A pudding may be cooked above the meat; for example, one of the baked custard or bread-and-butter pudding variety; or casseroled fruit. On top of stove, steam a pudding over the saucepan. In a pressure cooker allow a good hour.

OX-TAIL

This is also the season for the best English and Scotch ox-tail. Although less of a cheap meal than formerly, ox-tail is still reasonable, filling and delicious, and, so long as you put in enough water, the cartilaginous bones give you a helping or so of rich, jellied soup next day.

Prepare your braising pot as for hearts (see above recipe), but use 1 lb. carrots, 2–3 onions, water just to cover the meat, which you brown first as for hearts, and the juice of ½–1 lemon in place of the orange juice. Add 2 cloves, and ½ tsp. ginger to the pot. Cook for 4 to 8 hours (i.e. overnight if it fits your plans better), lowering the heat from 300° F, gas 2, after 1 hour, to 270°–250° F, gas 1–½, for the shorter time, but to 240° F, gas ¼, for the 8–hour stint. Half an hour before serving add ½–¾ oz. each margarine and flour that you have mashed together into a paste (*beurre manié*). Dot it all over the pot in small bits, then stir in until blended, and return to the oven for ½ hour to finish. Serve plainly cooked potatoes and additional root vegetables as for the hearts.

There is a useful alternative to potatoes if you are cooking the tail for 8 hours, and this is to cook haricot, butter or other dried beans in the pot at the same time. See instructions for pulse vegetables on p. 139, or the Baked Beans recipe on pp. 402–3. Remember the beans will absorb liquid and thicken the stew, so omit the *beurre manié*. Beans mean that you cannot cook the dish overnight, or if you were going to be out during these last 4 hours, for you must inspect the pot now and then during the last half of the cooking, to see if more liquid is needed. Also beans would probably absorb too much of the liquid to leave enough over for soup, though you should have spare beans for a second meal, to compensate.

Ox-tail responds well to pressure cooking. Use one pint water – reduce pressure after 1 hour, inspect and add more liquid if necessary. Cook further ½ to 1 hour. Thicken as instructed by makers.

ROAST AITCHBONE

Some butchers say they do not cut aitchbones owing to their size. The joint comes next to the rump, has a large area of lean, from which good slices may be carved, and is surrounded by fat, which is thick where it joins the bone. The proportion of bone is on the heavy side but, even when this, as well as the fat, is allowed for, good home-killed aitchbone is a splendid family and entertaining joint from the point of view of cost, tenderness, flavour and the big amount of lean meat that it yields. Butchers who cut aitchbones (alternative name 'edge bone') will usually allow you to buy a half (though the thick end will still be a large joint – 5–6 lb. untrimmed), and will usually bone them for you. As with all meat, however, the flavour is superior if cooked on the bone and, in this instance, the bone is not all that difficult to remove after cooking. On the other hand, as always, the boned joint is easier to carve. At the thick end, lean usually protrudes from the encasing fat and, being the next cut to rump, is very tender. Therefore, if your joint is Scotch or English, and bought from a good butcher during the height of the season, you can often cut a steak from this end which, beaten and fried in good dripping or oil, will make a little luxury meal for two.

Aitchbone was salted and boiled in the past and until very recently was regarded as a braising cut. Improved breeding and rearing has converted it, like topside, into a good roast, and some butchers bone and roll it and sell it as topside! In roasting it do not remove its fat but, during its longish cooking time, at a lower temperature than the better-known roasting cuts, start it off fatty side uppermost, turning it once or twice during cooking. This is one of the cuts where a roasting rack or grid in the tin is very useful. Best of all, you can lard it here and there through the lean. Remember to season the meat. Cook it at 325° F, gas 3, in the centre of the oven, allowing 20–25 minutes per lb. according to thickness, plus 25 minutes over.

Nothing from aitchbone is wasted in a family : the bones make stock or gravy and the dog gets them afterwards; the fat renders down into excellent dripping; the lean is of good flavour and plentiful hot, cold and for réchauffés.

Vegetables

LEEKS BAKED IN TOMATO SAUCE

Leek prices vary wildly, and one often suspects greengrocers of pricing them up in winter, their best season, when variety in vegetables is lacking. By cooking leeks in the method described here you make the most of a small amount, do justice to those grown in the garden, and provide a sauce without extra work.

Cut off the coarse leaves by cutting the tops of the leeks rather as if you were sharpening a pencil. Take care not to cut so much from the root end that the leek falls to pieces. Slit each leek in two lengthways, run the tap down them from the leaf to the root end and then soak in cold water for 15 minutes, swish about, and inspect between the leaves to ensure all grit is removed. Immerse in ½ pint cold salted water and quickly bring to the boil, drain and 'refresh' in cold water. Drain again very well. Lay the leeks in a fireproof dish, or put them in a saucepan. Add ¼ pint canned tomato juice made up to 8 fl. oz. with water. Shave ½ oz. margarine over the top. Cover and cook in gentle heat (oven 300° F, gas 2; on ring at simmering point) for ½ to ¾ hour according to thickness of leeks. When done, a knife or skewer point should go easily through the solid root end. If the sauce is thin pour it off and reduce by boiling until it is the desired consistency. For serving with lamb or beef the thinner sauce will do double duty as a gravy.

PARSNIPS AU GRATIN

Those who like parsnips probably know how to cook them plainly boiled and buttered like carrots, parboiled and tucked round a joint to finish as baked parsnips. But parsnips, like turnips, have enemies, and when parsnipophiles and parsnipophobes form warring sides of the same family, here's a way to cook them that may prove acceptable to both factions, enhancing the distinctive flavour for the first while disguising it for the second. It will make a complete vegetarian supper dish.

Scrape or thinly pare 1 lb. parsnips, split them into wedges and boil for 20 minutes until tender (7 to 10 minutes in a pressure cooker).

While they are cooking make the following sauce:

1½ gills milk	1–1½ oz. grated cheese
¾ oz. each margarine and flour	½ tsp. made mustard
	seasoning

Melt the margarine, stir in flour and mustard off the fire. Add milk, boil up, stirring smooth. Add all but 1 heaped tsp. cheese and mix well. Put cooked parsnips in heated gratin dish, mask with sauce. Mix rest of cheese with about 1 tbs. browned crumbs. Scatter over dish and grill until a brown crust is formed.

CORNISH SWEDES

Another vegetable that rouses strong passions. After eating them like this in Cornwall I became quite converted, and have converted others since. Belonging to the same family, turnips are excellent done the same way.

Swedes grow very large: a single root often weighs a pound. The root should be really hard, so refuse spongy specimens.

1 lb. swede	1 oz. margarine
2 tbs. cream, yoghurt, top milk or evaporated milk (in order of preference)	seasoning to taste
	black pepper

Thickly peel the swede. The outer rind is opaque-looking, the inner flesh a little transparent and finely 'veined'. It is essential to get off all the rind, which cooks stringily. Cut into inch pieces. Boil 20 to 30 minutes in salted water until quite soft (10 to 15 minutes in pressure cooker). Drain and mash with a fork, blending in margarine and seasoning as needed. Be generous with pepper. Reheat, pile in hot dish and top with cream or yoghurt, and finish with freshly ground black pepper.

Carrots

While new carrots are unbeatable cooked in the classic Vichy manner, old carrots with their richer flavour will respond to various treatments and are a useful and healthy winter standby.

OLD CARROTS VICHY

Thinly pare and cut the carrots into wedges. Boil about 30 minutes (15 minutes in pressure cooker) until the point of a knife easily goes through them. Drain off all but a tablespoon of the water, reserving the surplus for stock. Add ½ oz. butter/margarine for each 1 lb. carrots, 1 tsp. lemon juice, ½ tsp. sugar; season to taste. Shake the carrots in this over a fairly fierce heat until the water has evaporated, leaving the carrots glazed in a little syrup. Add 1 tsp. chopped parsley, shake again and dish up.

RINGED CARROTS

Slice the carrots in rings no thicker than a half-crown. Cook them in any well-flavoured meat or fowl stock, using just enough to cover them and cooking quite rapidly 15 to 20 minutes (5 minutes in pressure cooker). The liquid will reduce and thicken, making a sauce. Add salt only after tasting.

CARROTS IN WHITE SAUCE

See CARROTS IN BÉCHAMEL SAUCE p. 220

CARROT SALAD

Instead of the classic vinaigrette, make the dressing of 1 tbs. lemon juice to 2–3 tbs. oil (olive is best for this job, and nothing else. Grate the carrot of course.

STUFFED ONIONS

4 Spanish or large onions
1 heaped tbs. fresh
 breadcrumbs
seasoning

2 oz. grated cheese
1 oz. bacon dripping or
 margarine

Boil the onions in their skins for ¾ hour. Peel and cool. Scoop out part of the centres and chop them into the fat until small and well blended. Add to this half the cheese and half the breadcrumbs, and fill the onion cavities with the mixture. Put onions in a baking dish, cover and bake in a moderate oven (300–350° F, gas 3) for 1 to 2 hours according to size. Mix the remaining cheese and crumbs and, 20 minutes before the end, uncover the dish and top the onions with this mixture to finish cooking.

Obviously other fillings may be used: for instance cooked peas, odds and ends of bacon, sauces, fish or meat; but some of these would make a complete snack meal.

Potatoes

POMMES DE TERRE À L'AIL

A splendid aromatic dish for winter. I give it this name because I have met it as both 'Provençale' and 'Savoyarde', with milk and with stock. The great thing is the garlic and the grated cheese.

Peel and slice 1 lb. potatoes into rings. Very finely chop 1 clove of garlic, or crush it under salt if you want it in one piece to fish out before serving. Lay potatoes in a small well-buttered gratin dish, overlapping in layers with salt, pepper, chopped garlic and a good dusting of grated cheese between each layer (2 oz. in all), but not, at this stage, on top. If using crushed garlic, tuck it in the centre below the top layer. Put shavings of butter on top, and pour round a generous ½-pint of stock or good thin gravy. Cover with foil or greaseproof paper and bake 45 minutes at 375° F, gas 5. Remove covering, dust top thickly with grated cheese and return to oven for 15 to 20 minutes until top is brown.

MADAME MARTHE RIGOT'S
BURGUNDIAN POTATOES

Madame Rigot, now in her eighties, is the daughter and grand-daughter of famous Paris restaurateurs of the nineteenth and early twentieth centuries. Called Le Grand U, the restaurant was a meeting-place for writers, politicians and journalists. Such was the reputation of the Grand U's cassoulet (goose stew, to sum it up very, very crudely!) that the clientèle fought in the street on cassoulet days in order to get a place in the queue before it was all eaten up. Madame Rigot's grandfather was a Burgundian with his own vineyard, and it was, I gather, on childhood visits to the family property there that she first met the potato dish that follows.

No food can be exactly translated from one country to another, any more than language, the chief difficulty here being in the almost 100 per cent 'closed shop' for 'floury' potatoes in Britain – not only in shops, but in gardens (see p. 75). This means that the treatment I give here produces the nearest possible result to that of Madame Rigot.

Select nothing bigger than medium to small and very hard (a sign of freshness) potatoes. Steer clear of those plastic bags of spuds that have been hanging about long enough to get themselves washed, weighed, packed and turned green. Mud helps potatoes to stay fresh and firm. Discard any that have cuts or bruises. Scrub thoroughly 1 lb. and boil them 5 to 7 minutes in jackets. Remove the skins and slice slightly under ¼ inch thick, dropping the slices into ¾ pint seasoned milk, to which you have added no more than 1 tsp. finely chopped onion softened in ½–1 oz. butter/margarine. Bring the pan only just to a simmer, and continue cooking with the lid only half on the pan for about 30 minutes, until the milk has thickened, the potato become quite soft but not mushy, and the butter incorporated into the starch released by the potatoes. During the last 10 minutes add a pinch of dried tarragon (fresh, of course, if it is in season) and/or a little chopped parsley. You must carefully scrape a spoon across the bottom of the pan occasionally during cooking to prevent sticking and, if yours are gas-weight pans, put an asbestos mat beneath. The milk turns pale golden by the end, and the sauce is like cream.

Puddings

PINEAPPLE POLL

Perhaps I should claim for this the title of the only Pop Art pudding in the world. A surrealist nursery pud for adults.

Drain about 3 tbs. of pineapple pieces. (Pineapple 'pieces' are the cheapest form of tinned pineapple, and are wedge-shaped; if you have only chunks available cut them small.) *Very* thickly grease a pint pudding basin with good lard or shortening, a mixture of lard/margarine, or butter. With strips of candied peel and raisins make a face, upside down and inside out on one side or more of the pudding basin – up to 4 faces if you like, of varying expressions if you can. Cover the bottom of the basin with pineapple for hair, standing some pieces on end to make a fringe. Press the face well into the grease and keep chilled until the sponge is ready.

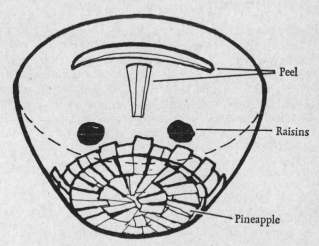

Face, upside down, set inside pudding basin

Prepare steamer and put on to boil. Have ready greased paper, foil, string, etc. for covering the pudding.

THE SPONGE. Make a 2 egg creamed or stirred sponge mixture as on p. 50f, adding 1–2 tbs. rum just before folding in the flour, and 1 tbs. pineapple, 1 level tsp. ginger and 2 tsp. baking powder with the flour. Fill the sponge mixture evenly up the basin by tablespoons so as not to displace the faces. Cover down, and steam 1 to 1½ hours. Before turning out, carefully free pudding from sides of basin to ensure the faces turn out intact.

THE SAUCE. ¼ lb. sugar dissolved in ¼ pint water to which is added the thinly pared or grated rind of ½ lemon. Bring to the boil. Add the juice of 1 lemon and 2 generous tbs. rum. Do not cook after rum is added. Serve in a heated sauceboat.

The sauce is a thin syrup, the pudding a light sponge that quickly absorbs liquid. Therefore keep the sauceboat – for a party 2 would be still better – circulating, so that sauce may be added little and often as the pudding is eaten.

COFFEE BREAD-AND-BUTTER PUDDING

Cut enough medium-thin slices of stale bread, brown or white, well buttered, to line a pint pie dish. Warm a spoonful or so from a pint of milk, and in it dissolve 1 rounded dessertsp. of powdered coffee. Next stir in 1–2 tbs. sugar according to taste. Beat 2 eggs well, mix with rest of milk and add to coffee mixture. Finely chop 3–4 walnut halves; cut into dice one thick slice of unbuttered bread; add these to pie dish. Pour in the milk mixture and set aside for ½ hour while bread absorbs liquid. Bake at 350° F, gas 3–4, for 40 minutes to 1 hour until the coffee custard (which this really is) part of the pudding is set.

APPLE FLANS

Less a recipe than notes, since the great variety to which apple lends itself would make it foolish to give merely one version.

Read the pastry notes on pp. 123–32.

PASTRY. Use shortcrust, flaky or a pâte sucrée. The following quantities are for the following-sized flan-rings (see section on equipment, p. 52) or tart plates, the pastry being rolled ⅛ inch thick at most, and they allow for lattices if desired:

Flan-ring	6-inch	7-inch	8-inch or fluted 7-inch	9-inch
Pastry	4 oz.	5–6 oz.	7 oz.	8 oz.
Basic amount of apple	just 1 lb.	generous 1 lb.	1½ lb.	2 lb.

FILLINGS AND FINISHES

À LA MÉNAGÈRE. The classic of all classic flans; carefully made and precisely arranged it is as ornamental as it is delicious. You may need rather more than the basic quantity of apple to allow for enough covering slices. 1–2 tbs. castor sugar, according to size. 1 tbs. sieved apricot jam in 1 tbs. hot water for glazing.

If you use method II you will need 1–2 oz. sugar for sweetening the purée according to *size*, not taste; too much sugar will make the filling too liquid and spoil the finish.

METHOD I Line the flan-ring and brush it out thinly with glaze. Peel, core and quarter the apples and slice them very thinly. Fill the flan-case higgledy-piggledy below, but reserve enough good slices to cover the entire top with closely and neatly over-lapped slices, either spiralling into the centre (starting from the outside) or encircling an apple-slice 'rose'.

Add no water. Dust over the castor sugar and bake in a moderate oven (375° F, gas 5) for 30 to 40 minutes. The edges of the slices and top of the pastry become darkly toasted, producing a black-and-white striped appearance, enhanced by the jam glaze brushed over the entire flan after baking, sides and all.

METHOD II. Exactly the same as above except that you cook to a purée (as in next recipe but omitting butter and marmalade) all but enough apple to cover the top. The advantage is that there is less chance of slices being displaced by sinking. The disadvantage is that it takes longer, especially as you must wait for the purée to cool before filling the case.

NOTE: A very fair result can be had minus the glaze, but even this small quantity adds to the flavour, and much to the appearance. The trick of brushing out pastry cases with jam glaze before filling them is worth remembering. It 'waterproofs' the case a little against the wetter type of filling.

À LA CONFITURE D'ORANGES. Shortcrust pastry is better for this one. Peel, core and cut apples up roughly into chunks. In a thick, covered pan over a mere whisper of heat *and with no water,* cook the apples down to a foam. You must stir them about occasionally, especially at the start. For each 1 lb. apples add 1–1½ oz. sugar to the hot foam, and stir until dissolved, then ½ oz. butter and 1 heaped tbs. coarse-cut marmalade. Cool the purée completely before filling the flan-case. From the pastry trimmings cut strips about ¼ inch wide (wider strips take less time, but give a clumsy finish) and make a lattice over the flan. Bake 30 minutes at 375° F, gas 5. Glaze when flan has cooled somewhat and lattice has hardened a little.

AUX FRUITS. As above, but instead of marmalade use dried fruits, slivered almonds, or a little sliced stem ginger. Any mixture of these will do.

BOURDALUE. The classic apricot bourdalue can be expensive and can involve making frangipan. This adaptation is, however, very pleasant. There is, of course, no compulsion to make proper confectioners' custard, and what substitutes you use is a matter between you and your conscience, but texture and the taste will suffer as much as you ought to do if you use custard straight from the packet.

Use rich shortcrust or flaky pastry, or pâte sucrée.
Line the flan-ring and bake blind (p. 127).
Meanwhile make confectioner's custard:

½ pint milk	1½ oz. castor sugar
1 egg	2–3 drops vanilla, or vanilla pod
1 egg-yolk	2–3 tbs. whipping cream or
½ oz. cornflour	substitutes (see pp. 62–3).
¾ oz. flour	

These amounts will be too much for the smaller flans, so make
half if you foresee no immediate use for spare. Excellent for
custard slices, éclairs and small light cakes.

Cream both egg-yolks with sugar and vanilla essence if used.
Reserve white. Add flours with 1 tbs. milk and mix to smooth
cream. Scald rest of milk with vanilla pod if used, pour on to egg
mixture and stir till smooth. Return to heat and bring just to boil,
stirring constantly. Care: this is when it lumps, which is fatal to
the subsequent foldings-in. Stir rapidly, whisk if necessary for
a few minutes to avert danger. Whip white stiffly; whip cream
only until it holds its shape. Add the white to the still hot mixture, fold in and, when cool, fold in cream.

Half fill flan-case with custard, cover with apple slices, which
you have cut medium-thin, poached in a stock syrup (made from
2 oz. sugar to ½ gill water) until just soft, but unbroken (in low
oven is a good way if only Bramleys are available), cooled and
drained. As before, make a neat top layer and brush with glaze.

Australian Sturmers are good for this when available. Also
Granny Smiths and similar sharp, crisp eating apples. Bramleys
are difficult to poach, and to handle after cooking, as they break
easily.

February

◆◆◆

Shrove Tuesday pancakes this month, so look up the notes on batter (p. 122), and put lemons and castor sugar on the shopping list for that day. St Valentine's Day, too, when many young people like to hold rather mad parties among themselves. A good, cheap and hot late-night supper can all be cooked in 2 big pots on gas rings by making the boiled chicken and rice on p. 189 – a 3 lb. bird will serve 6 to 8 and 3 oz. rice per person.

Soups
First read notes on pp. 112–13.

CELERY AND LEMON CREAM SOUP

A soup to make when you have had boiled chicken. A less nourishing version can be made from roast chicken remains. Although fresh to the palate, and therefore a useful soup with which to start meals, the full version has splendid nutritional value and is excellent for faddy children, the elderly (especially those who find it difficult to eat fruit or who dislike milk) and convalescents.

1 pint broth in which chicken
  has been boiled
¾ pint milk
3 outside sticks celery
  including leaves, or tops
  and leaves from inside
  sticks, as available
1 lemon
salt and ground white pepper

1 small or ½ medium onion
  finely chopped
1½ oz. each flour and
  margarine/butter
1 hard-boiled egg (optional)
1 egg, or 2 yolks
3 tbs. single cream or
  substitutes (p. 62).

Sweat chopped onion in half the fat, and celery, sliced finely, and turn about in fat. Add chicken stock and either pared or grated rind of lemon after you have squeezed and added juice. Bring to the boil and simmer 20 to 30 minutes until celery is quite tender. Meanwhile hard-boil egg where this is to be used. Put celery through finest Moulin-Légumes plate, or rub through sieve, pouring broth through afterwards. Melt rest of fat, blend in flour. The resulting roux will be very stiff so add milk gradually, stirring well with each addition, to avoid lumping. Bring to boiling point, continuing the thorough stirring, and adding the sieved celery and chicken broth, keeping soup just at simmering point. Continue simmering for 5 minutes. Adjust seasoning. Blend yolk or yolks with cream in small basin. If using hard-boiled egg, chop it finely and add to liaison. Pour on some of the hot soup, mix well and return to pan. Do not allow to boil after this. Serve with small fried croûtons, buttered cracker biscuits, or melba toast (p. 67) as required.

For very delicate stomachs use pared rind, removing before sieving, and yolks, to give a completely smooth soup; for heartier appetites, grated rind and hard-boiled egg. For the latter you may also put a little cooked rice and minced chicken meat in each soup-cup.

THE GARDENER'S WINTER SOUP

½ lb. leeks or onions	1 pint milk
½ lb. potatoes	1½ oz. margarine
½ lb. cauliflower	1½ oz. flour
½ lb. carrots	bayleaf
a few celery leaves	stalks of parsley
2 good tbs. chopped parsley	pinch of nutmeg
½ oz. butter	seasoning
1 pint water	

Reserve 1 small potato, 2 small flowerets cauliflower, 1 small carrot. Wash, pare and cut rest into quarters, tie the celery, bayleaf and parsley stalks in muslin. Simmer vegetables, with the herbs in muslin, in salted water for ¾ hour until tender. While they are cooking clean, pare and dice small the small potato and carrot, and divide the cauliflower into small florets, blanch them all for 1 minute, and soften them in the butter in a small covered pan over a low heat. Set this pan aside until the soup is finished. Remove herbs from boiled vegetables and put them, potato first, liquor last, through Moulin-Légumes or sieve. Melt the margarine, blend in the flour, add the milk and bring to the boil, blending the roux in smoothly. Add the vegetable purée and the herbs in muslin, adjust seasoning and simmer for 15 minutes. Just before serving remove muslin, add diced vegetables and parsley, and stir to mix.

TOURAINE

This tomato soup from southern France is a commonplace there in summer. Here in winter, when vitality and vitamins to say nothing of sunshine, seem conspicuously lacking, it brings a promise of the warmer days ahead. This is a quick version.

¾ pint canned tomato juice	1 onion
½ pint water	½ oz. bacon or pork dripping
½–1 oz. long rice, or	or lard
spaghetti broken small	seasoning

Slice the onion and soften it in the fat. Mix the tomato juice and water, and sieve the onion into the liquid. Bring to the boil, season, especially with enough pepper, throw in rice, and cook fairly quickly 12 to 15 minutes until rice is done.

MUSHROOM SOUP

¼ lb. mushroom stalks	1 pint milk
1½ oz. butter	½ pint stock or bouillon
½ oz. margarine	few strips lemon peel
1½ oz. flour	seasoning
1 tsp. chopped onion	parsley

Wash the stalks well, but do not break or bruise them. Slice them as thinly as possible in rings. Melt the butter, scatter in the onion and mushroom, and soften for 5 minutes. Pour off as much as possible of the butter into another pan with the melted margarine. Stir in the flour off the heat, add milk, returning to heat and blending smoothly until boiling point is reached. Gradually add the stock, mixing well and keeping at the boil. Pour back into mushroom mixture, season, add the lemon peel and simmer very gently 15 to 20 minutes, stirring occasionally. Before serving remove the lemon peel and dust in some finely chopped parsley.

NOTE: Later in the year this soup is particularly good if finished with a dessertspoon of chopped new mint instead of, or as well as, parsley.

GARBURE

Serves 8 to 10.

Also a soup of southern France, garbure can be made in several ways, but always contains cabbage, a starchy vegetable and a piece of pork or bacon. In summer you can concoct a light version with overblown peas, broad beans, or seeds from overblown French beans replacing the dried beans; with a few tomatoes to flavour, instead of root vegetables, and chives to decorate. But it is a splendidly filling soup in its winter dress.

½ lb. dried beans	1 clove garlic chopped finely
1 good-sized cabbage	into 3 sprigs parsley
1–1½ lb. pickled pork or	bouquet garni and 3 cloves,
bacon joint	tied in muslin
2 quarts water	1 tbs. olive oil (for preference;
1 large onion	corn or sunflower oil second
½ lb. potatoes	best)
2–3 carrots, turnips or a	salt
swede	pepper

Put the beans, prepared as on p. 139, into the water and bring to the boil, letting them simmer 2 hours before you add seasoning or any other ingredients. Add the pickled pork, the cabbage chopped small, the root vegetables cut into wedges, the onion quartered, and the bouquet garni. Pepper well, but add no salt. Simmer 4 to 5 hours. This cooking can be done in bits at a time at your convenience. Add the garlic and parsley, adjust seasoning and simmer at least another hour. Just before serving stir in 1 tbs. olive oil. The beans and potato should be mushy enough to thicken the broth. Serve a slice or so of the meat with each helping (unless you intend keeping this for a main dish).

In France there would be a long crusty baton loaf to accompany the soup. If there is nothing similar in your local baker's, at least you can serve your loaf crisp and warm as suggested on p. 66.

First Courses and Snacks

CORNISH PASTIES

In Cornwall they say: 'The Devil and all goes into a Cornish pastry.' And they pronounce it pahsty to rhyme with parsley. The secret of a true Cornish pasty is the raw ingredients for the filling. Cornish pasties did not start life as réchauffés made from leftovers, but as an ingenious way of providing a complete, hot and portable meal. The pastry case serves as cooking pot, thermal wrapping and dinner-plate all in one. The combination of the filling is as you please, but the ingredients must be those which can be completely cooked in *under an hour* at most. Pasties were sometimes taken by farm workers themselves, but more often it was the job of the children (at harvest time, of the whole household) to 'fetch father's dinner to the field' piping hot. The full size makes a hefty snack, but you can use a smaller gauge.

The traditional semi-circular pasty is cut from shortcrust slightly under ¼ inch thick, using a dinner-plate as diameter size-guide. On to one half of the circle thus cut out, whittle away, in small chippings, enough from a peeled raw potato (or turnip or carrot) to make a ½-inch-thick semi-circular layer. Salt and pepper (especially pepper in Cornwall) the potato, and on it put a thin layer of onion slices. Salt and pepper again. Then the meat. In Cornwall you ask the butcher simply for pasty beef. But it *must* be from a tender roasting or grilling cut, though you would probably succeed with first-quality skirt. The end cut from a home-killed aitchbone of beef as described on p. 163, would do nicely. You need about 2–4 oz. per pasty. Cut meat into big dice or smallish strips. Season again, then repeat the layers, with the onion next to the meat, and potato on the outside. To begin with, the whittling process can be slow, so it is as well to have both meat and onion ready beforehand, to prevent the first lot of potato from browning. Damp the edges of the circle and fold the uncovered half over the mound of filling, leaving a margin of the covered pastry to twist up over the top half. This twisting, which you do from one point of the pasty to the other, makes a good seal when completed. It must not be completed before you have raised the open end of the pasty and poured in about 2½ fl. oz. of water to make the gravy – more if you can, for a goodish bit of gravy in a meat pasty is highly prized. It soaks into the spuds and

Filling on one half. Damp edge. Turn over blank half leaving margin. Press.

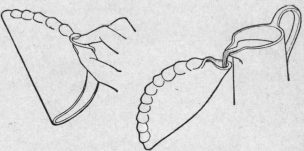

Twist to 1 inch from point. Raise open end of pasty and add
Leave open. liquid. Finish twist.

spreads the flavours. Not all Cornishwomen turn the pasty with its twist running cockscomb-wise across the top : flat pasties can be more useful when packing a basket. Brush over with beaten egg. Bake the pasty at 400° F, gas 6, for 20 minutes until pastry is set and brown. Lower heat to 275° F, gas 1, for another 30 to 35 minutes. If the pastry seems to be darkening too much, damp greaseproof, and cover tops loosely.

Fish makes a good pasty also. Small fruit pasties – use a side-plate for size, thicken juice with ½ tsp. cornflour per ½ pint, or boil down to syrup – make a change from fruit tarts and, when summer comes, are fine for picnic teas. Pasties of all sorts are a pleasant change from sandwich luncheons, especially if there are the means for heating them. Adjust sizes to appetites and occasions. 1 lb. shortcrust will make 4 dinner-plate pasties.

EGG AND BACON PASTY

This pasty is made differently – in a pie plate or flan-ring. The filling being very liquid, a deep shape would tend to produce a dryish top, or would need a disproportionate amount of egg to fill to the top.

For a plate 8 inches across the top (4 helpings):

8–10 oz. shortcrust or flaky pastry	6–7 rashers streaky bacon (rinds removed)
1 medium turnip	2 tbs. chopped parsley
1 medium potato	pepper
3–4 eggs	

Line the pie plate with ⅛-inch-thick (or less) pastry. This will take slightly more than half your ball of dough. Unless you like eating pastry without filling, do not take the dough out farther than ¼ inch over rim of plate. Roll out top to fit, and keep it cool.

Cut the bacon into ½-inch strips. Peel the vegetables, and keep in cold water until ready to use. Slightly beat the eggs, but do not overdo this: there should be streaks of white in the finished pasty.

(1) Whittle half the potato over the bottom of the lined plate.

(2) Cover with a layer of a third of the bacon strips all going one way.

(3) Dust with pepper and parsley.

(4) Whittle half the turnip on top.

(5) Lay on another third of the strips going at right angles to the first (so bacon is criss-crossed through the pasty).

(6) Whittle rest of turnip.

(7) Dust with pepper and parsley.

(8) Place last third of strips in same direction as first.

(9) Whittle rest of potato to cover.

(10) Dust with pepper and parsley.

(11) Whisk any remaining parsley into egg.

(12) Damp edges of pastry lid.

(13) Pour egg carefully and evenly over, pausing now and then to let egg sink down.

(14) Cover with lid and press edges together, knocking up with knife (p. 125), and decorating with fork.

Add pastry leaves from scraps if liked, but do not make a hole in lid. Add 1 tbs. water to egg bowl, and swish round to utilize dregs for brushing the top.

Bake in moderate oven, 375° F, gas 5, for shortcrust; 400° F, gas 6, for flaky pastry. After 25 to 30 minutes, or as soon as pastry is set and coloured, lower heat to about 325° F, gas 3, for a further 30 to 35 minutes to make about 1 hour in all. Excellent hot or cold.

DEVILLED CHICKEN (OR OTHER MEATS)

To devil meat or fish, first marinate for several hours in the devil – a hot, spicy uncooked sauce – then heat, usually by grilling. Small chicken joints can be used raw, but devilling is a fine way to use up cold meat. Serve salad only, if an accompaniment is wanted. Meat, off the bone, or fish can be served on hot toast, or fried bread. To devil minced or diced remains of joints, make half the quantity of devil, stir it into yoghurt – ½ a carton for a single-person household – and a little gravy, and heat in pan or oven.

DEVIL SAUCE (all spoons level)

2–3 tbs. salad oil or 1½ tbs. melted margarine
1 dessertsp. each of the following (or as many as possible):
thick Yorkshire Relish
Worcester sauce
Branston, Rajah or similar sweet chopped pickle or chutney (chopped *really* small)

1 dessertsp. cider or herb vinegar
1 tbs. each English and French mustard
½ tsp. Tabasco or sauce from hot Indian-made pickle
1 tsp. finely chopped onion
1 clove garlic chopped small
pinch salt
freshly-ground black pepper

Mix all very well together to produce a thick purée.

FOR CHICKEN JOINTS. Slash the flesh and cover with mixture, pressing it into slashes. Leave 6 hours before browning under pre-heated grill.

FOR STEAK, PORK CHOPS OR FISH. Spread mixture on both sides. Leave 6 hours, and grill, or bake in hot oven.

SAUSAGES AND BREAD SAUCE

A useful supper or luncheon dish to use up remaining sausages bought to go with fowl or for a buffet. Some people love bread sauce so much that they like an excuse for it anyway.

QUICKEST WAY. Grill the sausages, heat the sauce and serve.

VARIANT. Slip a sliver of garlic into each sausage before grilling.

BREAD SAUCE. This is one of England's two contributions to the world's classic sauces, the other being 'hard sauce' i.e. rum butter. Bread sauce is ruined by being over-refined. The texture should be rough, like thickish porridge. To get this, never sieve or grate the bread first, but proceed as follows (which is, hooray, much quicker):

Into a small lidded pan put ½ pint milk, 1 small onion stuck with 2 cloves, 1 oz. margarine/butter. Cut a slice of bread at least ½ inch thick and weighing 1½ oz. after de-crusting. Tear it in four, and drop into the pan. Add salt and white pepper. Put the pan on a very slow heat with the lid half on, and have both a small wooden spoon and a fork to hand. Keep an eye on the sauce and, as the milk heats, break bread down with spoon. As the milk comes to the boil, change to the fork and whisk the sauce until it is well mixed, but neither lumpy nor too smooth. Allow it barely to simmer for about 5 minutes, stirring the onion about. Put on the lid and stand pan aside for at least ½ hour, but the longer the better to develop flavour. Reheat very gently, adding a spoonful or so of milk if, when at boiling point, the sauce seems too thick. But it must not be in the least runny. Adjust seasoning, remove onion with cloves, and dish in a heated sauceboat.

WALNUT CHEESE TARTINES

PASTRY

4 oz. margarine	salt, pepper, 1 level tsp.
6 oz. flour	mustard powder
2 oz. grated cheese	4–5 tbs. water

Sieve flour, salt, pepper and mustard into mixing bowl. Rub in fat, stir in grated cheese, and mix to dough with water. Keep dough on the dry side. Knead smooth and rest in cool place for ½ hour if possible. Roll out ⅛ inch thick and cut into rounds 1½ inches in diameter or less. Set on baking-sheet and bake at 400° F, gas 6, for about 10 minutes until pastry is set but not coloured. Loosen with palette knife, but do not lift from baking-sheet until set. When cool pipe or mound on top the following mixture:

4 oz. curd cheese	salt, pepper, cayenne
2 oz. cake walnuts	

Press cheese through bowl-strainer. Season well with salt, pepper and cayenne. Chop the walnuts as finely as possible (almost to powder if you intend piping the cheese; a Mouli cheese grater or electric blender is excellent here). Mix nuts with cheese and top the tartines. For entertaining top the cheese with walnut halves.

Use as a savoury rather than a first course, or serve with drinks before the meal and omit first course.

Fish

First read fish notes on p. 86.

CREAMED SMOKED FISH (Garnished)

½ pint binding Béchamel
    sauce (p. 117)
4 kippers or their equivalent
    in Finnan haddock, or
    smoked fillets of any kind

4–6 tomatoes, tinned unless
    fresh ones are firm
¾ lb. well-made mashed potato
2 hard-boiled eggs

Barely cover fish with water, bring to boil, drain, skin, bone and flake it, and mix with sauce which you have thinned slightly with ½ gill warm milk. Reheat the whole on a low flame while grilling the tomatoes. Keep both warm while finishing or reheating the potatoes. Border a serving dish with the potato, pile the fish mixture in the centre, arrange the tomatoes down one side. Keep warm. Chop the eggs and put them in a band on the opposite side to the tomatoes. Serve piping hot, with cayenne pepper or Tabasco on the table for those who like them.

WHITING PIE

In a sense a variation of the above.

½ pint coating white sauce
    (any kind you fancy –
    cheese, onion, mushroom,
    egg)
2 lb. whiting (big fish are
    easier to bone) or other
    inexpensive fish obtainable
2–3 firm fresh tomatoes

¾ lb. good mashed potato – be
    generous with margarine/butter
2 hard-boiled eggs (unless you
    choose egg sauce)
1 medium onion (unless you
    choose onion sauce)
½ oz. margarine or bacon
    dripping to cook onion

Poach the fish in the oven. You will eventually need the oven at 400° F, gas 6, so put in the fish when you light the oven (if it is a whole big fish, just cover the bottom of the dish with water, otherwise water as in recipe p. 156). Cover dish. While fish is cooking (20 to 30 minutes), make the mashed potato, thinly slice the tomatoes, slice and soften the onion. Skin, bone, flake and mix fish with the sauce, and put mixture in a deep pie dish or gratin dish. Cover with tomato slices, salt them, then a layer of egg chopped or sliced. Scatter over this the onion, and top with mashed potato – prettily piped if possible. Set in the hot oven for 20 to 30 minutes until top is toasted.

NOTE: In both the above recipes the quantity of sauce is generous. Add sauce to fish until you think the mix is to your liking. Any leftover sauce is easily used up: add cooked mushroom, bacon, pasta, minced meat, etc. to make tea-time or supper snacks; add to soup or gravy to thicken; thin with a spoonful or so of milk for a sauce for vegetables.

Both recipes are also good examples of dishes which are a complete main course in one, and a very nutritious course at that. Calcium in the milk for the sauce, protein in the fish and egg, vitamin C in the potatoes and tomato.

And both recipes illustrate dishes that can be cooked on one day and eaten the next; or the components cooked in stages and the dish completed later. For example, make the sauce and cook the fish at one time. Hard-boil the eggs and boil the potatoes (in their jackets is best), at another. What is to be avoided is cutting the tomatoes or chopping the parsley very far in advance for both will lose juice and flavour, and also vitamins. Smoked fish has already been subjected to heat and may have lost some food value so, having cooked it, drain and cool it rapidly but leave it whole. Leave the fresh fish in its covered dish in a cool place – not at once in the refrigerator, however. The juices from it may be used in the sauce, in which case reduce the milk quantity.

SPRATS

Sprats are model food from every point of view but one. Tasty, nutritionally excellent, costing little, attractive and easy to cook, their one drawback is that the cooking is smelly. You must fry only so many at a time as the pan will hold in a single layer, and each fish must be turned once. This means the fat is on the boil for some time and, even with extractor hoods, fans and an open window, that fried-fish-shop odour wafts round the house, and clings to your hair and clothes. Your hair can be guarded by wearing your plastic bath cap, but clothes-wise, I fear, you can do no more than wear old things or something due for the wash tub.

1 lb. sprats will feed 2–3 people according to appetite. Work in this order :

(1) Cut thin brown bread and butter – 2–3 slices per person, cut across into triangles.

(2) Cut 2 lemon wedges (p. 105) per person.

(3) For each lb. sprats season 2 rounded tbs. flour with 1 level tsp. salt and ½ level tsp. pepper. Put in a flour-dredger if possible.

(4) Wash the fish in a colander under a fast-running cold tap. Drain, and dry them in absorbent paper (clean newspaper will do very well) or a cloth.

(5) Melt ½ inch fat in the frying-pan. Oil, lard or dripping will do, the first being best; the last should be melted down at a low heat, inspected and, if 'bits' are seen, strained through muslin. 'Bits' burn, and may taint the fat in the longish cooking time.

(6) Lay out the fish on a piece of dry kitchen paper, dust with seasoned flour, turn and dust other side.

(7) Put plates and a dish in oven. Scrumple up kitchen paper or newspaper on the dish to blot up surplus fat.

(8) When fat is really hot fill pan neatly from one side to the other with fish, leaving enough space between for turning them. Cook 2 minutes, turn in the same order as they first went into the pan, cook 2 minutes. The skin should be golden brown and crisp.

In a frying pan of 7–8 inches base you should get through 1 lb. sprats in three goes, the last lot not filling more than half the pan, so that 2 lbs. would probably be done in 5 goes – i.e. about 20 minutes' cooking time.

There is another, less smelly method, but you will not get quite the crisp finish. For this, preheat the oven to 425° F, gas 7. Heat ¼ inch fat in a big meat tin until smoking, or until 1 drop of water flicked in hisses loudly. Lay in the fish, cook 7 minutes, turn and cook 4 minutes. Remove carefully as they tend to break up. A tin will take a pound if some are fitted in round the sides.

LEMON SOLE AU VIN BLANC

There can be no doubt that for taste and texture, in particular for dishes of fish fillets poached and served with delicate sauces, Dover sole is the king of fish. Unfortunately the price of a Dover sole worth the filleting is also kingly. Luckily there are some near relations of the Dover sole that are often as cheap as cod or haddock. Of these the lemon sole is generally obtainable and, at this time of the year, specially good. Fillets of flat fishes are not intended for a hearty meal, but they are deceptively satisfying for their size.

A sole for filleting should be at least 11 inches long since, when the head and tail are off, you would otherwise have too tiny a fillet to be worth cooking. It should be thick through the 'shoulders' of the fish, and a pound in weight or more. A 1-lb. fish yields just enough for 2 people.

If possible get the fishmonger to do the filleting. I have done a bit of time, motion and wastage study on this matter, and have found that a skilled fishmonger (not all are) gets as much off the bone as I do, often more neatly, and in about one twentieth of the time. All one must do is to make sure he understands that you want the skin off on both sides – the black and the white – and that you want the head, backbone and skin for stock, the cat, or whatever.

Consult the filleting notes and diagrams (pp. 87–90) if you have to do it yourself.

Season the smooth side of the fillets, folding or rolling this side inside. Set them in a shallow fire-proof dish, and sprinkle them with 2 tbs. white wine. Trimmings, which enrich the liquor produced, are now added. Tuck head, well cleaned, alongside, add white skin, scaly side folded inwards so no scales fall into dish. Smear backbone with margarine/butter and put it on top of the fillets, and cover the dish with lightly buttered greaseproof paper or foil. Bake for about 15 to 20 minutes according to thickness at 325° F, gas 3.

Meanwhile, for 2 people, make sauce base in usual way (see p. 114) from the following:

187

½ gill milk
½ oz. each butter and flour   small slice of onion
small piece of bayleaf   salt and pepper

Boil bayleaf and onion in the milk beforehand if possible, otherwise put them in with the cold milk and leave them in until the sauce is completed, removing before serving. The sauce base should be the consistency of a binding sauce.

Remove fish trimmings and pour liquor from the baking dish into the sauce. Blend and bring to the boil. Taste, adjusting seasoning. Add another dessertspoonful of wine if liked.

Mask fillets, pour rest of sauce round, serve with well-made potato purée, or pommes duchesse piped into large rosettes, and browned in the oven, or piped round the dish and just toasted under the grill before serving.

Other classic sole fillet dishes include:

BONNE FEMME. As for Sole au Vin Blanc, but have ready some sliced small mushrooms (stalks will do for the family) and chopped shallot which you have softened in butter/margarine, and some chopped parsley and a little lemon juice. Add to the finished sauce.

DUGLÈRE. As for Sole au Vin Blanc, but add finely chopped shallot or very small onion sweated in margarine/butter to baking dish. (In summer, use chive and omit the shallot.) Have ready, for each 4 fillets, 1 concassed tomato (p. 15) and ½ tsp. finely chopped parsley. Cut the tomato into strips and add it with the parsley to finished sauce.

FLORENTINE. Omit the white wine, add juice of ½ lemon, proceed as before. Have ready a serving dish on which you have arranged a bed of carefully made spinach *en branche* (p. 15). Set fillets on this and pour sauce over. Also can be made with Mornay sauce.

MEUNIÈRE. See recipe for Haddock (p. 154).

SOLE MORNAY. A well-flavoured cheese sauce. Mask fillets as above, dust well with grated cheese and brown under grill.

ST GERMAIN. This is a gem of a dish. Use the fillets flat. Dip each in melted butter/margarine, then press on each side some fine browned crumbs. Grill, turning over once. Serve with thin brown bread and butter or tiny plain potatoes and a Béarnaise sauce (p. 119).

SOLE VÉRONIQUE. Proceed as for Sole au Vin Blanc but garnish the dish with bouquets of green grapes which you have pipped, skinned, and tossed in butter and lemon juice. This always impresses. Preparing the grapes is rather a fiddle, but use a (scalded) hairgrip to hook out the pips. Try out one of the grapes for skinning before you set to work and, if the skins won't budge, dip the bunch into boiling water for no more than 60 seconds, plunging at once into cold. Then pip, and lastly skin. Allow 4–6 grapes per fillet.

Meat

BOILED CHICKEN AND RICE

You need a big pot for this very simple, perfect dish to serve it in its traditional form: that is, with the chicken whole. For a family-sized bird of about 3½–4 lb. the pot will need to be at least 8 inches in diameter. The bird need not sit flat on the base of the pan, but the lid must close completely. These days, the difference in price between boilers and roasters is negligible, and I have seen boilers priced dearer than battery roasters; but there is often a gain in flavour.

Put your chicken into a pot of cold, well-salted water almost to cover it. Bring to the boil, adding any herbs you fancy tied in muslin, tarragon being particularly good, a few strips of rind very thinly pared from a lemon, pepper and a pinch of ginger. Simmer 1½ hours for battery birds, 3 hours for boiling fowls. Drain and dish the bird, covering with butter paper to keep warm.

Weigh 2–3 oz. per person of long-grain rice, then put the total amount in a liquid measuring jug. From the chicken stock measure three times the volume of the rice: that is for 6 *fluid* oz. rice you need 18 fl. oz. chicken stock. Do not wash the rice. The starch from it will thicken the liquid to provide the sauce. Add the juice of ½ lemon to each 1 pint stock used. Boil up the measured stock, add the rice and boil briskly 12–15 minutes until rice is done. Drain stock from rice, arranging latter in border round the chicken. Make up drained rice stock to ½–¾ pint with milk or more stock, make a roux of flowing sauce proportions (p. 113) and complete sauce, spooning some of this over bird and rice. Send rest to table in sauceboat.

Cauliflower makes best accompaniment if needed, or peas.

Use chicken joints, and reduce quantities for single-person households.

STUFFED SHOULDER OF LAMB

Bone or have boned a young New Zealand shoulder – at its best now, very modest in price, and with less fat than later in the year. See boning notes, p. 82. Try to get the butcher to bone meat for you to start with. This way you can watch him working and see how he often first skewers recalcitrant bits into place, giving him a hold while he makes firm ties. Firm tying is important because meat shrinks on cooking, its fibres harden back to their original 'lie', and so if you have tied loosely you can have a very messy joint to carve.

Well, you say, but I shall have to untie the butcher's efforts to put in the stuffing. So you will, but you'll find it easier to re-roll on the lines laid down by him than going it entirely alone. After a bit of experience you will be able to truss boned joints quite expertly.

Season the exposed surfaces and spread with this *stuffing*:

3 oz. walnuts very finely chopped (or put through Mouli or blender)	1 oz. margarine
	2–3 oz. fresh white crumbs (for speed add to blender with nuts)
grated rind of whole lemon and juice of ½	1 egg
	seasoning

Melt butter, blend in crumbs, nuts, juice, seasoning and lastly egg.

Fill cavities with stuffing but, in spreading it on rest of meat, keep well away from edges. As you roll up the meat, stuffing is pressed outwards to cover the edges while, if you start with stuffing spread to edges, it is pressed out, making everything sticky and slippery so it is difficult to handle and tie the meat. Roast as instructions on pp. 96–7.

SAUSAGE FRICADELLAS

1 lb. sausage meat	4 oz. fresh white crumbs
pinch sage	1 tsp. finely chopped onion
seasoning	⅛ pint milk
tomato sauce (p. 149)	½ carton yoghurt
lemon juice	3 green, 6 black olives

Mix all ingredients, but season only lightly as the sausage meat will already be quite well flavoured. Add half the milk to start with, as some sausage meat is more 'juicy' than others, and the mixture must hold together well. Mash all together a few moments to mingle evenly. Divide mixture into about 24 pieces, lightly flour hands and roll into large 'marbles'. Fry briskly, turning constantly just to toast the surface. Arrange in shallow dish and mask in ½ pint tomato sauce to which you have added 2 tsp. lemon juice and 3 chopped green olives. Cover the dish and cook in slow oven (300° F, gas 2) 25 minutes. Remove cover, marble (p. 107) sauce with yoghurt. Garnish with 12 black olive halves, and return dish to oven for 5 minutes to heat through.

The reason for the different coloured olives is simply that, while the black look better *on top* of the marbled sauce, the green look less curranty mixed *into* it. The difference in taste and texture is marginal.

Halve the quantities for a single-person household, except that you may like : so much you would like a second 'go'.

BAKED PORK WITH PRUNE FORCEMEAT AND ROSEMARY

3 lb. spare-rib or belly of pork.

PRUNE FORCEMEAT. Soak ½ dozen prunes for 1 hour. Stone and chop them and mix them with:

3 oz. fresh brown crumbs	2 or 3 rosemary leaves finely
1 egg	'minced'
seasoning	1 medium onion sliced and
1½ oz. margarine	sweated in the margarine

Spread the forcemeat thickly on the seasoned pork except where there is crackling. Oil any crackling. Cut butter paper or shape foil, to cover all but crackling surface of meat. Strew leaves, or lay a sprig of rosemary in the meat tin. Stand the pork on this. Add only enough water to cover the bottom of the tin. Roast by the Quick Method (p. 99). Occasionally brush the crackling with oil and, as the water evaporates, replace it, but never more than the original amount. Half an hour before the end remove the paper. The forcemeat will have a brown crisp top and there will be a rich fragrant sauce to serve with the meat. Dilute this (very carefully) if liked, to make a little more.

If you serve Jerusalem artichokes (next page) in Béchamel sauce with this, no other vegetable is needed. Don't forget mustard, though – plain English to contrast with the sweet and spicy tastes.

AMERICAN FRIED CHICKEN

A basic method suited to many besides the sauce given here.

Wash a chicken, jointed and divided into eight or ten pieces according to size. Drain, but do not wipe dry. Roll well in 1–2 tbs. seasoned flour. Fry about 35 minutes in a mixture of oil and butter/margarine until a good golden brown and crisp. Pile the joints as they are done in a serving dish in the oven.

CREAM GRAVY. Into the pan pour a scant ½ pint light stock and deglaze thoroughly. Add 1 tbs. lemon juice, blend well, finally adding 5 tbs. single cream. Spoon a little of this over the chicken before serving, just to give a shine, but not to sog the crispness, handing the rest in a sauceboat.

Sauté potatoes, peas, beans, a green salad are all good accompaniments. In addition, if the frying is not inconvenient, serve CORN FRITTERS. Easily made: all you do is drain a can of corn, or use frozen corn, drop it all into ¼ pint fritter batter (p. 123), stir well and drop by tablespoonfuls into deep fat, frying till golden, draining on kitchen paper.

Vegetables

First read sauce notes on p. 114.

JERUSALEM ARTICHOKES

You like or loathe them, and they you. They're individualists to cook, some taking longer than others although of even sizes. Allow for this in the cooking time, and allow 1lb. per 4 persons.

Peel them thinly, and drop into water acidulated with a little vinegar or lemon juice. Cut large ones in half. Bring to the boil in acidulated, salted water to cover them and cook 20 minutes. Test with knife point and remove those which are tender right through, continuing to cook the rest until done. Mask with ½ pint coating white sauce (p. 116).

Small artichokes may be baked in their skins in a greased baking tin or dish; about 1 hour at 400° F, gas 6. Large artichokes are good parboiled for 10 minutes in their skins, peeled, cut into thick slices and fried until golden in margarine or olive oil.

BROCCOLI WITH EGG AND LEMON

1 lb. broccoli spears	2 oz. margarine/butter
1 egg-yolk	seasoning
juice of ½ lemon	

Cook the broccoli spears in ½ inch salted simmering water until tender, about 20 minutes. Sometimes plants throw a mass of small spears: tie these in bundles to cook. Drain carefully. Hand the sauce separately.

SAUCE. Cream egg-yolk with salt and pepper in a basin or the lining of a double saucepan, or, provided that you have a mere whisper of heat or an asbestos mat, in a small saucepan. Cut the margarine into pieces and add these one at a time to the yolk over gentle heat, whisking or stirring continuously. When half the fat is incorporated add half the lemon juice. The sauce, which should be emulsion like, will thin down somewhat. Add the rest of the margarine, then the rest of the juice. Finally add a teaspoon or so of hot water until the sauce is like half-whipped cream.

Cauliflower may be divided into 4–6 large sprigs and served with this sauce. It is a good dish to serve as a separate course when the main course is better without a vegetable. Also excellent as the sole accompaniment to grilled meat or fish.

BEETROOT SOUR

Heat small tender cooked beetroots slowly by rolling them about in a covered saucepan in 1tbs. good oil. Chop finely 1 dessertsp. gherkins, capers or other sharp pickles, and 1 dessertsp. parsley. (In season, 1 tsp. tarragon or mint.) Add these to the pot with a good dusting of black pepper. Good single-person dish.

POMMES DUCHESSE

This is the classic method of making mashed potatoes. The egg helps the texture, binding and holding the mixture in shape for piped potato rosettes, which can safely be moved around like scones, and piled in a dish or used decoratively. It also, of course, enriches the dish, making it suitable for frail appetites and so on. You can use more yolks, or whole beaten egg if you like, though the latter can make rather an airy, unpredictable piping mixture; and can add various extras – e.g. grated orange peel and juice for game dishes. But there is no necessity for the full mixture in homely cooking, where nourishment is adequate via other things. Ordinary mashed potato, if properly mixed with hot milk, melted margarine/butter, and well whipped, will accompany most of the dishes in this book. It is the texture of potato purées that really counts: no lumps, soft, but not sloshy; and the flavour – creamy, not watery, well seasoned.

The full duchesse mixture is, for each 1 lb. potatoes:

| 2 egg-yolks | 2 tbs. top milk |
| 1 oz. margarine/butter | seasoning, nutmeg |

Pass the hot potato through the fine plate of the Moulin-Légumes, or a sieve. Heat milk and butter in a pan with ½ level tsp. salt, a good shake of pepper and dusting of nutmeg. (The heat helps to draw out the flavours of the spices, but is necessary to prevent the purée turning sticky instead of fluffy). Add potato and mix a little, off the heat. Then add yolks, and beat vigorously over gentle heat until potato leaves sides of pan and is light and soft.

If the finished purée is too stiff to be piped it may be necessary to add a teaspoon or so extra milk. If you have small or weak hands don't try to pipe too much at a time. It takes practice to get the knack, and may make your hands ache if you try to handle large volumes straight away. When piping pommes duchesse into rosettes make these good and fat, otherwise the baking will make them dry and brittle. Pipe rosettes on to lightly greased baking-sheet and brown in hot oven. Pipe borders to dishes as directed in individual recipes and brown in hot oven or under the grill. See also piping notes, (pp. 535–8); equipment (p. 56).

Puddings

APRICOT SNOW BREAD PUDDING

1 pint milk	1 rounded tbs. sugar for
2 eggs	custard
6–8 large slices about ⅛ inch	1–2 drops vanilla (or pod)
thick, from stale loaf,	2 oz. castor sugar for
buttered and de-crusted	meringue
	apricot jam

Well grease a pint pie dish. Spread the bread and butter with jam. Line the dish with some of the slices. Reserve one of the egg-whites. Cream remaining yolk and whole egg with 1 tbs. sugar and 1–2 drops vanilla. Scald the milk (with vanilla pod if used), pour on to egg mixture and return to pan, cooking very gently till mixture on back of spoon stays in two halves when a finger is drawn through it. Pour half into dish, add a layer of prepared bread and jam, pour in the rest. Set aside for 20 minutes for bread to soak up custard somewhat. Top with last layer of bread and bake in oven at 300° F, gas 2, for 3 minutes. Just before this time is up make the quick meringue on p. 409, spread or pipe over dish, and return to oven for a further 20 to 30 minutes.

BROWN BREAD PLUM PUDDING

4 oz. prunes	pinch each nutmeg and salt
3 oz. fresh brown breadcrumbs (see p. 67)	¼ tsp. baking powder
	2–3 tbs. milk
1½ oz. each margarine and castor sugar	1 egg
	grated rind ½ orange

(1) Soak and stew the prunes as directed on packet, drain, stone and halve them.

(2) Grease a pint pudding basin, assemble its coverings, prepare the steamer. Separate egg-yolk from white.

(3) Cream fat with rind, cream again with sugar until light and fluffy. Add yolk, beating well.

(4) Stir and mix together crumbs, baking powder, nutmeg and salt, and fold into mixture.

(5) Fold in prunes.

(6) Whisk white until stiff, and fold into pudding.

(7) Pour into basin, cover and steam about 1½ hours.

This is a light mixture, the prunes are comparatively heavy, so you must have everything to hand, and work quickly so that the pudding is on and cooking before the prunes sink through the mixture. It's not a disaster if they do, but a tribute to your skill and efficiency if they don't – and nicer to 'pull out a plum' throughout the pudding rather than having them on top like an upside-down pudding. You can lightly flour the prunes as you can cherries for cherry cake, but it doesn't always work, and may alter the light texture a little.

SAUCE. Make ½ pint of custard as on p. 137 from 1 whole egg, ½ pint milk, 1 dessertsp. sugar, 1 rounded tsp. cornflour. When cooked and thickened, stir in 1 tbs. of any wine available, or add some of the prune juice plus a teaspoon of rum, brandy or liqueur.

Turn out the pudding, and 'glaze' with a little sauce, handing the rest in a sauceboat.

Despite its humble ingredients this can be a party pudding. It can be steamed over something else for single-person purposes, quantity halved if necessary.

GOOSEBERRY MOULD

1 20 oz. tin gooseberries (Sainsbury's are excellent)
1 tbs. each Golden Syrup and syrup from stem ginger or ¼ tsp. ground ginger
1 dessertsp. lemon juice
½ oz. powdered gelatine (or 1 envelope) or a lemon or lime jelly dissolved in ¼ pint hot water. The latter is less good as the artificial flavour spoils the gooseberry taste, but useful in emergency

(1) Strain the gooseberry syrup over the gelatine in a small pan and heat very gently (p. 138) until dissolved.

(2) Stand gooseberries in warm place to take chill off and prevent their setting the gelatine before you are ready.

(3) Add the syrups and lemon juice to gelatine mixture and mix well.

(4) Turn fruit into pint measure and stir in the gelatine mixture gently. If the whole measures less than 1 pint make up with water.

(5) Give a gentle stir to see gelatine is evenly mixed through. Turn into wetted mould and chill until set.

Send to table with cream and crisp, digestive-type biscuits. Half quantity (small tin) for single-person households.

APPLE PAN DOWDY (American)

This is rather like a pudding made from toffee apples. A deep pie plate or sandwich tin is a good vessel to bake it in.

1 quart sliced cooking apple
(approx. 1 large Bramley)
4 tbs. soft brown sugar
4 tbs. black treacle
generous pinch each ginger,
cinnamon, nutmeg

2 tbs. cold water
1 oz. butter/margarine
6 oz. flaky or shortcrust
pastry
ice-cream

Mix together the treacle and water. Stir spices into sugar and add to liquid mixture. Fill pie plate with sliced apple and pour syrup mixture over. Cut fat in small pieces and strew on top. Roll pastry out just under ¼ inch thick, damp edges of plate and cover apples. Bake at 400° F, gas 6, for 30 minutes. Take a sharp knife and chop at crust to break it roughly into squares over which the filling seeps. Return to oven lowering heat to 350° F, gas 4, for 45 to 50 minutes until the top is brown and fudge-like. Serve hot on hot plates with a good tablespoon of fairly hard ice-cream for each person.

March

Though officially the first month of Spring, March is still a problem month in the kitchen. Green vegetables are limited in choice
and the cheaper sorts have been eaten, in various guises, all too
often. Salads are almost non-existent, but for the dearest varieties.
Potatoes are down to the oldest and most battered. Home-killed
lamb is at its dearest. Herrings are out of season. Only the most
ordinary fruits are plentiful, but they are imported and far from
bargain prices.

However, as always, there are compensations: this is the start
of the short whitebait season, and a small quantity of these tiny
rich fish goes a long way. Also in season in the fishmonger's are
mussels and mackerel, so there is a chance for a special treat or
two in the fish line.

The cold still makes soups and stews welcome, and these are
at their best made from cheap cuts of meat and old, strong-
flavoured vegetables. The British tea-table also comes into its own
with pikelets, scones and spicy fruit cakes, lardy and dripping
cakes, Sally Lunns, oatmeal cakes of many sorts, and other wintry
joys. For recipes of some of these see pp. 495–511.

Soups

First read the notes on soup on p. 112.

SOUPE A L'OIGNON

Not only is this one of the most delicious of soups, it is also cheap
and useful, since it can be made without stock, or you can use
good vegetable water if you like (preferably not strong cabbage
water). Stale bread and cheese are better for the finish, and preparation is simple.

½ lb. onions
2 oz. margarine or good
  dripping
1½ pints water or stock

½ oz. flour
½ bayleaf
seasoning

FOR THE FINISH

1 oz. grated stale or Parmesan
  cheese

2 rds. of stale bread, or 1
  slice French bread per
  person

Chop the onion finely. Melt the fat in a heavy pan, add onions and brown slowly on a low heat, turning them from time to time to prevent burning. Take pan from fire and dust in the flour evenly, stir well and return to heat just to 'toast' the flour. Pour on the liquid in small amounts, stirring out all lumps, and adding bay leaf and seasoning and bring to boiling point, stirring slowly. Simmer ½ hour. Meanwhile de-crust and quarter the slices of bread. Crusts may be left on French bread if the loaf is of small diameter, otherwise use a large pastry cutter to stamp off crusts. Pour finished soup into fireproof dish, cover surface with bread, cover bread with cheese, and brown under a hot grill.

MINESTRONE

Serves 10

The ingredients in minestrone can be varied to make use of what is in the larder and store-cupboard. For example, if you had some leftover brussel sprouts, or the outside leaves of a cabbage (not too leathery !), there would be no sense in buying cabbage specially. Macaroni is traditional, but rice, barley or spaghetti would do very well. In winter, tomato purée or tinned tomatoes are better than fresh (see p. 92). (In summer use fresh tomatoes.) Peas or beans of any sort, tinned or fresh, can go in; any sorts of root vegetables, diced; but if cooked vegetables are to be used as well as raw, the cooked ones should be added only 10 minutes or so before the end, as they may otherwise break down to a mush. Stock or vegetable water may be used, but are not necessary. Use bacon rind if only a 'starter' to a meal is wanted : but a good

minestrone can provide a luncheon almost by itself if diced bacon
or minced meat is also added.

2 oz. each carrot, celery,
  potato, leek, onion, cabbage
½ lb. tomatoes, minimum, or
  1 level dessertsp. tomato
  purée
2 rashers bacon diced
1 medium onion
2½ pints water

1½ oz. Quaker macaroni (or
  broken macaroni)
bouquet garni
large clove garlic
1 tbs. chopped parsley
2 oz. grated cheese for each
  3 helpings
minimum 1½ oz. margarine or
  bacon dripping or 1½ tbs. oil

Dice all the vegetables, except cabbage and tomatoes, and sweat
raw vegetables in the fat until just colouring. Meanwhile crush
the garlic well in salt, and put on the water to boil. Add boiling
water to sweated vegetables with bouquet garni, garlic, bacon,
macaroni, skinned tomatoes or purée, etc. and shredded cabbage,
and simmer 20 minutes. Adjust seasoning, adding salt cautiously
as some will have come from bacon. Simmer 10 more minutes,
throw in parsley and stir. Serve with a bowl of grated cheese on
the table.

For special occasions minestrone may be dished into individual
fireproof soup-cups with a little grated cheese added to each one
and browned under the grill. For slimmers, leave out any starchy
vegetable or pasta, but add a little extra cheese, or meat.

CARROT SOUP WITH ORANGE

1 lb. carrots
1 small onion
1½ oz. each margarine and
  flour
a few bacon rinds
1½ pints of liquid, which
  may be stock, water, or
  milk and water (for latter
  see second method)
½ bayleaf

1 level dessertsp. sugar
seasoning
1 orange
For entertaining, add a couple
  of tbs. single cream, top milk
  or yoghurt at the end, and do
  not boil up afterwards. (See
  note on 'marbling' cream,
  p. 107.)

STOCK OR WATER METHOD. Slice the carrots thinly, chop onion, sweat them in the margarine until the onion is soft. Off the fire add flour, stirring well. Add the liquid by degrees, stirring out all lumps. Bring to simmering point and simmer 25 minutes until carrot is tender. Put through Moulin-Légumes or sieve, add grated rind and juice of orange, sugar, and correct seasoning. Bring to simmering point, add cream just before serving.

MILK AND WATER METHOD. (Proportion: ¾ pint water to ¼ pint milk.) Slice carrots thinly, chop onion, sweat in fat until onion is soft. Add the water only and simmer 25 minutes until carrot is tender. Put through Moulin-Légumes or sieve. With a little of the cold milk mix flour to cream and add it with rest of milk to sieved soup. Add sugar, orange rind and juice, correct seasoning and bring soup to a simmer, cooking a few minutes to thicken flour. Add cream just before serving.

In both instances a pressure cooker may be used to cut time for cooking carrot (5 to 10 minutes according to thickness). For the first method omit flour before soup goes into cooker, adding it by blending to a cream with some of the stock afterwards, and simmering until it thickens. For second method simply use cooker instead of pan until thickening stage.

If liked, the rind of the orange may be needle-shredded (see p. 246) and blanched instead of grated. But the shreds will not float, so that they have little decorative value, and some flavour is lost in the blanching.

APRICOT SOUP

(See also Iced Fruit Soups p. 330.)

Everyone knows that tomatoes are 'fruit that are always used as vegetables', yet there seems a strange reluctance on the part of most members of most nations to try using other fruits in a 'savoury' way; to season them with salt and pepper instead of sugar; to mix them with onion, garlic or herbs. Even the fruit soups of Scandinavia and Germany are closer to English fruit fools than they are to soup. I have made a few experiments in the direction of using fruits with flavours other than sugar, and for other purposes than as puddings. Here is the result of one experiment. Dried apricots never seem cheap – and certainly those kinds that you can buy cheaply are not worth having – but when they are reconstituted they work out quite reasonable in price. For example, ¼ lb. of dried apricots soaked in twice their bulk of water will do the work of a pound of fresh, and usually taste better than the poor, stony, hard little brutes that often seem to find their way here. At the time of writing good dried apricots cost about 5s. per lb. They store very well in a screwcap jar, and are on hand to provide some of the most delicious of fruit dishes in the depths of winter. They make excellent jam; by themselves they make a party piece of yoghurt; in their dried state they can be chopped and added to meat stuffings, or filled with flavoured cheeses to make cocktail 'bits'. But first see how you like this soup.

¼ lb. dried apricots	2 tbs. single cream or 3–4 tbs.
delicate stock or water	top milk, or a little
1 small onion (in summer use	unsweetened evaporated
chives if possible)	milk, or yoghurt
¾ oz. each butter and flour	¼ pint milk
1 tsp. lemon juice	sugar, salt, pepper
	bayleaf

Put the apricots into a measuring-jug and cover them with twice their bulk in a lightly flavoured stock. (Use broth from a boiling fowl if available, or make stock with 1 chicken cube. Water can be used, but the flavour is not so good.) Leave overnight. If this is difficult, cover them 1 hour or more before using with twice their bulk in *boiling* liquid. It is here that you will discover the false economy of cheap apricots, if you've been tempted into buying them, for they can take as much as 48 hours to soften, and sometimes they don't at all.

Next day simmer them in the liquid in which they have soaked, made up to 1 pint. Season lightly, add sugar and bayleaf. When quite tender (about 20 minutes) put them through sieve, Moulin-Légumes or blender. While they are cooking, chop finely and lightly colour the onion in the fat. (Chives must be merely heated slightly to extract the flavour without spoiling colour.) Scatter in the flour off the heat, stir out all lumps. Add the sieved fruit pulp, return to fire and bring to boil, stirring all the time. Put through a bowl-strainer, rubbing the onion through with a wooden spoon. Adjust the seasoning, adding lemon juice and a little sugar to taste, and thinning slightly if necessary. Just before serving add the milk, reheat to simmering point, and add the cream, top milk or yoghurt. The addition of a few tarragon leaves or chives is attractive in summer time, and croûtons may be handed separately to provide further bulk and a finish in winter. The soup is also good in summer if chilled, when it may be thinned by adding more milk or water, 2 tbs. at a time, until the desired consistency is reached.

First Courses and Snacks

CURRIED EGG TOASTS

For each person :

one round of hot buttered toast	1 heaped tsp. of either cooked carrot, peas or potato, or corned beef
1 egg	
1 level tsp. curry powder	½ oz. butter or margarine

Boil the eggs exactly 5 minutes, transfer to cold water for a few minutes and shell. While they are boiling, make the toast, and put the other ingredients into a basin. As the eggs are shelled add them to the basin, and chop the contents together while eggs are still fairly hot. Pile on to the toast, reheat under the grill a few minutes, and serve with chutney (for a good home-made chutney see p. 545) and a stick of celery.

CHEESE FLOATS

Floats made from a yeast batter are one of the commonplace – and therefore appetizing – recipes of the West Indies. This is a simplified adaptation. West Indian floats are usually used as an accompaniment to a main course, but here the cheese makes them sufficiently nourishing for a snack.

4 oz. fritter batter (p. 123)
seasoned with salt and
pepper
cayenne pepper

4 oz. grated Parmesan or dry
Cheddar
made mustard

Put on the deep fat bath (see p. 103), and while it is heating stiffly whisk the egg-white. Add the cheese to the batter, with a little cayenne pepper and a teaspoon of made mustard. If you like you can add a chopped rasher of bacon to the mix, but in that case take care with salt. Lastly fold in the white.

Drop dessertspoonfuls of the mixture into the smoking fat. They will puff up, turn colour and float. When evenly golden, but not at all brown, they are done. Drain on kitchen paper and serve with Waldorf Salad (p. 448), or other vegetable accompaniment available. By making extra batter and reserving some before adding the cheese, you can dip onion rings in it and drop these into the fat when the floats are done. Also, although this would be less economical, being closer to a main dish, and would need extra cooking time, you can stir tinned sweetcorn into extra batter to make corn fritters, which go well. Drop one dessertspoonful of mixture into fat at a time, taking care not to overcrowd the fat bath – up to 4.

DEVILLED FISH

For each person :

¼ lb. coley
1 shallot
1 tsp. each tomato ketchup
and Worcester Sauce or
Yorkshire Relish

1 tsp. lemon juice
¼ oz. each margarine and flour
1 slice of bread fried in good
dripping for croûtons

Chop the shallot finely, fry in the fat until colouring. Skin and bone the fish (see pp. 87–9), add to the pan with the sauces and lemon juice, and as much water as you can shake from a wet hand.

Cook on a low heat to start with, stirring well all the time until the juices from the fish begin to run. Raise the heat and continue stirring until the fish is quite opaque and broken down into shreds. Off the heat scatter in the flour and stir for 1 minute longer over low heat, adjusting flavours to suit your taste. Keep hot while you fry croûtons. Serve very hot with a crisp salad as in the other snack recipes.

Fish

GRILLED MACKEREL

About ½ lb. of fish per person is the usual amount and, if the mackerel are very big, one will do between two. Some fishmongers are, others are not, good at filleting mackerel. They should not cut off a thick lump of the shoulder of the fish with the head, nor should they cut a thick slice from the middle of the back to remove the main bone. If they do this they will also chop off the connecting joints of the long bones, which will be left in the fish for you to pull out by hand. This is more trouble than learning to fillet your own mackerel, so if in doubt, try it yourself with the help of the drawings on pp. 87–90. Alternatively, ask the fishmonger merely to split and clean the fish (complete with head), and remove the bones yourself when the fish is half-cooked, but before it acquires its crisp brown finish. If you adopt the latter course, season only with a little salt and pepper at first, adding the lemon juice and spices after the bone has been removed.

Heat the grill for 3 minutes. Sprinkle the fish with salt, pepper, lemon juice, a little ground ginger, and a few cumin, dill, caraway, or coriander seeds. With oily fish like herring and mackerel additional fat is not needed. When the fish is opaque, but not yet coloured, remove bones if necessary and season as above. Add more lemon juice so that each fish has the juice of at least ½ a lemon. Continue grilling until the surface is well coloured and the edges slightly crisp. Serve with well-made mashed potato, or plainly boiled small potatoes (later in the year, obviously, new potatoes are best), or with thin brown bread and butter. Nothing else.

MACKEREL STEWED WITH WINE

From *Modern Cookery* by Eliza Acton.

Eliza Acton laid the foundations for the modern cookery book with its exact instructions and measurements. Her quantities, like Mrs Beeton's, were for families with perhaps seven young children and as many servants, but they can effectively be reduced. Her 'voice' comes to us, as C. V. Wedgewood so wisely suggests the voices of our forebears should come, not in the quaint period bleats invented by the B.B.C. drama departments, but full of sense, confidence, and an intelligent curiosity and appreciation of her subject.

This recipe is not for a large quantity, and was probably intended as one course at the ordinary four-course dinner of master and mistress of the house, when the children were in bed. Kitchen and nursery meals were less lavish in number of courses, and the fare cheaper and plainer, except that the servants sometimes finished, next day, the 'remains' of dining-room meals.

Notice the unusual method of making the sauce. 1 teacup of Spanish burgundy or a cheap vin ordinaire will replace the 3 wineglassfuls of claret. A mixture of margarine and butter replaces the butter.

Mackerel Stewed with Wine (Very good)
Work very smoothly together a large teaspoon of flour with two ounces of butter, put them into a stewpan, and stir or shake them round over the fire until the butter is dissolved; add a quarter of a teaspoonful of mace, twice as much salt, and some cayenne; pour in by slow degrees three glasses of claret; and when the sauce boils, lay in a couple of fine mackerel well cleaned, and wiped quite dry; stew them very softly from fifteen to twenty minutes, and turn them when half done; lift them out and dish them carefully; stir a teaspoonful of made mustard to the sauce, give it a boil, and pour it over the fish. When more convenient substitute port wine and a little lemon-juice for the claret.

Mackerél, 2; flour, 1 teaspoonful; butter, 2 oz.; seasoning of salt, mace, and cayenne; claret, 3 wine glasses; made mustard, 1 teaspoonful; 15 to 20 minutes.

WHITEBAIT

See note on sprats on p. 186.

¼ lb. whitebait per person	seasoned flour
oil for frying	lemon quarters

Wash the whitebait in a colander. Dry them well in an old tea-towel or paper towel. Season 2 heaped tbs. flour with salt and pepper. (This amount will flour about 1 lb. fish.) Spread it on a sheet of greaseproof paper and put about ¼ lb. of fish at a time on to the paper, bringing up the corners to form a sort of bag in which the fish are shaken until evenly coated in flour. Put them into a sieve or colander and shake slightly again over the paper to remove surplus flour. Fry in deep fat (p. 103). Cook only as much fish at a time as will cover the surface of the fat bath with room to move them about a little. When they are golden remove them to drain on kitchen paper in a warm oven. Serve with brown bread and butter and lemon quarters, and cayenne pepper if liked.

Mussels

Fresh mussels are tightly closed and, if put into a bowl of water, will sink to the bottom. Any mussel that floats should be discarded; likewise any mussel that, open, does not close if sharply tapped with a knife handle. Hanging from each shell is the blackish 'beard' of the mussel, which is a sort of filter. A sharp upward or downward pull removes the beard, which should also be discarded. Each shell must be thoroughly scrubbed and the mussels put into three changes of water to remove sand. Now and then sand gets into a mussel shell, and you should suspect this if one is exceptionally heavy, when you can open it separately and wash out the sand. Such mussels may be dead in any case, but if not, and if they opened in the pot with the rest, the sand would ruin your dish.

BASIC COOKING. Allow a generous pint of mussels per person. When well cleaned, put them in a large pan. Add to this a chopped shallot, parsley stalks, ½ teacup dry white wine, and 1 tbs. olive oil or 1 tbs. butter or margarine per quart of mussels. Put the pan on a fairly brisk heat and cook, covered, for not more than six minutes, moving them to see that any on top get down to the heat. The mussels will have opened in cooking and the liquor in the shells will have mingled with the rest of the ingredients to make a fine-flavoured 'stock'. The mussels can be finished in various ways of which two of the best follow. You may remove one or both shells for *marinière*, though children usually rather enjoy shelling them themselves. For the scalloped recipe remove the mussels entirely from the shells.

MOULES MARINIÈRES

Melt 1 oz. butter or margarine. Off the heat stir in ½ oz. flour. Take the opened mussels from their pan and keep them warm, after you have disposed of the shells if you prefer to. Gently pour the liquor on to the roux, stirring well to remove lumps. Heat the sauce just to boiling point and pour it over the mussels. For extra nourishment the broth may be thickened with 2 egg-yolks instead of the roux. If so, beat, stir in off heat; do not allow to boil.

SCALLOPED MUSSELS

In addition to the basic ingredients add a very finely chopped clove of garlic to the pan in which the mussels are cooked. Remove them from the shells, arrange them in a shallow fireproof dish and cover with a buttered paper to keep warm in the oven. Reduce the broth by about a third, add to it a tablespoon of finely chopped parsley and pour it over the mussels. Melt ½ oz. each butter and margarine and stir into this 2 tbs. fine breadcrumbs, off the heat, followed by 1½ oz. grated cheese. Spread the mixture over the mussels and brown it briskly under a hot grill.

Braised celery or salad may be served with this, but mussels are really best on their own, and you can serve a vegetable as a separate course where needed.

Meat

... he felt his belly crave for its food. He hoped there would be stew
for dinner, turnips and carrots and bruised potatoes and fat mutton
pieces to be ladled out in thick peppered flour-flattened sauce. Stuff it
into you, his belly counselled him.

James Joyce, *A Portrait of the Artist as a Young Man.*

Irish Stew, which is what half-starved young Stephen Dedalus was
hoping for, is one of the tastiest, cheapest and most quickly prepared of all meals. It is the product of a poor peasant nation, who
perhaps sent the recipe across the Irish Sea with her migrants to
become the slightly more sophisticated Lancashire Hot Pot; or
perhaps Lancastrians will say that Irish Stew is a reduced version
of Hot Pot. Delicious and cheap, whatever their history, there are
variations of both recipes. Some, like the James Joyce version,
have root vegetables added, others, like the versions given here,
consist simply of the three essentials – lamb, onion, potato.

IRISH STEW

1½ lb. scrag or middle neck mutton or lamb *or* 1 lb. best-end for a meatier, but dearer dish	¾ lb. onions
	¾ pint water
	salt and pepper
	heaped teaspoon of finely-chopped fresh parsley
1½–2 lb. potatoes	

Wipe the meat, which you should ask the butcher to chop as for
Irish Stew for you. Remove as much as you can of the fat. Put
meat into a stewpan with the water and a little salt, boil up and
skim. If the onions are large cut them in quarters from point to
root, but leave small onions or shallots whole. Peel half the potatoes cut them in thick slices or quarter them. Add these vegetables
to the pot with a little more salt and a good shake of pepper. Stir
the pot to mix all well, bring to the boil and simmer 2 hours. Half-
way through the cooking time add the rest of the potatoes on
the top of the pot, whole if small. Do not stir these in for they will

be dished by themselves. When the potatoes are cooked through, pile the meat and onions in the centre of the dish, the sliced and, by now, broken potatoes at one end, the whole potatoes at the other, and pour the sauce over the meat. This sauce will have been thickened by some of the sliced potatoes that will have cooked down to a mush, so there is no need to thicken further with flour. Sprinkle the parsley over the potatoes.

If you want to add other root vegetables, cut them into suitable pieces and add them with the sliced potatoes at the beginning of the cooking time.

LANCASHIRE HOT POT

1 lb. best-end neck of mutton or lamb *or* 1½ lb. scrag or middle-neck	1 outside stick of celery
	1 oz. seasoned flour
	¾ pint water
1–1½ lb. potatoes	1 tsp. chopped parsley
½ lb. onions	1 oz. good dripping

Have the meat chopped by the butcher as for Irish Stew. Dip the prepared meat in flour, well seasoned with salt and white pepper. Put the whole peeled potatoes and onions into cold water just to cover and bring them to the boil, simmering for 5 minutes. Use this water for your hot pot. Slice the potatoes and onions in rounds about ¼ inch thick. Cut the celery rather more thinly. Arrange meat and vegetables in a cocotte in layers, but reserving enough potato slices to cover the top in an overlapping spiral. Pour in the cooled stock, made up to ¾ pint with water if necessary. Melt the dripping and run it over the potato top, cover with lid, or a twist of greaseproof or butter paper. Foil can be used, but it seals in steam, so that the final browning of the top may take longer. Cook in a moderate oven (375° F, gas 5) for 2 hours, uncover ¼ hour before the end and transfer the casserole to a higher shelf, or slightly increase the oven temperature, and cook for about ½ to ¾ hour longer, until the top is turning colour. If the food comes to the top of the cocotte, and it is not made of glass, you may obtain a richer, more crisp and even finish by putting the dish under a preheated grill for a few minutes.

(Oven glass frequently cracks if exposed to direct heat.) Scatter on the parsley just before bringing to table.

Other versions of hot pot include root vegetables and sliced sheep's kidney.

Pig's fry

One of the most savoury, nourishing, and, except in certain districts, forgotten of all pork dishes. The fry may be composed of several different sorts of pork offal: heart, liver, kidney, melt (absurdly reserved for 'pet food'), and the 'curtain', a lacy sheet of membrane and fat attached to the melt. In my opinion liver is essential to the flavour, while the heart can be a nuisance, because all heart requires longer cooking, although it is excellent if time is immaterial.

For the recipe given here I am indebted to my sister, who brought pig's fry to my notice in the first place.

JOY MANSFIELD'S RECIPE FOR PIG'S FRY

6 oz. pig's liver
4 oz. melt
2 oz. bacon (which may be the cheap 'pieces' most grocers sell for about 6d. a lb., or it may be cut from a knuckle, it may be rashers or a piece)
some pig's 'curtain'
2 large or 3 medium onions

4 oz. kidney
4 oz. heart (optional, but then make up with extra of the other ingredients)
½ pint lightly flavoured stock or water
1 oz. flour
salt, pepper
sage or thyme
bayleaf

Cut the offal into neat strips about 2 inches long and ¾ inch wide. Slice the onion, dice the bacon. Using some of the strips of curtain (unless there is only enough for the crisp titbits described below) and adding good dripping as needed, fry the ingredients a good brown in order of the length of time they take to cook, but starting with the onion and bacon to flavour all the meats. Next heart, kidney, melt, liver. Remove some as the pan becomes full, and keep hot in cocotte in the oven. When all are browned scatter in the flour off the heat, stir in well, and return to heat until nut brown. Add the liquid by degrees, stirring out any lumps, and carefully scrape down the caramelled juices from the sides and bottom of pan to deepen colour and flavour. Pour the resulting sauce over the meat in the casserole, add a little thyme or sage (fresh when possible), some pepper and the bayleaf. Return to oven and cook 1 hour or longer in a slow heat (300° F, gas 2). Correct seasoning. It is important not to oversalt this dish as there is often enough salt in the bacon. Ten minutes before serving fry the rest of the curtain until the pieces are brown, curled and crisp. Hand them separately on a small hot dish or saucer. (They are also excellent as titbits with a drink, or for high tea.)

For entertaining, add a spoonful or two of wine or sherry. Also, if liked, a crushed clove of garlic may be added with the herbs.

ACCOMPANIMENTS: Croûtons of fried bread for hearty eaters; plain boiled potatoes, skins left on; new potatoes in season; any plain cooked green or root vegetable; in season, tomatoes simply baked whole in skins.

Spiced beef

A few years ago at a time of stress I was looking in an antiquarian bookseller's window in search of distraction, when I saw a hand-written notice clipped to a book: 'Eliza Acton. Older than Beeton. 21s.' I buy old cookery books only if they are practical in some way for modern needs, but I bought the Acton without bothering to assess the text, because of the charm of the engravings: diagrams for carving fish, bottle jacks for roasting, jelly moulds looking like a design for a concert-hall organ, and decorative vignettes that really were decorative. However, I had read only a few pages when I recognized that here was a master.

Eliza Acton was very keen on spiced and pickled beef, and she gives many versions. The value of preserved meats in the days before domestic refrigerators is obvious, but there are still many families who cannot afford, cannot house, or do not want a refrigerator. They would find home-pickled beef as useful as the Victorians found it. Better still, it is very good eating.

Victorian recipes deal with amounts of 12–20 lb. Today this would be far too much, unless you were to make the dish between friends, when a butcher might consider giving you a special rate per pound for such a large quantity. However, as with many dishes, there is a size below which the recipe seems to spoil. A joint of 5–8 lb. is a good size for a family, and, as Eliza Acton says, the meat will keep well for a fortnight. I have also given a recipe for spicing 2 lb. of beef, for the two- and single-person households. This is not perhaps quite as succulent as a bigger joint, but will make a most tasty dish from which you can feed over several days, useful when one is busy, and much superior to the rather crude salted 'boiling joint' offered by most butchers and supermarkets.

The usual rule for pickling meats is that they should be in the pickle for a day for each pound in weight, but if the small quantity is very thick break this rule in favour of a longer time. Vary the spices according to your preferences, and what is available in your locality. But remember, if you are stuck for spices, or even for herbs, to consult your chemist. Many spices and flavourings used in the kitchen are used in medicines. Elizabethan and Georgian women made physicks more often than her doctor made them; in some instances the chemist's shop took over recipes from the kitchen.

Until recently you could buy bay salt for pickling. This was sea salt as it came from the ocean, often seaweed and all, and was said (is said by the over-sixties, who sampled food pickled with bay salt) to give a far better flavour than common salt. As far as I have been able to discover, sea salt in quite this unrefined form is no longer obtainable. The nearest is the 'rock salt' sold by health food stores. If you own an electric blender with the right attachment or instructions, you can grind your own spices and salt very easily. If you have an Indian grocer in the neighbourhood get the spices freshly ground from him. Pound them yourself by hand with pestle and mortar, or even between two old metal spoons. But ready-ground spices will still give you a good result if freshly opened and of good quality.

Cuts of beef for pickling are: brisket, silverside, topside, flank. The cheaper rib joints, boned and rolled, would make a rather special dish of spiced beef. In theory Argentine chilled beef should be an economical buy for pickling, but the thawing makes the juices run freely out of the meat, and this gets the dish off to a bad start with less flavour than it might have. As it is, the preliminary salting causes quite a bit of the blood to run from the meat – one good reason for not wasting top-quality beef on pickling. Does the meat lose some of its nourishment from preservation? Yes. But you can't have everything! Preserved meat is a convenience; it makes a tasty dish of otherwise inferior cuts, rendering tender what otherwise might be too tough to use at all.

SPICED BEEF BASED ON ELIZA ACTON'S RECEIPTS

5 lb. lean brisket, silverside, etc.
1 tbs. crushed juniper berries
1 level tsp. each ground mace and black pepper
1 rounded tsp. ground cloves
½ small nutmeg grated
pinch cayenne pepper

3 oz. brown sugar
¼ lb. rock salt, crushed powder
¾ pint stock (can be from meat cube)
1 small onion
2 medium carrots
bouquet garni

NOTE: If brighter, redder meat is preferred add ¾ oz. saltpetre to spices, but flavour will be slightly altered.

If you have to buy from a non-family butcher on whose meat you cannot rely, hang the meat 2 days in an airy place (see p. 40), first untrussing, and spreading it well out. Next rub all surfaces with a little ordinary cooking salt and return to the hook overnight. Next day run quickly under tap, and wipe dry. Mix well all the ground spices (not the salt) with the sugar, and rub mixture well into surfaces of meat. Rest on dish, again in a current of air and covered, to keep insects away, for 3 days, turning once. Rub in the rock salt, but see that the sugar mixture is spooned back evenly over the meat also – it will be a sort of syrup by now. Leave meat one day for each pound in weight, turning once each day.

Rinse off the pickle, tie and skewer meat back to shape. Put in a pan not much larger in diameter than meat itself, but as deep as you like, so that the limited amount of stock comes up round the meat. Do not add more liquid or you weaken the flavours. Boil up slowly over low heat to avoid scorching the surface of the meat resting on the bottom of the pan. When fiercely bubbling, scum will begin to form and, after a few minutes, tends to thicken, when it is easy to remove. Add onion, carrot and bouquet garni, and reduce the heat gradually over about 10 minutes, putting a lid on the pan between inspections, until the meat is merely 'shaking' in the broth. Continue this gentle cooking for 3 to 4 hours depending on the thickness of the joint, until a thin metal skewer will run easily from top to bottom of the joint. During the cooking time inspect again at intervals to see that water is neither bubbling too fiercely, nor has stopped moving altogether, and loosen meat if it has stuck to base of pan. Taste stock. If very salt, pour off into measure, dilute with equal quantity of boiling water and return 3/4 pint of this diluted broth to pan bringing again just to simmering point. Turn meat over about once an hour.

If you are serving the meat hot, you may steam small potatoes in their skins – well scrubbed – on top of the pot about 1 hour before the end. But do not try to cook root vegetables or dumplings in the pot while meat is cooking. Pasta or rice go well with the beef, and as they, like small dumplings, cook in 10 to 15 minutes they are delicious cooked in the broth when you have removed the beef to a hot dish in the oven. Dumplings, made as in the recipe on p. 157 but with half brown breadcrumbs/half flour, a generous measure of baking powder, a big pinch of herbs, and formed about the size of your top thumb joint, are as attractive to look at as to eat.

For serving cold, put the meat into a clean pan or deep dish, and pour the broth over it, leaving it to get quite cold and firm, when it will carve as thinly as ham. The broth can be used as a stock for soups. Beetroot, made with a lemon vinaigrette, is an excellent accompanying salad; also beetroot and potato diced and mixed with mayonnaise.

BRAISED SPICED STEAK

2 lb. Scotch or English stewing steak in one piece all spicing ingredients in above recipe but in half quantities	2 oz. fat pork cut into 2 thick slices (a useful way to buy this would be to buy a good-sized belly of pork for roasting and get the butcher to cut you two thick rashers from it)

Proceed as in the above recipe, but leave the meat, in the first sugar mixture 1½ days, and in the salt mixture 2 days, turning once. (If very thick, allow extra ½ day in spices, 1 day in salt.) Having rinsed off the pickle, place the steak on one piece of fat pork and cover with the other. A useful dish in which to braise the steak would be an oval fireproof vegetable dish, covered with foil. Pour round the stock (water would do if stock is difficult to manage) and, using an asbestos mat, boil up and skim. Add the vegetables cut in halves or quarters. Cover and cook preferably in the oven 300° F, gas 2), for 1½ to 2 hours until meat is tender.

The suggested accompaniments are the same, but for bedsitting-room life pasta are easier to manage than dumplings, and if you are feeding visitors you may have to add some water to your broth to cook enough of them. Also vinaigrette will do very well on the potato-beet salad if mayonnaise is a bother.

Serve the steak in thick fingers if hot; slice it rather more thinly if cold.

NOTE: All these recipes for the meat course may leave you a residue of stock or gravies. As I pointed out in the general notes on making economies (pp. 65–7), such remains may be added to, or diluted to make a cup or two of soup. For instance, the Hot Pot and Irish Stew liquors can be expanded, with the aid of pearl barley and water, to make a type of Scotch broth; or with more onion, potato and water, to make potato soup. Half a tin of ready-made pease pudding stirred into the beef liquor makes lentil soup. And such soups may well be more nourishing than those based merely on bone stock, as you will see from these notes.

LEEK AND BACON ROLL

Into an 8 oz. quantity of savoury suet pastry (p. 133) mix, at
the dry ingredient stage, one medium leek or onion chopped fine,
and 2 rashers of bacon or 1½ oz. ham also chopped. Season well.
Form the finished dough into a roll to fit into a large pot or
steamer. Wrap in 2 coverings as usual, tying the ends or twisting
them and making generous folds to seal the wrappings. Steam
1–1½ hours. Serve with plenty of good thickened gravy. This
dish, said to be a Sussex recipe, is at its best with gravy from the
Sunday roast, expanded if necessary with stock (you need plenty
of gravy).

TRIPE

You need about 2 lb. tripe for 4 people. That called honeycomb
is usually the favourite. The basic preparation is to blanch, then
simmer it in barely enough water to cover, with about ½ lb.
onions – more if liked – seasoning and a dash of lemon juice, for
2 hours. Then :

(a) for classic tripe and onions, blend into it ¼ pint good binding white sauce. Serve with pommes purée and peas, or carrots,
or hot toast for a change.

(b) for piquant tripe, well brown 1½ oz. flour, blend into the
stew, then add 1 tbs. Worcester sauce, 1 tbs. vinegar, 1 tsp. chopped
capers or mustard pickles. Serve with pommes purée etc., as
above.

Vegetables

Most of the vegetable recipes given for the entire winter quarter
can be used in March, but roots are getting coarse, whilst late
frosts can make the last of the winter greens scarce even though
they, also, are getting past their prime. These suggestions, therefore, help to disguise faults with good flavours.

CABBAGE WITH BACON

Dice a cabbage finely (smooth cabbage is preferable to savoy) by shredding and then cutting across shreds. Cut into ¼-inch dice about 2 oz. flank bacon, which should have a little lean included. Chop very finely a good sprig of parsley, together with a little of onion. On a low heat cook the bacon until the fat runs well, but do not allow to colour. Raise the heat and throw in the parsley mixture, cooking for a few seconds only. Now add the cabbage in two or three lots, turning well so all is coated with the contents of the pan. Shake in some pepper, cover tightly and cook very slowly for seven minutes, occasionally lifting the lid to stir and make sure the heat is low enough not to catch the cabbage. If there seems insufficient fat, add a little margarine. Taste, and add a little salt if necessary. Cover again and continue cooking 5–8 more minutes until cabbage is tender. Taste again and adjust seasoning. Serve very hot.

A supper dish may be made by adding more and better-quality bacon. Pile the cabbage and bacon in a hot dish surrounded by croûtons fried in a well-flavoured dripping : that is dripping that has been used to fry onions; beef dripping; or chicken fat.

SPROUTS WITH BUTTER AND LEMON

Throw the well-washed sprouts (1 to 1½ lb.) into boiling salted water and cook for five minutes. In another pan melt ½–1 oz. butter according to the amount to be cooked. Turn the drained sprouts into this, and stir to cover all with the butter, taking care not to break the outer leaves. Season, and squeeze over them 2 or 3 tsp. lemon juice. Fit well down on to them a piece of buttered paper or foil, and cook over a low heat until tender. Frequently lift the paper and carefully turn the sprouts. This will help to cook them evenly, and prevent them steaming and so turning an unattractive colour.

CARROTS IN BÉCHAMEL SAUCE

Cook 1½ lb. carrots in the usual way, and when tender drain and shake them in a very little sugar. Make a Béchamel Sauce (p. 117), mask them with this and serve.

HOT BEETROOT

Skin 2–3 medium cooked beets. Cut into large dice, and heat in ½ oz. well-seasoned margarine. Pile them in a dish and spoon down the centre a thick band of plain yoghurt into which you have stirred 1 tsp. lemon juice, 1 tsp. sugar and a good grinding of fresh black pepper. Return to oven to heat through.

Puddings

COCONUT FLAN

This recipe is a favourite with the children in my family, also with the men.

Bake blind an 8-inch shell of shortcrust, pâte sucrée or flaky pastry (see pp. 129–32).

Meanwhile mix in a basin 1 teacup (8 fl. oz.) each desiccated coconut and castor sugar, 2 well-beaten eggs. If liked add either a few drops of vanilla when beating the eggs, or a teaspoon or so of lemon juice to finished mixture. Do not add lemon juice to raw eggs for fear of curdling them. Don't economize on the eggs. If you do you will not get the lovely squishy texture which is a feature of this recipe. Turn the mixture into the shell and cook in a low oven (300° F, gas 2) about 35 – 40 minutes until the eggs have set and a golden crust has formed on the top, but not long enough to dry the mixture. The time depends a little on the size of the eggs.

ORANGE FOOL

From Mrs Peel's 10/– A Head for House Books

The juice of five large oranges, the yolks of two eggs, one table-spoonful of castor sugar. Mix all together, and stir over a slow fire until it thickens. On no account let it boil. Pour into custard glasses (large wineglasses will do) when still warm. It should look like a rich thick custard.

I found I needed two whole eggs and two yolks. Perhaps modern oranges are juicier. This may not seem very economical, but it is one of the dishes that give a little glamour without extravagance, provide a lift to wintry days and solid fare, while at the same time being excellent nutritionally, especially for children, the elderly and invalids.

BREAD AND JAM PUDDING

Also one of Mrs Peel's recipes.

Take some pieces of bread and soak in milk flavoured with lemon peel; fill a shallow pie-dish nearly full of this mixture, bake for a few minutes, cover the top with jam, then a layer of bread crumbs, and return to the oven until crisp and brown on top.

Good with Golden Syrup also.

APPLE AND ORANGE FOAM

Wash, quarter and core 1 lb. cooking apples. (In season, this is a good dish for windfalls or spoiled apples, for those with gardens. It can also be made from withered eating apples, such as haunt many households after Christmas.) Put them into a small heavy pan with no more water than you shake from your hand, or than clings to the apples from washing. Over a very slow fire cook them down to a mush, inspecting the pan and stirring them about now and then. Beat well with a fork and, as you do so, add brown sugar and a few drops of vanilla. The mixture should be reasonably sweet, but not enough to make it runny. For very

sweet palates stir in a pinch of bicarbonate of soda, which counter-
acts the acid. Grate the rind of one orange, squeeze out the juice,
stir into the apple, and sieve the mixture. If you have a spare
egg-white, or can use an egg-yolk for another dish, a whole egg
is not necessary, but otherwise stir one yolk in, just warming the
mixture to set the egg, but on no account heat enough to scramble
the egg. Now whisk the white with a rotary beater a little, and
when bubbly add one by one 6 tsp. castor sugar, beating all the
time. Turn into the apple mixture and thoroughly fold in. Set
aside in a glass serving dish or individual fruit cups until quite
cold. Where possible chill in a refrigerator. Serve with shortbread
fingers (pp. 325–6).

DÉLICE D'ORANGÉS

Fill ramekins or small apéritif glasses with 2 heaped tbs. chunky
marmalade of good quality. Top up with about the same amount
of double cream. If liked this may be lightly, but on no account
stiffly, whipped, with a dash of rum, wine or about 2 drops of
vanilla added, but no sugar. Serve chilled with shortbread biscuits,
or crumble shortbread thickly on top.

April ·

++

April in England is usually the first month that feels like spring; the month when we can safely think of chimney sweeps, lawn mowers, mothballs and lighter clothes and food. Chickens often agree, and lay a glut of eggs (sometimes even earlier, in March) so, and especially if you make a lot of cakes and puddings, you might consider pickling a few dozen eggs while the price is low (p. 547). Vegetables are getting more varied and cheaper, in particular imported salad vegetables. English and Welsh lamb begins its season, but is dear. New Zealand lamb, however, is at its best for both quality and price, and a prime leg of lamb for Easter is well within range of the moderate family budget.

Soups

First read soup notes on p. 112.

POOR MAN'S POTAGE ST GERMAIN

the outer leaves from an
   endive
1 14–15-oz. tin of peas, with
   enough light stock to make
   up to 1½ pints liquid
good handful frozen peas

6 spring onions or 1 shallot
1 oz. each butter/margarine and
   flour *or* 1 yolk, 2 tbs. top milk
mint if using dried peas
seasoning

Tinned peas, if thought of as peas, are, to me, the most awful of all the *bad* convenience foods. (About good convenience foods I say my say on p. 462.) However, I keep a tin of so-called garden-grade tinned peas in my winter tin store against some unimaginable disaster, and provided I think of them as a quite different article altogether from fresh peas, they can be turned into something tolerable.

223

This recipe can also be adapted for use with ¼ lb. dried or split peas cooked as on p. 139, when the flavour will be much the same but the colour yellower. (Note the bluish liquid in the tin !)

In full and late summertime Potage St Germain is made with peas that have got rather overblown – for those who have enough space to grow successions of peas, or whose holidays coincided with final pickings. On a hot day thicken with a yolk and cream liaison and serve chilled with a fresh mint leaf in each soup-cup.

Strain off the liquid from the peas into a measure and make it up to 1½ pints with light stock. Very well wash the endive leaves, picking over to remove browned edges, discarding withered parts. Trim and wash the spring onions, cut them into about 3-inch lengths, and chop the endive medium fine. Cook endive, onion (and mint where used), in 1 pint of the liquid for 12 minutes. Cook the frozen peas in remaining ½ pint, straining this back with the rest when peas are tender. Set them aside. Put the tinned peas through a sieve or Moulin-Légumes, followed by the endive and onion, but discard the mint. *Do not pour the liquid through if using flour.*

FOR FLOUR LIAISON: Melt the fat, stir in the purée of vegetables, then the flour, lastly adding the liquid. Bring to the boil, stirring well. Sieve again.

FOR YOLK LIAISON: Pour liquid through Moulin or sieve, return soup to heat and bring just to boiling point, stirring well. Adjust seasoning during this operation. Pour a little hot soup on to the mixed yolk and milk, pour back into pan and stir about 30 seconds over very low heat.

Add the cooked frozen peas. They are not just a garnish but add another dimension to the texture. Tiny croûtons can be used as a garnish for entertaining purposes.

CRÈME DUBARRY

1 small cauliflower (curd *only*)	2 tbs. cream (or substitutes)
¾ pint each light stock and milk	½ oz. cornflour
juice and thinly pared rind of ½ lemon	1 oz. butter/margarine
	seasoning

Divide cauliflower into sprigs and turn them for 3 minutes in the melted fat. Meanwhile boil up stock, pour this on to the cauliflower, adding lemon rind and juice, and simmer, covered, for about 10–12 minutes or until sprigs are tender, but not broken and mushy. Reserve a few sprigs for garnishing. Remove rind, put soup through Moulin or sieve. With a spoonful or so of the milk, slake cornflour. Heat rest of milk, pour on to cornflour and then add to puréed soup, mixing well, and bringing to boil. Take off the boil, stir in the cream and the garnishing sprigs, which you have divided into very small flowerets, and return to low heat 2 minutes.

SHARP POTATO SOUP (German Swiss recipe).

1 lb. potatoes	vinegar
1 onion	1 oz. butter
1 pint stock (mutton stock,	bayleaf
fat removed, will do)	seasoning

Slice and sweat onion in butter. Put peeled, quartered potatoes into stock with bayleaf. Season with pepper and a very little salt, bring to boil, adding onion and butter, and cook until potato is tender – about 20 minutes. Remove bayleaf, put through Moulin. Reheat, stirring in 1 or 2 tbs. good vinegar, and tasting to adjust seasoning, so that the soup is both just sharp and just a little peppery. Its non-creamy, piquant taste and texture make it refreshing and very spring-like. Sprinkle a little chopped fresh chive, tarragon or chervil as available on each soup-cup.

FISH CHOWDER

More a meal than a soup, chowders are a fine American contribution to gastronomy (although the word is said to come from French *chaudière*). The characteristic ingredients are fish – shell or non-oily – crisped salt pork (green streaky bacon at a pinch), potato, milk and dry biscuit. As with any foreign recipe this can claim to be no more than a translation. 8 to 10 helpings, but it is a nourishing and 'different' dish that can be nicely managed on a gas ring, so single-person households are urged to try it (quarter quantities).

2 lb. saithe	1¾ pints milk
¼ lb. pickled pork (or green streaky bacon)	8 fl. oz. cup evaporated milk (or single cream)
2 medium onions	seasoning
16 fl. oz. diced raw potato	cracker or small cheese biscuits

Poach the fish in salted water in the oven or on top of the stove. Skin, bone and flake it, leaving to cool in its liquor. Cut pork into inch dice and fry until crisp. Remove and fry chopped onion in the fat from pork. Add potato dice, turn in the fat, add enough fish liquor to cover, and cook until tender but not broken – about 12 minutes. Return fish to pan, add milk and cream, season well and bring just to boiling point. Serve with a few crisped pork dice on each soup-cup and hand a plate of cracker biscuits.

Some recipes say crumble the cracker biscuits over the soup. Others recommend serving pickled cucumber or gherkin as an additional accompaniment.

First Courses and Snacks

ŒUFS À LA TRIPE

Turn-of-the-century Mrs Beetons include recipes for this excellent dish, Boulestin gives a version in A *Second Helping*, but the recipe given here follows one taught at the Cordon Bleu, London. Sieving the yolks gives a better finish, I think, than the more usual chopping, and the cheese gives an extra turn of the screw to consistency and taste.

1 bunch spring onions – avoid the very thin kind as they are fiddling to prepare – or 2–3 medium ordinary onions or in season, white part of young leeks	4 hard-boiled eggs
	1½ oz. margarine
	generous ½ pint milk
	1 oz. grated cheese (p. 65)
	1 oz. flour
	seasoning

Shell the eggs, remove yolks from whites, and press the former through bowl-strainer. Thinly slice whites and put them over the bottom of a small well-greased gratin dish. Scatter yolks over, and slip the dish into a polythene bag to prevent drying. Cut spring onions into 2-inch lengths (slice ordinary onions). Sweat in the melted fat, add flour off heat, blend, add milk, bringing to boil while stirring well. Season. The sauce must be somewhere between a coating and a flowing sauce, so if too thick add a spoonful or so of milk. Spoon sauce over eggs; thickly dust with grated cheese. Put into a hot oven (400° F, gas 6) for 15 to 20 minutes to heat through thoroughly, finishing under grill for a crisp browned top.

A good dish to make in advance: prepare up to stage of masking with sauce, omitting cheese until just before putting into oven.

Also a dish that can be fitted in with a variety of cooking plans: for instance you could make a double quantity of Béchamel sauce, using half for the eggs and simply adding the sweated onion. You could use cheese sauce, scattering the onion on to the egg-whites, yolks on top of onion, for the components would be the same and all blend together when the sauce seeps down. For a change, omit onion and make a good parsley sauce instead; or add a very little finely chopped tarragon to sauce, and omit the cheese.

Very useful for single-person households, though gas-ring cooks would have to forgo the browned cheese on top, stirring in cheese to the hot sauce instead – a little more than 1 oz. of Cheddar is needed for this. Also a good first course where the main course is on the light side.

RÉMOULADE OF SAUSAGES

An invention resulting from a slightly obscure reference in his novel *Clem* by the French writer Henry Muller. Hungry young men will eat any quantity you like to prepare. A useful dish to bring on mid-way through an informal party. Good for single persons. Polite quantities here are suitable for luncheon appetites.

For each person allow 2 Frankfurters or pork sausages and about 6 oz. peeled potato.

For each lb. potatoes allow the quantity given here of rémoulade sauce :

2 hard-boiled egg-yolks	seasoning, garlic, mustard
up to ¼ pint oil	powder
1 tbs. vinegar	

For cooking the sausages : enough white wine or cider to come about half-way up them (choose the smallest baking dish or tin you can manage with, obviously; or saucepan if cooking them on top), 1 tsp. finely chopped onion, or chive.

Roast pork sausages first in a lightly greased baking tin or dish in the oven at 425–50° F, gas 7–8, for 20–25 minutes, turning once to brown evenly. At this half-way mark stir the onion into the fat that has run from them. (If using chives add with the wine after the full time.) After 20 minutes add wine to browned sausages, and cook a further 5–7 minutes, lowering heat until the potatoes are ready. If cooking on top of stove fry sausages, add wine, cook covered, keep hot.

Cook frankfurters in wine with onion (omitting preliminary browning) at 325° F, gas 3, for 15 minutes, or simmer in wine on top of stove 10–15 minutes.

While sausages are cooking, boil potatoes in their jackets, cutting large ones in half. Do not allow them to overcook. Drain potato water into second pan over low heat, standing plate or colander over it to act as warmer for potatoes while you prepare them for the sauce. Strip off skin, holding hot potato in cloth. Cut up roughly into inch pieces and return to warmer. When all are ready mix, while good and hot, into the rémoulade which you have prepared while they were cooking.

RÉMOULADE. Cream yolks with 1 level tsp. mustard powder mixed to a thick paste with vinegar, salt and pepper. Work into this the oil and, now and then, a little of the vinegar until all are smoothly blended. Crush a clove of garlic in salt and stir it about in the sauce until the salt has all dissolved from it, when it is discarded.

(N.B. Garlic is not usually added to rémoulade sauce, but is an improvement for this hot potato salad. Some rémoulade recipes insist on the addition of anchovy-essence or chopped fillets. Not suitable here.)

Pile the hot salad in the centre of a large heated dish, encircle with the sausages, over which spoon the wine liquor from the cooking dish or pan.

OATMEAL BLINI OR PANCAKE SCONES

Makes 16.

Typical Russian blini are raised with yeast or made with buck-wheat flour. They are about the size and thickness of pikelets or drop-scones, being cooked in the same way. In Russia they appear in many guises and for many different meals. Two can be sand-wiched with a filling and eaten in the fingers, a few may be layered with filling and masked with sour-cream sauce, and they accompany caviare. They can be sweet or savoury. For those who want the real thing there is a recipe for a blini batter in *Russian Cookery* by Nina Petrova.* However, the distribution of buck-wheat flour in the British Isles being dubious, and yeast mixtures having drawbacks, I put forward as a simplified alternative an oatmeal drop-scone recipe.

2 oz. plain flour
2 oz. fine or medium oatmeal
1 egg plus 1 white
½ gill milk

½ level tsp. bicarbonate of soda
½ level tsp. salt
1 level tsp. cream of tartar

Sieve thoroughly all dry ingredients. Beat the whole egg and milk together, make a well in dry mixture, and pour in, beating until a perfectly smooth, thick batter results. Grease a thick

*Penguin, 1968.

frying-pan by rubbing it over with larded paper; or you may use a well-cleaned solid electric, or range hotplate direct, greasing in the same way. Scotswomen will use a girdle. Whisk the egg-white and fold into the batter. Drop batter by the tablespoon on to the cooking surface, turning when bubbles burst on the upper side. Allow about 2 minutes for the first side when cooking begins, and a little less for the second side. But as the cooking surface heats up, less time than this will be needed. Grease between cookings. Lower heat if batter starts burning, raising it again as necessary. (ts. p. 339)

Blini should be slightly thicker and airier than drop-scones, so do not spread the mixture as you spoon it on to surface, but hold point of spoon over one spot so batter piles up slightly forming its own small circle.

Keep hot in clean cloth on cake rack.

FILLINGS. All manner of odds and ends make good fillings, provided they are cut up small, well flavoured and put on to the blini piping hot. Make all the blini first, then fill them, lastly mask with any sauce being used. Glaze suitable blini-in-sauce under the grill for a final finish.

SUGGESTED FILLINGS:

Poached fish flaked into prawn butter (p. 266).

Minced or chopped liver, fried in margarine with a little onion, tomato and marjoram. More fried tomato to garnish.

Leftover ham or bacon, peas, sweated onion, spoonful of stock to moisten.

Minced lamb, a spoonful or so of gravy, a little chopped hot chutney.

Leftover curry. Mask with curry sauce thinned slightly with milk.

Mushroom and bacon, masked with mushroom sauce.

Minced beef and onion heated in yoghurt with ¼ tsp. paprika.

Spinach purée, masked with cheese sauce.

4 oz., *total weight*, of filling will fill enough blini for 4 for luncheon, 6 to 8 for first course. As a luncheon dish serve green salad, cucumber or tomato salad, etc. as accompaniment.

Sweet blini make a delicious pudding. Sandwich pairs of them with fruit purée and top with honey, yoghurt, whipped cream or ice cream : blini and filling hot, of course, topping cold; or, if syrup or honey, just warmed. Ordinary drop-scone batter, which includes sugar, may be used for the sweet kind.

Like pancakes, these blini may be made several hours beforehand – even overnight. Here they have an advantage over the yeast-raised 'real' ones, for all yeast mixtures are at their best when absolutely fresh. You can make them the evening before if you like. I've made them 48 hours before very successfully. All that is required is to keep them wrapped in their cloth. But don't put them in foil or polythene when they are still hot for the steam will make them soggy. To reheat them, overlap widely in a lightly greased gratin dish or shallow tin, with foil or a buttered greaseproof tucked over, and slip in the oven – 325° F, gas 3 – 8 to 10 minutes.

Useful for single-person households.

Salad hors-d'œuvres or crudités

At a time of year when we cannot altogether abandon hot main courses, a light start is often preferable for entertaining, and is often more convenient than serving a pudding course for the family. Raw vegetable salads, called crudités these days in Paris, are excellent for the purpose.

Cucumbers are cheaper now, and the two cucumber salads suggested as curry accompaniments (p. 154) are good examples, so is the carrot salad on p. 166. By the end of the month Dutch tomatoes are cheaper and, if regarded as the fruit which they are, compare well with other fruits on sale. Tomato-growers themselves usually prefer tomatoes at the orange end of their colour spectrum, when the flavour is sharper, the aroma delicious, the flesh firm, pips small and skins easy to lift (see p. 104).

SWEET AND SOUR TOMATOES

| 3 medium tomatoes for 4 people | salt |
| mint | sugar |

Skin and thinly slice the fruit, arranging slices overlapping on small plates or on a serving dish. Dust the slices with salt (rock salt is best), a very little demerara or granulated sugar, and freshly chopped mint. Chill. The sugar and salt are better if coarse as they do not quite dissolve, giving a pleasant texture on the palate.

SPRING VEGETABLE BOWL

1 young carrot
½ bunch radishes
½ bunch spring onions
3–4 tightly closed button
  mushrooms
1 tbs. chopped fresh herbs
  (any mixture)

½ level tsp, granulated sugar
juice of ½ lemon
1 tbs. oil
garlic
lettuce leaves

Scrape carrot. Wash, top and tail radishes and onions. Wipe mushrooms gently, but do not skin or stalk. Slice carrot and radish quite coarsely; cut onions into ½-inch lengths, quartering bulb ends if these are fat. Slice mushrooms through from cap to stalk fairly thinly.

Rub a salad bowl with garlic, swirl round it the oil to take up the flavour. Add the lemon juice and mix for a minute. Put in the vegetables and turn them well. Add a little more oil as necessary to give a good shine to the salad. Sprinkle with sugar, dust over with herbs, turn once again, and serve on a lettuce leaf on small plates or in fruit glasses.

Fish

GRILLED SAITHE STEAKS TARTARE

8-oz. piece of saithe fillet per
  person
¾ oz. margarine per fillet
1½ lb. potatoes for each 4
  persons

1 oz. each lard and butter for
  cooking them
½ pint tartare sauce for each
  4 persons
parsley

Boil the potatoes for 15 minutes. Drain and cut them into inch pieces.

.While they are boiling, skin the saithe, put it on a well-greased grill grid, season and dot with margarine. Heat the grill and cook the fish on one side for 3 minutes. Turn, season other side, baste with fat from the grill pan, and grill at full heat for 4 minutes or until fish is browning well. Lower heat slightly and continue until top is evenly browned, and a small pointed knife easily passes through the thickest piece of fish.

While the fish is grilling complete potatoes: heat lard till smoking hot in frying-pan, add butter, and when bubbling, tumble in potatoes to cover evenly with fat. Then leave them unstirred until they brown, when they may be tumbled over once more. Sauté potatoes must not be treated like chips, and browned all over evenly, but fried and unfried surfaces should be piebald in a perfectly haphazard way. Dust with salt and chopped parsley.

TARTARE SAUCE. This is the moment for being able to make your first-of-the-season real tartare. Tarragon and parsley will both be well up in the garden, and there will probably have been a ray or so of sun to give them aroma. At this time of year I use chives in preference to shallot. For the base of the sauce you can, if you have some made, use the thick salad dressing (p. 250) for economy and speed. But it is inferior, naturally, in taste and texture to a true mayonnaise base.

½ pint mayonnaise (p. 248)
A ravigote of :
1 tbs. each minced shallot, chopped tarragon and parsley

1 rounded tsp. good Dijon mustard
few drops herb vinegar

Thin mustard slightly with vinegar, stir in the ravigote, blend in the mayonnaise.

BRILL

Some compare brill to turbot, others to Dover sole. It has not quite the rich glutinousness of turbot, but big brill can be cut and used in much the same way. On the other hand the flesh has all the flavour and firmness of Dover sole, and a small brill, which will be the size of a large sole, is not so hopelessly dear as Dover sole. Brill seems a much too little known fish in view of its excellencies. Ask for it, therefore, at your fishmonger's, and try for a small one. Cook it in any of the ways suggested for lemon sole (p. 188) or plaice (p. 281).

Scallops (*Coquilles Saint-Jacques*)

Prices of scallops should be at their most modest now, and for a little special dinner won't break the bank. Two a-piece may not look much, but scallops are unexpectedly satisfying. This is a dish that calls for pommes duchesse.

COQUILLES SAINT-JACQUES AU GRATIN

Serves 2.

4 scallops (select the heaviest and see you get the deep shells)	5 tbs. each white wine and water
1 level tbs. browned crumbs	1½ oz. butter/margarine
1 tsp. minced onion or chopped chive	¾ oz. flour
handful of mushroom stalks finely sliced in rings	seasoning
	1 lb. pommes duchesse (p. 194)

Melt butter, sweat onion and mushroom. Separate 'yolk' from white of scallops, slicing through horizontally to make 2 whites and yolks per scallop. Add to pan and sweat 5 minutes. Stir in the flour off the heat, add the wine and water and mix smoothly. Return to heat, but allow to come barely to boiling point. The liquid should just move as an occasional bubble breaks the surface. Cook thus 5 minutes. Fill back into the shells, which you have well cleaned. Pipe a border of pommes duchesse round the edge of the shells. You may have more sauce than you can put into the shells, before piping the potato. If so, add it after piping when the potato will hold it. You should also have some potato over, which may be piped into rosettes on a damped baking-sheet, and browned in the oven, to be eaten next day.

COQUILLES SAINT-JACQUES EN BROCHETTES

Poach 2 scallops per person in 1 gill mixed wine and water, lightly seasoned, for 6 minutes. Separate white from yolk, split, wrap each piece in a thin rasher of bacon and skewer them. Dust with flour, and egg and crumb each skewerful. Grill, turning often, or fry in deep fat. Handling hot skewers with care, slide fish neatly off on to individual plates on which you have prepared a bed of mashed potato or well-flavoured rice (e.g. add to rice a little softened onion, a pinch of caraway seed, dried herbs, saffron, etc. to taste), or dish on skewers on serving dish, with potato or rice bed. In this instance, the server should have ready on the table a clean cloth or thick tissue napkin to hold skewers, and a wide-pronged fork for sliding the fish off.

SOFT ROES ON TOAST

Herring roes from frozen blocks can be quite tasteless if they have been hanging about too long, and impossible to handle if chopped from block when solid. Buy only from reliable shops. ½ lb. for 2 for a snack, ¼ lb. for a savoury. For each ½ lb. melt ¾ oz. each margarine and butter. Season lightly with salt, add a dash of cayenne or tabasco. Turn roes in this for about 5 minutes over gentle heat. Serve on fingers of buttered toast with lemon wedges and cayenne pepper.

MEAT

Paschal lamb

Consult the notes on lamb (p. 20) before choosing a whole leg of young lamb for your Easter week-end joint. Here are three ways to dress it as a hot roast, followed by some réchauffé recipes for finishing it later in the week.

LAMB WITH ROSEMARY AND GARLIC

Split a clove of garlic into 6 thin slices. With the point of a small knife raise an inch of the meat from the shank bone at the knuckle end and insert the first sliver against the bone. Make a similar insertion between two sections of lean at the chump end. Insert two each just under the skin at different places on the top and underside of the joint. Pick spots where there is a little patch of fat as this will melt and distribute the aroma evenly round the joint. Take six rosemary leaves and insert them in a similar way. Season the meat and roast as directed on pp. 96–9.

ACCOMPANIMENTS: Small roast, or boiled new potatoes, peas. Mint jelly. Make plenty of gravy as suggested on p. 99, so that you can reserve some for the réchauffés.

LAMB WITH WINE AND WALNUT DRESSING

leg of prime young lamb
1 clove garlic
1 tsp. minced onion
good sprig parsley chopped fine
pinch thyme (optional; fresh for preference)

8 walnut halves chopped medium fine
½ gill Spanish burgundy
grated rind and juice of ½ lemon
1–2 tbs. redcurrant jelly (or, if you make it, good mint jelly as on p. 554)
1 oz. butter/margarine

Spike lamb with garlic as in previous recipe and roast as on pp. 96–9 for 1 hour.

Meanwhile prepare dressing. Melt fat, sweat onion, stir in rind and juice of lemon, wine, herbs, walnuts and lastly jelly, tasting to see if you need more than 1 tbs. The dressing should strike a nice balance between sharp and sweet. Whip jelly with a fork before adding, otherwise it may prove reluctant to dissolve. Add also any blood that may have run from meat before it was cooked. Simmer the dressing 5 minutes. Remove joint from oven, turn the underside uppermost, spoon over it 1 tbs. of dressing. Return to oven for 10 to 15 minutes. Carefully turn joint over so as to dislodge as little of dressing as possible, spoon 2 tbs. dressing over upperside of joint, and return it to oven for rest of cooking time. This procedure does not interfere with any roasting of potatoes that may be going on in the meat tin.

Dish the joint, and rest it as usual. Pour off surplus fat, add 5 tbs. water to meat tin and cook down pan juices with remnants of dressing fallen from joint. Add this to remaining dressing and heat through gently, sending to table in heated sauceboat. Spoon juices that run from meat, on carving, into dressing, before handing the sauceboat.

ACCOMPANIMENTS: Potatoes as before. Buttered cauliflower or, after meat course, green salad.

GLAZED GIGOT

France and Scotland both use this term for leg of lamb.

Prepare and roast joint 1 hour as in previous recipe.

Mix 1 rounded tbs. of English-made 'French' mustard to a thinner consistency with 1 tbs. pineapple syrup from a tin of pineapple pieces. Add 1 small tsp. lemon juice and 2 tsp. demerara sugar. Spread this first on underside of joint, returning to oven, then on upper side to finish, as previous recipe. Make gravy in tin as follows: pour off all but 1 tsp. fat, in which brown 1 tsp. minced onion, dust in ½ oz. flour, finally adding ½ pint light stock.

ACCOMPANIMENTS: A platter of various spring vegetables – baby carrots, turnips, spring onions – fattest available – plainly boiled and finished by browning and glazing in 1½ oz. margarine/ butter, ½ tsp. sugar, seasoning; baby beets, boiled then tossed in butter, lemon juice and parsley; new potatoes. Vary this how you like with what you can get and prefer (½ lb. of each sort; 1½ lb. potatoes will serve 4).

Réchauffés

Lamb reheats best of all meats, and recipes are endless. But the best réchauffé recipes ever are Boulestin's. So good indeed is

Mouton à la Bourgeoise that I sometimes roast a joint of lamb expressly in order to make it. And it is positively made for the larger joints needed for big families, for autumn lamb past its first youth and for 'bargains' that turn out not to be.

Shepherd's Pie may seem almost too ordinary to need a recipe. However, as wrong proportions, careless preparation or badly timed cooking can render the simplest dish unpalatable, and as Shepherd's Pie is so good when well made, I have included it. It also illustrates all the rules for classic réchauffés.

THE REHEATING OF MEAT. Beef is often wrongly used for Shepherd's Pie – as the name suggests. On reheating, even the tenderest, most finely cut meat hardens at first, due to changes in the protein. This accounts for the texture of incorrectly cooked réchauffé dishes. Whereas reheated lamb becomes tender again in a comparatively short time, beef requires quite a long recooking. These facts are important also when grousing about large-scale cooking such as school dinners or 'the firm's canteen'. In order to serve 300 diners who are allowed, say, only ¾ hour for lunch, roast meat must be carved in advance and, of course, kept hot. This is commonly done by putting the slices in hot gravy, nutritionally sensible since the juices in the joint mix with the gravy and are not lost. But even 10 minutes of this is enough to toughen beef, as you can try for yourself with your very next joint by cutting a couple of thin slices, and putting them in a covered dish in the oven. To make them as tender again as the joint from which you are eating, you will need to add liquid, and leave them to stew for over an hour. Lamb slices are cut thicker, and they too need an hour. But *minced* roast lamb will cook, in a liquid, in 30 to 40 minutes, whereas minced roast beef needs an hour or more.

The only method of reheating roast meat very quickly – but this is suitable only for family meals – is to make *boiling hot* a fair quantity of a good, suitable sauce, have ready the meat, minced or thinly sliced, put it in a preheated dish, pour the sauce on to it at once, and serve immediately on hot plates. This method is helped by including wine, cider or beer in the sauce, for they act as tenderizing agents.

Rissoles are acceptable only because the grilling or frying renders the outside crisp and very savoury, while the heat penetrates to the inside only enough to warm it without reaching a temperature that hardens it. For these reasons rissoles should be cooked quickly at very high temperatures, and should be thick.

Much is heard nowadays against the reheating of food because it has sometimes been the cause of food poisoning. But in the conditions of the normal domestic kitchen, food poisoning is unlikely. Essentials to follow are:

(1) Cool the joint quickly, covered from the atmosphere if you have no larder, and in summer cover it even in the larder (p. 40).

(2) Store the cold meat in a properly constructed cool larder or food safe, covered as above, or refrigerator – also covered.

(3) Follow scrupulously the advice on kitchen cleanliness in dealing with all réch**a**ufféing.

(4) If you want to keep meat longer than 2 to 3 days you should store it in the freezing compartment of the refrigerator.

You must use judgement in interpreting these points in relation to time of year, and the position of, for instance, your larder. On a very sunny winter's day a west-facing larder can become quite warm, whereas in a very cold spell north- or east-facing larders can be colder than the main compartment of a refrigerator.

The loss of flavour in refrigerated food matters less for réchauffés since their sauces and components are well flavoured to offset this.

GENERAL RULES FOR RÉCHAUFFÉS

(1) All components must be cooked.

(2) Skin, gristle and large pieces of fat should be removed from meat.

(3) Food must be suitably seasoned, and proportions nicely balanced: e.g. avoid small quantities of meat swimming in sauce or overwhelmed with vegetables, croûtons, etc. Avoid making meat 'go further' by adding large amounts of breadcrumbs or potato.

(4) See that the sauce or gravy consistency is appropriate: e.g. avoid serving mashed potato, or coated fried foods, with watery gravy. Serve fried croûtons or sauté potatoes, for example, with réchauffés heated in white sauces. Serve sharp thickened sauces with coated fried foods.

(5) If you intend to use up potatoes by mashing and spreading or piping them, this can only be done hot. Therefore try and make the purée while potatoes are still hot as they sieve more easily, and it is easier to reheat the purée. Always store potatoes, whole or mashed, well-covered as they dry quickly.

A REMINDER: onion and potato sour quickly, therefore store them, or sauce or stock containing them, in the cold.

SHEPHERD'S PIE

½ lb. cold roast lamb or mutton
1 medium onion
½ pint good gravy or stock
¾ lb. potato purée (p. 155)

¾ oz. bacon dripping (for preference) or margarine
1 slice bread dried crisp, but not coloured, in the oven
seasoning

Remove skin, gristle and larger pieces of fat from meat. Leave some fat however. Mince the meat, ending by mincing the bread, which 'cleans' out mincer and thickens stock. Chop and fry onion in dripping until browned. Add to meat, stir in gravy, adjust seasoning, and put in pint pie dish. Pipe or spread potato on top. If you have used the correct amount of margarine/butter in the potato mix it is unnecessary to dot more fat on top. But should you have beaten egg left over, an attractive finish will result from brushing over the top with this. Bake at 400° F, gas 6, for 30 to 40 minutes. Grill top if not evenly browned enough.

NOTE: Where gravy or stock is insufficient or non-existent add ¾ oz. flour when browning onion, stir in, and cook until the flour browns also. Add a total of ½ pint liquid, making up gravy with water or using bouillon cube or paste. Bring to boil, stirring well, and proceed as rest of recipe.

MOUTON À LA BOURGEOISE (Boulestin)

Boulestin does not indicate quantities, and while I agree that finicking exactitude can be overdone, young or novice cooks like guidelines. Reckon, therefore, on 2–4 oz. cooked meat per person in réchauffés which do not include pastry or potato as an intrinsic part of the dish. 2 oz. is certainly enough for young children, but boys and girls from 12 years old to their lower twenties are growing and/or full of energy and activity. They usually love tasty réchauffés, and 4 oz. of meat is not too much for ravenous appetites. (Information included for the benefit of anyone expecting young visitors and not used to feeding them. By the way, one of the oddest Victorian relics is that women have smaller appetites than men. Popular, of course, with restaurateurs.)

¾ lb. cold roast lamb or mutton cut slightly thinner than when hot – gristle, etc. removed	2 good sprigs parsley, chopped
	1 medium onion or 2 shallots, minced
1½ oz. butter/margarine	½ pint stock or thin gravy
1 level tbs. flour	1 tbs. olive or good salad oil

Melt the butter and briskly fry the slices of meat just until they brown. (They will also shrink somewhat.) Remove them to a hot gratin dish, and return this to the oven, which you have set at 300° F, gas 2. Mix onion and parsley and fry them briskly in the pan for about 1 minute. Scatter in flour off heat, add liquid and bring just to simmering point, stirring till smooth. Pour over meat, cover and cook 1 hour, lowering heat to 250° F, gas ½, after 20 minutes. 10 minutes before serving remove covering, stir in olive oil, and return to oven to finish. Gas-ring cooks can do this in a stout pan with lid, or oven dish on an asbestos mat. Low heat.

Boulestin rightly states that the dish, obviously a favourite of his, is at its best accompanied by tomatoes. Grill, fry, or bake whole as for jacket potatoes, with neither fat nor water, in the lower part of the oven. Jacket potatoes are themselves good here: medium sized, started off at least 1½ hours before the time of the meal, and moved up or down in the oven according to their progress.

The recipe demands plenty of 'blotting-paper' in the form of plain potatoes or good fresh bread to take up the tasty sauce. Spoons for slimmers.

CURRY

Roast mutton is much better than beef for currying. Cut in thick slices, dice, or fingers, and cook gently in the curry sauce on p. 152 in a covered dish or pan for 1 hour. Accompaniments to choice as for the curried fish.

MIROTON OF LAMB

Make as for Beef Miroton (p. 453). I find that very thinly sliced cold potatoes overlapped over the top, basted with melted margarine and finally browned very lightly under the grill, go well with lamb miroton.

Cauliflower, basted finally in its serving dish with a little melted butter, lemon juice, parsley and seasoning, makes a good accompaniment.

Vegetables

A tomato dish on the lines of following two recipes is in Janet Ross's *Leaves from our Tuscan Kitchen* of 1905, so, although I first heard of them at a Women's Institute meeting in Sussex, the origins are probably Italian.

TOMATO CHARLOTTE I

½ lb. tomatoes, fresh or canned	2 oz. suet
about 1 level tsp. salt	pepper
2 oz. fresh breadcrumbs	pinch thyme or marjoram
	½ oz. margarine

Grease 1-pint pie dish or soufflé dish. Skin and quarter fresh tomatoes, chop up tinned ones roughly. Season to taste. Mix crumbs, suet, herbs and seasoning. Starting and finishing with crumbs, fill tomato and crumbs in layers into dish. Depending on shape of dish you may find you have simply a sort of tomato sandwich. Press down lightly, dot top with margarine, and bake at 350° F, gas 4, for 40 to 50 minutes.

TOMATO CHARLOTTE II

½ lb. tomatoes (fresh or
canned) skinned, seasoned
and softened in a little
margarine

3 oz. browned crumbs
2 oz. butter/margarine
seasoning

Melt 1½ oz. butter, stir in crumbs and seasoning, heating gently
until fat is well mixed, and crumbs start to separate again. Line
a greased pint plain mould (or very small cake tin) with medium-
thin coating of crumb mixture, but see that bottom of mould is
well coated. Fill mould with layers of crumbs and tomatoes. Dot
top with rest of butter and bake 20 to 30 minutes at 375° F, gas 5.
Turn out.

NOTE: If liked, vary the flavours by the addition of herbs, a
little minced onion, a pinch of spice, a little sugar – whatever is
to hand.

CAULIFLOWER FRITTERS

Excellent with réchauffés and fish, but make them only when
you can fit them in. For example if you are frying in any event,
when fat bath and coatings are on the go; or if you have made
your main dish in advance and so are feeling energetic. Avoid
them as an accompanying vegetable for a dinner-party – too
much trouble and space are needed, too much smell generated.
Make them as a main dish for luncheon, plus a cheese, mushroom,
or egg and lemon sauce.

Separate cauliflower into flowerets. Blanch for 5 minutes in
salted water. Drain, and pat gently dry in a cloth. Dip in fritter
batter (see p. 123), or coat with egg and breadcrumbs, and fry in
deep fat. Drain on absorbent paper.

Vegetable salads and salad dressings

Not all salad vegetables are yet in profusion, but now is the time
to get your hand and mind tuned in to the salad season, and to
make a stock of dressings. English salads are one of our failures.
Good salad, like good sandwiches, needs care. Most Englishwomen

take great trouble with sandwiches, but their idea of a salad is a hasty jumble of clumsily hacked up vegetables sent to table with a bottle of Somebody's Salad Cream.

To me these bottles of goo always have something scented and sweetish about them, reminiscent of face-cream, gents' hair oil and a loathsome emulsion I had to swallow as a child. I get great amusement from the eternal Briton's wail of 'greasy' if you mention vinaigrettes. Do they never look at labels? Bottled salad creams are full of oil. They *have* to be.

Salad vegetables must be clean, and kept crisp and cool until ready to serve. See notes on food storage, p. 41.

GREEN SALAD

Means what it says. Lettuce, watercress, the small cresses, dandelion, endive, chicory. Any of these or a mixture of some, but nothing else. Wash thoroughly, shake drops out, pat dry in a cloth. Nothing nastier than watery salad. Break or tear up big leaves and sprigs. Mix with vinaigrette (pp. 247–8) only just before serving.

MIXED SALAD

Wash and dry medium-sized lettuce leaves. Make radish flowers (see diagram on p. 106), prepare slim spring onions by slicing off roots and all but 1 inch green tops, thinly peel about 3–4 inches cucumber and cut in ½-inch dice, skin and cut 1–2 tomatoes in eighths. In this sort of chopped salad your aim should be similarity of size and weight of the ingredients, as they mix better that way. Just before serving mix lettuce leaves with a little vinaigrette, toss the other vegetables in a sugar vinaigrette. Arrange lettuce in bottom of bowl and fill with mixed vegetables so that it resembles an opened flower – the lettuce leaves being petals, the rest stamens. If tomatoes are scarce and expensive, segment an orange (p. 104) instead.

POTATO SALAD

¾ lb. medium potatoes
1 dessertsp. minced chives or
   onion

¼ pint mayonnaise (pp. 248–50)
   rémoulade or thick salad
   dressing (pp. 250–51)

Boil potatoes in jackets 25 minutes. Skin and cut in ½-inch dice or pieces, put in mixing bowl. Mix chives with dressing in small basin and add to potato, while latter is still warm, by the table-spoon, turning over until potato is coated to your liking. Leave to get cold before serving. Make in bigger quantities as desired and store well covered in refrigerator for several days. Later on, use the 'chats' – the tiny potatoes clinging to the roots as you dig them up, and which usually get thrown out. Fiddly to scrape, but lovely to eat, and pretty !

CUCUMBER BOAT

½ cucumber*
8 fresh chive blades
6 blanched, toasted almonds
2 tsp. seedless raisins

2 oz. curd cheese
lemon juice
sugar
seasoning

Pare cucumber and split in 2 lengthways. Scoop out seeds. Sprinkle inside and out with salt, pepper and a very little sugar and tip up on the rim of a plate to drain off some of the juice. Meanwhile very finely chop chive, almonds and raisins. Mash the cheese, season it, and work in lemon juice to taste. Reserve a pinch of chives and a level tsp. of mixed nut and raisin. Mix rest of all three into the cheese. Pat the cucumber with kitchen paper to dry. Fill cavities with cheese mixture, butt cucumber halves to-gether to form a boat, sprinkling top of filling with nut mixture, lastly with chives. Chill and serve.

*Most people buy cucumbers half at a time, so the directions are for that. If you use a complete fruit you will be saved the butting operation.

LETTUCE GARNISH

Many recipes for cold food give directions for dishing 'on a bed of lettuce'. There are various ways to deal with the lettuce in these cases, and as the lettuce is often not intended to be eaten, or you may have to assemble the dish sufficiently far ahead for the lettuce to wilt somewhat, you can use outside leaves for the purpose; not, of course, damaged or discoloured specimens, but the coarser, darker leaves.

(1) Remove the thicker part of centre rib of leaves, shred them as finely as possible (technical name: 'needle shreds'). When you know garnish will be eaten, dust with salt.

(2) Use whole leaves, breaking across rib if required to lay flat.

(3) For individual plates of salad or cold food – e.g. dressed fish – lightly salt medium inner leaves, and use as cups to hold the food.

The very finest lettuce for all purposes is the Iceberg or Webb's Wonderful type. It is as crisp as cos lettuce, has as good a flavour and, when well grown, has a huge centre as firm as Dutch salad cabbage. The shape of cos lettuce is sometimes a drawback, but otherwise it is always preferable to the ordinary cabbage lettuce. Webb's Wonders are beginning to be readily available in London, and once the provincial housewife makes her preference for them known, they should spread to other towns. Both Webb's and cos 'stand' longer after dressing, and wilt less quickly if storage is difficult. So far, however, they seem not to be favoured for cultivation under glass, so we have to wait for them until mid-season.

Single-person households should not be put off by the size of these two lettuces. The outside leaves can be cooked like spinach, used for soup (see the Poor Man's St Germain a few pages back), and cooked in with peas to give a nutty flavour and extra bulk. Squeeze cooked lettuce as for spinach, chop and flavour it similarly

Dressings

It is a counsel of perfection to make vinaigrettes fresh for each salad, and do so by all means if you have the strength (the French say 'courage', a nice linguistic difference), or are entertaining. Busy housekeepers should mass-produce and bottle the stuff. When French friends come to stay they make up a bottle for me as they do for themselves in Paris. Theirs is mysteriously much better than mine. The ingredients are all provided by me, so the mystery doesn't reside in 'unobtainable excellence. But I avoid watching the process, for the treat would become a commonplace once I learned the secret.

Make, also, more mayonnaise than you need, since this keeps splendidly in the cool if well covered. Those plastic containers with snap-on lids are ideal ('Airfix' is Woolworth's brand). It is supposed to be risky to keep mayonnaise in the ice-box as it may separate. I seem to get away with it, but I put it in the warmest part – in my machine the lower part of the door.

You need a larger container for the thick salad dressing given here; or emptied pickle jars, if the lids are intact with plastic sealing strip and anti-vinegar lacquer.

TARRAGON VINEGAR

Easily made and, on the sunny April evening of a fine day, the new shoots of tarragon will be in perfect picking condition. Cut a good one and thrust, still sun-warm, into scant pint of white vinegar. Leave 2 to 4 weeks. Some cooks – particularly in East Europe – mature herb vinegars and other pickles in the sun.

PLAIN VINAIGRETTE

To fill ½-pint bottle

1 clove garlic	6 fl. oz. salad oil
1 rounded tsp. Dijon or made English mustard	2 fl. oz. vinegar (herb, wine or cider vinegar for preference) or
¾ tsp. salt	1 fl. oz. each vinegar and lemon juice
½ tsp. freshly ground black pepper	

Crush the clove of garlic in some of the salt and put it into a basin with rest of salt, mustard and pepper. Mix with a few drops of the vinegar to dissolve salt and thin mustard somewhat. With a wooden spoon or small whisk beat in 1 tbs. oil, followed by a little more vinegar and oil until all is smoothly blended and thickened. Pour into a screwcap bottle or jar. Remove garlic or not as liked, or leave it for 24 hours before removing. It will not go off, as the vinaigrette ingredients act as a pickle. If you like garlic, fish for it, at your convenience, to chop finely and spread on meat or fish just before grilling.

Shake the bottle thoroughly before use.

SUGAR VINAIGRETTE

Sugar vinaigrettes have limited uses and are not worth making in quantity as sugar takes away the refreshing sharpness of classic vinaigrette, modifies the taste of the vegetables dressed with it, sometimes to their detriment, and so spoils one of the points about vegetable salads – the contrast of their flavour with rich dishes. One use for them is when you make a big hors-d'œuvre of various cold dressed foods, and need to ring the changes on dressings. The Eliza Acton Brawn Sauce (p. 400) is essentially a sugar vinaigrette, giving you a hint that dressing of the genre is suitable for salads served with pork or other similar meats.

3 dessertsp. oil	other ingredients as for plain
1 dessertsp. vinegar	vinaigrette but reduced in
½ level tsp. castor sugar	proportion

Make as plain vinaigrette above.

MAYONNAISE

1 egg-yolk	¼ pint salad oil
1 level tsp. dry mustard	1–2 tsp. lemon juice
¼ tsp. salt	1–2 tsp. tarragon vinegar
pepper	

248

Cream the yolk with the mustard, salt and pepper in a small basin. Stand it on a cloth to prevent slipping. Put the measured oil into a lipped vessel. Have a teaspoon to hand. Mix the vinegar and lemon juice in a cup. Take up a rotary whisk. Add 1 tsp. oil to egg and whisk well. Repeat this until you have added 8 tsp. and a thick emulsion forms. Add 1 tsp. vinegar to mixture and whisk. Sauce will thin a little. Add 8 more tsp. oil, and another of vinegar, by which time half the oil will have gone in. The whiskings must completely incorporate the fresh teaspoon of oil or vinegar, but there is no need to whisk on after this point. Now add 1 dessertsp. boiling water and whisk briskly. The sauce will thin dramatically. After this, however, you can add rest of oil by the tablespoon, ending with rest of vinegar, and the sauce will thicken again perfectly.

In electric blender : use 1 whole egg, ½ pint oil and double rest of ingredients. Put in egg and all seasonings, and 1 tsp. vinegar. Add only enough oil to cover bottom blade of blender. Blend well. Add rest of oil about 1 tbs. at a time to start with until good and thick, then vinegar, then rest of oil quite quickly. Needs thinning – as above.

In electric mixer : ingredients as above. Put egg, seasonings and 1 tsp. vinegar in bowl. Start beaters at fast speed, adding oil in continuous but slow, thin trickle direct on to moving beaters. When half oil is in add rest of vinegar, then rest of oil much more quickly. Needs slightly less thinning than blender mixture.

If disaster strikes there are several ways to try and 'bring back' curdled mayonnaise :

(1) Add 1 tsp. very cold water.

(2) Add from 1 tsp. to a complete raw egg-white (this slightly lightens the texture, but not enough to matter).

(3) Add 1 coffee-spoonful mustard.

(4) Start again with fresh ingredients and, when the new sauce is completed, whisk in the curdled sauce by the tablespoonful.

To basic mayonnaise may be added tomato juice, shellfish coral, ravigotes of chopped herbs and pickles; it may be set with gelatine for decorating cold food; cream and Béchamel may be added for binding savoury mousse and so on. Thin mayonnaise by adding boiling water teaspoon at a time and whisking in.

MOCK MAYONNAISE/HOLLANDAISE/BÉARNAISE
(Cooked)

2 oz. margarine or white shortening (a proportion of butter improves)
2 standard eggs (if only very large or very small eggs, adjust fat)

1 tbs. tarragon vinegar for mayonnaise; lemon juice for Hollandaise; wine or herb vinegar for Béarnaise (as below)
seasoning

Before making Béarnaise Sauce you must prepare the wine or vinegar: chop finely 1 tsp. onion or shallot, sprig each thyme, parsley, and tarragon; put into small pan with 2½ tbs. dry wine (red or white) or good vinegar (no need for tarragon if tarragon vinegar is used), pinch salt, good sprinkling black pepper; boil fast until only 1 tbs. remains. This process gives a concentrate of flavours. Strain the vinegar, add 2 tsp. cold water and proceed as below.

Cut fat into large chunks and put with all rest of ingredients in a basin over a small pan of simmering water. *The water must not touch the basin.* Whisk steadily until mixture thickens – about 10 minutes. For mayonnaise continue whisking off heat until sauce has cooled somewhat.

Makes about ½ pint. For a limited number of people, use half hot as Hollandaise or Béarnaise, leaving rest to get cold for extra flavoursome egg 'mayonnaise' next day.

As with lemon curd, made on the same principle, the keeping quality is of short duration, a few weeks at most and the colder the better. Tends to thicken, but thin as ordinary mayonnaise: a teaspoon of hot water at a time well stirred in.

THICK UNCOOKED SALAD CREAM

The original of this recipe was American, but I have modified it to suit the less sweet-toothed. The quantity given will fill a 2-lb.

jam jar or, better, 2–3 medium-sized pickle jars. Halve the quantity for small households.

1 pint salad oil	3 fl. oz. water
2 tbs. tarragon or other good vinegar	1 rounded tsp. dry mustard
	1 level tsp. castor sugar
2 oz. Marvel or Sainsbury's milk powder (or similar)	½ tsp. each salt and pepper

Essential equipment for this recipe: a rotary whisk (or electric mixer).

In a small basin whisk *very well* the milk powder and water until a thick froth forms on top. Whisk in the mustard, sugar, salt, pepper. Transfer to a larger bowl. Add the oil about 4 fl. oz. at a time, whisking really well with each lot. The mixture will become thick. Lastly whisk in the vinegar.

The dressing is the colour of cream. You may add, say, ½ tsp. extra sugar, 1 dessertsp. extra vinegar at the end, if you want it sweeter or sharper. You can use 3 largish tbs. yoghurt, or 3 fl. oz. evaporated or condensed milk instead of the powder. Use *no salt* and *scant* spoonfuls of vinegar if using yoghurt; use *no sugar* if using condensed milk.

It is much better to test for flavour if you have on hand some cubes of cooked potato on which to dab the dressing. Salad dressings of this kind are greatly modified in flavour by the food they dress. Avoid drowning food in thick dressings.

PLAINLY COOKED POTATOES

In several other recipes, something has been said on various plain ways to cook potatoes, and this summarizes the points made, and adds a few more. Potatoes are a staple of our diet, so no apologies for plenty of space spent upon the basic methods of cooking them.

Whatever way you cook them it is obviously simpler to have potatoes of even sizes. Old potatoes to be cooked in their skins are, for most purposes, better if of medium size and without irregular humps, dips or large blemishes, since one can then be sure that they do not take too long, all will be done at the same time and they will be clean and wholesome right through. If very large, potatoes for boiling can be halved or quartered lengthways. Halving widthways will not necessarily reduce the thickness enough.

LARGE POTATOES. On the other hand, if you want to go out for an evening, or, indeed, come home from your job, and find potatoes ready and waiting, choose big ones, put them in a low oven in a wide tin – just in case they should burst – or wrapped, not too closely, in foil. Exact timing is impossible to give, so much depends upon age, freshness, type, soil and the climate. Extra dry, wet, or cold weather affects vegetables as it affects all living organisms. However, the following is a rough time-guide for cooking whole medium to large potatoes in their skins. (Jacket potatoes also cook well in the ashes beneath solid-fuel fires. Allow at least ½ hour longer than times for slow oven.)

Weight of each individual potato and cooking times

		5–6 oz.	7–8 oz.	10–12 oz.	about 1 **lb.**
BAKED	Moderate oven	1 hour	1½ hours	2 hours	2½ hours
	Slow oven	1½ hours	2 hours	2½ hours	3 hours
BOILED	Ordinary pan	40 mins.	1 hour	1¼ hours	1½ hours
	Pressure cooker	15 mins.	20 to 25 minutes	30 to 35 minutes	40 to 45 minutes

SERVING. These large potatoes need plenty of dressing, which may be butter; cream cheese or yoghurt, with or without extra flavourings of herbs, onion, capers, etc.; mayonnaise; or gravy from the main dish. They are convenient to handle if sent to table in a foil 'nest' or on a side-plate, and slashed across the top with some of their dressing packed into the cuts where suitable.

PLAIN COOKING SMALLER OF CUT AND/OR
PEELED POTATOES

Method of cooking	Old Potatoes	New Potatoes
Boiled in skins	Soak in cold water if possible. Scrub well. Cut large ones in 2 or 4 to match size of smaller. Cold salted water to cover, cook 20 minutes after coming to boil (Pressure cooker: 7–10 mins.)	If from garden stir round with stick in cold water so friction takes off grit. Rinse. If from shop soak a little, and wipe with cloth to remove mud. Cut extra large in half. Boiling salted water to cover, sprig mint. 12 to 20 minutes according to size. (Pressure cooker: 5–7 mins.)

Skinning. Hold in cloth pull away skin with aid of small knife.

	Send butter to table separately.	Turn in seasoned melted butter and chopped fresh parsley.

Laughing Potatoes
(Irish): Simmer 1 hour, steam over hot water further 30 mins. until skins split. (Pressure cooker: 20–30 mins. according to size.) Press round split to emphasize the 'grin', send to table in skins, butter separately.

Steamed in skins	Preparation as before, cook in steamer, colander, plate or inverted pan lid (covered) 1–1½ hrs.	Preparation as before, cook as for old potatoes 45 minutes to 1 hour. Choose even sizes.

Serve as for boiled, skinning or not as preferred, beforehand. A useful method for gas-ring cooks.

Method of cooking	Old Potatoes	New Potatoes
Boiled after peeling	Pare thinly, cut out blemishes. Boil and serve as above.	Rub or gently scrape off skins. Boil and serve as above.
	Olives: Halve or quarter large specimens, pare away edges until shape of large olives. Cold salted water to cover, simmer 12 mins. Or blanch 1 min. and steam about 20 mins. (Pressure cooker: 3–4 mins.) Serve buttered as under New potatoes boiled in skins.	
	Purée or Mashed: Boil in or out of skins as above. Heat 2 tbs. milk, ¾ oz. margarine/ butter. Beat sieved hot potato in this. Season.	Not suitable for mashing.
BUTTER COOKED (neither boiled nor baked)	Dice into ¾-inch cubes turn well in 2 oz. melted, lightly seasoned butter/margarine in thick, covered pan over low heat 30–45 mins.	Use only small sizes. Rub off skins, proceed as under Old potatoes.

Method of cooking	Old Potatoes	New Potatoes
Roast after Peeling	Size *very roughly* 2 ins. diameter. Very large roast potatoes look unappetizing. Parboil 5 mins, in or out of skins. (Pressure cooker: 1 minute.) Drain well. Skin if necessary. Gently shake together in colander, slightly to roughen. Have dripping or lard smoking in tin, turn potatoes in this, roast 35–40 mins turning once. Dish, salting lightly.	Will not roast or bake satisfactorily.

TESTING. Use a narrow-bladed, pointed knife in preference to either fork or skewer, which easily break the potatoes. The blade should meet no more resistance from the centre of the thickest potato in the pot than from a slab of butter. In a pound of new potatoes sizes may be unavoidably mixed between small and very small. In that case test a smaller one after 12–15 min. and, if done, remove, leaving larger to finish cooking.

The skins of baked potatoes come away from the flesh as they cook, and when the skin is thus 'lifted' all round, and the potato, taken up in a cloth in the whole hand (rather than prodded with one finger), 'gives' on gentle pressure, it is done. Always allow plenty of time, giving extra if in any doubt, as there is something specially depressing about half-cooked baked spuds (or apples!).

Puddings

RHUBARB

The first outdoor, home-grown rhubarb is being pulled in respectable quantities by now.

Cut off every scrap of leaf since it is poisonous. Wipe the stalks and trim off the dryish 'wings' at the foot of them. Cut into 2-inch lengths.

The best method of cooking is in a cocotte in a low oven, for this ensures that the rhubarb remains unbroken. If cooked on top, use an asbestos mat, thick pan, low heat. Rub the bottom of the cooking pot with a little butter, put in the rhubarb and scatter over it 3 oz. castor or fine brown sugar for each 1 lb. fruit. Cook about 20 minutes. Stir once round, very gently, with a wooden spoon to mix in sugar that may remain undissolved on top. Strips of lemon or orange peel give a good flavour; clove, cardamom, coriander, mint if liked; later on, best of all, a spray of elder flower.

The stewed rhubarb may be served as it is, hot or cold, with cream, yoghurt, shortbread biscuits (pp. 325–6), ice-cream and so on. Or, of course, in a pie dish instead of a cocotte, covered in pastry in place of a lid (p. 102), for rhubarb pie. Or this stewing may be the first stage for fool, mousse, mould or flan.

RHUBARB FLAN

Thoroughly cool and set the rhubarb so you can lift out the pieces whole to make a neat filling. Slake 1 tsp. arrowroot or cornflour with 1 tbs. juice, boil up rest, add cornflour and cook until it clears. Cool a little. Use a blind-baked flan-case but reserve some paste to make lattice after case is filled. Fill with fruit, spoon over thickened juice to fill almost level. Roll out and cut lattice, damp ends and arrange strips, allowing a little slack for shrinkage, since the case has already done its shrinking. Bake 5 minutes at 425° F, gas 7. Brush very carefully, while hot, with rest of juice, covering lattice and sides.

RHUBARB MOULD
First read gelatine notes on p. 138.

Use rind and juice of 1 orange and rind of ½ lemon to flavour, or orange and elder flower when available. Cook up to 2 lb. rhubarb (to make a 1–2 pint mould) and, in this instance, break up into pieces while hot. To each 1 pint purée allow ½ oz. gelatine. Dissolve it with some of the juice to make mould in usual way.

Blanch 8–12 almonds, cut into slivers, and toast under the grill. Care: they burn very abruptly. Turn out the mould and spike with almonds. Serve with whipped cream – no substitutes – and thin shortbread fingers or ratafias.

TOFFEE FRUIT ROLL

¼ pint fruit purée
grated rind of a lemon,
   orange or grapefruit, or
   1 tbs. marmalade
2 oz. fresh white crumbs (or
   stale cake crumbs)

½ lb. shortcrust or suet
   pastry (i.e. make suet
   crust with all flour instead
   of flour and crumbs)
½ lb. Golden Syrup
1½ gills milk

Roll pastry into an oblong just under ¼ inch thick and about 12 by 7 inches area. Spread with syrup, leaving a 1-inch margin all round. Mix purée with peel and crumbs and spread over syrup. Damp top edge of pastry, roll up and press damped edge to seal. Put into a narrow baking dish or tin, pour the milk round and bake 1½ hours at 350° F, gas 4.

BANANA CHARTREUSE

I really ought not to include this recipe. It may lead you down paths that, perhaps, it would be kinder to leave undiscovered. It is a trouble to do, ice is a must and, while not expensive, it is not one of the cheapest of puddings. It is, however, a delightful period piece so decorative. Belonging to all that is most amusing and fantastic in Victoriana, it is a splendid bit of show-offmanship and, for those rare moments when you have time to indulge your design sense, gives that a little outing. Two mixtures are involved – lemon jelly and banana bavaroise.

First a little bit about the jelly. You can use two packet jellies if you like – either lime or lemon flavour. Or you can make your own lemon jelly.

MAKING JELLY. Perfectly made jelly including aspic is a chef's test-piece, a darling of cookery examiners. It is not set as an item by itself, but merely as part of a dish which is part of a course, which is part of a menu. This very Banana Chartreuse is a favourite example, and you are expected to make it at the double, between thickening sauces, slicing onions, deep-frying fillets, piping canapés *et al*. It takes years, after your finals, before you see anything to like about jelly-making.

Nevertheless real lemon jelly is a gourmet's pleasure. It is as pale, clear and sparkling as good hock to look at, and as fresh to the taste. When you are not being badgered, it is fascinating to make.

To get that perfection of translucence, all equipment must be surgically clean, soap or detergent-free. So one assembles large saucepan, hand whisk and jelly-cloth, and boils them for 5 minutes. Pour off water and leave to cool. Also scald two mixing bowls.

If you have a proper felt jelly-bag, so much the better. If not, a yard square of old and not-too-worn blanket will serve. This may need more than one scalding to clear the water completely. Some instructions advise that an old tea-towel doubled will do but, whenever I have seen this used, cloudy jelly has resulted. The thick density of matted wool fibre makes a second filter, perhaps, to the whites and shells. You can sew your blanket into a deep bag if you like, or simply attach ties to the corners and let the square drop into as deep a 'hammock' as possible, so that liquid goes down through filter. Professionals have special metal stands on which bags hook and in which bowls rest. If you are going to go in for much jelly, aspic and jam making you might like the full outfit. Otherwise invert a chair on the kitchen table and fasten the bag to the legs. Here is what it will look like :

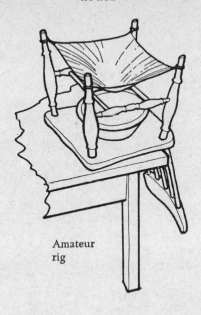

Amateur
rig

LEMON JELLY

1½ pints cold water	1 inch *stick* cinnamon
⅛ pint lemon juice (about 4 lemons)	2 cloves
	1 gill sherry (optional)
thinly pared rind of 2 lemons	1¾ oz. gelatine (2 oz. in warm conditions)*
6 oz. sugar (loaf recommended)	shells and whites of 2 eggs

Put all ingredients except whites, shells and sherry into scalded pan over gentle heat and, without allowing mixture to become hot, stir with whisk until sugar and gelatine are completely dissolved. Withdraw from heat. During this time you will have wiped carefully 2 eggs, separated whites from yolks, crushed the shells and set them aside. Shells and whites are now added to

*For first attempts at Chartreuses the larger quantity of gelatine may make handling easier.

pan, which is returned to a brisk heat, and whisked steadily until boiling point is almost reached. Stop whisking and let the mixture froth up, draw aside and let subside. Repeat this frothing and subsiding twice more. Leave 3 minutes before pouring through jelly-cloth. Scrape all shell fragments and scum from pan into jelly-cloth. This is the filter which clears the jelly. The steady whisking ensures that the whites and shells are broken down small and that they are distributed through the mixture thoroughly to pick up all impurities and particles. It is fascinating to see the grud in the cloth and the clear jelly running from it into the bowl beneath. (And, by the way, do see there is the bowl beneath!) When jelly ceases to run through, but only drips through, carefully remove the first bowl, replacing with a second. Pour liquid jelly through cloth again, adding sherry.

Keep jelly in a warm place until you are ready to use it. Should it set, stand the basin over a pan of simmering water until it dissolves. Avoid all temptation to stir it about during this process. This introduces air which makes bubbles, completely spoiling the clarity of the jelly. For the same reason when filling moulds, do so gently, close to the mould, by spoonfuls if need be, for splashing will also make bubbles.

LINING THE MOULD. The classic shape for Chartreuse is the straight-sided, flat-topped charlotte mould. But any fairly simple 1½-pint mould will do – a pudding basin if necessary, though thick moulds are slow to set and sometimes obstinate to turn out.

Pour ½ inch jelly into bottom of mould, set in refrigerator. Arrange a decoration on this from very thin slivers of almond, angelica, citron, pistachio nut. (Glacé cherry should be avoided in this instance, when the filling is to be a pale yellowy colour. Cherry could be included in decoration for a raspberry mould.) Let the decoration suit the shape of the mould top, and keep it delicate. A thin skewer is a great help in moving and placing the slivers. It will help if you pour a little cool jelly into a spoon and dip each sliver before placing it. When the decoration is complete, chill (but do not set) jelly by the tablespoon on a cube of ice, and carefully cover the decoration. Return to fridge to set thoroughly. Add another ¼ inch of liquid jelly so that decoration is well covered, and set.

Select a basin, a second plain small mould, or a very plain handleless cup or beaker, so long as it is at least an inch smaller in diameter than your main pint mould and, when stood inside, leaves a half-inch margin all round. Put this second mould to chill well in the coldest part of the refrigerator so that, when it is stood on the set jelly it will not melt it and spoil the pattern. Put a small weight in the basin to keep it in place, and fill up round it with cold, almost setting jelly to come to about ¼ inch below the top of the outer mould. Return to refrigerator to set thoroughly. (To divide up the work conveniently, you could get to this point one day and complete the pudding the next.)

BANANA BAVAROISE FILLING. Bavarian creams were a great feature of cold buffets up until the Second World War. They are basically a custard, flavoured well, enriched with cream and set with gelatine. In this instance the custard is replaced by banana purée.

¼ pint banana purée (2 bananas)	1 tbs. water
	1 tsp. castor sugar
¼ pint double cream	1 egg-white
¼ oz. gelatine	

Put the bananas through a Moulin or sieve and beat with sugar until liquid. Whip cream very lightly until it barely holds shape, fold into banana. Melt gelatine in water and add to mixture. Whip white until stiff and fold in. Keep in warm atmosphere until required, to prevent setting.

FINISHING. Take mould from cold, wring out a cloth in very hot water and, removing weight, fill centre mould with cloth until inner mould comes away leaving the outer mould thickly lined with jelly. Very thinly slice 1–2 slightly chilled bananas, completely lining the exposed surfaces of the jelly with them. Do this neatly, overlapping the slices so that inner surfaces of jelly are quite covered. Spoon the bavaroise into the banana-lined cavity and return to cold to set.

Turn out only just before serving, as standing often causes the jelly to split, owing to the weight of the filling bulging slightly against the lighter jelly walls. For this reason use patience and care in turning out. Have the mould in the warm kitchen about

7 to 10 minutes before turning out. This will mean that less direct heat is needed to get it to move, so less risk of melting some jelly from the sides, which makes splitting more likely. Dip the mould in hot water almost to the top, about 5 seconds only for metal, 8 to 10 for china moulds. Invert damped serving dish over top and turn over. Give one hard, but not violent shake and it should move. If not, repeat dipping, but for a shorter time. Or invert mould on damped dish and swathe it in a cloth wrung out in very hot water, leaving a moment or so before shaking. (N.B. The dish is moistened so that mould can be centred, should it turn out off centre.)

Have ready chopped up any spare jelly (to chop use a wetted knife on wetted greaseproof paper), and put it round the Chartreuse. The pattern on top appears to be floating, the banana slices look intriguing in their 'aquarium' and the chopped jelly sparkles brilliantly.

Later in the year you can make wine jelly and use red fruits.

And now down to earth for a final pudding for the month, and a further use of batters (p. 123).

PINEAPPLE FRITTERS

Fresh pineapples are about often quite cheaply in early spring. Cut the pine into rings ½ inch thick, put each slice flat on a board and thinly cut round rind and remove. Cut out hard core in centre. Care: If you make the centre too big, with fresh ripe pineapple, the circle of fruit may break.

Make ½ pint fritter batter for each 8 rings. Dip the rings and fry in deep fat. Cover your hand as frying basket is lowered, for fritter batter sputters. When golden and puffy, drain on kitchen paper and send to table with plenty of castor sugar.

May

For those with limited incomes May can herald a season of mild martyrdom in the kitchen. The shops are piled with tempting but expensive fruits, vegetables and fishes. The lovely long days make the cook resent each moment she is forced to stay indoors at a stove.

My advice is: treat yourself to a few gorgeous summer foods, making them go as far as possible, obviously, and I suggest ways of doing this throughout the book; so recap, as they say, on various subjects. Plan kitchen work ahead, aiming at spending, say, a long half-day twice a week in the kitchen, rather than two or so hours every day, 'mass producing' as far as possible (see pp. 68–9). And why not switch your hot meal to the evening during the summer?

Because many people like to know, I give directions for garnishing and dishing attractively or formally, where necessary. But, if it is a choice of half an hour extra in the sunshine or trimming an already tasty dish, of course choose the sun!

Some recipes for using summer fruit and vegetables and various fishes may sound extravagant to town dwellers who must buy everything they eat. I hope they will bear with these recipes without too much impatience (or envy!) for, as I have mentioned in the introduction, a book of this kind must also cater for those with gardens, or with access to local specialities.

Some years, as every gardener knows, you can have gluts of fruits and other crops to such an extent that you don't know what to do to avoid throwing good food away. But even when yields are merely average, there is enough to allow you to be lavish with fresh fruit puddings, and usually to consider making a little jam later on. The section on preserves on pp. 539ff. is selective rather than exhaustive, but now is not too soon to study recipes. Anyone with a really big kitchen garden will find the

Ministry of Agriculture's *Domestic Preservation of Fruit and Vegetables*, H.M.S.O., 5s. (postage extra), an invaluable guide.

Soups

First read soup notes on p. 112.

LIGHT SPINACH SOUP

1 lb. spinach	½ oz. margarine
1 tsp. minced onion	*Liaison* :
½ pint stock or water	2 yolks
1 pint milk	2 tbs. single cream
grated rind of 1 lemon	seasoning
juice of ½ lemon	

Sweat onion in fat. Wash spinach in 3 changes of water, shake or drain off surplus, add to pan and cook spinach only in what water clings to leaves, for about 12 minutes. Season lightly. Put through coarse plate of Moulin-Légumes, or chop to fine mince. In the latter case squeeze out liquid and add it to stock. Return spinach to pan, add stock and lemon and, lastly milk. Stir well and bring just to simmering point. Pour a little soup on liaison, pour back into pan and heat gently, but on no account boil. Serve hot or chilled.

Note for those unused to dealing with spinach : spinach cooks down dramatically as it contains a large amount of moisture. Start cooking over low heat, adding big handfuls as it cooks down, turning it over, and bruising with a wooden spoon. Once moisture begins to run raise heat. Do not add too much salt before spinach has cooked, but adjust seasoning when it is ready.

OUTSIDE LEAF OF LETTUCE SOUP

½ pint each stock and milk	2–3 good sprigs each mint and parsley, chopped fine
undamaged outer leaves of lettuce weighing anything between 3 and 8 oz.	1 oz. margarine/butter
	1 egg-yolk
1 small onion, minced	2 tbs. top milk
	seasoning

The method is as for preceding recipe, but add chopped herbs with milk, and simmer 3 minutes to cook them. Serve hot or chilled, and garnished with mint leaves.

SHELLFISH BISQUE

First read notes on shellfish on pp. 271–8.

Has there ever been a nation dwelling on a small island so averse to and ignorant about fish as we English? (It makes matters rather worse than better that we evolved the kipper, and that, in recent years, more men fish than watch football.) The Scots and Irish seem more appreciative of fish, perhaps because fishing has figured more prominently as an occupation among them. Welshmen are rich in streams and rivers, and perhaps this has made them more inclined to fish. The English, notoriously, throw back much of the coarse fish they catch on the ground that it is 'muddy'. Even so, throughout the British Isles, fish has never had the attention paid to it that has been paid to meat, and we are rightly called beefeaters. The percentage of the population that has never heard of, let alone tasted fish soup must be in the region of 90. Yet elsewhere fish soups are regarded as a delicacy, often as a looked-forward-to treat – e.g. the clam chowders of New England.

Light, subtle and delicate bisques are among the luxury soups, but this version costs almost nothing for it utilizes parts of fish usually thrown away. Because you can make something so good from the shells, you can afford the extravagance of an occasional shellfish mayonnaise in the summertime, and also will feel less resentful at the time needed to dress crab – the poor man's friend in the shellfish world.

FOR THE STOCK:

1½ pints water
⅛ pint white wine
bayleaf
slice of onion
seasoning (use white peppercorns for preference)
several parsley stalks

about ½ lb. good fish trimmings (e.g. plaice, turbot or sole; your fishmonger will probably give you some free of charge with your other purchases)

Put all ingredients into a pan, bring to the boil and simmer 25 to 35 minutes. Leave to cool. (The stock turns to jelly when cold, and keeps well in a covered bowl in a refrigerator.)

FOR THE BISQUE:

fresh shells from any of the following (including small claws, etc.): 1 crab, 1 lobster, ½ pint prawns
3 oz. margarine/butter
1 oz. flour

¼ pint milk
Liaison:
1 yolk
3 tbs. thin cream
seasoning

The carapace and exo-skeleton of all shellfish are lined with a buttery or oily substance, mostly of the same characteristic bright colour, after cooking, as the external layer of the meat – call it shellfish marrow for want of a better term – and of excellent flavour. By pounding the shells over heat with butter this marrow may be driven out to mingle with the butter and form the basis for soups and sauces.

Break up the shells somewhat, if they are very large and rocky, before beginning to cook them. It is not essential to remove the black, rounded eyes of prawns and shrimps if you dislike the task, but be careful they do not get into the sieved butter as they are hard and will spoil the appearance of your dish. Remove also – and taking care not to pierce your fingers – the sharp small feelers and long sweep-like antennae of prawns and shrimps, as these are dry, and can also be sharp, and they easily get through the mesh of the sieve.

Heat the fat in a heavy pan, add the shells, and stir and pound away at them until the fat is a rich reddish-orange. Turn on to a sieve, scraping out pan, and rub on the sieve to extract as much as possible of the fat and grud. This is a clumping, inelegant process, and you must not expect to get back much over half your quantity. Leave to harden. Leave shell on sieve.

MAKING SHELLFISH BUTTER: Weigh 1 oz. of the hardened butter, melt it in a large pan, add flour to make roux. Add milk and blend to a panada or binding sauce. Heat the fish stock just to boiling point, and pour it slowly through shells left on sieve. This collects a little more of the shellfish essence, also straining the stock at the same time. Pour stock on to roux, stirring smooth and boiling up as usual. Add some of the soup to the liaison, mix, return to pan and heat without boiling, adjusting seasoning.

The bisque should be slightly thinner than most cream soups, and of delicate flavour. Serve hot or chilled. Bath Oliver biscuits are a good accompaniment.

SPRINGTIME BROTH

6 to 8 helpings.

1 pint lamb stock cleared of fat	handful of young peas (or frozen)
1 pint milk	2 small carrots
3 oz. mushrooms (or stalks)	1 oz. each margarine and flour
2 oz. rice	
6 fat spring onions	mint
2 very small beetroots	2 tsp. lemon juice

Cut the cleaned carrot into ¼-inch dice. Put it into the stock or cook gently. Dice and add the beetroot; finely slice and add the mushroom. Add the rinsed rice. In a second pan melt the fat and add the onions cut in thickish rings. Sweat for 3 minutes, turning as necessary. Add flour off heat, then milk, and blend together carefully. Add the peas and simmer 5 minutes. Meanwhile finely chop 3 sprigs mint.

When the rice has been cooking 12 minutes, test it, giving 3 more minutes if needed. Pour contents of one pan into the other and stir until blended. Add the lemon juice and serve with a small teaspoon of chopped mint on each soup-plate. The soup has a pinkish colour and a fresh flavour.

First Courses and Snacks

FISH TARTLETS

A general idea for using up the odds and ends of shellfish; for making something rather special from the lovely fresh fish that children often bring from a day's fishing but that otherwise would be too small for all the family to share; and for making a family dish from such fishmonger's bargains as small lobsters and salmon heads.

4 oz. shortcrust or flaky pastry (pp. 127, 130)	¼ pint mayonnaise or thick salad dressing – preferably
2–3 oz. cold cooked fish, flaked and seasoned	including lemon juice
	1–2 hard-boiled eggs

Thinly line 8 patty-tins with the pastry and bake blind. Fill them ¾ full with mayonnaise. Chop the egg fairly finely and cover the mayonnaise with a layer of this, finishing with fish. If you want to prepare the dish in advance, keep all chopped ingredients in covered basins or cups to prevent drying and put together just before serving.

Stuffed eggs

A standby for single-person establishments if ever there was one. The amounts of flavourings needed are very small. Preparation can be divided up easily to suit circumstances, and can need no more apparatus than a fork, knife, cup and one small saucepan.

Stuffed eggs can form part of a mixed cold hors-d'œuvre, or they can be the focus of a decorative salad platter, or be served alone. They keep and transport well, and are easy to eat in the fingers, making them a perfect picnic item. The fillings can be varied to suit all tastes and there's even enough filling over from, say, six to make a sandwich for next day's luncheon or tea.

If they are served on their own table, hand thin brown bread and butter; for picnics, cut rather thicker slices. For slimmers, accompany them with young crisp lettuce leaves.

Eggs these days seem to take longer to cook than formerly, and I find the standard 10 minutes for hard-boiled eggs seldom enough to cook the yolk completely; 12 to 15 minutes according to size seems surer. Plunge into cold water to prevent overcooking. It is a good idea to roll the eggs about during the first 4 minutes' cooking, as this helps to centralize the yolk, giving an even thickness of white all round. Crack shells well all over, rub between palms to loosen skin, and peel off shells.

AUX FINES HERBES.

6 hard-boiled eggs	1 tsp. each minced chive
1½-2 oz. butter/margarine	and parsley
seasoning	½ tsp, minced fresh tarragon
	pinch of paprika

Halve eggs 'round the equator' (see p. 105). Drop yolks into a small basin. Stand whites on the serving dish. Mash yolks, add butter, and continue until mixture is like whipped cream. Add herbs and seasoning, and mix well. Fill into whites (pipe in if liked), piling up slightly and finishing with a few grains paprika on top. This and the following alternatives are enough for a first course for 6.

Some alternatives:

ANCHOVY. 2 anchovy fillets pounded into yolks and butter. or 1 level tsp. good anchovy paste.

CHEESE. 1 oz. *finely* grated *dry* cheese.

CURRIED. 1 level tsp. curry powder or paste.

HAM. 1 oz. lean ham well pounded, ½ tsp. dry mustard.

SMOKED FISH. 1 oz. kipper, buckling or haddock fillet.

SARDINE. 1½ sardines; 1 tsp. lemon juice; little cayenne pepper.

TUNA. 1 oz. tuna fish; 1 minced black or green olive.

WALNUT PICKLES. 2 pickled walnuts chopped fine; 1 tsp. minced chive.

CHEESE PUDDING

Quickly made and cooked, easy to digest yet nourishing, this is really a simplified soufflé and a useful dish for those first summer afternoons when you want to get out as soon as possible; or for a late supper when you have stayed out as long as possible. A good idea, in the latter case, to make crumbs and grate cheese before leaving the house.

4 oz. fresh crumbs (white
  or brown)
1 pint milk
1 oz. margarine
2 eggs

4 oz. grated cheese
cayenne
½ tsp. dry mustard
seasoning

Soak crumbs and melt margarine in well-seasoned warmed milk while you prepare rest. Light oven and set at 375° F, gas 5.

Grease 1½-pint pie dish or soufflé case. Separate yolks from whites and whisk latter stiff. Mix mustard into cheese, add to crumb mixture with yolks and mix well. Lastly fold in whites. Bake 40 to 45 minutes until risen and browned.

AVOCADO PEARS

About now, in bigger towns and cities, you may find avocados coming down in price, since they should be coming to this country from several sources. They differ from most dessert fruits (which is what they are) as they have a fairly high protein content, while being low in sugar and carbohydrate. This makes them a good food for slimmers. But they are also rich in vitamins A, B, C, D and E, which makes them good for everyone. Finally they are soft and usually eaten with a teaspoon, and this makes them particularly valuable for the elderly, who have problems with the raw foods they really ought to eat.

If you have never tried avocado, you will find its preparation couldn't be simpler. Choose your fruit by holding it in your whole hand, and very gently pressing the whole of it. If ready to eat it will 'give' like a packet of not-too-soft butter. But even if hard, 3 to 4 days in a warm room or airing cupboard will do the trick. Avoid prodding at the top, as many people do with pears. It merely bruises the fruit and tells you nothing. Some avocados have blackish patches when ripe. These are quite harmless and, in fact, taste virtually the same. Some people advise shaking the avocado and listening for the stone to rattle, but some fruits are ripe before, and over-ripe at this stage.

Slide a knife point into the top of the fruit and cut it down the centre until you hit the point of the stone. Let the knife continue halving the fruit all the way round down to the stone. Take the fruit in your hands and twist gently, when it will come apart. Insert the knife point behind the stone remaining in one half, and flip it out. (Plant the stone and grow a pretty indoor plant.) Stand each half in a small plate, hollow uppermost and standing level. Squeeze a little lemon juice in each hollow and run this over the whole surface with a finger tip, to keep the colour. Season well. The centres may be filled with :

(1) Vinaigrette – the best-liked filling of all.

(2) Flaked fish, especially mackerel in mayonnaise or dressing. (Salmon head is good for this.)

Avoid the popular and mistaken predilection for prawns and shrimps in avocados. It is a snob choice merely. The unique nutty blandness of the fruit is drowned by the saltiness of the fish, while the butteriness of the fruit 'absorbs' some of the bite of the fish – a double loss. I also think mashing, heating, or mixing with salad vegetables are all detrimental to avocado.

A good single-person supper dish. The second half may discolour, but will be perfectly sound next day : sprinkle with lemon, enclose in food bag or foil.

Fish

Killing shellfish

A live lobster, for most people, is not *sympathique*. Ink blue-black, with patches of white and merely pinkish intimations of its magnificent hue when cooked, it glides on thin feelers over the sea floor and lurks in its rock lair ready to savage any intruder. It has no appealing ways, is good for nothing but eating and, for those who have to buy theirs, very expensive at that. All that can be said in favour of crab, which isn't even such a fine sight on the dish as lobster, is that it isn't so dear.

Yet I have heard that in one of the marine laboratories they keep a lobster as a pet, as I was once tempted to do. He was promised for supper two days ahead, and was brought in a pail of sea water. Each day this water was tipped into the washing-up bowl for his swim; each night he snoozed in a wet sack in the fridge. He was so strange a companion that, with Fabre, he changed for ever my relations with the natural world. Man, says The Good Book (conveniently written, edited and translated by Man), has dominion over the beasts, but long before he taught himself how to draw out Leviathan with an hook, man had given sufficient evidence of power without responsibility, and we deserve to be apprehensive as the researchers translate the language and account for the laughter of dolphins. It will serve man right if one day he finds nothing left to subject to his nasty sovereignty.

SHELLFISH LORE. My lobster was caught by a fisherman friend who set his pots off the Sussex coast. How accurate was his fascinating crustacean lore I cannot say, but understanding something of their structure and habits helps the kitchen work. The larger shellfish, he said, can live a long time, and he claimed to have caught specimens over 20 years old. Every so often crustacea cast their shells – their external skeletons – to allow for growth. Therefore never buy a soft-shelled specimen, since its whole organization is occupied with the formation of a new shell, and the meat will be scanty and of poor quality. Good and sensible fishermen throw such specimens back, hoping to catch them when they've become a better bargain. Crustacea are fitted with 'radar', small feathery antennae in the head, and the long-shaped shellfish have the familiar sweeps, as long as their bodies, for detecting when there's a porpoise close behind them. Each differently constructed, left and right claws are used variously for holding, crushing and cutting. The 'tail', small and almost all shell in crabs, but containing the best meat in other crustacea, is jointed and armoured like the rest of the carapace, makes for strong propulsion in swimming, and turns under to help protect the softer belly. The long types of shellfish have a form of spinal cord, and all have the boot-button, horny, pivoting eyes. If you are an evolutionist you relate prawn and lobster to garden woodlouse, crab to spider.

WHAT NOT TO DO. Shellfish indeed lack the winsomeness that charms sentimentalists. Were a cookery book to appear in which the recipes for, say, duck began with the instruction:

'Bring a large pan of water to the boil and throw in the live bird'
what an outcry would follow! Yet this preamble is a commonplace of shellfish recipes.

If you wade among pools left on the sand by an outgoing tide
you may see small crabs scuttle away leaving a claw behind.
Naturalists suppose this a sign of fear, the creatures hoping to
confuse an enemy by the stratagem. It is also a sign of pain,
which is usually caused by an enemy. Hence, when flung into
boiling water, shellfish often throw claws. Further, as the heat
strikes through the shell, the poor creatures struggle to get out of
the pot until extinct – a full minute at least. Also you may hear
the horrible noise of air in the shell being driven suddenly out,
said to sound like screaming. In the last few years efforts to stop
the barbarity – the result of ignorance rather than indifference
– have been intensified by the Universities Federation for Animal
Welfare, who have publicized a method of cooking shellfish discovered to be painless at least thirty years ago, but largely ig-
nored. Cookery writers and gourmets must take some of the
blame for this since some of them still give currency to the legend
that boiling alive produces better flavour. I should like to attend
the taste-test where some expert picked out the dishes made with
shellfish subjected to this drawn-out agony, from those made with
fish cooked in the approved way, which is described below.

THE RIGHT METHODS. Don't cook live crustacea until the
last possible moment. Like all fishes moisture is vital to them.
They will keep very well for up to two days in the refrigerator
between thick layers of sacking soaked in mild brine or sea water.
The time limit is absolute, however, for after that they begin
to live off stored nourishment and will lose both flavour and
meatiness.

There are two ways of killing lobster, so if you are lucky
enough to have a source of reasonably priced lobsters, choose
the method most suited to your dish. Crabs may also be killed
in both ways, but the first way is easier with them, the second
needing experience and anatomical knowledge.

(1) This is the method recommended by U.F.A.W. and for
most dishes is all the cooking required. Put the crustacean into

a pan of cold salted water well covering it. Stand the pan on an asbestos mat over very low heat. The water must take at least 4 minutes to reach 70° F. At this temperature the creature 'faints', and when the water reaches about 75° F it stifles, dying long before the water reaches a temperature to cause it the least discomfort. There are no signs of distress, the flavour is excellent, and there is an abundance of the curd-like substance which, a sign of health, makes the texture of shellfish so good when mixed into the rest. When the water has come to boiling point simmer for 20–30 minutes according to size.

(2) A swift and sure way of killing lobster, and better for dishes like Thermidor, where cooking should preferably be by frying the raw lobster meat in butter (rather than reheating meat that has already been cooked by boiling), is to pierce the spinal cord. In the centre of the main section of carapace will be seen a whitish indented cross. Holding a cloth over the back and tail to counteract the reflex jump, drive the point of a knife or skewer through the centre of the cross. Split the fish in half lengthways for cooking, frying first the cut side, then the shell side in hot butter until the shell becomes the typical brilliant red.

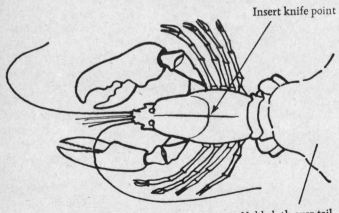

Insert knife point

Hold cloth over tail

In dealing with crustacea you must often pick them up. Should the claws not be pinioned, you will come to no harm provided you hold them across their backs, as in the sketch. A very fresh lobster, pinioned or not, may give a sudden strong thresh of the tail, so be ready for this and keep your hold, for dropping it may damage the shell and hurt the creature. Crabs' tails are less powerful, but the sudden movement is startling.

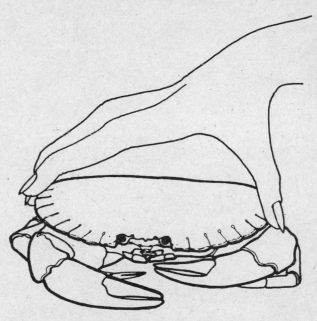

Hold shellfish over the back – they cannot lift their claws upward

Once cooked, shellfish become highly perishable and should be eaten the same day. Treat with great caution advice from a fishmonger that you can keep his cooked shellfish overnight, even in a refrigerator. This is advisable only when you are sure the fish has been freshly cooked. Never buy shellfish from any but the most reputable shops.

DRESSED CRAB I

The full method, for special occasions. A crab 2½–3 lb. in weight will serve 4. Pick up one or two from the fishmonger's slab, and choose the heaviest for its size. Despite the labour involved, prefer 2 medium-sized crabs to one huge one for larger numbers of diners.

1 hard-boiled egg	made English mustard
lettuce to garnish	½ cucumber
2 oz. margarine/butter	1 level tbs. fresh crumbs
parsley	(brown or white bread, and
seasoning	less if preferred)
¼ pint mayonnaise	anchovy paste to taste (optional)

Work all the time with a cloth to protect hands

(1) Open cooked cold crab by using thumbs to prize out round body section from underside. Fishmonger will do this if asked.

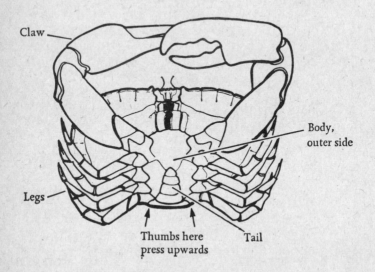

Claw

Body, outer side

Legs

Thumbs here press upwards

Tail

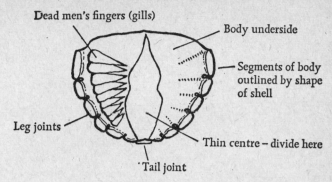

Dead men's fingers (gills)

Body underside

Segments of body outlined by shape of shell

Leg joints

Thin centre – divide here

Tail joint

(2) Have ready : 2 basins or plates for meat, dark meat from shell, white meat from rest, copy of *The Times* for refuse, tea-spoon. Twist off claws, legs and tail as close as possible, if possible including last joint (shown in diagram, still attached to body). Set aside the main shell, covered, in cool place while working on body – the longest job; and claws – the toughest.

Remove and discard beige spongy gills lying flat against inner side of body shell. These are not poisonous, but you might as well chew the dishmop. You will then see that the body shell has undulations corresponding to the position of the claws and legs. These lead towards the thin, dipped centre of the body section. With a heavy knife split down this thin line to cut body in half. You now have two semi-circles, thicker at their circumference than their centre. Each semi-circle is divided inside by thin shell partitions into four segments (very roughly !).

Body divided in half. Thin shell walls approximately as shown

Split through the semi-circle horizontally, when you can scoop out meat from between partitions with the spoon handle. A proper fiddlin' little job, as the Cornish child said of the creation of the house-fly. But the greater part of the best 'white' meat lies herein. Fishmongers haven't time to pick the body section, which is why you get less for your money when a shop dresses crab.

(3) To crack claws, fold double newspaper over them and whack with hammer or other heavy object (scale weight is ideal). Controlled violence wins the day, for overmuch zeal results in a shattered mass of shell and meat. Fishmongers will always do claws for you, when you may merely need to help on the work with nutcrackers, or an extra tap or two.

Each joint contains good white meat. (Small legs and tail contain a little, but it is better to use these for decoration the first day, keeping in refrigerator overnight and using for snacks next day; but see notes pp. 266–7, 275). You should also scrape the pinkish curd from the inside of the shell fragments; it is moist and tasty, adding greatly to the texture of the dryish white meat.

N.B. *This pink curd, present in all crustacea, dries up quickly, and its absence denotes staleness in cooked shellfish.* Its presence in abundance indicates not only freshness but quality. Note also that the pointed, extreme ends of claw meat should be quite jelly-like and drip with moisture in freshly cooked crustacea. Dried clawmeat means a very stale specimen which you would

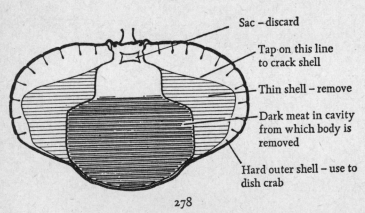

Sac – discard

Tap on this line to crack shell

Thin shell – remove

Dark meat in cavity from which body is removed

Hard outer shell – use to dish crab

be unwise to eat. If you cannot return it at once, to prove your point, telephone at once with a complaint, so that you can at least return next day and claim your money.

(4) Remove and discard the small greenish-brown sac below the head, and the antennae attached to the head. Spoon out the soft, darkish, greeny meat from the main shell. Tap sharply round the line you can see which follows the shape of the shell, indicated by the thin lines in the diagram. This line divides slightly thinner from thicker area of shell. The former will break off neatly, leaving you with a natural crabshell dish on which to arrange the meats. Well scrape all meat from shell. Scrub it under running cold tap, likewise small legs to be used for garnishing.

(5) Mix dark main-shell meat with crumbs, season well, and fill into centre of shell in broad raised band. Blend 1 level tsp. mustard with 3 tbs. mayonnaise, and mix white meat well with this. Fill into shell at either side of dark meat. Cream butter with seasoning, anchovy paste, or coral of crab should any be present. Pipe round edge of shell. Finely chop white, sieve yolk of egg, and arrange in bands where dark and white meat join. Lastly sprinkle a thick line of chopped parsley down centre of dark meat.

Set crab on bed of shredded lettuce (p. 246).

Make a cucumber salad (pp. 154 and 231); cut thin brown bread and butter to accompany. Good potato or green salad may also be served, but anything else spoils the flavours.

DRESSED CRAB II

A less elaborate version. Prepare exactly as above, but omit piping butter, and chopped garnishes. Use Thick Dressing (p. 250) in place of mayonnaise, and decorate the dish with egg slices or quarters.

ALFRED EARNSHAW SMITH'S DRESSING FOR CRAB

This may have been a familiar East Anglian accompaniment for crab in the past, since my husband's family comes from

Cambridge. Splendidly simple on its own with brown bread and butter; for more substance, add cucumber and potato salads.

Prepare and dish meat in shell, omitting all garnishes. Send to table with freshly made mustard and good mild vinegar (avoid brown malt vinegar), and brown bread and butter.

Each person mixes to his taste, as often as he needs it, a little mustard and vinegar at the side of his plate, taking it with the crab as horseradish with beef, or mixing crab into sauce.

NOTE: Mustard greatly enhances the flavour of crab, and should always be used in crab sandwiches.

Spider crabs

These look as their name suggests, and they are large with rocky shells. They do great damage to inshore fishing, but as a notion persists that they are poisonous most fishermen kill those they catch and throw them back, although sometimes keeping the claws for eating. In fact, much tinned crabmeat is from spider crabs, which are excellent eating, so if you get the chance of one take it. Anatomically, preparation is the same as for ordinary crabs. Fishermen often smash the shell hoping this will kill them, so cook as soon as possible.

Lobsters

These have almost no 'body' meat, and what there is is not worth the trouble of extracting. The greatest amount of meat is found in tail and claws. Split the fish in half lenghways, lift out and slice the tail meat in thick chunks, which may then be replaced in the shell for serving. The green meat is found in the 'head' section of shell. Stomach, dead man's fingers (in corresponding positions to crab) and string-like spinal cord, running down tail, are discarded. A respectable sandwich may be filled from the feeler claws of larger specimens, if these are picked clean. Wrap in foil or polythene in the refrigerator for keeping overnight, as they dry out quickly – but see note on pp. 267–8.

PLAICE DUGLÈRE

For a main course of fish.

1 plaice about 2 lb. in weight (filleted)	chopped
	7½ fl. oz. milk
2 tomatoes concassed	5 tbs. white wine or juice
½ small onion minced	½ lemon
3 sprigs parsley finely	seasoning

Fold fillets in three (and see p. 90) points under, broadest third uppermost. Avoid small, ready-done fishmonger's fillets. They will not be skinned, will probably be double-filleted, and when you have skinned them will be revealed as too small and insubstantial. Oven-poach with wine, etc. as in the Sole recipe on p. 187. Serve with new potatoes.

COLD FRIED PLAICE

Few people seem to know this excellent method of frying fish to be eaten cold, when it is, if anything, superior in flavour. Coated fried foods make very pleasant alternatives to the more usual picnic fare, and are useful for summer suppers. My mother used always to make a large batch of 'cold' fish of several kinds, all filleted: plaice, sole, turbot, haddock. As it keeps very well stored in the cold, it was then ready, over about three days, for beach and country expeditions, unflustered luncheons and late suppers.

Plaice fries better than it poaches to my mind, so it makes a good choice. Large fillets for preference. Oil for the frying is essential, and be generous with egg.

Very well coat the fillets first in seasoned flour, then in beaten egg. Deep fry until golden. Drain on cake rack under which you have put two layers of absorbent paper.

Serve with green salad, hard-boiled egg halves, dill-pickled cucumbers or gherkins, tarragon mayonnaise, tartare sauce, potato salad, beetroot in vinaigrette, etc., according to your fancy. Lemon wedges are essential, however, whatever else is served, unless you are serving some Indian Lime Pickle as on p. 154, which goes very well indeed.

Two Victorian Fish Sauces for Summer

GOOSEBERRY SAUCE

Traditionally served with mackerel; good also with herrings, halibut and skate.

½ lb. green gooseberries
1 oz. butter
½ oz. flour
1 level tsp. minced onion

grated rind ½ orange
1 tsp. sugar
pinch ginger

Cook gooseberries without water as for apples on p. 172 (about 20 to 30 minutes). Put through Moulin, or into electric blender, adding sugar while still hot. Meanwhile fry onion in butter until golden, blend in flour, add gooseberry purée, orange rind and ginger, stir over gentle heat for few minutes to cook flour. Serve hot or cold.

CUCUMBER SAUCE

½ cucumber
1 oz. margarine
½ pint Béchamel sauce or
  white sauce made from
  milk and fish stock

1 tsp. lemon juice
1 tsp. chopped parsley or
  (better) parsley and
  tarragon
1 tsp. minced onion

Peel and cut the cucumber in halves lengthways. Discard the centre containing seeds. Cut into inch lengths and soften with onion in margarine until tender, over very gentle heat. Press through bowl strainer. Add Béchamel, mixing smoothly over low heat. When simmering add lemon juice and herbs. Dish in sauceboat hot or chilled.

If no white sauce is to hand, scatter 1 oz. flour into the vegetable, add ½ pint mixed stock and milk and proceed as usual, seasoning well, sieving at the end.

Meat

RABBIT AND BACON — A BRAISE

Trouble-free for the cook, starch-free for slimmers, light on the purse provided you avoid hutch rabbit. Avoid also very dark, imported rabbit which is better for more highly seasoned dishes.

RABBIT. Use approximately half the quantity of bacon to rabbit by weight. Therefore buy your rabbit first, and note the weight. Rabbit leg portions are very meaty; the saddle is considered choice. Most shops insist on your buying a mixture of frozen rabbit pieces. For big appetites, allow, say, a leg each, or 1 each shoulder and saddle portions. A single portion of saddle for a younger child will usually be enough.

BACON. Best for this is green (i.e. unsmoked) streaky. It must be in the piece. Rashers are no good in this instance. A second choice would be smoked streaky; third choice, pickled pork, which is the same cut (belly of pork in fresh meat). Remove the bones. They run in just the same way as the bones in breast of lamb, p. 82.

A very cheap dish will result from using a flank joint of bacon. The flank lies between the streaky and the gammon. It is very fat at the streaky end, but often carries an excellent cushion of gammon-like lean at its gammon end. Fat is necessary to all rabbit dishes as rabbit is very dry; to this dish it is essential. In addition, the rind of the bacon helps to make the gravy. Unless you are catering for about six, you will not need all your flank joint, so cut away some of the fat (render down for frying). If there is a large piece of lean, you may like to cut yourself a gammon steak from that end for next day's luncheon or supper.

ONION. About 1 lb. onion for a dish for 4. Try for big bulbs, which look more attractive and save work.

SEASONING. Ground white pepper only.

Choose a close, deep cocotte or saucepan to cause the limited amount of liquid produced to come up well round the meat. Starting and ending with ¼-inch-thick slices of bacon, fill the pot with alternate layers of bacon, rabbit, and onion sliced in rounds, peppering lightly between each few layers. Cook in a slow oven, 300° F, gas 2, for 1 hour; or on top of stove on asbestos mat, and with foil or greaseproof under the saucepan lid, on a very low heat. After first hour, when liquid has begun to form in the pot, lower heat and continue cooking 2½ to 3 hours. About half-way through it is a good idea to lift out the layers and put the top layer to the bottom.

Taste the liquid. If very salt (as is sometimes unavoidable where choice of bacon is restricted) pour off into measure, and add an equal quantity of boiling water, returning to pot for 10 to 15 minutes.

Serve with new potatoes, spring cabbage or cauliflower.

Only the most virulent fat-haters object to the bacon fat in this dish. Most of the fattiness seems to be blotted up by the rabbit, while the flavour is chicken-like and quite delicious, with the light, yet rich liquor.

2–3 joints rabbit, 4–6 oz. bacon will make 2 meals for single person. If very low heat is possible, the dish may be left cooking all day.

Parsley sauce goes well with it, alone or used to mask cauliflower or, in season, broad beans.

COLD RABBIT PIE. A lovely cold pie results from boning the rabbit joints before they are cool, and rearranging the layers in a pie dish. Have ready short or flaky pastry, and the oven heated to 375–400° F, gas 5–6. Cover the dish and glaze with egg (p. 106), bake 25 to 30 minutes until the crust is a nice colour. Leave overnight, when the liquor will have set to strong clear jelly.

Minced beef

Cheap, versatile and nutritionally excellent, good minced beef is a bargain when offered by a reliable family butcher. Classic mince dishes include rissoles (usually made from joint left-overs), hamburgers (U.S.), dolmas (Middle East), meat balls (Scandinavia) and meat loaves, galantines and meat rolls of many sorts. The following are a selection. Most are good for small households.

HAMBURGERS

½ lb. raw minced beef
salt and black pepper (freshly
  ground)

butter
fried onion rings

Well season the meat with salt and black pepper. Shape it into 4
flat cakes. Grill 2 minutes each side under preheated grill. Spread
butter on each steak, garnish with onion rings. Serve at once.
The meat should be brown outside, pink inside.

ACCOMPANIMENTS: New or mashed potatoes; salad; Dijon
mustard.

DOLMAS

½ lb. raw minced beef
1 clove garlic, minced
pinch fresh thyme or little
  grated lemon rind

salt, black pepper
2 tbs. uncooked rice
a few good cabbage leaves
tomato sauce (p. 149) or juice

Mix meat, garlic, rice, flavourings. Blanch cabbage leaves. Remove centre rib of leaves, halve big leaves. Put 1 tbs. meat mixture on each leaf, and fold up like a parcel. Pack closely in a small
oven dish or thick pan, cook in tomato sauce or juice, barely to
cover, in low heat 1 to 1½ hours. Can be done on top of stove.

BEEF FRICADELLAS (or RUSSIAN TIFTCHI)

½ lb. raw minced beef
4 tbs. yoghurt
garlic salt, or Lawry's
  Seasoned Salt; or crush 1
  clove garlic and a selection
  of pinches of herbs with
  salt, and soak 10 to 15
  minutes in the yoghurt,
  afterwards straining it

¼ pint vinaigrette made with
  ½ lemon juice/½ vinegar
crumb from 1 stale white
  roll, or thick slice bread, soaked
  in water
black pepper
dried crumbs
oil for frying or butter for
  grilling

Mix mince, bread, yoghurt, black pepper and salt as for Sausage

285

Fricadellas, p. 191. Form mix into 'marbles' and leave to marinate in the vinaigrette 1 hour or longer, turning once or twice. Drain, roll in crumbs and fry or grill. Serve with peas.

STEAKLETS

½ lb. raw minced beef
1 chicken liver, or 2 oz.
   other liver

½ oz. dried breadcrumbs
2 tbs. tomato ketchup or juice

Chop or mince liver, mix all ingredients, form into flat cakes and grill or fry 2 minutes each side. Serve in unsweetened 'bun rolls', with onion rings and sweet mustard pickle, or with fried potatoes of any kind. Crisps are useful here.

MEAT BALLS

¾ lb. raw minced beef
1 egg
1 small onion
fat for frying, including at
   least 1 oz. butter
¼ lb. minced fat pork (e.g.
   belly) or sausage meat

1½ slices stale white bread
1 boiled mashed potato
½ pint water
1½ tsp. salt
¼ tsp. white pepper
1 level dessertsp. made mustard

GRAVY

1½ oz. margarine
2 oz. flour

1 pint stock
seasoning to taste

Soften bread in water. Brown onion. Mix all ingredients in large bowl and knead by hand until smooth and spongy. Divide into 8 portions and roll in palms of hand to form balls. Heat fat and fry quickly till well browned, moving round at first to harden outside to a good round shape. Put into a saucepan. Heat margarine for gravy in the frying-pan, add flour and stir until flour is just turning colour. Add stock gradually, whisking and stirring with fork to avoid lumps. Add to meat balls and simmer 1 hour. Add a few thinly sliced mushrooms to gravy for variety.

MEAT LOAF

¾ lb. raw minced beef
1 tsp. garlic salt or other
   seasoned salt, or ordinary
   salt crushed into garlic and
   herbs
1 beaten egg

5 tbs. tomato juice or
1 rounded tsp. tomato purée,
   thinned with water to make
   5 tbs.
3 rounded tbs. porridge oats

Mix all well. Pack into small loaf-tin and bake at 350° F, gas 4, for 45 minutes. Rest 5 to 10 minutes to 'set' before slicing. Serve hot with good gravy, peas, sweet corn, rice, mashed potato flavoured with chives and parsley, etc. Serve cold with salads.

SUSAN POTTER'S SPANISH EGGS

The name is my own. The real name, like the exact recipe, I stupidly failed to get from the clever young cook who made the dish for me. She learned it on holiday in Spain, and, for all I know, her version was already an adaptation. It is an incredibly messy recipe to handle, and you must simply giggle your way through, sustained by knowing that it is most delicious and unusual to eat.

FILLING (or yolk of the 'eggs')

½ lb. raw minced beef
1 tsp. tomato purée
pinch each of nutmeg, ginger,
   allspice
seasoning

small onion, minced
1 level tsp. dried, or rounded tsp.
   fresh marjoram
1 oz. bacon dripping or margarine

COATING (or white)

3 oz. long-grain rice
1 small egg
1 tbs. flour
seasoning

saffron : if strand saffron, soak
   a pinch for 3 to 4 hours in
   water barely to cover, or overnight; if packeted, 1 tiny packet

(1) Soften onion in dripping. Mix rest of filling ingredients

and add onion. If the meat compacts to a lump loosen with fork. Leave for flavours to mature, covered, in cool place.

(2) Cook rice, drain and mix with beaten egg. Scatter in flour and mix well. Flour and egg must form thick batter to help hold coating and cook to even colour. Add saffron (including water). Season.

(3) Put on deep-fat bath to heat. Oil is best for this dish. Form meat mixture into balls in floured hands. Coat with rice mixture only at the minute you are ready to cook, for it easily tumbles off. Flouring meat ball and hands helps somewhat, but you must keep spoon to hand to scrape your hands as necessary.

(4) Put two 'eggs' at a time into frying basket, lower carefully into fat, hand covered, to avoid spluttering. Fry till golden. Loosen from bottom of basket carefully, to turn once. Drain on absorbent paper. Serve hot with peas, young carrots, hot baby beets, or green salad. A cream gravy (p. 192) or tartare sauce is excellent.

Breast of lamb

Let me say at once that I find breast of lamb the least sympathetic cut of any meat I know. However, such is its ridiculously low cost, those of modest means cannot afford to neglect it. Nutritionally, of course, it is as good as the better cuts, so let no one worry on that score. But it is dreadfully fatty, it is laced with bones and (worst, as far as I am concerned) each layer of lean is enclosed by a membrane, one of which is quite thick and rubbery, runs the length of the joint and is removed only by picking the whole thing to pieces.

From this it may be guessed that breast of lamb needs careful preparation for most recipes. It also needs, in my opinion, far longer cooking than is recommended in most recipes.

Many butchers reckon breast of lamb a cold meat cut, and I have included suitable recipes. Some butchers, who have a call for it, sell breast ready boned, stuffed and rolled – a good and trouble-free bargain, making a useful mid-week roast or braise for a family, a weekend 'joint' for the single-person household.

The usual time given for breast of lamb plus stuffing is 40 to 45 minutes per lb. at 350° F, gas 4. For my taste this is not enough, and I ignore the weight, giving *any* roast breast 1½ hours at 325° F, gas 3, but allowing for additional time if the fat is not crisp, or if a skewer will not push completely through the joint and leave it again easily.

Methods other than roasting are also given.

Boning of breast is shown on pp. 83–4.

WARNING: Many supermarkets sell packets of lamb breasts which have been chopped along their length between the riblets. They will be useless for the recipes given here using whole breasts, but may be of very slight help for those cut up and fried. Some butchers cut the thin flap off breasts. Avoid these. They will not make enough to eat and are difficult to roll up.

ROLLED AND STUFFED ROASTS, OR BAKED JOINTS

Preparation is the same: bone, remove excess fat, outer skin and any other membranes you can get at. Spread the stuffing, not too thickly, down the centre, and roll from thick to 'flap' end as tightly as possible, skewering and tying as in diagram. Make spare stuffing into boulettes with floured hands, or into a sort of croûte on which to stand the joint during roasting. Add boulettes about ½ hour before the end.

Despite all the fat in the joint, it is much improved by a basting or two during cooking. However, if more than a covering of fat over the bottom of the roasting tin runs from the meat, pour off excess.

Add bones to roasting tin – and if possible start them before the meat – and cook them a good colour, making stock for gravy from them. Most of these recipes call for plenty of good gravy, in this instance thickened with nicely browned flour. Plainly boiled small potatoes are the best accompaniment where no others are given.

ENGLISH THYME AND LEMON STUFFING

2 rounded tbs. fresh white crumbs
1 small egg
1 rounded tsp. fresh, or level tsp. dried, thyme

grated rind of 1 lemon
1 tsp. minced onion, chives or middle part of spring onion
1 oz. margarine
seasoning

Melt the fat, soften the onion (but not chives). Stir in crumbs. Add well-beaten egg, lemon rind, thyme and seasoning.

Peas, broad beans, carrots or cauliflower to accompany.

A little lemon juice added to the gravy is specially good.

SPANISH STUFFING

crumbs, egg, onion, fat as above, plus:
1½ oz. shelled chopped walnuts

generous pinch rosemary, black pepper, salt

Tiny glazed onions, button mushrooms and whole baked tomatoes to accompany. Or cold with salads, including Sweet and Sour Tomato Sauce (p. 231).

MINT AND MUSHROOM STUFFING

Crumbs, egg, onion fat, seasoning as for English Thyme and Lemon Stuffing (above) plus: 3 oz. mushroom stalks minced and sweated 15 minutes in fat. Add rest of ingredients and 1 tbs. chopped mint.

Peas, young carrots or turnips to accompany. Or cold with salads, including a Potato Salad.

The above stuffings may also be used for two lamb breasts prepared as the following recipe, which serves 6 to 8.

BREAST OF LAMB SANDWICH

Ingredients as for English Thyme and Lemon Stuffing, except use half the quantity of crumbs, and knead all into 2 oz. good beef or pork sausage meat.

Bone, de-fat and skin the two breasts. Season them lightly on the boned side. Put one, boned side uppermost, in tin. Spread thickly with stuffing, lay second one on top, boned side to stuffing, just securing at ends and in middle with string to prevent curling. Roast very well (see pp. 288–9).

ACCOMPANIMENTS: Tomato Charlotte (pp. 242–3), ratatouille (pp. 403–4), braised onions, spinach, or anything in season that has a little sharpness. Some tomato juice used in place of some stock in the gravy is good. Excellent cold with salads.

NOTE: All the foregoing and most of the following may, with advantage, be baked in covered roasters or foil-covered baking tins, or in thick pans on asbestos mats on top of the stove (pot-roast). Moreover, they may be cooked for some hours in this way, at the lowest oven settings, or on very low top heat. The latter method will produce a slightly stewed underside (unless the joint is raised on a grid, etc.). On the other hand, this may be a minor price to pay for being able to come home to a hot roast meal ready and waiting. Root vegetables may be put in the pot below or round the meat.

NON-STUFFED BRAISES AND STEWS

The breast is boned or not, browned in fat and cooked in a cocotte or saucepan with generous amounts of accompaniments or flavourings.

ESPAGNOLE. Cut in broad strips between the riblet bones, through the breastbone. Brown in hot fat, set on mirepoix of thick onion and carrot rings, also browned, light stock just to cover vegetables, and mixture of :

3 oz. quartered mushrooms	½ pimento sliced very thinly
4 whole small tomatoes	6 olives stoned
minced clove garlic	salt, black pepper

Rice instead of potatoes to accompany.

BONNE FEMME. Preparation as above, including browning also 12 tiny onions and inch cubes of fat bacon (streaky or collar in the piece).

ACCOMPANIMENTS: peas, broad beans, new potatoes.

BOULANGÈRE. As foregoing, but ½-inch potato dice are added to pot, and some butter is added to give the characteristic Boulangère taste, especially to the potatoes.

CURRY. Stew the breast or breasts in really well-flavoured stock with some lemon juice included, about 2½ hours until it is easily boned and thoroughly skinned. Use only the lean, cut into longish squares. Curry as usual (p. 152ff.).

FRIED DISHES

The procedure is similar for all the following. The meat is pre-stewed, boned and cut in pieces, then coated and shallow-fried or grilled, and served with sauces, etc. The coated portions will also grill successfully if a little melted margarine is run over them beforehand.

FLORENTINE. Stew, bone and cool under weighted board. (Stewing should be in salted, flavoured water as usual). Cut in portions, coat with egg and crumbs to which 1 dessertsp. grated very dry cheese has been added. Fry in butter and dish on a bed of spinach.

ACCOMPANIMENTS: New or sauté potatoes; tomato sauce or tomato-flavoured gravy.

MADÈRE. Stew, bone etc. as above, adding grated rind of orange instead of cheese to coating crumbs. Serve on bed of mashed potatoes, surrounded by butter-fried small onions and mushrooms, adding ½ gill sherry or madeira, 1 tbs. orange juice to gravy.

NAPOLITANA. Fried as above, served on dish of spaghetti in good tomato sauce.

SOUBISE. Fried as above, dished in border of mashed potato (for entertaining, piped, brown Pommes Duchesse, pp. 194–5), the centre of which has been filled with peas, accompanied by onion sauce (p. 118).

Vegetables

SPINACH

Always wash spinach in three changes of water: for some reason the last vestiges of grit will not depart in under three. Boil it

down in no more water than clings to its leaves, salting to taste.
Press very well in colander, or squeeze in the hand. You could
never get all the moisture out of spinach unless you dehydrate
it to a point of unpleasantness. A reasonable test is to relax pressure and chop it slightly. If it is still slushy, press again; otherwise
it will be dry enough.

The ways of finishing are mainly varied by whether you sieve,
chop or leave it whole. The first is called *purée*, the second and
third *en branche*.

PURÉE. Add any or some of the following to each 1½ lb. sieved
spinach : 1–1½ oz. margarine or butter; 1 dessertsp. minced onion
sweated in the fat; salt, pepper, nutmeg, ginger (and for those
who find spinach bitter 1 rounded tsp. sugar quite wins them
over); 1–2 tbs. milk, cream or substitutes; 2–3 yolks.

The egg-yolks, plus *beurre manié* or a panada, enable you to
turn the purée into greased castle-pudding moulds, or a loaf-tin,
and cook *au bain-marie* to make spinach timbales or loaf. Good
with a little grated cheese on top, tomato sauce round, Mornay
sauce mixed in, to make luncheon dish with poached eggs, bacon
joint, etc.

EN BRANCHE. Add any or some of the following to each 1½ lb.
chopped or whole-leaf spinach : 1–1½ oz. butter/margarine;
1 dessertsp. minced onion sweated in the fat; seasoning and
spices; 1–2 tbs. milk, cream or substitutes.

NAVETS PRINTANIÈRE

1 lb. new small turnips	¼ pint coating Béchamel
1 tsp. each chopped chive and	sauce (see p. 117; use scant
parsley	½ oz. flour, generous
lemon juice	¼ pint milk, so sauce is on
¼ oz. butter	the thin side)

Thickly pare and boil the turnips whole in salted water just to
cover, to which a squeeze of lemon juice has been added, for
20–25 minutes (10 to 15 minutes in pressure cooker). When
tender turn in melted butter. Add chopped herbs to hot sauce.
Set turnips in dish, pour sauce round them.

GLAZED ONIONS

1 lb. onions about the size of golf balls	1 tsp. sugar
	1 oz. butter/margarine
seasoning	chopped parsley

Blanch onions 1 minute, put into fresh salted water, bring to boiling point and simmer about ¾ hour or until a thin skewer will easily pass through from side to side. Drain well, reserving water for stock, but putting 1 tbs. into a frying-pan with the sugar. When sugar has dissolved add fat and melt. Add onions, season and cook on medium heat, turning carefully to brown all round in the caramelizing sugar. Pour glaze over onions in serving dish, and decorate with parsley.

POTATOES

New potatoes are at last really down in price, and there is no better way to serve them than as they are with plenty of butter.

Puddings

The sight of gooseberries in front of the greengrocer's shop quite consoles me for being unable (as I am certainly unwilling) to pay for early English strawberries. It is true I must wait for July for those best-of-all giant, yellow, squashy, dessert goosegogs that rank among the aristocrats of fruits, but green gooseberries make some of the best dishes the English have contributed to the table.

GOOSEBERRY SUET PUDDING

Awful if badly made, a triumph if well made, fruit-filled suet puddings are an English speciality. The method of work is exactly the same as that for the savoury puddings (see Steak and

Kidney Pudding, p. 431), and the same proportions of suet, crumbs, flour, baking powder and water are used. But add 1 tbs. castor sugar to the suet mixture with the dry ingredients, omit pepper, and cut the salt to a pinch. 1 tsp. ginger and/or grated rind ½ lemon may also be incorporated if liked. An 8 oz. quantity of crust will line a 1½-pint pudding basin, and 1 lb. gooseberries will fill it well, as they must, since the fruit shrinks on cooking, its juice being partly blotted up by the crust.

Top and tail the gooseberries and add 3–4 oz. sugar to the fruit, in layers as you fill the basin. Add an elder flower when possible.

Tie down as for Steak and Kidney, steam for 1 to 1½ hours – longer does no harm. As it is easier, for serving, to turn the pudding out, remember to grease the basin well. Loosen edges gently, invert a heated plate or shallow dish on top and turn the whole thing over as for a jelly. It is a mark of a well-made fruit pudding that it neither collapses nor splits on being turned out; but serve quickly in any case. Cream is a must, and send extra sugar to table.

ELIZA ACTON'S GREEN GOOSEBERRY PUDDING

Boil together, from ten to twelve minutes, a pound of green gooseberries, five ounces of sugar, and rather more than a quarter of a pint of water: then beat the fruit to a mash, and stir in to it an ounce and a half of fresh butter; when nearly, or quite cold, add two ounces and a half of very fine bread-crumbs, and four well-whisked eggs. Bake the pudding gently from half to three-quarters of an hour. To make a finer one of the kind, work the fruit through a sieve, mix it with four or five crushed Naples biscuits, and use double the quantity of butter.

I find that 2 oz. crumbs, 3 eggs and the 1½ oz. butter do excellently, particularly if you separate yolks from whites, stiffly whisking and folding in the latter just before baking at 325° F, gas 3, in the upper half of the oven. Use 4 sponge finger biscuits in place of the 'Naples biscuits', or 'Lincoln Creams' at a pinch. Serve with cream.

GOOSEBERRY FOOL

1 pint sweetened gooseberry purée	¼ pint cream
¾ pint boiled egg custard (p. 137)	single cream for serving burnt almonds (optional)

Mix all together. Chill. Coarsely chop some toasted almonds and strew on top just before serving with thin cream. The cream may be marbled on to the fool instead of decorating with almonds (p. 533). Chill in individual fruit glasses if preferred.

GOOSEBERRY FLAN

Use 5 to 6 oz. pâte sucrée to line 7-inch flan-ring, baked blind (p. 127). Cook the fruit (1 lb. fruit, ¼ pint water, 4 oz. sugar) *en cocotte*, to ensure its keeping whole. Arrange neatly in case, and fill with the juice thickened with arrowroot, brushing some over sides of flan case also.

NOTE: Make pie, charlottes, or crumble with gooseberries, and these are also good, when served hot, with a blob of plain ice-cream. The Gooseberry Mould on p. 197 can be successfully made with fresh fruit if the fruit is cooked *en cocotte*, but the fruit must be absolutely cold before being handled or it will break easily. Make up the juice to 1 pint as for the canned version.

Two recipes for keen pastrycooks

GOOSEBERRY CURD BOUCHÉES

Make small bouchée cases from puff paste as usual. Fill them with this curd:

1 pint sieved gooseberry pulp (cook fruit without water in oven)	2 eggs 3 oz. butter/margarine 10 oz. sugar

Melt butter over low heat in thick pan. It must not boil. Add beaten eggs, purée and sugar. Cook gently until mixture thickens (about 30 minutes). Pot or seal at once, if it is not all to be used immediately. Not a long-keeping preserve.

GOOSEBERRY CURD GATEAU

A mille-feuille cake, so not suitable for eating without forks. An attractive cold buffet item.

Cook 3 layers of mille-feuille, round or oblong. Spread first layer with gooseberry curd, second with whipped cream or confectioner's custard (p. 173). Ice top with white glacé icing (pp. 527–8). Decorate with ½-inch band of crushed pastry crumbs or chopped burnt almonds round edge of top.

APRICOT (OR PLUM) DUMPLINGS

In Bohemia, where I was first introduced to them, these dumplings are often covered in one of the traditional yeast-raised doughs. An Austrian or German version given by Lady Sysonby in her admirable *Cook Book* (Putnam, revised edition, 1948) covers them with choux paste. I cover mine in thinly rolled suet crust made with all flour and no breadcrumbs. This is a very attractive way to use the rather unripe, tart apricots that come from southern Europe from the end of May to July, and for the cheaper plums in the autumn. It's a useful recipe, also, for anyone without an oven, providing a hot fruit pudding in exactly the amount needed.

Make the suet crust as on pp. 133–4. 8 oz. will cover 8 fruits. Roll out the paste thinly, and cut it into squares. Wrap a fruit in each square, pinch edges of paste to seal, then roll lightly in floured palms. Drop into slightly sugared boiling water. When they float they are done – about 5 to 7 minutes. Do not let the water boil fast or the paste may break up. Lift out and drain. Run a little melted butter over them and serve with cinnamon (or other spiced) sugar and cream or egg custard sauce (p. 137).

CUSTARD PUDDINGS

A pudding on their own, one of the variations of baked or steamed custard (p. 137) also makes a useful 'stretcher' for expensive soft fruits. Single-person puddings *par excellence*, they may be cooked on top of the stove in a covered pan (lay foil or buttered greaseproof paper right on top of the mould(s)), or even in the cups of an egg-poacher. Special ramekin dishes are not necessary. Tea-cups do very well even though lacking in elegance, and soup-cups are of course excellent.

The various bread-and-butter puddings, Cabinet Pudding, Crème Caramel, and others can be steamed as well as baked, the chief difference being that, in steaming, the top must remain covered to prevent condensing moisture dropping on the mixture and making it pappy on top.

Use a steamer, or stand the moulds on something to raise them from direct contact with the bottom of the pan – old saucers, a small meat grid, or a folded cloth. Cover moulds. Cook in just simmering water 30–40 minutes for big dish, 15 minutes for individual dishes.

PETITS POTS DE CRÈME

A richer mixture with a bland flavour and velvety texture. (Incidentally, good invalid fare.) To each 1 pint milk: 3 whole eggs, 3 yolks, 1½–2 tbs. sugar. Vanilla, coffee, almond, liqueurs, citrus rinds, etc. to flavour. The flavour must be of 'good quality': avoid artificial essences. Rinds are heated with the milk to extract flavour; powdered coffee may be creamed with eggs or dissolved in milk; liqueurs and other flavours are added at the end of the mixing. The process is the same, but the little pots should cook *au bain-marie* in 10–15 minutes or steam about 20–25 minutes. Best served cold. Garnish them with something suggesting the flavour: coffee-bean dragées, paper-thin slivers of candied citron, a few thin spikes of toasted almond, candied rose or violet petals; one or two only to each small pot. If delicately done, a few drops of appropriate colour may also be added. Put a few drops of colour in a spoon, mix in well, adding more if needed in the same way. The method guards against a sudden gush of colour falling irremovably into the mixture.

June

The first two months of summer are very easy on the cook who has no budgeting problems. Who needs to think very hard, still less to work hard in the kitchen, when strawberries, raspberries, asparagus, French beans, lobsters and salmon can be bought in plenty? Needless to say, if you have a vegetable plot you can enjoy generous supplies of summer fruits and vegetables even on a tight budget. What's more, they will probably be better varieties, with finer flavour, than any you could buy. However, even those who can enjoy all these delights only by buying them may, with a little foresight, still make much of what they are able to afford without too much labour.

Avoid recipes that want you to cook summer fruits (Summer Pudding is the exception); or that drown them in sweet syrups, mock cream, and large amounts of cake or pastry mixtures. Resist the temptation to stretch fresh cream by mixing sugar or cream substitutes with it; when, that is to say, the recipe gives fresh cream to be used as a garnish or accompaniment. When cream is used in the dish – e.g. mousses – half cream/half substitute may often be used. Care, though, where cream in a recipe must be whipped. (See notes, p. 62.)

As with fruits, so with other summer luxuries, let your watchword be little and good. Most luxury foods are rich and satisfying anyway, but it is self-defeating to promise a treat by way of special taste and texture and then to ruin both by additions to make mere bulk. Much better add an extra course to your meal. Nor should this involve vast preparation: a little plateful of crisp radishes with a thick finger or two of lavishly buttered fresh bread; a simple stuffed egg (pp. 268–9) on a Webb's Wonder lettuce leaf; a small cup of jellied soup (p. 302) or chilled fruit juice will do the trick.

This, above all, is the time of year to plan to :

(1) cook ahead;
(2) cook at night;
(3) mass produce !

for your own sake more than anyone else's.

Refrigerators come into their own, naturally, but for those without there are many dodges for saving work. For instance: bake a flan-case or two, store in polythene in a tin. Make some shortbread rounds and fingers for accompanying fruit. Pick over and wash radishes and put in polythene. Make a quantity of Béchamel sauce, a trifle thinner than usual, and bring it just to scalding point each day to keep it. Use slightly more gelatine or slightly less liquid for jellied or set soups or puddings, putting them on the floor of the larder overnight to set: something between 5 tbs. and ¼ pint less liquid, depending on the temperature of both the day and your larder; ¼ oz. (½ envelope) more gelatine per pint of liquid or purée. Make two small moulds of jellied dishes rather than one larger one. Not only will the smaller amount set more readily but, if you set enough for two days in one mould, it is more likely to lose shape or split once turned out, and so will be less appetizing on its second appearance. Try to have half a dozen hard-boiled eggs ready to hand for quick dishes and as 'extras' in salads. Salad dressings and creams keep excellently without refrigeration so it is well worth making a supply. Potato salad, dressed while the potatoes are still hot so that the dressing soaks in well, will keep for about 3 days since the dressing acts as a pickle.

Soups

Chilled and jellied soups deserve wider popularity. Certainly I never knew anyone not converted to them once tasted. Many soups are delicious chilled provided no fat is left on top; chilling makes this easy to remove since it hardens and can be lifted off. Broths are too thin, and their colour – cloudy grey mostly – not attractive. If, however, they are strong enough to jell on chilling, you can clear them with egg-white and tint them with a little Marmite or caramelized sugar, when they will resemble true consommé. Never add ice to soup to chill it as this merely dilutes the fine flavour.

The turtle consommé is an example of a good 'convenience food', the mock turtle is a good example of cheating. These, the cucumber and the avocado are quickly made.

TURTLE CONSOMMÉ

Jellied soup is filling, and this quantity should serve 6.

2 tablets Lusty's Turtle Soup   juice of ½ lemon (maximum)
(sold in cartons of 4)   pepper
1 pint water

Place the tablets in a pint measure. Pour on ¼ pint boiling water. Stir until *completely* dissolved, for you need all the tablet to get a good set. Make up to just 1 pint with cold water. Add lemon juice and pepper to taste. Pour into a basin. Chill, and spoon into soup-cups when set. Serve with lemon wedges, cracker biscuits, or Bath Olivers.

VARIATION 1. Add 5 tbs. sherry instead of lemon juice, and salt. Serve with lemon wedges.

VARIATION 2. For a more substantial course place a neatly trimmed poached egg in the bottom of each soup-cup, pour soup on top when half-set. Chill. Accompaniments as before.

MOCK TURTLE CONSOMMÉ

2 rounded tsp. Marmite   juice ½ lemon
½ oz. (1 envelope) gelatine   white ground pepper

Dissolve the Marmite in ¼ pint boiling water. Dissolve the gelatine in the lemon juice plus 1 tbs. water. Mix these two liquids. Make up to a scant pint with cold water. Add pepper. Proceed and finish as preceding recipe.

CHILLED CUCUMBER CREAM

½ pint coating Béchamel
  sauce
½ pint light stock
½ hot-house cucumber or
  two small 'ridge'
  cucumbers from the garden

1 tsp. minced onion or shallot
green colouring
mint leaves or strips cucumber
  peel

LIAISON:

1–2 yolks

2–3 tbs. thin cream or top
  milk

Hot-house cucumber need not be peeled if you use an electric blender, or if you do not mind the tiny speckles of darker colour that finely sieved skin will leave. The flavour may well be superior where the skin is used.

Cut the cucumber in inch pieces. Simmer it with the onion in stock for 20 minutes (5 minutes in a pressure cooker). Put through fine Moulin plate or sieve or in blender. Reheat, and gradually and smoothly incorporate Béchamel, or add to blender all at once. Bring just to simmering point, pour a little on to liaison, mix well and return to rest of soup, stirring over low heat for 1 minute. Adjust seasoning, colour a delicate green. Chill. Serve garnished with mint leaves or a few thin strips of cucumber peel.

This soup may also be served hot, although its delicate flavour is rather lost.

ICED BEETROOT SOUP

1½ pints light stock (chicken
  for preference)
2 medium raw beetroots
1 clove garlic crushed with
  salt
1 tbs. tarragon vinegar *or*
  1 tbs. dry white wine or
  cider, 1 tsp. chopped fresh
  tarragon
2 tbs. sherry

1 chopped shallot
seasoning
1 level dessertsp. sugar

To clear soup:
1 egg-white
1–2 crushed egg-shells

To garnish:
2 tsp. finely chopped chives
2 tbs. yoghurt or single cream

Thoroughly scrub the beets and chop them medium coarse on a plate to retain juice. Put them in pan with stock, garlic, vinegar, shallot, seasoning and sugar. Simmer 1½ hours. Allow to cool completely. Add white and shell and bring to boil whisking steadily to distribute white evenly through the soup. As it boils up stop whisking, taking off heat as soon as it foams up in pan. or piece of clean, scalded blanket. (For method see p. 259.) As soup runs through add sherry. Chill thoroughly. Serve in soup-cups or glass goblets with a whirl of cream or yoghurt run on to surface at last minute and a light sprinkling of chopped chives. The pleasure of this soup is almost as much in its clear burgundy appearance as in its delicate flavour.

AVOCADO SOUP (UNCOOKED)

Like bananas, avocados discolour readily, and it is impossible to leave this soup overnight – even in a snap-closed plastic container in the ice-box – without some discoloration. The flavour, however, is not impaired. The top discolours most, but the effect is lessened by thorough stirring. For a good colour make as near the meal as possible. Over-ripe and battered fruits do just as well (not mouldy specimens, though!), although the colour may be less green.

3 to 4 helpings.

1 medium-sized ripe avocado (p. 270) or 2 small or battered fruits	juice of ½ small lemon
	8 fl. oz. light stock
	½ carton yoghurt
1 tsp. minced spring onion, shallot, or chives	⅛ pint milk
	2 tbs. single cream

Halve the avocado, remove the stone, slip out of skin and mash. Also scrape inside of skin, as the darker green, which helps to make the attractive colour, clings to the skin. Mash, add rest of ingredients and pass through sieve or put in blender. Chill and serve.

First Courses and Snacks

KEDGEREE

Spelt 'kitchuree', 'ketchuri' and similar variants in some Victorian books, the dish was, perhaps, brought from India by a Scotsman, for it is best known made with 'finnan haddie', and often thought of as of Scottish origin. In fact it can be made with various meats or fish, the next best to smoked haddock being one of the many smoked sausages from Europe – Frankfurter, Polish boiling ring, German ham sausage, cervelat and so on. Liver and kidney are liked by some, but to me this is too near to risotto. Black pudding is also excellent, as are white fish – the coarse-textured bream is splendid because it doesn't break up too small – shrimps, prawns and cockles. What distinguishes kedgeree from other rice dishes is the hard-boiled egg, the generous quantity of butter (use half margarine if necessary) and above all the curry powder and cayenne. Of rather dearer items, such as ham-sausage or prawns, use half quantity if you like. Use very little salt if your chief ingredient is salty, e.g. prawns. Ask for Continental sausages in the piece, remove their casing (except Frankfurters) and cut in ½-inch dice. Gas-ring cooks can simmer the eggs and haddock one after the other, with the rice steaming in a colander or bowl strainer over the pan; or tied in muslin actually in the water. The rice can continue cooking while the haddock is flaked and the eggs shelled. Thus only one pan is needed for the meal.

The following quantity is enough for luncheon or supper for 4; a first course for 6–8.

1 lb. poached finnan haddock	1 heaped tsp. curry powder
2–3 hard-boiled eggs	½ tsp. grated nutmeg
½ lb. cooked Patna rice	squeeze lemon juice
4 oz. butter/margarine	

Skin, bone and flake the fish. Halve the eggs lengthwise and slice thickly. Melt the butter, stir in the curry powder and heat very gently for 5 minutes. Stir in egg and fish; fold rice in lightly.

Adjust seasoning, add nutmeg and lemon juice. Heat through gently, turning carefully to distribute ingredients without breaking up rice.

To reheat kedgeree the best plan is to stand the bowl or dish containing it, covered, in a pan or tin of hot water, and heat (on top or in oven) for about ½ hour at a low temperature.

FRIED SANDWICHES

Perhaps this is going to sound terrible to you. All I can say is that it doesn't *eat* terrible ! In fact, it's very good and very quick, the preparation having all been done the day before for another meal; and very cheap, the cost having also been calculated for another meal. And it is gratifying to have neither the labour of sandwich-making nor the ingredients wasted. For a luncheon snack one round of sandwich each is necessary, plus accompaniments. But those with good appetites may need more.

Cut each half-round sandwich in half again. For each eight of these small sandwiches allow 1 beaten egg plus 1 dessertsp. water. But heat up only 1 egg at a time for the bread quickly blots up the egg. Allow 1 oz. butter/lard for frying each 12 small sandwiches.

Beat the egg on a plate, heat the butter/lard mixture (or butter/oil) in a frying-pan. Rest the plate of egg at an angle so that you can control the amount of coating put on each sandwich. Brush each side well with egg, and fry golden, turning carefully to avoid disturbing the filling.

Serve with a dish of runner beans, peas or a salad – according to the filling of the sandwiches. For instance, fried chicken sandwiches accompanied by orange and Belgian endive salad. If there is a good gravy or sauce on hand serve it also : e.g. egg sandwiches with tartare sauce.

Sweet sandwiches, such as jam, chocolate, brown sugar, banana, make a good pudding treated like this. Serve with cinnamon-sugar, chocolate sauce (p. 436), jam sauce (p. 120). etc.

BAKED SANDWICHES

The principle is that of bread-and-butter puddings, but as there are sometimes more left-over sandwiches to use up than the amount of bread used in bread-and-butter pudding, you must consider using a larger dish and more liquid.

Grease a pie dish (with good dripping if suitable) and arrange the sandwiches in it. Fill it with gravy or a thin sauce for savoury sandwiches; milk, sugar and an egg (or 2) for sweet sandwiches. Flavour the dish further by herbs, or essences and so on, sprinkled on the layers. Run melted margarine on top and bake until browned and crisp.

OMELETTES

If you want to produce a completely even-coloured, not-at-all-browned omelette you must have a thick small pan. Cast iron is unbeatable because the heat is spread evenly and, once hot through, the metal acts like a girdle, and it is that rather than the heat source itself that does the cooking. Indeed, the heat can be kept quite low during cooking. Thinner pans allow the heat to come through so that the centre of the pan over the flame (or element, etc.) is hotter than that of the perimeter. Cheap or gimmicky pans may be of uneven thickness, to make matters worse. Therefore if you go in much for omelettes it will pay you to buy the best pan you can possibly afford (8–9 inch in diameter, no bigger).

NOTE: an 8-inch omelette pan takes 2 large eggs, 3 'standards' at a pinch; a 9-inch pan will take 4 eggs, such omelettes usually being intended for 2 or more people depending on the course; a 2-egg omelette is usually enough for each person for a main course.

Use a small basin for each 2-egg omelette when making several. Line them up whisked, seasoned, etc. Have the cooking butter ready in ½ oz. portions; the filling keeping hot in covered pan on very low heat, or in a double boiler; a ladle to hand to spoon it out; plates in the oven. The diners must eat as they are served. Polite waiting for others won't do with omelettes.

Butter is a must for omelettes: the better the better, and unsalted for preference.

Don't beat the eggs too long; but the white must be broken down beyond the stage when it can make unpleasant white strings through the omelette. I like to add a little water to the mix as I think it helps to distribute the white through the yolk, and also gives lightness.

The method of adding the flavouring or filling varies according to their character. Some may be stirred into the raw mixture, others are added at the end just before the omelette is rolled or folded. Seasoning must always be added to raw eggs.

There are two well-known methods of moving the egg in the pan during the cooking. One is to stir, all over the surface, with fork or palette knife in a series of small circles. The stirrings must break through the cooked egg to allow the uncooked to go down to the heat of the pan. The second is to lift or 'pull' the cooked edges inwards allowing the raw mixture to run underneath. Either way the purpose is the same: to make the omelette thick, and to keep any portion of it from remaining so long in contact with the heat of the pan that it colours.

Lastly, there must be a layer of half-cooked egg over the centre, to be folded inside as the omelette is dished. If you are adding filling at the end, the heat of this will (if it won't it's not hot enough) cook some of the liquid egg, so allow for this, and stop the cooking when there is a little more liquid egg than you think agreeable to eat. Exception: 'Spanish' Omelette.

There is no disgrace in being unable to turn an omelette out of the pan without the help of a palette knife or whatever. Deft pan-tapping techniques are less important than the safe arrival on the plate of an omelette neatly folded, neatly filled, succulent and hot.

Sauté potatoes or thin brown bread and butter and a green salad make the best accompaniments for savoury omelettes; the salad should preferably follow the omelette, but do at least serve it on a side-plate rather than risk eating lukewarm lettuce and vinaigrette-soaked omelette.

Hand extra sugar or sauce, as appropriate, with sweet omelettes.

Some suggested fillings for savoury omelettes
per 2-Egg Omelette

Mixed with the raw egg :
FINE HERBS. Chop finely a mixture of any fresh herbs to
give 1 dessertsp.
CHEESE. 1 tbs. grated dry cheese of which some should be
Parmesan if possible. Dry stilton is also excellent.

Scattered on to omelette half-way through cooking :
FRIED CROUTONS – little-finger-nail size. 1 rounded tbs. per
omelette.
CHEESE. As above.
POTATO. 1 tbs. small dice of boiled potato heated in butter.
BACON. ½–1 rasher diced and fried crisp.

Folded into omelette at end of cooking :
TOMATO. 1 per omelette, concassed, seasoned and softened
in butter/margarine.
MUSHROOM. Finely sliced, softened in butter and milk, seas-
oned, 1 tbs.
HAM. 1 tbs., after it has been chopped and heated in a little
Béchamel sauce.

Sweet omelettes

Use plain beaten egg.
JAM. 1 tbs. heated, added before folding.
BANANA. ½ banana, sliced, softened in butter, squeeze lemon
juice, dash rum (optional), added before folding. For a very special
dinner whip 1 tsp. castor sugar, dash rum, into cream, chill, and
add a dollop as you serve the omelette.
RUM OR BRANDY BUTTER. Useful post-Christmas omelette.
1 dessertsp. hard sauce (p. 473) added on folding. Dish quickly.

For a pretty finish to sweet omelettes, dust with icing sugar.

BACON POTATO ROLLS

POTATO PASTRY

3 oz. each self-raising flour
and sieved potato
½ tsp. baking powder
1½ oz. margarine or lard
pinch salt, pepper

water
FILLING
¼ lb. thin rashers of bacon
made mustard

Stir flour, baking powder and potato together with pinch of salt and a good shake of pepper. Rub in fat. Mix to firm dough with about 2 tbs. water. Roll out thinly and cut into strips slightly larger than the rashers. Lay a rasher – rind removed – on each strip, lightly dab with mustard. Roll up. Bake at 375° F, gas 5, for about 20 minutes. Serve hot with green beans; cold with salad.

NOTE: This is the stylish version, but you can dice the bacon and make simply 'potato cakes'. Flaked smoked fish is also excellent as a filling. Make into fish-cake shape, and fry where no oven is available.

Fish

Sea- or salmon-trout

One of the finest fish in the world for flavour, appearance and meatiness. Although slightly cheaper per lb. in the shops than salmon, this is offset by the fact that you must buy the whole fish, and a 2-lb. fish is about the smallest you ought to have. Deep-freezing of sea-trout is now a commonplace, resulting in the high prices that seem always to follow the process, coupled with the fact that you may find it difficult to tell if you are being offered 'new season's' article. But, as I have said, in this book I am not proposing to deal with luxury foods, and am thinking of sea-trout solely from the point of view of those whose family or friends fish, and so bring them direct from river to kitchen.

DECORATED SEA-TROUT

When the fish is really fresh you need nothing more than salt in the cooking water. I favour the heavy brine of p. 337. Fish-kettles are no longer a commonplace of private kitchens, but a covered roaster might fit or, if desperate, a meat tin. If you have to use a saucepan, and thus curl your fish round very much, you may have to forgo removing the bone.

Fit the fish into the cooking vessel, put in cold water to cover. Take out the fish, measure the water, and add the salt accordingly. While the brine is coming to the boil prepare the fish.

Gut it carefully, making as short an opening as you can. This helps to keep it together later on when you are handling it. Trim the tail and snip out the brown feathery gills. Wrap the fish in muslin so the fold comes on top for you to grasp when lowering in and lifting out.

Cook, slightly curved, in the fast-boiling brine 15 to 25 minutes according to the thickness of the fish. Lift out carefully, and prop in position on a flat dish or board. Gently turn back the muslin when cold. The skin may peel off with it, otherwise peel it, leaving only head and tail as they are. Remove the eyes. Run a small pointed knife carefully along the division down the back until you can just see the bone. At the head junction insert a pair of scissors and snip through the thick centre back-bone. With the knife to help, loosen the bone a little until you can take it between finger and thumb. Pull gently upwards and towards tail, easing as needed with knife, and finally snipping again at tail end.

Make up ½ pint aspic jelly (Maggi for speed) and, when cool, run a little on the serving dish and leave to set. For speed stand on ice. Using two fish slices, or similar, lift the fish on to the dish, and decorate it as you fancy and with what you have to hand. The important points to decorate are along the back, the eye-sockets and the mouth. And you can set thinly sliced decorations along the fillet division down the side of the fish. Stick to a few restrained colours.

Here are a few examples: A whole green olive in the mouth;

rings of green and black olive down the back; piped aspic mayonnaise in eye-sockets and along sides.

A lemon butterfly in the mouth (p. 105); thin circles of cucumber overlapping just where fish meets dish; small segments from lemon slices set in a crest down back; half-circles of stuffed olive down sides; circles of stuffed olive in sockets.

A prawn in the mouth; crest of shrimps or prawns down back; needle shreds of green pepper 'seaweed' scattered where fish meets dish; circles of pepper in eye-sockets, piped round with aspic mayonnaise; piping also along sides.

ASPIC MAYONNAISE is made from equal quantities of aspic jelly and mayonnaise plus ½ tsp. extra gelatine to each ¼ pint aspic. Melt the aspic, scatter in the gelatine and melt it. Cool, and mix with mayonnaise just before it sets.

ACCOMPANIMENTS: These must be good and simple: cucumber sliced thinly and simply seasoned; tiny new potatoes tossed in mayonnaise; thin brown bread and butter; green beans in good vinaigrette; green salad.

But not tomato, not beetroot, no dressing with sugar, no form of raw onion, nothing crudely vinegary. All such drown completely the delicate flavour of the trout.

GENEVA SEA-TROUT

A favourite Victorian recipe.

Butter a large baking tin. Put in a layer of thin rounds of carrot, onion and celery. Tie in muslin a bouquet of thyme, parsley, a bayleaf, 2 cloves and a blade of mace. Place the gutted and prepared fish on this, season, thickly butter a paper, and lay over the whole. Bake in low oven for 30–40 minutes according to thickness. Lift out the fish, skin all but head and tail, remove eyes. All this should be done on the serving dish, which is afterwards cleaned with a damp cloth dipped in salt. Keep warm, covered with butter paper. Add to the baking tin a large glass of dry white wine and another of light stock or fish stock. Simmer 10 minutes. Strain off liquid into small pan and thicken with a *beurre manié* made from 1½ oz. butter, 1 oz. flour. Just mask the skinned part of the fish with this; serve the rest in a hot sauceboat.

ACCOMPANIMENT: New potatoes or brown bread and butter.

GERMAN HERRING SALAD

A version of this is very popular with office workers who lunch at the German Food Centre near Hyde Park. Quantity for 4–6 main-course helpings, 6–8 first-course helpings. Use a breakfast-cup or ½-pint measure. Use any form of pickled herring – rollmops, bismarks (fillets), raw filleted kippers, or bucklings.

1 cup (½ pint) diced pickled herring	
2 cups diced cooked potato	piled lightly in measure,
2 cups diced cooked beetroot	not pressed down
1 cup chopped sharp crisp apple	
2 tbs. thinly sliced small or spring onions	1 carton yoghurt 4–6 tbs. thick dressing
1 chopped pickled cucumber	freshly ground black pepper

Mix all well together. Serve individually on a crisp inner lettuce leaf. Serve thin brown bread and butter (or pumpernickel if possible), Bath Olivers, rye bread or crispbread.

Very useful, reduced in quantity, for the single-person household.

RED MULLET

The West Country is the place for these at their best, and they are in season there now. As with all fish they may be had imported and frozen at other times of the year, but then they are not very cheap. Correctly prepared, they are gutted and cleaned, but the liver is left in them. They are slashed diagonally across the sides – about 4 cuts – and grilled or baked. But they are at their best, in my view, if first marinated for about an hour on each side in a marinade of 2 tbs. olive oil, juice of ½ lemon, pinch chopped cumin or caraway seed, pinch ginger, ¼ tsp. salt and freshly ground black pepper. They are then grilled about 7–10 minutes each side under a hot grill. Baste with the marinade now and then.

Serve with plain potatoes.

CRAB OR CRAWFISH NEWBURG

First read notes on shellfish on p. 271.

This is, of course, better with crawfish or lobster, because the meat is in chunks, not flakes. However, the taste is still delicious with crab, and it makes a wonderful treat at the end of one of those disappointing cold, grey holiday days. If using crab, stir the green meat in with the cream at the end.

1–2 shellfish to weight 2 lb. Crawfish or lobster are best if killed by piercing (see p. 274), put raw into the butter to cook, shelled afterwards	2 oz. butter (or margarine up to half the amount) 1½ oz. for crab ¼ pint single cream ⅛ pint sherry 2 egg-yolks

Melt the butter in a small frying-pan.

For cooked shellfish : slice the tail and claw meat, where suitable, into inch pieces. Put all white meat into the butter and heat well.

For raw shellfish : cook until the red colour develops strongly, then remove from pan, shell and slice the flesh. Return flesh to pan. After this the method for both is the same. Pour on the sherry and heat to boiling point, to drive off the alcohol. Add the cream off the heat, stir and add the yolks. Return to a very low heat, and stir just to thicken – but do not let the egg scramble. If you have enough large pieces of shell use them to serve the fish in, or scallop shells if available. Whatever happens, it must be really hot when served, and some people like to put gratin crumbs on the top and give a final grilling before serving.

Thin brown bread and butter is the best accompaniment. A green salad to follow is good.

Meat

Grilling

Grilling cuts are always expensive, more so in summer when the demand for them is at its highest. There is no cheap way round; indeed nothing is more wasteful than attempts to find one. All I claim for the Cutlets Fines Herbes below is that it is a cheaper dish than some and waste is minimal. If you decide on a grill buy the best, buy enough, and economize on something else.

One of the most extravagant items, for example, often mistaken for cheap, are lamb best-end cutlets. Their price per pound is lower than chops only because they carry a large proportion of bone and fat to lean. One best-end cutlet may feed a young child, but a schoolboy or girl, an adult after a day's work, will easily eat two of larger size, and will need generous accompaniments as well. These cutlets are all very well in a mixed grill, but no one pretends that a good mixed grill is a cheap meal.

If you do have cutlets at any time, you will gain from buying the complete piece of best end, and preparing it yourself. For example, careful chining – removal of the backbone – will give you every scrap of the good fillet meat which forms the 'eye' of the cutlet. Butchers in a hurry can easily chop away quite a lump of this, leaving it attached to the chine bone, where it can be put to no better use than providing a luxury snack for the dog.

Because of its cost the grill needs perfect cooking, and it is here that many come to grief because they confuse speed and ease with that peculiar clumsiness that is the curse of English cooking.

There is nothing complicated to grilling, but the preparation of the food should be precise, the timing exact and, above all, the heat fierce. The original and still the best method of grilling is by sitting the meat actually on glowing charcoal, as with barbecues. In a Paris household recently I had fine grills cooked on the gadget described on p. 55. It was used always in preference to the grill itself. However, used properly, the grills on modern cookers give excellent results.

(1) See that all accompaniments, sauces, etc. are at a stage requiring little or no attention after you have finished grilling; any first course should be ready to serve. Have all dishes, plates, etc. ready warming in the oven, but never keep grills hot for long, or in high heat. Have the table laid.

(2) Have all items to be grilled completely ready to be cooked and, if there are many, decide how much you can fit on the grid at one time.

(3) Turn on the grill to its highest setting *at least 5 minutes before* you begin cooking.

(4) If your grid is of the flat metal sheet type, be sparse in greasing it before laying on the food, since cold food absorbs fat. Reheat the grid for a few seconds before putting on the food. *Do not put any fat or seasoning on the meat at this stage* as it spoils searing which seals juices in meat, and is vital for the fine flavour and tenderness of a good grill.

(5) Grill first any accompaniments – e.g. tomatoes, mushrooms.

(6) Put the meat on the grid, and begin with the grill-pan and grid in their highest position under the fierce heat, so that meat is as close to flame as possible. Leave it thus 2 or 3 seconds only. Withdraw grill-pan and brush surface of food with oil or butter, return and let it flame up for about 1 minute so that it is seared completely, being singed black here and there. Season it, lower the position of the grid and/or grill-pan, but not the heat, unless your grill positioning is poor. Continue cooking in accordance with the times set out in the table below. Then turn the meat and repeat the process for the second side. This will give you a grill correctly and appetizingly charred on the outside, pink and juicy within.

NOTES: Never use a fork for handling grilled meat, for you may pierce the seared surface, in which case the juices will escape and spoil the grill.

Note that lamb and pork should never be underdone: lamb should be no more than a pale shell-pink inside; pork should be completely white through.

Sausages should be greyish white at the centre.

Kidneys should have no more than beads of blood on the cut side. Note that the cut side of kidneys is cooked last.

Liver is very much better fried in my opinion, but should be done enough after merely searing; unlike other meats it is better painted with oil or melted butter before being cooked. It should be still very pliable and soft to the touch when cooking stops. Reject thick slices of liver: fried or grilled, they tend to be over-cooked outside and repulsively raw in the centre. Butchering of liver is one of the worst examples of the decline of skill in the trade since the rise of supermarkets. You will do better to buy liver in the piece, and slice it yourself – not more than ½ inch thick.

Mushrooms, likewise are better fried or, best, baked in a shallow, covered dish or plate in a little milk and butter. If they must be grilled, paint both sides first with butter and put a nut of butter in the cap.

Tomatoes, like kidneys, are cooked skin side first, cut side last. Paint with fat, and season straight away.

Times per side for grills (but allow for variation in quality of meat, efficiency of grill).

Steaks ¾ to 2 inches thick:
Underdone (*Bleu*)	3–4 mins.
Medium (*Saignant*)	3½–4½ mins.
Well done (*Cuite*)	4–5 mins.
Lamb cutlets ½–1 inch thick	2½–3½ mins.
Lamb chops 1–2 inches thick	4–7 mins.
*Pork chops ¾–2 inches thick	5–10 mins.
Sheep's kidneys	2½ mins.
Veal kidneys	3–3½ mins.
Sausages, according to thickness and 'breadiness'	5–8 mins. total time

Bacon: grill crisp. If local bacon is invariably salt, blanch rashers ½ minute, blot on kitchen paper, then grill.

*Note that for the thicker pork chops the heat itself would need to be reduced after about 5–7 minutes in addition to lowering grill/ grid position.

Frying

All the above items may, of course, be fried (see p. 103). Liver should be lightly floured first. The times will be about the same as for grilling.

Accompaniments

GRAVY. This is made from the juices in the bottom of the pan. Pour off fat. Add ¼ pint stock and boil, scraping the coagulated juices from sides and bottom of pan. Add a dash of sherry, wine or cider if available.

SAVOURY BUTTERS. Make these in advance and leave in the cold to harden. Cream about 2 oz. butter/margarine (some butter must be included) for each 4 to 6 people. Season, and add : 1 tsp. fresh herbs, mixed or of one kind; ½ crushed and minced clove of garlic (especially for lamb); 1 tsp. anchovy paste; 1 tsp. lemon juice; 1 tsp. parsley.

POTATOES. Duchesse, mashed, new, sauté, chipped.

SALADS. Anything except crude, vinegary beetroot.

CÔTELETS FINES HERBES

4–6 helpings.

3 good-sized English (or first quality New Zealand) middle necks of lamb

2 good sprigs parsley

1 small twig rosemary

few leaves tarragon or small sprig fennel or dill

8 chive blades

(herbs may be varied to taste)

1 clove garlic

1–1½ ozs. butter according to number of cutlets

seasoning

Each middle neck of lamb will yield two conventionally – and one slightly eccentrically-shaped (but meaty) double-width cutlets; that is, cutlets two bones wide. Allow two of these per person for adults, one large one each for younger children. Ask the butcher to avoid gashing the eye of the cutlets in chining the meat (or do this yourself with a small meat-saw). It is better to do the dividing up into cutlets yourself, unless yours is a skilled butcher. Remove the chine-bone completely, and divide the meat into double-width cutlets. The small end of the necks, together with the chine bones, go into the stock-pot for broth, or to make a lamb stew. Trim off all fat and gristle possible from cutlets, leaving only as much as attaches them to the bones. Very finely chop herbs, cream garlic in salt. Heat butter in small saucepan and simmer herbs and garlic in this for 1 minute with a shake of pepper. Meanwhile have grill heating. Cook cutlets as general directions, then spoon a little herb butter over each. These thick cutlets have 3 surfaces, grill each surface 60 seconds, buttering each. Dish in the butter, with new potatoes, and a salad or young vegetables.

COLD SUMMER JOINTS AND POULTRY

Read notes on meat and roasting on pp. 96-7.

By midsummer English lamb is plentiful; 'cheap' and 'expensive' roasting joints of beef are at average prices; pork is often very reasonable, partly because the old idea lingers that it 'goes bad' in summer, and so it is not as popular as other meat. This is a good moment, therefore, from every point of view to enjoy a cold roast at its best, which is when it has been left to become cold without any cutting to let out the juices. The flavour and succulence of such cold roast joints is unbeatable, and to take one as the centrepiece to a picnic makes a memorable meal. Moreover, by cooking the joint late in the evening you avoid an unwelcome, hot chore during a fine summer's day.

Choose the lower temperature method where possible (p. 97). A big joint, kept in the refrigerator and allowed to thaw out for about an hour before it is wanted, will provide a series of cold luncheons or suppers, saving work for several days, while naturally, réchauffés can be made as usual. The juices in chicken, lamb and pork set to jelly. Sandwiches made from these roasts are at their best.

A small chicken is a good choice for the single-person household.

Summer stews

Stewing cuts of beef are at their cheapest and, with the often
chilly evenings of the summer in these islands, stew is welcome.
As stew may be left in the oven at its lowest setting for many
hours, a hot meal in the evening is often a convenience all round.
Keep the stew light in flavour and not over-thickened. Use small,
young vegetables. The juice of an orange or half a lemon will
give a summery character to the dish. Note also that there is no
preliminary frying.

This example is adapted from Eliza Acton.

WELSH STEW

1½ lb. stewing beef (chuck or buttock steak for preference)	8 each baby carrots and turnips
	12 new potatoes
	juice of an orange
1 dozen button onions	seasoning
1 pint stock or water	

Put all into a cocotte or covered pan and cook gently for 3 to 6
hours according to convenience. For long cooking on top of the
stove use an asbestos mat, or Mijoska.

Vegetables

Asparagus and artichokes from the garden

The standbys for asparagus in limited quantity are eggs. Mount
a couple of sticks on scrambled egg; fold three thin ones into an
omelette; set 3 stalks, cold, on a lettuce leaf, add 3 slices of egg,
a spoonful of mayonnaise and you have an appetizer. Chop a
few with diced fried bacon to garnish grilled fish etc. When the
stalks sprout in half-dozens no harm is done if you wrap them in
polythene in the refrigerator until a second half-dozen are ready
a few days later.

The nice thing about English garden asparagus of the dark green sort is that the stalks are tender much further down their length than most of the imported stuff. Even a modest number of stalks makes enough for a small first course.

Globe artichokes are less of a problem for, when the whole thistle is served, one is enough for each person. Indeed for a small family with a single vegetable plot one plant, well established, is enough to provide an annual 'taster' of artichokes, provided you don't insist upon eating only the 'fond', the thick base of the flower. Of course this is the choice bit, but you need quite a lot of space to grow enough of these big plants to keep you in 'fonds' for the season.

The cooking of these two luxuries is by simple simmering in salted water – boiling when the vegetables are put in, no lid. Asparagus takes 12 to 20 minutes, artichokes 20 to 45, according to size.

Serve hot with melted butter. Lemon juice, added by some, is considered sacrilege by others. Serve cold with mayonnaise or vinaigrette. Hot plates are important to keep melted butter melted.

Commercially grown asparagus is fairly uniform in length, and several inches should be cut from the root end before tying with soft string or tape, in bundles of suitable size for individual helpings. Garden asparagus, however, varies in length, so uniform trimming will be likely to be wasteful. Two strings should be tied round longer bundles. See the water does not gallop, or the precious heads will drop off.

Jellied salads

First read notes on Gelatine on p. 138.

Setting fruit in jelly, or making jellies from fruit, is a commonplace. In America they do the same with vegetables, and also with combinations of meat, fish, vegetables and fruit. Jellied salads are as delicious to eat as they are attractive to look at. The simple ring jellies given below can be varied by setting suitable foods in them, as well as filling the centres as suggested. The vegetable loaf, also, could have chopped ham, fish, etc. added to it, thus making a complete luncheon dish.

TOMATO OR CUCUMBER ASPIC RING

ASPIC:

1. *Cider Aspic*
1 pint water
¼ pint cider
2 tbs. cider vinegar
1 piece root ginger
1 tsp. celery seed (or a few dried celery leaves)
sprig tarragon (or dried)
1 small onion quartered
1 dozen peppercorns
1 chilli
salt

⎱ All tied in muslin

½ oz. gelatine (1 envelope)
1 tbs. lemon juice
Method below.
2. *Simple Aspic*
¾ pint water or light stock
5 tbs. pint each sherry and herb vinegar
rind and juice of ½ lemon
1 oz. each carrot and onion
salt
1 oz. gelatine
1 egg-white and shell
*Method as lemon jelly
p. 259.*

FILLING:

¾ lb. tomatoes – concassed (p. 15) and cut into strips *or* ½ hot-house or 1 large ridge cucumber – sliced paper thin (hot-house need not be peeled)

Alternative for tomato where fresh are difficult or expensive
1 pint canned tomato juice in place of tomatoes and water, to be made up to 1 pint after cooking herbs and spices in it

*Simmer the herbs and spices, covered, in the liquids for 20 minutes, then strain carefully. Melt the gelatine in the lemon juice and 1 tbs. of the liquid. Add to liquid. Add the tomato or cucumber. Pour into wetted pint or 1½-pint ring-mould and leave to set.

Turn out on bed of shredded lettuce, or lettuce leaves. Fill centre with mixture of cooked diced meat or flaked fish etc., diced potato, chopped green beans, broad beans, peas, etc., with the addition of, say, a little chopped pineapple, or handful of large raisins, sliced peach, stoned chopped prunes, dried figs or dates. Turn the mixture in vinaigrette, mayonnaise or other dressing.

Alternatively the aspic may be set in small individual moulds.

VEGETABLE LOAF

Serves 8 to 10.

ASPIC

Liquids, flavourings, gelatine and lemon juice as above, but in double quantities.

Dice:

½ peeled cucumber
4 small cooked potatoes (must not be floury or broken)

4 medium cooked runner beans (or 6 french beans)

Slice:

1 dozen stuffed olives
¼ each red and green pepper
4 concassed tomatoes

2 new small carrots
8 radishes
6 fat spring onions

Add whole:

2 tbs. cooked broad beans

Proceed as in previous recipe, stirring vegetables into the liquid very carefully to avoid clouding too much. Set in a large loaf-tin or deep square dish, or in individual moulds.

NOTE: This is a full version. Use vegetables as available, with more or less liquid.

Serve with cold, thickly sliced meat, cold fried fish (p. 281), hard-boiled eggs, fingers of cheese, cold Frankfurters etc. Hand mayonnaise or thick dressing (p. 248) separately.

A good dressing with these jellied salads is

YOGHURT DRESSING

1 carton yoghurt
1 tbs. tarragon vinegar or lemon juice
1 clove garlic crushed in salt, or 1 tsp. minced onion

8 chives finely chopped
big tsp. made mustard
salt
black pepper

Combine all together, removing garlic after an hour or so.

BROAD BEANS

There are people who don't like them. We others can, as a rule, seldom get enough.

Cook them 10 to 20 minutes according to size in boiling salted water just to cover. (Save water for stock.) Finish by dressing in a good parsley or, better, savory (the herb) sauce; in melted butter into which two rashers of frizzled streaky bacon have been crumbled; in 1 tbs. or so thin cream, warmed with 1 dessertsp. chives and piled on to a croûton of fried bread – this served as a separate course, for which broad beans are excellent. They go particularly well with ham and bacon, and during the short season they have in most gardens, a boiling joint of bacon (pp. 349–50) with broad beans makes a feast at very modest cost.

Puddings

SUMMER PUDDING

To make a really first-class Summer Pudding you need raspberries, red currants *and* cherries. Cherry juice contains a substance that seems lacking in the rest of the prunus family. Being no chemist I cannot tell you what it is, only what it does. Cherry juice has a caramel-like quality that, cold, seems to stick things together, and when caramelized seems to retain its brittleness even if exposed to dampness. There is a marvellous pudding of Rosemary Hume's (not in *Penguin Cordon Bleu Cookery*, I fear) called Cherry Pain Perdu which demonstrates this odd quality of cherry juice, for you cannot successfully make the pudding with any other fruit. The essence of the pudding is the crispy juice-soaked bread. Use plums, say, or apricots, and all you get is soggy bread.

One of the warnings issued with most recipes for Summer Pudding is that it is difficult to turn out as it falls apart easily. If a proportion of the fruit is cherries this is less likely.

Where all the fruit must be bought, Summer Pudding is far from cheap, but for those with a few raspberry canes and a currant bush (white currants are just as good for flavour, but blackcurrants too overpowering) it is as useful as delicious, you can make a rare treat from the 'stragglers' at the start and finish of the season.

half a loaf of stale bread
¼ pint heavy stock syrup
(p. 526)

¾–1 lb. red fruit (preferably raspberries, redcurrants, cherries)

Stalk currants and cherries (stoning the latter is not necessary but nicer), pick over the raspberries for odd stalks or mildewed specimens. Put all into a cocotte. Set oven at 300° F, gas 2. Boil up the syrup, pour it over the fruit and set the cocotte, covered, in the oven for 15 to 20 minutes. This heats the fruit, allows its juice to run somewhat, and the syrup to penetrate, without breaking it. Leave to cool a little. Meanwhile cut the bread in $\frac{3}{16}$-inch slices – it must bend to the shape of the mould, hold its shape, but not be so thick that it either cracks across, or is stodgy from lack of juice to soak it through well. De-crust the bread, gauge the size of the bottom of a 1-pint pudding basin with a plain pastry cutter and cut a circle of bread to fit. Use the rim of the basin to cut a circle (probably over 2 slices) to fit inside the top. Line the basin completely with bread, butting the joints firmly together. Pour in the fruit, leaving about half a tea-cup of juice for finishing. Fit the top, and spoon the remaining juice over, especially the top edges. Put a small saucer on top and a weight on that so that the pudding is under slight pressure to force the juice through bread. Leave till next day, keeping as cold as possible. Turn out, and serve with a generous bowl of half-whipped cream and another of castor sugar.

STRAWBERRY SHORTBREAD

SHORTBREAD:

4 oz. plain flour
4 oz. butter
2 oz. castor sugar
pinch salt

2 oz. rice flour (where supplies are difficult semolina (preferably) or fine oatmeal may be substituted)

325

Cream the butter and sugar. Turn on to a board. Mix salt and flour and, with palette knife in one hand to clear board, use other hand to work flours into fat mixture until an even dough is formed. Cut in half and form each half into a round about 6 inches in diameter. Use a flan-ring or cake tin as guide so that edges are even. The rounds should be about ⅛ inch thick, and may be rolled out or knocked out into shape with the heel of the hand. Lift very carefully on to baking-sheet lined with grease-proof or Bakewell paper (p. 53). Prick surface. Bake 15 to 20 minutes at 325° F, gas 3, until set and golden but not brown. Cool on the baking-sheet. Handle carefully.

FILLING (to be added not more than ½ hour before the meal):

6–8 oz. strawberries 2 oz. castor sugar
¼ pint double cream

Keep 6 well-shaped strawberries whole and cut the rest into small pieces on a plate, or crush with a broad-tined fork, sweetening with 1½ oz. of the sugar. Whip the cream until it just holds its shape, fold in rest of sugar. Reserve a good third of cream for the top, spread the rest thickly on a shortbread round. Cover with the crushed strawberry. Set second round on top, spread with cream and decorate with whole strawberries. Large rosettes of cream may be piped if preferred.

A luxurious version may be made by using toasted ground almonds or hazelnuts in place of the rice flour. The resulting pastry is very delicate to handle and very absorbent, so finishing as late as possible is essential. Toast hazelnuts in hot oven in their skins until skins go black – about 15 minutes – when they rub off very easily. Blanch almonds before toasting to remove skins – 1 minute in boiling water. Grind nuts in Mouli Grater. (Buy nuts from health food stores as they're often less expensive.)

Even the first recipe is not cheap, but it will give 6 people a fine strawberry-and-cream feast costing less than neat fruit and cream.

VACHERIN

This is the same idea as above, but meringue takes the place of shortbread. You do not sweeten the fruit or cream as there is enough sugar in the meringue. This dish is well known to Australasians, in a slightly different shape, as Pavlova Cake, and I am always surprised it is not better known in England where 'what to do with egg-whites' is a frequent question.

MERINGUE

3 egg-whites	large pinch salt
6 oz. castor sugar	¼ pint double cream

With a rotary whisk beat the whites and salt until the foam no longer moves when bowl is inverted. Add 4 oz. sugar, 1 tsp. at a time, whisking in. Add 1½ oz. all at once and whisk in lightly. This gives a very good piping consistency. Over-whisking is one of the causes of meringue oozing. Another is cooking at too high a temperature so that the outside hardens leaving the inside uncooked when, on cooling, it reverts to liquid and oozes through the hard shell. Using a large piping bag and a ½-inch plain nozzle, pipe two 7–8-inch circles on well-oiled paper on a baking-sheet. Better still, use Bakewell paper. Draw the circles if liked, but pencil may come off Bakewell on to bottom of meringue. It is harmless and unseen, however. Start piping at centres of circle, and spiral outward keeping the spiral touching. Avoid unevenness and breaks by not drawing away from piping, and pipe fairly thickly. Imperfections are inevitable at first, but not difficult to disguise. Dredge with remaining ½ oz. sugar. Use the less good circle for the bottom layer. Bake at 250° F, gas ½, for about 2 hours, with oven door ajar. When top is quite firm, peel off paper and invert the circles, piercing here and there so that drying out is helped. Cook for a further ½ to ¾ hour until firm. Cool.

Spread whipped cream thickly on bottom layer. Into this half drop strawberries, sliced fresh peaches, whole raspberries, stoned poached cherries. Use most of the cream for this filling. Put on the top meringue circle. Pipe 6–8 large rosettes of cream round the edge and on to each put a whole fruit or slice.

PEACHES

Peaches are particularly good with Vacherin (above) as their bitter-almond taste offsets the sweetness of the meringue. They are also cheaper than soft fruits at this time as a rule, and 3 small or 2 medium peaches will fill a 7-inch Vacherin.

Douse peaches in a bowl of boiling water 1 minute and drop into cold water to skin. The blush stays on the flesh if peeled thus, which helps the garnish. Marinade them in a little white wine or dry sherry (drink it while finishing the garnish) for an extra fillip.

Make a form of fresh peach bourdalue (p. 172) by pressing shortbread mixture, made with almonds, into a 6-inch flan-ring, baking blind, half-filling with confectioner's custard, covering with halves of peeled small peaches and finishing with apricot glaze scattered with toasted almond flakes.

Take the chance of fresh peaches to make your own Melba – virtually a different article from the sickly tinned concoction of most restaurants and tea-shops.

Fresh peaches and raspberries are natural allies, and where few raspberries can be afforded make them go further with a couple of small sliced peaches.

TOFFEE AND CHOCOLATE CHERRY PIE

½ lb. flaky pastry
1 lb. cherries
¼ lb. sugar
pinch of cream of tartar
¼ lb. plain chocolate
chopped walnuts or hazelnuts
cream

Line a shallow oblong tin or dish with flaky pastry and bake blind. Meanwhile pip the cherries and leave them to dry out somewhat. Using half, arrange them in two wide bands: one at one end of the pastry case, leave pastry blank for an equal width, then put on the second band of cherries, so that there is a second blank at the other end of the flan-case. Melt sugar in a small pan in 2 tbs. water with cream of tartar over a slow heat, moving pan *slightly* as sugar melts and begins to colour. Allow barely to colour and spoon over the bands of cherries as evenly as possible, re-warming if the caramel sets too quickly. You need rather a lot of caramel for this sort of thing, but the sugar need not be wasted, as extra water boiled in the pan will melt it down to a syrup for other uses, such as pouring over puddings or using as a sweetener.

Let the caramel set. Meanwhile melt the chocolate in another small pan over hot water. Dip the remaining cherries in the chocolate, cool them, and arrange them in the blank spaces between the bands of toffeed cherries.

Chop the nuts, and put a neat line of them between the bands of cherries. Brush the edges and sides of the pastry with a red jam glaze. (p. 526). Hand whipped cream separately.

July

Soups

ICED FRUIT SOUPS
See also Apricot Soup, p. 202.

In Scandinavia and Germany they make a feature of fruit soups and juices; fruit-growing for the latter, in particular, being an agricultural staple. The fruit you grow in your own garden seldom wants for willing hands to pick it, and when crops are heavy fruit soups are a pleasant way of ringing the changes. Where fruit is limited cook with vegetable marrow to make bulk.

The basic quantities are:

1 pint fruit juice or pulp, or mixture of both
½ pint water
1 oz. cornflour, arrowroot, potato flour or sago
about 2–3 tbs. sugar
Additions to choice or for modifying flavour:
lemon juice
wine or liqueur
raisins or sultanas, chopped

Accompaniment and garnish:
almond paste balls (or made into fruits to match soup or into fingers etc.)
ratafias (p. 516), shortbreads, ginger snaps, or dry biscuits spread with cream cheese
cream, yoghurt, herb leaves, petals, etc.

Where necessary (e.g. apples, apricots, rhubarb, plums) the fruit must be stewed in water – 1 pint or to cover – until tender and then sieved. But fruits such as raspberries may yield enough neat juice if pressed well through a fine nylon sieve or put into the electric blender – depending on pips and coarseness of skins.

Cook the thickening (cornflower, arrowroot etc.) in the ½-pint water, stirring out all lumps.

Add the fruit to the thickening, heat through just enough to melt sugar and sweeten only just to taste, for the soup starts the meal and should not resemble a sweet pudding. Add lemon juice to sharpen and to keep the colour bright. Add dried fruits to soften, or in place of some of the sugar, and to make a 'texture'.

Chill, serve in soup-cups or glasses, garnished with yoghurt, mint leaves, rose petals or other suitable decorations.

Some people add spices to the fruits during cooking, but I think it is a pity to spoil the fresh fruit taste.

TOMATO CONSOMMÉ (HOT OR COLD)

1 lb. tomatoes, chopped	salt
1 medium onion, chopped	juice of ½ lemon, sprig of
1 pint light stock or water	tarragon or
5 tbs. sherry or dry white wine	2 tbs. tarragon vinegar

1 chilli
few seeds from cardomom pod
piece ginger root
blade mace
pinch carraway or cumin
6 peppercorns (crushed)
2 sprigs mint
rind of ½ lemon
1 egg-white and crushed shell

as many of these as you like, tied in muslin with the tarragon where used

Except for the lemon juice or vinegar, sherry and egg, simmer all the ingredients together 1 hour. Remove herbs and spices and put through Moulin-Légumes, or sieve. Return to pan with egg-white and shell and lemon juice, and boil up as for jelly on pp. 258–9. Add salt to taste. Pour through a fine strainer or jelly-bag, adding sherry at the same time. It does not matter if the soup is not clear of sediment as a jelly, but it should not be cloudy. Serve hot or cold with melba toast, or fingers of rich cheese pastry (p. 183) which has been rolled very thin. A handful of cooked rice may be added to hot soup; or pasta shells, vermicelli etc. This soup can be made out of season with canned tomatoes or juice.

331

MINT AND MUSHROOM SOUP

¼ lb. mushrooms (or stalks)
2 tbs. finely chopped mint
1 lb. potatoes
1 small onion
1½ pints light stock or
   ¾ pint water and ¾ pint
   milk

1 oz. butter
¾ oz. flour
rind of ½ lemon
1 clove
1 tbs. lemon juice
seasoning

Scrub the potatoes, halve them, cut the onion in half, and simmer these with the lemon rind, clove, seasoning, in stock or water until tender. Mince the mushrooms, melt the butter and cook them in it very slowly 10 to 15 minutes. Remove potato skins, sieve vegetables, and return to liquid, adding milk if used. Scatter flour on to mushrooms, add the soup and bring to boiling point, stirring smoothly. Add lemon juice, and lastly mint, which should not be chopped until wanted.

First Courses and Snacks

POTTED SHRIMPS

1 pint shrimps measured
   after shelling
¼ lb. unsalted butter (or
   ½ butter / ½ margarine)
pepper
cayenne pepper

ground spices to taste – e.g.
   mace, nutmeg, ginger (a
   very little clove or
   cinnamon may be included,
   but can be overpowering)
lemon wedges

Melt butter, add spices, and allow to simmer to develop flavour. Add a few shrimps and taste, adjusting flavour. Lower heat, add shrimps, and turn them over and over in the spiced butter without allowing it to bubble. After about 15 minutes taste again and, if to your taste, fill into small pots (yoghurt or cream cartons will do). Add extra melted butter so that shrimps are covered completely. Keep in refrigerator freezing compartment according to star rating; in main cabinet about 2 weeks; in cold larder about 10 days. But once unsealed use within 48 hours. Serve them with hot toast and butter, handing cayenne, black pepper in the mill, and lemon wedges.

EGGS IN ASPIC (ŒUFS EN GELÉE)

I think every food shop in every town in France must have its own *œufs en gelée* recipes. Although they are so useful, variable, easy to make and eat, only a minority in the British Isles seems so much as to have heard of them.* They keep well, so make a batch. Set them in a meat tin or shallow dish, or in individual moulds for easy transporting. The small-sized plastic cream cartons are very useful here. Turn out on to lettuce leaves or thin crisp biscuit at home, eat from container at picnic.

8 œufs mollets (p. 148)
(*important: not hard-boiled eggs*) ·
1–1½ pint aspic (see below) according to size of moulds
2 slices ham; or pressed beef, chicken etc.; or
16 prawns or shrimps or about 2 tbs. crabmeat; or

8 thin small slices of smoked or Cheddar cheese; or a small quantity of any other well-flavoured ingredient as available
thin slices drained cucumber, slivers green or red pepper, cooked peas, slices olive, etc.

Make Maggi aspic unless you happen to have on hand some good clear (or clearable) jellied stock, in which case strengthen it with the addition of ¼ oz. gelatine per pint, colour with Marmite and flavour with 1 tbs. each tarragon vinegar and sherry. Fish stock makes excellent aspic, being, indeed, better when fish is included in the recipe. Or make the simple aspic on p. 322.

Set a ½-inch layer of aspic first, setting a few strips of pepper,

* Shortly after this was written there was a fine Gilbertian row in the House of Commons over the withdrawal of *œufs en gelée* from the Commons' Dining-Room menu.

a few peas etc. as a pattern if liked. When firm, put in the cold eggs with aspic to come about half-way up. Leave to set. Cut the meats into small slices about the size of the eggs. Cover eggs completely with aspic and set. Arrange the meat above the eggs, cover with aspic, finishing with more vegetables and aspic to fill the mould(s).

The mould(s) must be filled gradually otherwise the various ingredients simply float about higgledy-piggledy. This may not bother you in individual moulds, but would make a large dish difficult to serve and less attractive. There is no need to set a pattern or, indeed, any vegetables in the bottom of the mould(s) if you are not turning out the aspics. Nor need you make a fussy design in any event. But, for example, you could put green and red colour in separate lines down a big dish; set a big circle of cucumber with peas and slices of black olive filling the centre. A haphazard mosaic of small-cut pieces of all colours scattered over the top of a large dish is very gay and quickly done.

N.B. When you wish to keep jelly of any sort for a day or so, cover the moulds well, or the top shrivels and goes leathery.

A good dish for single-person households.

KIPPER FRANÇOISE

1 packet kipper fillets
¾ lb. potatoes
1 heaped tsp. minced onion
2 large sprigs chopped parsley
vinaigrette dressing in which are crushed 2 big cloves garlic

Boil potatoes in jackets until just cooked but not at all mushy. Skin, cut in rough ¼-inch dice and turn while still warm in the well-mixed vinaigrette with the onion and parsley. Leave to cool for flavours to be absorbed.

Skin the kipper fillets and divide them along their natural divisions, removing any stray bones, in particular fin bones, which tend to get left in.

Allow 2 strips per person arranged on individual plates with a good tablespoon of potato salad, for a first course, 4 strips (or 2 plus a hard-boiled egg) and 2 tbs. salad for lunch.

This is a highly-flavoured, satisfying first course. I would use it to start a meal the main course of which is a grill or simple roast to be accompanied by salad or green beans, without potatoes for once. Beer is fine with it, but wine would be wasted. It is a great success with the hungry young as a mid-party reviver.

COLD RISOTTI OR RICE SALADS

First read note on cooking rice, p. 139.

These consist of a basis of cooked cold rice with all sorts of 'bits' added and tossed in dressings (8 oz. raw rice for 4).

(1) Always turn the cooked rice first in a little salad oil, no matter what the dressing is to be, for otherwise it can be a sticky recalcitrant lump, especially if you are using up yesterday's rice, which breaks up as you make your additions and try to mix them in.

(2) Whatever the additions, check the final seasoning, adjusting as necessary.

(3) Vary dressings to suit additions (see pp. 247ff. for dressings). For example:

INGREDIENTS	DRESSING
Cold diced roast beef, diced beetroot, broad beans, chopped raw mushroom	Vinaigrette with parsley or vinaigrette mixed with parsley sauce
Flaked white fish, hard-boiled egg, peas	Mayonnaise
Flaked smoked fish, hard-boiled egg, peas	Yoghurt dressing, (p. 323) with 1 tsp. curry powder added
Chicken, diced cucumber, pineapple, green pepper	Mayonnaise, or lemon vinaigrette with 1 tbs. tomato ketchup
Cold roast lamb, sliced green beans, tomatoes, canned sweet-corn	Thick dressing, 1 tbs. each mint, parsley

Fish

FISH MOULD
First read gelatine notes on p. 138.

CREAM

½ lb. coley (salmon heads for luxe version)
½ pint binding Béchamel sauce
juice ½ lemon or 2 tbs. dry white wine or dry cider

½ oz. (1 envelope) gelatine
½ carton yoghurt or 3–4 tbs. single cream
1 egg-white
shavings of butter
seasoning

DRESSING

¼ pint thick dressing (p. 250) (mayonnaise for salmon)
1 level tsp. each: capers; chopped chervil, tarragon or fennel; chives; parsley; or other fresh herbs to hand, except sage or rosemary

GARNISH

1–2 sliced hard-boiled eggs
¼ cucumber thinly sliced, salted lightly and drained

Poach fish (in the oven, or on top) with lemon juice, shavings of butter on top and seasoning. No *water*. Skin, bone and flake. Pound into thick Béchamel. With poaching liquor melt gelatine, and add to mixture, pounding again. Add cream or yoghurt, adjust seasoning. Whisk white until stiff and fold in as the mixture begins to set. Turn into plain wetted mould and leave to set (overnight if you have no refrigerator). Mix herbs into thick dressing. Turn out the fish mould and mask with dressing. Edge the serving dish with the garnish.

Serve with potato salad, green salad etc.

NOTE: Chicken or other poultry is excellent done like this.

SHELLFISH PUFFS

¾ lb. flaky or rough
  puff pastry (pp. 130–32)
½ pint shrimps or prawns
  or 4 good tbs. crabmeat

¼ pint well-flavoured white
  sauce – coating consistency
cayenne pepper or Tabasco;
  or soy sauce
beaten egg

Roll out pastry, keeping in a square, ⅛ inch thick. Divide large square into four smaller squares. Sprinkle fish very lightly with Tabasco or cayenne, or fairly lightly with soy, and turn well. Add white sauce and mix well. Put a good tablespoonful of mixture on one angle of each square, keeping well clear of edges, and piling up (this raises the puffs). Damp both edges of the angles, bring over the free half and knock together, using knuckle to press and seal edges. This gives a triangular puff. Paint tops well with beaten egg. Bake 400° F, gas 6, just above centre of oven for 20 minutes.

Serve hot or cold with cucumber salad (p. 337) and broad beans (the latter either hot with butter and parsley, or cold with vinaigrette). Alternative fillings according to season:

    late spring: lemon or witch sole fillets;
    early summer: herring roes;
    autumn: turbot, halibut (cheaper cuts) with egg and lemon
      sauce;
    winter/spring: plaice fillets, brill, mussels, white wine
      sauce.

HERRINGS LOWESTOFT

The name is, I think, invented rather than indigenous, the inventor being a Herring Industry Board copywriter; at any rate it was from a leaflet published by the Board that I got this method of cooking herrings. It works equally well for other 'oily' fish – mackerel, sea-trout and salmon for instance – producing fine flavour while reducing oiliness. The heavy brine prevents the water from permeating the flesh, which is firm, well flavoured and does not break up in cooking.

For each pint of water, 1 oz. cooking salt. Bring to the boil. Clean, but do not decapitate the fish. Put them in and boil at the gallops 6 minutes. Drain. Remove heads and trim before sending to table hot or cold.

When cold, boning is easy: open along centre back, lift top half away from bone, lay open, lift bone from lower half. Put fish together again. Place fish on a bed of lettuce and surround with bouquets of potato or Russian salad; with hard-boiled egg quarters; with stuffed tomatoes and so on. Serve dishes of cucumber, radishes or olives; green salad, beetroot salad, or rice salad; thin brown bread and butter.

Served in this way herring become as elegant looking as they are excellent eating.

GRILLED FISH

As for meat, the grill must be red-hot before you put the fish beneath it. The grid *must* be greased.

FISH STEAKS AND CUTLETS. White fish need fat added. Either paint with good salad oil, melted margarine or butter, or good dripping or lard; or dot the surface with small pieces of the hard fats. Sear the surface right in the flame for a few seconds, then season, and cook in fierce heat until the surface is lightly browned and even slightly charred. Turn, repeat the process, but continue the cooking until the fish is cooked through. Fish breaks easily once cooked, so if you want to colour both sides of a piece of fish it is better to turn it before the first side softens up too much, giving the second side rather longer to ensure thorough cooking. The second side will be the side uppermost in serving, for you cannot turn again.

Fish an inch thick will need about 8 minutes' total grilling; more or less for thicker or thinner fish, but make allowance for solidity of the flesh. Frozen fish may need slightly longer. Test by running a skewer through the fish: it should come out easily.

'Oily fish' – herring, mackerel, salmon, sea-trout – need not have any fat added before grilling.

When grilling whole fish, after cleaning and thoroughly scaling them:

make slashes along the length of round fish at about 1½ inches apart and diagonally on either side;

make a cut down the centre of small flat fish following the centre bone;

make this central cut plus a few crosswise slashes on a large flat fish (e.g. brill, 2-lb. plaice).

see that the cuts are seasoned, and receive some of the basting fat.

Again, cook the first side for a short time, turn and complete cooking on the second side. Since you must serve your fish with this second side showing, make up your mind, with flat fish, which side you wish to finish uppermost, and remove the skin from that side. It is usual to remove the black skin. You may remove both skins, but then will need extra care in dishing. A very well coloured and crisp surface adds to flavour and appearance where suitable.

Seasoning may include the additions of chopped herbs, lemon juice, flavoured salts or butters, and spices; for instance, garlic salt. Butter or oil in which onion, herbs, garlic etc. have been heated is excellent brushed on the fish.

SAUCES AND GARNISHES. Savoury butters such as those mentioned in the grilling notes on p. 318 are also used for fish; ravigote, tartare and shellfish sauces are well-known grilled fish dressings; other dressings include:

Anchovy, Curry or Mustard Sauce (pp. 117–18)
Devil (p. 181)
Chive and Mushroom (fried in butter)
Chive and Chervil or Fennel in white sauce or melted butter
Lemon juice and melted butter (1 tbs. to 2oz.)
Bed of spinach purée
Small triangular or round croûtes fried in flavoured oil

These suggestions merely scratch the surface of possible accompaniments for grilled fish. Classic lists number dozens, so if you run out of ideas take a look at the cookery shelves in your library.

Meat and Poultry

MAYONNAISE OF CHICKEN

When this fine dish fails it does so for two reasons: dryness; badly made salad accompaniments. A third mistake is often the dressing – for this dish you really must use genuine mayonnaise, not even home-made thick dressing; chicken is cheap enough to allow you to be generous with the sauce.

QUANTITIES. For 6 helpings you need a 3½–4 lb. bird, and at least ½ pint mayonnaise (Method A), or ¼ pint each aspic and mayonnaise (Method B). For 2 helpings buy chicken joints and make ¼ pint mayonnaise (Method A), for you cannot easily make less than the ¼ pint each mayonnaise and aspic, so that Method B is not recommended for small households. However, both being useful dressings, any excess can soon be used up.

COOKING THE BIRD. See p. 100 for roasting notes. The watchword is: keep it moist. And do so, too, by retention of the natural juices. If you roast a whole chicken do this 24 hours ahead and let it get really cold so that the juices set inside as jelly before carving. Seal a boiling fowl, seasoned, in foil or parchment, cool undisturbed in the wrapping, resting in a colander over the pot, so cooling is gradual, and any escaping broth drips back into the pot. Use any jellied juices (from either) in aspic where used. Chicken joints should also be sealed in foil or parchment for baking or boiling, and allowed to become absolutely cold before being unwrapped.

Where available insert a sprig or leaf of tarragon in bird, or wrapping, and a small onion, or slice of onion.

PREPARING. Have ready the mayonnaise (p. 248) and, where used, the aspic – Maggi's will do very well, unless you have jellied stock to use up (p. 322).

Some like the dramatic look of a whole chicken masked in mayonnaise but I think this also needs decorating, when the decoration, unless served immediately, will need coating with aspic to keep it from drying or displacement. In addition, much of the coating sauce will come off during carving, so the appearance is short-lived, and extra mayonnaise must be handed. If you mask a whole bird you must use Method B. (You *can* carve the cold bird, stick it together with strong aspic, and mask, when serving will not knock the coating off very much. But I think this is strictly for what caterers call 'banquet service'!) The usual way is to carve the portions, and mask them by Method A or B.

A third way, perhaps the best for a big family party, is to carve the bird and remove meat from bones, masking on the lettuce bed, by Method A, if for immediate serving; on the bare dish, by B, if preparing the meal far in advance. The latter is less satisfactory from the point of view of garnishing, and also may get slightly dryer.

It is usual to remove chicken skin for masking. This is essential for boiled fowl, and where you bone the chicken. But it is not essential – if you like skin – for a whole roast bird or joints. Cut off protruding joint bones.

If you want to decorate the meat, Method B is essential.

MASKING. *Method* A. If the mayonnaise is as stiff as whipped cream, thin it slightly so that will just drop from the spoon. Arrange chicken on a bed of plain lettuce on serving dish, but not piled up so that some portions get no sauce. Use a tablespoon held low down on handle close to the 'bowl'; drop from side of spoon in a broad band, and try to cover the area in one go. If only a tiny bit is not covered leave to the end to see if mayonnaise spreads over it. Retouch with small blobs dropped from point of spoon close to the meat surface. Much retouching looks messier than gaps.

IMPORTANT. Vinegar thins mayonnaise, so it is unwise to dress the lettuce base, or any garnish that is to go on the dish, with vinaigrettes of any sort.

Method B. When the aspic is half-set mix it with the mayonnaise, and work quickly from then on. Have the chicken or joints on a cake rack with dish beneath. Spoon the now-thickening sauce over the chicken, as above. Remove the whole contraption to a cool place to set – about 1 hour. If decorating, do this only when sauce is well set. For this use paper-thin slivers of pimento, olive, almond, pickles (patted dry), etc. Keep the pattern and colours simple and uniform on each portion. Brush decoration with, or spoon over it, half-set aspic. Leave to set. If the decoration is to be left all day add a second coat of aspic when first has set. Lift on to prepared serving dish very carefully with fish slice or palette knife.

This method is to be preferred only for more grand occasions. The extra work does not improve either the flavour or texture of plain mayonnaise, which is one of the greatest of sauces and, with chicken, one of the happiest culinary marriages. The aspic method is merely useful in some circumstances.

ACCOMPANIMENTS. For family meals one filling salad and one lightweight. For example: rice salad (simple slivers of pimento, tomato, beans) and vinaigrette dressing; or potato salad in mayonnaise, with watercress and orange, or green salad in plain vinaigrette.

Add one of these for entertaining: diced cucumber, pineapple, almond slivers – mayonnaise; skinned and pipped green grapes, diced cucumber – salt, pepper, little sugar, lemon juice; lettuce salad; orange and grapefruit segments tossed in olive oil, toasted almond flakes scattered over; peas, sliced beans and broad beans in mayonnaise.

RAISED PIES

Don't be put off by the apparent length of this recipe. Dealt with fully here to demonstrate alternative methods of making and of fillings, it is really several in one. Not expensive, but one of the exotics of the English table, raised pies are near relations of pâtés, and you will often see pâtés in French delicatessens enclosed in decorative pastry crusts. Making raised pies satisfies one's creative urges and calls out one's imagination in the matter of fillings and finishes. Their cheapness begins, for example, with the hot-water pastry, which is improved by a proportion of dripping whilst among the best fillings are pigeon, hare and rabbit, cheap cuts of bacon, pork and veal.

HOT-WATER CRUST. In her instructions for raising pies,
Eliza Acton says: 'When the crust is not to be eaten it is made
simply with a few ounces of lard or butter dissolved in boiling
water with which the flour is to be mixed.' She goes on to advise
a good French *pâté brisée* for pies where the pastry is to be eaten.
This perhaps explains why the standard recipes for home-made
hot-water crust become hard on cooking. (Notice that the pastry
used for their pork pies by Messrs Harris, Wall and Sainsbury is
solid, but not at all rock-like.) As with shortcrust, I have long
used a higher proportion of fat for hot-water crust, and got over
the trouble.

12 oz. flour
scant 7 oz. fat (may be lard,
  lard and dripping, lard and
  butter, or all three, but
  lard should predominate;
  melt and strain dripping
  through muslin let harden; less
  tasty if clarified

scant ¼ pint water
1 egg-yolk (2 yolks are still
  better, but reduce water
  by 1 tbs.)
½ tsp. salt

Sieve flour and salt into a mixing bowl, making deep well in
centre. Heat water and fat slowly to boiling point and allow to
boil until water bubbles and crackles. At once pour liquid into
flour and mix with a wooden spoon, adding egg-yolk after a few
minutes. The heated liquid will swell the flour, partly cooking it,
and lumps soon form. Work these smooth and, as soon as possible, take over the mixing with the hands, being wary of heat in
the centre of the dough. Knead smooth. The dough will be soft
and oily.

RAISING THE PIE. This must be done while the paste is still
warm, so work quickly in one of the following ways, first cutting
off about ¼ of the dough for the lid (⅓ if the pie is long and shallow), which must be kept warm and covered.

By hand. Form the dough into a shortish, thick cone, turning
it several times in the palms to smooth the sides. Then press or
punch the top of the cone down steadily with your fist, turning
with the other hand, until the cone of dough is hollow in the
centre. Continue turning with one hand and shaping with the

343

other, potter-fashion, until you have a thick-walled flat-bottomed 'cocotte' of dough. The pastry should be moulded until it is $\frac{1}{4}$–$\frac{3}{16}$ inch thick. Points to watch are the junction of sides with base, which should not be too thick; but rather this than so thin that when the filling is pressed in it will pierce through, causing gravy to leak out.

Over a jam jar or tin. Turn a 2-lb. jam jar or 5-inch cake tin or soufflé dish upside down. Lightly grease and flour. Put the dough on top and roll it out evenly to the edges, moulding it down the sides by hand. To get enough dough to the edges and to keep even thickness, roll over the base from time to time with a rolling-pin. Leave to get quite cold. Very carefully slip a palette knife round to loosen sides and shake gently just above pastry-board to detach from bottom of mould.

In a raised pie mould or tin. Raised pie moulds are, like flan-rings, bottomless. *They must be stood on a baking-sheet and kept centred as you work, since they cannot be moved, once filled.* They are in two sections, hinged or pinned together, usually oval and 'waisted' with fluted or patterned sides. (Very attractive, not cheap.) A small straight-sided tin or dish will do as well. (I have used an oval cocotte successfully.)

Roll the dough ¼ inch thick and fold lightly in four, dropping centre in centre of mould, and then unfolding and pressing the dough against the sides and into the junction of base and sides Gradually work dough up to top, keeping it even, and ending with it just under ¼ inch thick. If you use a raised pie mould or loose-bottomed cake tin you can cook the pie in it; but from a fixed-base vessel remove the shell when cold and set, stand on baking-sheet and support with double thickness greaseproof band for cooking.

INGREDIENTS FOR FILLING. *Important:* have this ready before raising the pie. Keep covered in foil or polythene.

1 lb. meat (see below)	dissolve ¼ oz. gelatine in
1–2 hard-boiled eggs	it)
(optional)	½ glass sherry (or wine)
scant ½ pint strong clear	seasoning, herbs, spices
stock (if only light stock	

A common fault of home-made raised pies is the dryness of their filling, because not enough fat is put in. The popular factory-made pork and veal-and-ham pies contain generous proportions of fat, which accounts for their excellence. To make a good pie, then, stick to the high proportion of fat given. Another mistake is that the filling is frequently cut too coarsely; mince it if you doubt your skill or judgement in this matter.

The pound of meat should be made up of 10 oz. of the characteristic meat – pigeon, hare, etc. – 4 oz. *very fat* pork or bacon, or pork sausage meat, and 2 oz. ham, tongue, pressed beef or beefsteak. Cured or smoked lean meat gives flavour and texture, while lean fresh beef adds to the flavour of the jelly, and gives body to the filling.

When using pigeon I buy 2 or 3 as they are so cheap, and use the breast meat and livers for the pie (if your poulterer is to draw the birds, tell him you want the livers or he may not bother to keep them), the rest to make the stock, as there is little meat on the legs. This may yield only ½ lb. meat, when you must make up with extra beef steak. Skirt is excellent for pies.

If you cannot buy portions of hare, use the saddle for the pie (jug the rest), with belly of pork or flank bacon for the fatty meat.

You will notice that pork is not my first choice. It is hard to better the good commercial pork or veal-and-ham pie. A home-made pie of this kind has a different texture and appearance, which sometimes disappoints those who expect a sort of super shop version. Provided this is not expected, home-made pork or veal-and ham pie can be very good indeed.

For the lean pork for a pork pie a good idea for a family is to buy a hand (equivalent to shoulder of lamb, but much, much leaner; and cheap owing to its awkward size and the proportion of bone), and cut the 10 oz. of lean from this, roasting the rest. Get the butcher to chop off the shank for you, and from this make the stock, as it will give you good jelly.

A fine raised pie can be made during the summer from a guinea fowl, with fat and lean bacon as for the other meats, and dry white wine in the stock – made from the fowl bones and giblets. (See more about guinea fowl on p. 351.)

FILLING THE PIE. The meat may be put into the pie in distinct layers: slices of bacon, followed by game, followed by ham, seasoning and herbs between each layer, starting and finishing with bacon. Or the meats may be mixed together with the seasonings. Whichever way is preferred – the first being more attractive when cut, the second ensuring even distribution of the all-important fat – the cutting-up is of first importance. If sliced, the slices must be cardboard thin, even if you put them in several deep; while chopping must be really fine. This sounds odd until you come to fill the pie and, later, cut it. Thick or lumpy pieces of meat will not compact down or fit in corners, and are likely to push through the pie crust when pressed down. They are solid when cold, making cutting difficult, and, being loosely packed, fall out of the slices, making serving messy: both points a nuisance at picnics or parties. (Notice the same reasons hold good for cutting meat thinly for sandwiches.)

For sliced layers I cut the fat bacon really paper-thin, and distribute it between every two slices of the other meats; this keeps them beautifully moist and tender and salts them, whilst itself 'melting' almost to invisibility.

Eggs, whole or sliced, are placed in the centre of the pie.

When using sausage meat roll it out thinly and line bottom and sides of pie with it, reserving enough for a layer half-way up the pie, and another to cover the top of the meat after the stock has been poured in.

Having packed in the filling add enough stock mixed with sherry to come half-way up the meat or a little over. You may have to insert a skewer gently here and there to make the stock go down if you have done your packing well.

FINISHING. Roll out the lid, reserving a very small quantity of pastry for leaves and tassel. Damp top edges of pie-casing and edge of lid and 'pinch' the lid on. There are many ways to make this edge both decorative and also the good seal it must be. The pinching will give a quite wide stand-away frill, and this may be patterned by small cuts at ½-inch intervals, the pastry being given a slight curl or twist up or down, towards or away from you, which will make a fancy edging. Or you can pinch with two fingers against a third, or against your thumb, or mark with a fork or knife blade. With the spare pastry make leaves, and a rose or tassel, to adorn the central hole in the lid that lets out steam. Make this hole large enough to take the tassel easily. Twist a knife point in it to enlarge.

Georgian pie-makers used to make wonderfully ornate edges and decorations, and Eliza Acton shows a pie wreathed in a pastry bas-relief of grape vine.

Tassel in place with 'cable' round, circle of leaves, cut edging, knife point pattern. Caution: don't cut sides too deeply. Could stick leaves round (with egg white).

LEAVES

Thin strip of pastry cut

One segment marked with knife point to make leaf

TASSEL

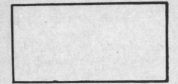

Strip of pastry 2 x 1 inches
⅙ inch thick

Cut it down ¾
depth in fine strips

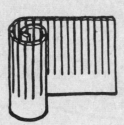

Roll up

Uncurl

ROSE

Strip as for tassel. Cut at wide intervals, roll, uncurl petals.

Pin a band of well-greased double greaseproof paper round pies not in mould or tin. Bake for 20 minutes at 425° F, gas 7, lowering heat to 350° F, gas 4, for 1 hour, then 325° F, gas 3, for 1½ hours. During this last period of cooking rest a sheet of damped greaseproof paper over the top of the pie to prevent it darkening and drying too much, and remove the collar of double greaseproof so that the pie walls colour well. Half an hour before the end of the cooking mix an egg-yolk with 1 dessertsp. water and a good pinch salt and brush over the whole pie thoroughly. Return to oven without covering, to cook the glaze. Tassels and roses need not be added until about 1 hour before the end of cooking.

After the pie has cooled slightly, very gently lift out the tassel from the centre hole, insert a funnel (make one from thick greaseproof paper or double foil) about 1 inch down into the pie and pour more stock in gradually until it can be seen in the funnel on a level with the crust but not brimming over. Leave the pie to get cold, putting back the tassel when the stock has settled a little. Leave till next day before serving.

BOILED BACON

Slipper and gammon hock, collar, or a piece of forehock, are all medium-sized, moderately priced and meaty cuts of bacon for boiling; slipper, for example, weighing about 2 lb., while forehock can be cut into pieces anything from 2 lb. (boned) to 8 lb. (whole). Back can be bought in the piece, as can of course streaky, the former being rather fat, the latter often fairly fat but very cheap. Corner gammon is dearer, weighs about 4 lb., but is good value, being boneless and lean, for a family. Boiled bacon is a most useful summer joint; it is light in character when hot, while its virtues cold are too well known to need enumerating.

I have referred elsewhere to the treatment of over-salt bacon. If this is a problem when bacon is only one of the ingredients in a recipe, it is crucial when bacon or ham is the principal item on the menu. A whole joint of over-salted meat is impervious to any treatments I have managed to devise – they include the essential soaking for several hours or overnight, changes of water, blanching, adding sodium bicarbonate. The Danes have, in the last few years, very greatly reduced the amount of salt used in bacon curing in response to public taste. There is also the newish British 'sweetcure' method, which usually gives a mild joint, but bacon cured by this method is not to be found everywhere. Unsmoked or green bacon is not necessarily any less salt, for salt goes in during curing, and this takes place before smoking. Look with suspicion on dark red, raw-looking, wettish bacon, often a sign of too much salt.

In any event soak the joint for a minimum of 6 hours in lukewarm water, changing this if possible more than once. Untie larger joints for soaking, re-tie before cooking.

Put the joint into cold water with an onion stuck with 2 cloves, carrot, celery (leaves or seed, when fresh unavailable), 1 tbs. brown sugar, ⅛ pint tarragon vinegar or ¼ pint dry cider. Paradoxically, because it acts as a slight tenderizer the acid helps in releasing the salt into the water, and, of course, adds greatly to flavour. Cook for a minimum of: 1 hour for joints up to 1 lb.; 1½ hours for joints up to 2 lb.; 30 minutes per lb. for joints over 2 lb., plus 30 minutes. Remove rind while hot, and coat fat in browned crumbs.

For eating cold, however, skin, return to pot and leave to get cold in liquor, crumbing the outside fat next day.

The broth makes excellent stock for cooking lentils for pease pudding or soup, or for cabbage soups (pp. 142–3, 177).

Parsley sauce is hard to better with boiled bacon, in particular when broad beans are the accompanying vegetable. Pineapple, also, is particularly 'right' with bacon, and a salad of crisp lettuce with a couple of spoonfuls of chopped fresh pineapple turned in the leaves is excellent. I give also a sauce that was originally made for roast guinea fowl, but which goes well with ham or bacon.

BROWN CHERRY SAUCE

For roast game, grilled ham, etc.

½ pint stock
½ small onion, sliced
¾ oz. butter/margarine
¼ oz. lard
1 oz. flour
1 level tbs. rowan jelly
   (optional)
bouquet garni

1 small tsp. black treacle
seasoning
grated rind and juice ½ orange,
   and ½ lemon
½ lb. white heart cherries,
   stoned
a dash of brandy (or sherry)

Heat the lard in a small saucepan. Add the butter. In this cook the onion until soft, scatter in flour and cook until nut brown. Add stock by degrees, stirring out all lumps. Add rest of ingredients and simmer gently ½ hour. Remove bouquet garni, strain sauce, sieve liquid part, keeping cherries warm. Return all to pan and reheat before dishing in heated sauceboat.

Cooking, or morello, cherries give a particularly good flavour to this sauce, but you may like to increase the treacle, or use some sugar as well, to offset the sharpness. Any sort of good canned cherries may be used (but not the watery, bright red 'fruit salad' kind as they have no taste), and extra lemon juice will be needed in that instance.

GUINEA FOWL

(*French – pintade.*)

So called because they were first found in the wild state in Guinea, these plump meaty birds are on the borderline between game and poultry. They are reared for table now in the manner of free-range poultry. Flavour and texture are something between chicken and pheasant, but as they are considerably cheaper than the latter, and as well-covered, or better, as the former, they are a very good buy. At their best in the summer, they make a perfect hot-weather roast for a special occasion.

The flesh is on the dry side. Larding is recommended in older cookery books, but if you adopt the method of slipping a piece of fat under the skin, as described on p. 85, and of cooking the bird breast down for the first 20 minutes of roasting you will get a satisfactorily moist result. Season inside as for chicken. Roast at 325° F, gas 3, for 40 minutes, raising heat to 400° F, gas 6, for the final browning of the breast. Baste two or three times, and cover breast with larded paper until final browning stage, when dredge lightly with flour and baste, before returning to the oven.

Make gravy in the roasting tin and serve with game chips or potato crisps, browned crumbs, bread sauce, watercress and green salad. (Thinly sliced orange salad or fresh peaches, skinned and sliced, either of these then being lightly arrosé with brandy or Cointreau, aren't half bad either, as an extra.)

As a change try the Cherry Sauce on p. 351.

Vegetables

Marrows

Ever since the twenties it has been the fashion to admonish the English horticulturist – amateur or professional – on the large size of his vegetables as compared with those on the Continent. It seems to me that too many of these critics are ignorant of gardening.

To begin with, things grown in a hot dry climate set seed and ripen quickly. In such a climate the best varieties to grow are those which produce a multitude of small fruits (in case you've forgotten your school biology, I use the word fruit here in its widest sense). In the rainy cool of the British Isles you can successfully use varieties which have larger and fewer seeds and seed heads, and bring these to fruition in a state of perfection as far as tenderness and flavour are concerned. It is just not true that flower-show judges award the prizes to marrows left so long on the plant that they attain size by becoming coarse and hard. Anyone who has grown marrows of various sorts, including zucchini or courgettes, knows that you would wait for ever for them to grow beyond their allotted size. Big marrows quite quickly attain their maximum size and, picked then, are so tender and juicy that, if you mean to exhibit them, you handle them as cautiously as hothouse grapes. The least scratch of fingernail will blemish or pierce their skins. Cooked at this moment they can taste like melted butter.

No, the objection to giant marrows for the kitchen is that they need large numbers to eat them. The real problem for those who must buy from shops is that the small marrow they have chosen has been too long *picked* and is hard and dried.

A fresh young marrow will 'bend' if you press the ball of your thumb on top of one of its ridges, it will have a shiny skin, the tiny stalk will still be green and fat, and it will not have callouses where the skin has been damaged. The last is not a very reliable guide, for callouses can also be the result of damage to the surface of the fruit when small. (It used to be a favourite trick of country children to scratch their names on just-formed marrows so that, as the fruit swelled, the callouses over the wounds writ the name large along the side of the marrow.) No need to peel a really fresh marrow.

STUFFED MARROW

Make ordinary sage and onion stuffing (p. 485; use approximately ½ lb. onions), cut out an oval lid almost the full length of the marrow. Do not peel it. Scoop out all the seeds, season the walls of the fruit, stuff, replace lid, tie round with soft string at two places and bake in meat tin at 325° F, gas 3, for about 1½–2 hours according to size. Marrow takes quite a lot of baking, and is as delicious when thoroughly cooked as it is nasty when half-done. Test with a skewer which should go completely through at the rounded end as if through softened butter. The marrow may sag at the sides if a wide lid is cut. In this event support it with a foil case twisted round, or use a narrow fireproof dish.

Marrow may, of course, be filled with meat mixtures for a main course (p. 401).

MARROW FLORENTINE

Based on a recipe from *Leaves from our Tuscan Kitchen.*

Halve, seed and cut the marrow into inch-thick slices. Peel if necessary. Blanch for 5 minutes, drain and return to pan with 2 oz. butter (or ½ butter, ½ margarine), a sprig of fine-chopped marjoram or basil, about 6 chive leaves, chopped, or 1 tsp. minced onion, a little salt and pepper. Turn slices well in this mixture, and simmer until the marrow is absolutely tender, 20–30 minutes. Add 2 tbs. light stock (chicken for preference), 2 of thin cream (or substitutes) and 1 tsp. lemon. Reheat and serve.

Both these are useful single-person dishes. With sausages (English or Frankfurter, etc.) they make a good main meal.

MARROW AND TOMATO

Any combination of these two goes well. This recipe can be done on a gas ring if an asbestos mat is used, but the crumb top would then need a grill, or would have to be omitted.

Fill a fireproof dish with alternate layers of peeled and sliced marrow, skinned sliced tomato, paper-thin rounds of onion, shavings of margarine, seasoning. When the dish is full, thrust a crushed clove of garlic through the centre. Cover with foil and bake at 325° F, gas 3, for 45 minutes. Remove foil, and scatter over top 1 oz. browned or dried breadcrumbs mixed with ½ oz. grated Parmesan or 1 oz. dried Cheddar. Dot with margarine and return to oven, turning heat up to 400° F, gas 6, for 15 minutes or until top is browned. Or finish under grill.

Tomatoes

This is the peak of the English hothouse season when, in my opinion, the best flavoured tomatoes in the world are plentiful and cheap.

RAW STUFFED TOMATOES

Sharp as they are, salt enhances their flavour still more, so that two of the best fillings for hollowed out raw tomatoes are shrimps or prawns. Turn these in a little mayonnaise, or lemon juice and cayenne, and pile into large tomatoes from which you have cut the tops – the flower end, as the stalk end makes a good standing base – and hollowed out the divisions and pips, skimming finally with care – don't let them split down the sides.

Chopped ham or boiled bacon turned in a little parsley sauce; flaked smoked fish in white sauce; a mixture of young vegetables, or chicken and mushroom, with rice in mayonnaise – all make good fillings, and the fillings may be varied to make complete courses for light meals or accompaniments. Filled raw tomatoes are very good with grills of all kinds.

COOKED STUFFED TOMATOES

Hollow out as above, but do not skin, and fill with: chopped liver, or kidney and bacon, in white sauces, sauce espagnole (p. 118) or orange sauce (p. 487); flaked fish in good Béchamel (p. 117) with a few peas, diced carrot, or sliced beans; cauliflower, broken down into small florets, in cheese sauce; a small egg broken into each tomato, topped with a square of bacon rasher; rice mixed with curry leftovers; the remains of risotto or kedgeree – all to be baked uncovered, except for the tomato tops, 10–20 minutes at 375° F, gas 5, according to filling.

WHOLE TOMATO SALAD

Sometimes you will see tiny 'chats' tomatoes on sale, and they are very cheap. Skin them by dropping into boiling water 1 minute – no more – and at once into cold. Turn them in a vinaigrette made with lemon or orange juice in place of vinegar and serve with thin brown bread and butter, or thin crisped oatcakes and butter.

BUTTERED CHATS

Melt 1½ oz. butter in a shallow pan or dish which you can cover. Skin ¾ lb. chat tomatoes as above. Chop finely 6 blades chive and 2 sprigs mint, basil or marjoram. Mix all well with the butter, season, cover the pan, and cook gently 12–20 minutes, turning the tomatoes from time to time. Good with baked or grilled white fish.

TOMATOES NATURE – TWO IDEAS

(1) While the season is on, nothing beats tomatoes eaten just as they are with salt and hot toast and butter – plenty of butter. Make each slice of toast fresh as it is wanted, and put a dish of tomatoes on the table. As a course at tea instead of bread and jam, most children can't have enough, and you can make a splendid summer breakfast of it.

(2) There are yellow tomatoes to be had, in rare instances in shops, but certainly you should grow some yellow and some red if you grow your own, for the great pleasure of looking along the row at the regal colour. For a summer dinner adorn the table with golden and red tomatoes heaped on dark leaves, to be eaten as dessert with sugar – and *vin rosé*.

Peas

The most delicate method by which to cook precious garden peas is that known as *à la française*. The details in recipes vary, but the essence of the method is as follows:

2 lb. peas (in the pod)	1 tsp. chopped mint (optional)
1 oz. butter	1 tbs. stock or water
1 tsp. minced onion *or*	
4 spring onions, *or*	optional
1 dozen chive blades	
1 lump sugar	seasoning

A small lettuce (good way to use up 'thinnings'; or buy one of the hearts of lettuce to which greengrocers reduce wilting lettuces on Mondays at bargain prices.)

NOTE: If you cannot get good fresh peas, you certainly will save money nowadays by buying a plastic sackful of frozen. At this time of the year they are in tip-top condition, and save time and work.

Quarter the lettuce, trim or chop the onions, and put them with the butter and sugar over low heat in a thick pan. When the butter has melted and the lettuce wilted into it, add stock and peas, seasoning very lightly. Cover and barely simmer ½ hour, less for very tender peas, 15 minutes for unthawed frozen peas. Pour off the liquid and reduce it until no longer watery, adding the mint. Pour over peas and lettuce, which you have kept warm in a heated dish.

Omit onions and mint to make a change and enjoy the nutty sweet taste of the peas and lettuce alone.

Another nice way with peas is to make a flowing consistency Béchamel sauce (p. 117), omitting the bayleaf from the bouquet garni, but adding a goodish pinch of ground mace or a generous grating of nutmeg. Turn the cooked peas in this, and surround them in the serving dish with a border of tiny fried croûtons.

SUMMER VEGETABLE POT

Useful for gardeners, and after a week-end of visitors when there may be varied leftovers of vegetables.

6 oz. shelled peas	¾ oz. margarine/butter
¼ lb. button mushrooms	1 rounded tbs. flour
½ lb. broad beans	2 tbs. top milk or single
(shucks included if tender)	cream
2–3 sprigs mint, marjoram or	seasoning
parsley	

In a deep saucepan or cocotte melt the fat. Season well. Add the mushrooms, washed, but otherwise left untrimmed. Cook gently, covered, 2–3 minutes until juice begins to run. Add the peas and beans and as much water as you can shake from a wetted hand, turning all well until shiny with fat. Cover, and continue cooking on a mere whisper of heat (use asbestos mat if necessary) for 15 minutes. Meanwhile chop mint finely. At end of cooking time scatter in flour off fire, stir well, add cream or top milk and mint, stir again, return to fire 2 minutes. This forms a sauce round the vegetables. Those who insist on onion may add a few chopped chives, spring onion tops, or a *small* amount of onion bulb – more delicious without though.

Serve as a separate course with thin brown bread and butter – Hovis is particularly good. This is a dish that warms up perfectly. (First made for coming home to after the opera, in the interval of which one has a light supper and so, although one wants only a small, quickly produced snack, something more imaginative than sandwiches is needed especially if the singing wasn't up to scratch . . .)

THE GARDENER'S OWN POTATOES

The first root or two of home-grown potatoes should be shared by all the family perhaps, or by one's two most appreciative friends. But then, make this special dish for the gardener's private consumption, as a reward for labour and an encouragement for next year.

2 lb. freshly dug new potatoes	¼ pint single cream (no
sprig of mint	substitute)
1½ oz. salted butter	1 level tsb. chopped parsley
½ oz. flour	seasoning

Boil the potatoes with the mint as usual. Drain them. Melt butter in a big pan and put in the potatoes, rolling them carefully until all are coated in butter. Scatter in the flour, roll gently to mix. Pour in the cream, add the parsley, and season. Keep on gentle heat 3 minutes, moving just enough to prevent sticking, and mix and thicken the flour. Serve hot on their own, or with a plain very good grill – fillet steak, chump chop; a choice cut of salmon or turbot; fried chicken. And a bottle of *Bourgogne Blanc*, say, or Muscadet, and forget all about balancing the budget for the evening.

Puddings

GERTRUDE GOSLIN'S BLACKCURRANT KEESEL

July is blackcurrant month. Not a classic keesel, but that is the nearest generic term for it. The tapioca in this recipe softens the tartness without in any way interfering with the lovely flavour of blackcurrants, and the textures melt into one another. Possible, but not nearly so good, with the various blackcurrant syrups.

½ pint boiling water	2 tbs. seed tapioca
7½ fl. oz. cold water	4 tbs. sugar
½ lb. black currants	

Into ½ pint boiling water scatter 2 tbs. seed tapioca, stir, see none sticks. Add the black currants and the cold water. Boil up, lower heat to a whisper (use asbestos mat if necessary), simmer not less than 20 minutes. Frequent scraping across the base of pan is essential as the tapioca tends to sink and stick. When tapioca grains are seen to be clear, stir in sugar, continue simmering few minutes to dissolve sugar, then boil up 2 minutes. Cool slightly before pouring into individual glasses, or pour into wetted mould, chill well and turn out. Serve with unwhipped cream. Cream substitutes spoil the flavour.

This is a soft mould and does not turn out successfully if the currants are over-ripe, or the season rainy, when blackcurrants may contain a high proportion of water. It is just as attractive, however, served in the dish.

LINZER TORTE

PASTRY

6 oz. flour	4 oz. butter/margarine
½ oz. finely ground coffee	3 oz. castor sugar
(not instant powder)	1 egg-yolk mixed with 1 tbs.
½ tsp. cocoa	water

MARMALADE OF RASPBERRIES

8–12 oz. raspberries	1 round tbs. sugar

Cook raspberries gently with sugar but no water until sugar melts, then boil fast 3 minutes and leave to cool.

Mix cocoa, flour and coffee thoroughly, turn on to pastry-board and make into a circle. Into the centre of this put egg, sugar and butter. Pinch these together with fingertips of one hand only, until they are mixed. Using palette knife in clean hand, gradu-ally push ring of flour in towards centre, pinching it into rest, scraping board to incorporate all ingredients. When all is to-gether in one lump of dough, scrape hand, flour both hands, and gently kneed into smooth ball. Roll out $^3/_{10}$–$^1/_4$ inch thick, and line a 7 to 8-inch flan-ring – a fluted ring is particularly attractive for this – reserving pastry trimmings for a lattice. Fill with the rasp-berry marmalade, cover top with coarse lattice of $^1/_2$-inch-wide strips. Bake at 375° F, gas 5, 30 minutes. Cool well before sliding off baking-sheet. Brush over whole with glaze made from 1 tbs. sieved red jam, or whisked redcurrant jelly, and 1 tbs. water heated together. Serve with whipped cream.

The dough for this pastry is very soft when raw, and brittle while warm, so needs gentle handling. It is beautifully crunchy and short to eat, and the coffee flavour and texture a unique combination with the raspberries. Tinned or frozen raspberries do very well, but the syrup of the former may need reducing somewhat. If so, remove the fruit from the syrup first. Thaw frozen raspberries before adding sugar, since they will probably need rather less. The fruit will sink down in flan after cooking.

REDCURRANT WINE JELLY

1 packet red jelly
$^1/_2$ pint sweet red wine or
1 pint jelly made as on p.
   259 but with $^1/_2$ pint port
   (cheapish kind and 5 tbs.
   lemon juice instead of
   lemons

$^1/_2$ lb. redcurrants
3 oz. sugar
$^1/_4$ pint water

Make a syrup of the sugar and water, bring to the boil, pour over all but 2 dozen of biggest prepared redcurrants in cocotte. Put in gentle oven 250° F, gas ½, for 15 minutes. Allow to get completely cold. Strain off juice carefully to avoid breaking the fruit, and melt the jelly in the juice, adding wine and water to make up a scant pint. Add the cooked currants, and pour into a wetted 1½-pint mould. Lastly add the raw currants. The cooked currants sink, the raw float, and between the two is a clear layer of jelly. The sharp currants offset the sweetness of the jelly. Serve with castor sugar and cream.

FRUIT MOUSSES

There are several varieties, some with a custard base which are really cold soufflés, others frozen and rather like ice-cream. The variation given below is practical, as it can be made by those without refrigerators and makes use of those egg-whites which one so often has spare. Any fruit may be used – fresh, bottled or canned.

For preparation of soufflé case and general instructions, see p. 419.

¼ pint fruit purée	flavouring to taste (e.g. 1–2
1 oz. castor sugar	drops vanilla added to
¼ pint double cream (or	apple, ½ tsp. lemon juice
substitutes, p. 62)	added to raspberry, 1 tsp.
½ oz. (1 envelope) gelatine	white wine to strawberry,
2 tbs. water (or fruit juice if	1 tsp. sherry to redcurrant,
available)	orange to rhubarb, almond
2–3 egg-whites	to cherry)

Put the flavoured purée and sugar into mixing bowl; melt the gelatine in 2 tbs. water and stir into purée. Whip whites stiffly, whip cream until it barely holds shape. Fold each, in that order, into purée, and pour into a prepared soufflé case or serving dish. Leave to get as cold as possible. Decorate as for a soufflé or in any other way preferred, suiting decorations to flavour. Cream, wine or fruit sauce may be handed separately : see overleaf.

WINE SAUCE

5 tbs. sherry or table wine	1 tbs. lemon juice
– generous measure	2 yolks
5 tbs. water – very mean	1½ oz. sugar

Whisk yolks and sugar in a small basin over, but not in, simmering water. When you can write your initial on the froth, pour slowly in the wine, water and juice mixed, whisking non-stop. Serve hot or cold.

FRUIT SAUCE

5 tbs. fruit purée	¼ pint water
juice of half a lemon	1 tbs. rum or brandy
2 oz. sugar	(optional)

Whisk all ingredients over gentle heat until the sugar dissolves. Serve hot or cold.

Pour a little of either of these two sauces over or round an unmoulded pudding, sending rest to table in a sauceboat. Fruit Sauce may be thickened with arrowroot for masking puddings, where suitable.

Soups

CLEAR PARSLEY CONSOMMÉ
(Chilled or hot – Useful for gardeners.)

1½ pints good chicken stock such as is left from boiling a fowl; or made from giblets and bones of roaster)

¼ lb. parsley (more may be used but not much less)

the green top of 1 spring onion or 8 chive blades, chopped

1 tbs. lemon juice

5 tbs. sweet white wine, cider, or dry sherry

1 level tsp. salt

¼ tsp. pepper

½ tsp. sugar (optional, but not more)

1 egg-white and crushed shell

¼ oz. gelatine if stock is rather a soft jelly

double cream (optional)

Wash and finely chop the parsley including stalks. Add all ingredients except wine to stock in large pan and bring slowly to the boil, whisking continuously and following jelly method (p. 258) to clear the soup. Pour through jelly-bag or cloth, adding wine. Serve just chilled but still liquid, with a spoonful of cream marbled on at the last minute; or completely set without garnish; or hot with cheese straws or Bath Oliver biscuits. Improve colour if liked with green colouring.

Another, more usual Parsley Soup is on p. 412.

CREAM OF PEA-POD

2 lb. young pea pods (pea pods will keep a day or so in polythene in the refrigerator)
1 pint stock (or bouillon cube)
green tops from 2 or 3 spring onions

¼ pint milk
2 good sprigs mint
salt, pepper, sugar
½ carton yoghurt
½ oz. each butter and flour
or 2 egg-yolks

Wash pods, put in pan with onion tops, and just cover with boiling water. Add 1 level tsp. salt, ½ tsp. sugar, good shake of pepper, 1 sprig mint. Simmer about 1 hour until soft flesh will rub off inner fibrous lining of pods. Remove mint. Pass through Moulin-Légumes, and afterwards through bowl-strainer or sieve, to make sure all fibrous pieces are cleared. *Either:* Melt butter, add flour off fire, stir in milk and bring to boil stirring out any lumps; add stock and purée and bring to boil, stirring in yoghurt, and finally adding remaining mint chopped finely. *Or:* Heat stock, stir in purée, add milk and bring just to boil. Whisk yolks with yoghurt and pour hot soup on to them, finishing with mint as above.

TOMATO SOUP

This recipe, in almost identical words, appears in both Mrs C. S. Peel's 10/- *A Head for Housebooks* of 1899 and Janet Ross's *Leaves from our Tuscan Kitchen*, edition of 1905 (first published 1899), the latter being claimed by its author as largely compiled from the recipes of her old Italian chef, or from *Come si Cucinano i Legumi* published by the Fratelli Ingegnote of Milan. So where the recipe really originated – like many these days, also – I am unable to say. But it tastes nice, which is what matters.

1 lb. tomatoes
1 pint stock
bayleaf, parsley, celery seed
   or 1 stick (or dried leaves) } Tie in muslin
   6 peppercorns
1 tsp. sugar
1 sliced onion
1 oz. each dripping and flour
salt

Put tomatoes and flavourings in stock and simmer until tomatoes are soft – about 20 to 30 minutes. Meanwhile sweat onion in dripping, add flour and simmer it until it turns straw colour, but not any darker. Add some of the cooked soup, mix, and pour back to rest of soup, mixing well over gentle heat. Remove muslin and add salt to taste. Sieve, reheat and garnish with tiny croûtons.

That is the original version. I like to use stock that has had bacon in some form in it; or I add bacon rinds, tied together, while the tomatoes cook; or chop up a rasher, cook and sieve it with the rest. As a variation, and for those who like it, a crushed clove of garlic – removed before sieving – adds greatly to the interest.

MIDSUMMER SOUP

Gertrude Goslin's recipe.

1 quart stock
2 tomatoes (skinned and sliced)
seasoning
good pinch caraway seed
1 tbs. tarragon (or similar) vinegar
1 rounded tsp. mixed pickle (chopped finely)
faggot of mixed fresh herbs
as available (or pinch dried)
8–10 prunes soaked ready for use, or plums stewed but not mushy
1 each medium carrot, potato (diced), onion (sliced), clove of garlic (chopped finely)
1 oz. margarine
½ tsp. curry powder

Soften onion and garlic in margarine, add carrot and potato, and continue gentle cooking 5 minutes, turning about to coat with fat. Pour over these the stock, and simmer 10 minutes. Add rest of ingredients, except prunes, season and continue cooking 10 minutes. Remove faggot. Adjust seasoning. Put a prune in each soup-plate, and stir the soup before each helping, as there is no thickening to hold ingredients in suspension through the liquid.

First Courses and Snacks

SALAD NIÇOISE

There are variations in the ingredients for this favourite hors-d'œuvre, but it should include tuna fish, anchovies, green beans, black olives and tomatoes. It may also have hard-boiled egg, lettuce (as a foundation, shredded or not), broad beans, peas, pimento, cucumber. You can make a version with sardine or salmon, and substitute green for black olives – though this really is a loss.

Build up your Niçoise in layers in a shallow dish, more or less how you please but the anchovies and stoned olives should go on top –in a pattern or casually. For example:

(1) Layer of mixed beans and peas.

(2) 2 small tins of tuna, flaked with a little of the oil, over bottom of dish.

(3) A scattering of needle-fine pimento shreds (from ¼ of a pimento – never overdo this ingredient).

(4) Slices of hard-boiled egg (2–3) and skinned tomato (2–3), alternating and overlapping to cover surface completely.

(5) 4–6 anchovy fillets halved and strewn over with stoned halves of olives.

Make a good lemon vinaigrette (p. 229), add 1 tsp. fresh chopped herbs and spoon over. Melba toast is good with it.

WINE-PICKLED HERRING FILLETS

A classic Polish hors-d'œuvre, which also appears in various versions in Scandinavia.

Make a marinade of : ¾ gill olive (or good salad) oil, 2 tbs. lemon juice, 3 tbs. white wine, 1 dessertsp. chopped chive, salt, freshly ground black pepper. Fillet 3 herrings (p. 90). Lay fillets in shallow dish, pour on the marinade, whisking well just beforehand. Cover completely with greaseproof paper and leave for at least a week, turning often. Foil may be used in refrigerator, but care must be taken that temperature is not cold enough to congeal the oil.

Serve garnished with minced spring onion scattered lightly over fillets and thinly sliced radishes. Hand brown bread and butter, brown toast, or blinis (pp. 229–31).

TOMATOES BONNE SANTÉ

4 large tomatoes	1 oz. butter/margarine
½ lb. spinach	6 blades chive or ½ tsp.
1 egg	minced onion
1–2 oz. grated cheese	seasoning
(according to strength)	

Cook down the spinach, drain and squeeze out moisture well. Melt butter, chop spinach into it, season and chop again over slight heat. Add chive, mix over heat. Cool a little. Add cheese and beaten egg. Cut tops off tomatoes, hollow out, add chopped pulp and strained juice, but not pips, to spinach. Season insides of tomatoes and fill with spinach mixture. Put on tops and bake at 375° F, gas 5, for 20 to 25 minutes. Serve on fried croûtons or buttered toast if liked, or on bed of green beans turned in butter and well seasoned.

Good vegetarian and single-person dish.

MACARONI GEORGINA

The quantity given serves 2 for a luncheon dish, and 4 as a first course with the addition of 2 more eggs.

6–8 oz. macaroni
2 cloves garlic
2 large eggs 'mollet' (p. 148)
   (duck's eggs where
   available)

3 oz. mushrooms (or stalks)
2 oz. margarine/butter
1 oz. butter
freshly ground black pepper
salt

Cook macaroni *al dente* (i.e., so that it is just tender, but not mushy – biteable in other words). Meanwhile chop garlic and soften in 2 oz. margarine, wash and cut mushrooms in ½-inch pieces, and soften in 1 oz. butter. Shell eggs and keep warm covered with butter paper. Drain the macaroni, return to pan, strain garlic butter on to it, discarding garlic. Add mushrooms and their butter. Pepper well, add salt to taste, mixing all over gentle heat, and taking care not to break up mushrooms. Pour round and over eggs, return to oven for a few minutes.

Also good for vegetarians and single-person households.

As a variation, fry 2 diced bacon rashers with mushrooms, using only ½ oz. butter.

Either version reheats well.

Fish

TRUITE AUX AMANDES

Serves 2

Fishermen and fishmongers tend to think alike on the subject of trout bought in shops: overrated. My fishmonger says he would rather have a fresh herring any day, and has a shrewd suspicion that many of his customers buy trout as a status symbol. He's very happy, of course, to supply them. Fishermen say trout should be cooked on the river-bank to be really good. I agree with both these authorities, though I think smoked trout delicious. If not quite addressed to camp-fire cooks, this best of all trout classics is included for catch-it-yourself cooks.

2 trout
8 blanched almonds
salt and cayenne pepper

heavy brine (p. 338)
1½ oz. butter
about 1 tbs. lemon juice

Gut the fish, saving any roe (to be cooked in butter and added to the serving dish as an extra garnish), cleaning well and snipping out gills. At this point put almonds to soak in warm water. Boil fast as for Herrings Lowestoft (p. 338), 6 minutes or until eyes are completely white. Remove at once, drain, and carefully remove skin leaving it only at head and tail. It should be easy to remove fin bones during the process. Trim tail, remove eyes, cover closely with butter paper and keep warm. Cut the almonds into long slivers. Heat butter and fry almonds until just colouring. Add lemon juice, a dash of cayenne and spoon over the fish. Serve on hot plates.

SOUSED HERRING OR MACKEREL

4 herring or 2–3 mackerel (depending on size)
about ¼ pint each vinegar and water
1 small onion sliced thinly in rings
1 tsp. brown sugar
1 tsp. pickling spice including small pieces ginger and 1 chilli

1 bayleaf
2 fennel or dill sprigs (pinch seed in winter) if available
for herring: strips of orange rind, juice of ½ orange
for mackerel: strips of lemon rind, juice of ½ lemon

NOTE: When available I use the vinegar and spices from a jar of home-pickled onions (p. 546), adding only bayleaf, lemon or orange, fennel and sugar. The onion flavour and all the spices have, of course, already mingled and matured, so cooking the vinegar is unnecessary. The result is particularly mellow.

Lightly crush the spices between two spoons, and simmer with peel, onions and sugar in liquids for 5 minutes. Pour over fish, and cook on top or in oven for anything from 20 minutes at medium heat, to 6 to 8 hours at lowest oven setting, or over minimal burner heat with asbestos mat if necessary. The long version will 'melt' the bones – useful for children, and if cooking is done overnight, for a hot breakfast. Serve hot or cold, usually without any accompaniment other than brown bread and butter. However, a dish of buttery new or mashed potatoes can be excellent, or sliced tomatoes dressed very simply with salt, pepper and sugar.

Useful single-person recipe.

DABS AND FLOUNDERS

In both July and August small – or indeed any-sized – boys holidaying along the coasts bring home catches of these small and delicious plaice-like fishes. Sometimes they appear in town fish shops. They are tastier and firmer than plaice, but are usually too small to fillet. They need no elaborate cooking, being at their best grilled or fried *à la meunière* (p. 154), or deep fried – with egg and breadcrumb coating, or with flour and egg (pp. 103 and 281) – and served hot or cold with any of the sauces used for lemon sole, with flavoured butters, or with salads.

A pleasing variation, if deep frying, is *au Colbert*. Split down centre on one side, and lift flesh from bones either side of centre bone out as far as fins, making a pocket (below). Egg and crumb fish, including the inside of this pocket; when fried it will curl away from bone. Just before serving put a pat of *maître-d'hôtel* butter on top. If fish is thick and big enough, the centre bone may be removed before serving, but with most dabs this is not a good idea.

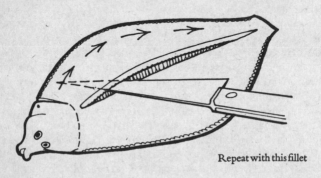

Repeat with this fillet

A DELICIOUS COLD FISH STEW

Gertrude Goslin's recipe.

1 lb. 'fat' fish according to
season : halibut or turbot
'cutlets', brill, salmon
heads (about 3), mackerel
(not quite so good)
1 Spanish or 2 smaller onions
2 oz. butter (proportion of
margarine may be used)

2–3 eggs
1 rounded tsp. cornflour
(optional)
juice of 2 lemons
salt, pepper
½ level tsp. ginger

Slice onion in rings, not too thick. Sweat in butter. Add fish on
the bone. Barely cover with water. Season, including ginger.
Cook on top or in oven very slowly with gentle heat, about 35 to
40 minutes so that fish is tender but firm. Drain fish, boning
where possible, or necessary, for example with heads, and put to
get cold on serving dish. Remove onion rings from liquor and
reserve, covered, in a cool place. Pour liquor into saucepan
through strainer to get rid of stray bones. (Use double saucepan
if working with egg mixtures bothers you.) Beat eggs and add,
with lemon juice, to liquor. Heat gently, stirring constantly,
keeping below boiling point until mixture coats back of spoon.
Alternatively slake cornflour with a little of the cooled liquor,
and stir in with other additions, when curdling of eggs should
not occur. Pour sauce over fish, scatter the onion rings on top
and leave until cold. Slightly chill before serving if possible, but
do not serve too cold.

Accompaniments : potato salad with vinaigrette dressing,
cucumber with salt and sugar, or green salad.

Meat

English, Scotch, Welsh lamb, all three are now at their peak.
The latter is worth holidaying in Wales for if you have never
had any, and it's very difficult to come by outside Wales. Any of

the lamb recipes given elsewhere should be consulted : pp. 235–42, 288–92, 318, etc.

SANDWICHES

Meat sandwiches are often badly made because, I think, it is thought that the filling is good enough to tell its own story. This is a fallacy. Meat sandwiches, like any others, need : thinly cut bread, thickly spread *butter* (*please not* margarine with meat), good seasoning of salt and pepper, crusts cut off when made.

In addition there should be further flavouring to suit the meat, and a useful way to incorporate this is to spread it on one of the two slices of bread; for example :

thin mustard for bacon, ham, pork, beef;
medium horseradish sauce for beef (one slice horseradish, one mustard);
mint or redcurrant jelly for lamb, hare, pork (other slice mustard for pork);
apple sauce or rowan jelly for pork, duck, goose, game (other slice mustard for pork);
bread sauce for chicken, pheasant;
mayonnaise for fowl – or mix the meat into it;
chutney juice for lamb or pork (no mustard, if hot chutney).

Vegetable or fruit additions to meat sandwiches should be nicely prepared; for instance :

tomato; skinned, thinly sliced, seasoned, for lamb;
paper-thin, salted and peppered beetroot for beef or hare;
paper-thin pickled cucumber for goose;
pineapple; crushed to flakes, thinly spread, for ham or bacon (mustard on other slice);
prunes or plums; mashed, thinly spread, for duck or goose (French mustard on other slice).

Day-old sliced loaves are a great help when making any quantity of sandwiches. In any event try to buy the proper sandwich loaf, as the square shape ensures quicker work; day-old also.

Having reckoned up how many rounds to make, use 'production-line' methods. That is:

(1) Do all the slicing.

(2) Keeping loaf in its order as cut, open out pairs of slices, butter them all, and put them conveniently to hand, laid out in their pairs.

(3) Carve the meat (as far as you can calculate the amount) very thinly. (Avoid chopping, for the little bits tend to fall out.) You may prefer to do the carving before cutting the bread, but it's a moot point whether thin meat or sliced bread dries quickest, and I find it helps carving calculations to fill one sandwich first.

(4) Spread all left (or right) hand slices with the mustard, sauce or whatever; opposite slice with second spread, when using.

(5) Put meat on right (or left) hand slice, seasoning each layer if double – as thinly carved fillings should be. Put any other addition on top.

(6) Cover with left (or right) hand slice, and press down well with whole hand.

(7) Pile up 3 to 4 sandwiches in an even heap (keep loaf order as far as possible; you will now see why, especially if yours was not a sandwich loaf), and with a large, very sharp cook's knife, not a saw bread knife, and pressing flat of hand on centre of heap, thinly trim off crusts, and cut sandwiches in triangles, halves, thirds or quarters as preferred.

For picnics, wrap in greaseproof paper, and slip into polythene bags or sandwich boxes, or wrap in foil. It is a good idea at a big picnic where there are children to make up a bag for each child containing his allotment of each sort of sandwich, cake, fruit, etc., putting name slips in the bags. Nothing damps family picnics more than squabbles over the food.

Any sandwiches that are to be made some time in advance must be kept from drying. Wrap arranged buffet plates completely in foil, and store in cool away from flies. Meat sandwiches made overnight for office or school lunches should be foil or polythene wrapped, and stored in cold larder or refrigerator.

BLANQUETTE AND FRICASSÉE OF VEAL
(CHICKEN OR RABBIT)

The best definition I know of these two rather obscure terms is given by Len Deighton in *Où Est le Garlic?* :

I have known cooks with some pretty wild ideas about how fricassées differ from blanquettes, but the only difference is that for a blanquette [sautéeing in butter] is replaced by a blanching of the meat for 5 minutes in water. Confusion is fomented by some French chefs who seem to reserve the word fricassée for fricassées of chicken, but this is just a fashionable trend, so take no notice.

A common mistake is to heat up chicken in white sauce and call it a fricassée. In fact, well-made blanquettes and fricassées must be made from raw meat and choice vegetables and are every bit as delectable as the now fashionable *bœuf stroganoff*, which bears a family resemblance to them, differing most of all in the expensive meat needed for stroganoff, and therefore in the cooking time.

1 lb. stewing veal (imported pie veal is best, being boneless and lean)	1½ oz. butter
	1 oz. flour
	2 egg-yolks
4 oz. each button mushrooms and onions small/medium sized	5 tbs. single cream or yoghurt, etc.
	juice ½ lemon
½ pint chicken stock (from cube will do)	parsley
	border of good pommes purée made from 1 lb. potatoes
1 clove, 4 peppercorns, salt	

Melt 1 oz. butter and cook veal until it hardens and turns a greyish colour. Scatter in flour, add stock and bring to boiling point. Press peppercorns deep into one of the onions, stick clove into it, add to pan. Simmer ½ hour. Meanwhile quickly fry rest of onions in rest of butter until just coloured, add mushrooms and cook gently a few minutes. Add all to meat with lemon juice and continue cooking further ½ to 1 hour until meat is perfectly tender. Meanwhile make the potato purée or pommes duchesse mixture, and pipe (or spoon it, forking it evenly) round edge of serving dish, in a thick border that will 'contain' the sauce when

meat is dished. Put dish in top of moderate oven just to colour
the potato lightly. Strain sauce from meat, discarding the spiced
onion and, if thin, reduce sauce by boiling until syrupy. Meanwhile blend yolks and cream. Correct seasoning of sauce, cool 1
minute, and pour on to liaison of yolks and cream. Reheat without boiling, adding meat mixture. Spoon into centre of serving
dish. Garnish with chopped parsley.

A rather elegant alternative to the mashed potato border, if
you happened to have some spare dough on hand, is to make a
circle or oval (or whatever is the shape of the dish) of puff or
flaky pastry about 1½ inches wide, ⅛ to $\frac{3}{16}$ inch thick, score it
fairly deeply into a pattern of triangles (as diagram), brush with a
little egg and water glaze and bake in a hot oven. Or make
fleurons of the paste if a gratin dish is to be used.

BŒUF EN DAUBE

Pretentious recipes abound for this. In fact it should be made
very simply and cheaply for the peasant dish it is. This version
uses stewing steak, and the quantities can be reduced or increased to suit numbers. But you cannot do with less than ¼ pint
wine quantity for marinade for it must come up round the meat.
This 'sausage-meat sandwich' version gets round the larding-
needle question. If, however, you have a larding needle you can
use simply a thick cut of lean beef and lard it.

2 large slabs of stewing steak
  (buttock, chuck, skirt)
  weighing about 1 lb. each
¾ lb. pork sausage meat
½ pint any dry wine or cider
2 tbs. salad oil
1 tbs. minced onion
1 clove garlic minced
bayleaf
pinch caraway seed
strips lemon rind
4 black peppercorns crushed
1 tsp. brown sugar
big pinch salt
½ pint stock
2 cloves garlic
vegetables as preferred or
  available
faggot mixed herbs

MARINADE
Wine, oil and onion
  essential, rest adaptable,
  but no more sugar or salt.
May be heated to just
  below boiling point, then
  cooled completely before
  use.

Trim the steak a little so that both pieces correspond in size and shape. Roll out sausage meat to fit, chopping trimmings, and pressing them into sausage meat. Put sausage between steak, tie round like a parcel and further secure with short poultry pins. Mix the marinade, put meat in pot or dish that fits it closely, and pour marinade over it. Leave 12 hours, turning as often as possible. Thickly slice ½ lb. each carrot and tomato (or other roots in winter). Place in bottom of cocotte, or pan to fit meat as closely as possible. Put meat on top. Crush 2 cloves garlic in salt, and add. Mix about ½ pint stock with marinade, and pour over, to come about half way up meat, so that top layer of beef is just reached. Damp one side of a thick sheet of greaseproof paper slightly larger than top of pot. Put it over pot then fit lid on. If only kitchen paper is available, use double, and damp both sides with milk. Or you can fit foil beneath lid, but careful that thin metal edges don't cut the foil. This paper layer seals the pot. Cook in or on very low heat for 4 to 5 hours. Leave to get cold, when fat is easily removed. Cut in slices downward through the 'sandwich'.

You can use it hot, but one then cuts it thicker and, although rich and satisfying, it tends to be eaten extravagantly, indeed greedily, whereas cold it makes many helpings, lasts well and is of superb flavour.

Vegetables

Other sorts of spinach

The seed catalogues these days offer many varieties of spinach. Most people know 'spinach beet', indeed it is more commonplace now in shops than 'summer spinach', probably because the latter is a sort of catch crop, short lived and therefore wasteful of labour. I have also seen 'Swiss Chard' or seakale spinach in shops. These spinach varieties are good value in garden or shop. They are less watery than summer spinach, so less goes farther, every bit can be used and, provided they are not left 'standing' once fully grown, when cooked and chopped, are equal in flavour, texture and appearance.

Spinach recipes, p. 293.

SWISS CHARD OR SEAKALE SPINACH

The leaves are very large, broad and spear shaped, with wide white corrugated stalks running up into the leaf as a centre rib. There is also a red variety.

The whole may be cooked and used like spinach, but the leaf should be stripped from the stalk and rib, and the latter cut across in ½ inch strips, and cooked first for 3 to 4 minutes in ½ inch boiling salted water. Pour off this water before adding the leaf, bruising all well as it cooks down, exactly as spinach.

Or strip off the leaves and use as spinach, but use the stalks as seakale. That is: boil them whole (or halved if very wide) in salted water 12 to 20 minutes, tied in portion-sized bundles. Serve on very hot plates with melted butter, seasoned and sharpened with lemon juice to taste.

NEW ZEALAND SPINACH

This one spreads out flatly over the ground, having 'thick, soft, fleshy leaves with a crystalline appearance', as my seedsmen have it. Another name for it is 'Cut and Come Again' indicating its profuse growth. A bit of a bore to pick though due to spread. No bonus here by way of stalks, but when cooked it is indistinguishable from spinach, and any spinach recipe suits it. It can contain quite an amount of water and makes excellent spinach soups. Keeps growing until severely frosted.

BEETROOT LEAVES

Add them to spinach. If you happen not to be cooking spinach at the time when you find beet leaves on your hands, cook them down, sieve, add pinch sugar, salt and pepper, little minced onion softened in butter and use to fill omelette or, with 1 tbs. white crumbs and few chopped mushrooms stalks, use as stuffing for a breast of veal or lamb.

Cucumbers

These recipes are intended for outdoor ridge or pickling fruit; but could be adapted to 'frame' cucumbers.

CUCUMBER FLAN GARNI

Author's recipe.

3–4 ridge cucumbers (according to size)
½ pint Béchamel Sauce (p. 117)
1–2 small eggs or yolks
lemon juice to taste

6 oz. flaky or rich shortcrust pastry (pp. 129–30)
4 rashers streaky bacon
1 ¼ inch slice from large white loaf

378

Bake a 7 to 8-inch flan-case of flaky or rich shortcrust. See that sides come well up (slightly above rim of flan-ring).

Pare cucumbers, slit through lengthways into four and remove seeds. Cut in inch lengths and throw into boiling salted water just to cover. Cook 15 to 20 minutes until tender but not mushy. Meanwhile make sauce. Drain cucumbers and pat dry on kitchen paper, filling neatly into flan-case. Beat eggs lightly and add to sauce adjusting seasoning and adding lemon juice. Pour over cucumbers and put in moderate oven (350° F, gas 4) to set egg for 10–20 minutes. Meanwhile quarter rashers, cut bread into ¼ inch dice. Roll up bacon and either bake in top of oven, or grill crisp. Fry bread until golden. Scatter both over surface of flan just before serving.

A delicious supper with any kind of sausages, with liver, kidneys or a plain grill. Pastry and croûtons replace potatoes. Can be made with courgettes (don't peel). Additions can be varied for vegetarians.

STUFFED CUCUMBERS

4 ridge cucumbers	3 sage leaves
1 medium onion	seasoning
1 oz. fresh brown breadcrumbs	½ oz. butter/margarine
	2 tbs. milk

Cut a small oval 'lid' from each cucumber and scoop out pips, invert and leave fruit to drain. Mince onion and sage, soak crumbs in milk. Soften onion in butter and mix with crumbs, sage and seasoning. Lightly season inside cucumbers, fill, replace lids, bake 1 hour at 300° F, gas 2.

CONCOMBRES INDIENNES

4 ridge cucumbers	½ oz. flour
1 medium onion	1 tsp. curry powder or paste
1 oz. margarine	lemon juice, sugar
½ pint stock	1 level tsp. desiccated coconut
½ carton yoghurt	(optional)
1 egg-yolk (optional)	seasoning

Pare cucumbers, cut in 4 lengthways, remove seeds and cut in inch lengths. Cut onion in thin rings and brown briskly and well in margarine. Add cucumber and brown, add curry powder and cook over very low heat 3 minutes. Stir in flour off heat, add stock and rest of ingredients, except yolk where used. Bring to simmering point and continue cooking 20 minutes, scraping across centre of pan to prevent sticking, but carefully so as not to break cucumbers. Cool 1 minute and stir in egg yolk.

Good with plainly grilled or poached fish; eggs; gammon steaks.

CREAMED CUCUMBERS

Prepare cucumbers as above, sweat in 1 oz. butter. Add 1 oz. flour, stir in 1½ gills milk and bring to boil without lumps. Add seasoning, a little nutmeg and a few chopped tarragon or fennel leaves. Simmer 15 minutes or until cucumber is just tender. Add 1 yolk and 2 tbs. single cream or substitutes. Serve very hot; by itself on buttered toast or with plainly grilled or roasted fish or meat.

Courgettes and Little Gem marrows

The growing of these is exactly as for marrow – see section Growing it Yourself, pp. 71–6, but cooking is somewhat different.

COURGETTES

Although there are many more involved recipes, this will bring out all the delicate flavour and pleasant texture.

Wipe 1 lb. courgettes. Cut or snap off stub of stalk, shave off scar at flower end. Cut in 3 to 4 slanting pieces. Blanch for 2 minutes. Drain. Melt 1 oz. butter in small saucepan, and add courgettes, turning to coat all in butter. Season lightly. Finely chop 1 sprig each parsley, tarragon, thyme, 2 rosemary leaves, 6 chive blades – or ½ tsp. minced onion – and stir in. Lower heat to mere whisper (asbestos mat if necessary), cover pan, and cook about 30 to 40 minutes, inspecting and turning often, as the sugar in courgettes catches easily. Serve in the sauce resulting from the cooking. Adjust seasoning as necessary. Zucchini are virtually the same and may be treated the same way.

LITTLE GEM

These round, usually apple-sized marrows take on a rich custard-like texture when cooked, and have a sweet nutty taste. They are far superior to marrow, in my opinion, and equal to, though different from courgettes. Their size is also most useful. Allow one per person of orange-sized specimens (two for hungry *appreciative* men!), more of the 'littluns'. Wipe them and simmer very gently in salted water about 25 to 30 minutes until soft when lightly pressed with back of spoon. Serve whole, handing butter, melted or not, salt and black pepper in pepper mill. No need to remove seeds from young specimens.

All these sorts of marrow produce abundant flowers. In Italy unwanted blooms are picked, dipped in thin batter or egg-white and deep fried; also stuffed and baked.

ROAST OR TOASTED MARROW SEED

Around the Mediterranean they often cannot afford to waste anything that can be turned to use for food. Poverty apart, hot, dry, sparse soils produce only so much vegetation, so what there is is prized. Here is a use for the vast masses of seed produced by the marrow family. Separate seeds from the stringy pulp holding them together, rinse and pat them dry. Spread them on a tin or dish, salt lightly and roast or toast until barely coloured, turning once to mix in the salt, serve with drinks. Avoid seed from older fruits as these develop husks.

Puddings

SKIMMING WHEEL TART

An old-fashioned recipe ideal for using up dishes of jam skimmings, or the quarter pots that always accompany jam made at home. An excuse, also, to sample or show off your jam.

Use a flat pie plate if possible. Line with ⅛ inch shortcrust pastry, about 8 oz. will be enough altogether. Keep a quarter in reserve. Using half this, roll with flat of hands on. table to a long thin strip. Damp ¼ inch round edge of pie, and press strip on. This makes rim of wheel. Roll out the remaining paste into an oblong also ⅛ inch thick. From this cut very neat ⅛ inch wide strips. With a small brush or ball of little finger damp one edge of a strip and form it into a circle about ¾ inch in diameter in the centre of the pie, laying it damped side down and just pressing enough to stick it. Damp rest of strips and lay from rim of pie to centre circle to make eight 'spokes'. In each space between spokes fill with as many jams as you have, repeating flavours in rotation. Fill centre with mincemeat, cherries, honey, or whatever is available and different from the jam. Brush pastry lightly with milk to glaze, and bake in a hot oven for about 15 to 20 minutes.

NOTE: Jam is a great boiler-up-and-over, and spreads readily when hot. About 1 tbs. per section will be found plenty, however mean it looks before cooking.

MELON COOLER
First read gelatine notes, p. 138.

Serves 6 to 8.

As elegant as it is refreshing, and as simple to make as glamorous in appearance – especially if you can find a tall-shaped mould. I've made it in a tumbler-shaped flower-vase with great success. (Clean vase thoroughly, of course.) The melon may be cubed, but better still if you have one of those round vegetable

scoops (Tala make them), use the larger end. 2 pint capacity
mould. Use an 8 fl. oz. teacup.

1 oz. (2 envelopes) gelatine
dissolved in ½ teacup water
2 tbs. castor sugar dissolved
in ½ teacup liquid made up
from strained juice of 1
lemon and water

2 'split'-sized bottles
Schweppes dry ginger ale
1½ teacups melon balls cut
from medium-sized *ripe* melon
powdered ginger
castor sugar

When the gelatine and sugar are dissolved, mix liquids and add
melon balls. As jelly starts to set, push melon down evenly
through mould. Do this with something thin but not sharp –
for example a dinner knife – so as not to create air bubbles in
jelly. Leave to set. Turn out, and border dish with a sprig or so of
mint or basil leaves etc. Stir ½ level tsp. powdered ginger into 4
tbs. castor sugar and hand separately.

Lemon Puddings

Lemons are often very cheap at this time of year as they come
into the country from several sources and certainly this is when
their sharp delights are most welcome.

The basis of many of the best puddings is lemon curd and
that given here is from an early Beeton recipe. Many people
seem to think there is something difficult about it. In fact it is
very easy and quick, the large proportion of acid appearing to
work in some sort of reverse fashion which *prevents* curdling.
Home-made lemon curd recipes often omit what Mrs Beeton
points out: that its keeping qualities are short-lived, so there is
no point in making a huge batch as for jam. (It makes a welcome present if you have any spare.) Once you have lemon
curd, Lemon Meringue Pie is simple.

LEMON MERINGUE PIE

4 oz. shortcrust or pâte sucrée *thinly* to line 7 inch flan-ring,
coming above the rim; bake blind. ¾ fill with lemon curd. Make

meringue by whipping up 1–2 whites and adding 2–4 oz. sugar; pile on pie, and 'dry out' 45 to 60 minutes at 275° F, gas 1.

LEMON CURD

¼ lb. butter	grated rind of 2 lemons, juice
1 lb. loaf sugar	of 3 lemons
5 small eggs – whisked lightly	

Put all ingredients into a saucepan (enamel for preference) and stir over gentle heat until sugar is dissolved and mixture begins to thicken. Continue until the consistency of honey. Put into jam jars and cover down in the usual way. Will keep up to 3 months in cold dry store.

To make lemon cheesecakes add a few pounded almonds, or candied peel, or grated sweet biscuit. Line some patty pans with good puff-paste, rather more than half fill with mixture and bake ¼ hour in a good brisk oven.

Mrs Beeton c. 1898

LEMON CREAM

An extravagance which ought not to be included, perhaps, but is too good to leave out. Versions appear in many old books.

½ pint double cream (tinned does well)	2 oz. castor sugar
	1 lemon
1 egg yolk	½ oz. (1 envelope) gelatine

Grate lemon peel. Put with cream, sugar and gelatine into enamel pan (for preference) and stir continuously over low heat on asbestos mat (or in double pan) about 10 minutes until no more gelatine or sugar grains are seen over bottom of pan. Do not allow to boil. Water in double pan should barely simmer. Cool slightly and pour some of mixture on to yolk in a wide jug or basin, mix well, add rest, and put jug into pan of boiling water. If using double pan return mixture to this. Continue gentle cooking off the boil until mixture coats back of spoon. Squeeze lemon and strain juice into basin. Gradually pour on to it the cream mixture, stirring well. Have ready a thoroughly, but lightly oiled mould, pour cream in and leave to set. Turn out and send to table with single *fresh* cream. Decorate with any suitable yellow sweetmeats – jelly slices, sugar 'mimosas' or thin fresh lemon decorations.

LEMON SPONGE PUDDING

2-egg creaming or stirred
method cake mixture (pp.
498, 507) flavoured with grated
rind of 1 fresh lemon

1–2 tbs. lemon curd

SAUCE

juice of 1 lemon
½ pint water

2 oz. sugar
½ oz. cornflour

Get the steamer ready. Prepare pudding basin and covers. Put curd in bottom of greased basin. Make up pudding mixture, creaming rind with margarine at beginning. Turn this into basin. Cover and steam 1 hour or longer if convenient.

Dissolve sugar in water and juice. Slake cornflour with 2 tsp. cold water. Pour a little of the boiling syrup on to this, return to pan and boil up, stirring briskly. Pour into heated sauce boat. Turn out pudding and serve.

LEMON MOUSSE OR SOUFFLÉ MILANESE

2 eggs
2 oz. castor sugar
¼ oz. gelatine
3 tbs. water
¼ pint double cream (or
suitable substitutes for
whipping)

grated rind and juice of 2
small or 1½ larger lemons
prepare a pint soufflé case
(p. 419) separate yolks
from whites, dissolve
gelatine in water, keep just
lukewarm

Beat lemon rind, juice, sugar and yolks in mixing bowl over a pan of water taken from the boil. Bowl must not touch water. Whisk until you can 'write your initial' with the trail on top of rest of mixture. Remove from hot water and whisk until quite cool. Half whip cream. Stiffly whisk whites.

Fold cream into yolk mixture, then gelatine, pouring slowly, then whites. If possible, stand bowl on ice while doing this. Turn into soufflé case. When set, remove paper and decorate 'raw' edges with chopped toasted almonds, cake crumbs, etc. Decorate with large whorls of whipped cream, 'mimosas', etc. Or send single fresh cream to table.

September

✦✦

Some claim that September is the richest month of the year in the kitchen. Game, gourd fruits, prunus, some of the choicest vegetables in the garden, English apples and pears and, in the heart of the country, sloes, brambles, nuts and edible fungi, free for the picking. It is a month for bottling garden produce, which has flavour unequalled in the best of commercial brands – tomatoes, plums, blackberries, pears. It is the great pickling month – for example you will not find pickled damsons on the shelves in the supermarket, and nothing rivals their subtle delicacy as a relish for cold roast pork, cold pies, turkey and goose. Recipe for them, and other preserves in the section beginning on p. 539.

Soups

BORTSCH

Serves 8 to 10.

Many ways to spell it, many ways to make it, most Russians or Polish versions are *pots-aux feux*, meals in themselves, with joints and a fowl cooked in the soup, and contributing to the stock. They include juice squeezed from raw beetroots, a *julienne* of several other vegetables, sausage added at the end and, almost invariably, sour cream. They are big soups in every way, intended for a big family, to last several days, and needing the resources of a big kitchen, with more than a single pair of hands.

Add what you like to this minuscule version for today's small households.

1 lb. mince or stewing steak
cut into strips
2 medium beetroots (raw for
preference)
1 medium onion
3 carrots
1 stick celery or ½ small
celeriac root (when these
are available)
1 oz. margarine or bacon
dripping

¼ small cabbage
sour cream or yoghurt
seasoning
faggot of fresh herbs (or
dried in muslin)
pinch caraway or cumin seed
pinch celery seed
1 quart good stock (if possible
from fowl)
bacon rinds or bone

Dice beets, slice onion, scrape and quarter *one* of carrots. Put them into a big pan with meat, pour on stock. Add bacon, faggot of herbs, seasoning and seeds. Bring to boil, reduce to simmering point, removing any scum remaining after 15 minutes. Simmer 2 hours. Meanwhile cut vegetables into neat *julienne* strips, fry lightly in fat. Lift out bacon, quartered carrot, muslin. Add *julienne*. If liked, also dice the carrot cooked in the soup and return to pan. Continue cooking about 30 minutes or until meat is quite done. Stir in sour cream. Serve very hot with pieces (or spoonfuls) of meat included in each helping.

To make a complete meal add 1 frankfurter (halved) for each person 10 minutes before serving, and hand French, black, or rye bread and plenty of butter.

GAZPACHO

Outside Spain, and perhaps to make this unusual and ancient dish more acceptable to tourists, gazpacho is known as a soup. When I first had it, in this country, I thought how like a salad it seemed. Not long afterwards, in reading Santayana's autobiography, I came to this:

That oil and water will not mix is disproved ... by a salad, gazpacho .... Bread, tomatoes, and cucumbers, with oil and vinegar, and some slivers of raw onion, if you were not too refined, composed its substance, all floating in an abundance of water; so that if hunger was partly mocked, thirst at least was satisfied, and this is the more urgent need in a warm climate.

If you like salads you'll love it. As many of the following as you like, although I consider that tomatoes, either fresh, canned or juice, are vital, while the garlic and pimento loom large in many gazpacho recipes. Olive oil is specially good, but other salad oil plus an olive or two chopped into the mixture is a good substitute. The colder the soup (or salad !) the better.

2 tomatoes concassed, juice strained into soup, cut small
1 onion minced
1 ridge cucumber ¼ inch diced
½ pimento minced
1–3 courgettes or ½ small marrow or 1 Little Gem, ¼ inch sliced
2 tbs. wine or herb vinegar
1–2 cloves garlic minced

1 teacup (8 fl. oz.) cold water
freshly ground black pepper
paprika
cayenne or tabasco
salt (rock salt where possible)
1–2 tbs. chopped fresh herbs (my mix includes few leaves tarragon, large amount of parsley and marjoram, young leaf or two rue)
3 tbs. olive oil (or salad oil and minced olives)

Mix all ingredients except oil in a big bowl, and season well to taste. Finally add oil by spoonfuls whisking in with hand beater. Chill if possible, handing melba toast with it. Chilled, very dry sherry goes well (especially if you are lucky enough to take your first course outdoors on a warm September evening).

PLUM MULLIGATAWNY

1 lb. plums stoned
1 small onion sliced
1 oz. each margarine and flour
1 chilli or ¼ tsp. cayenne pepper
1 pint stock or water

2 oz. sugar or to taste
1 rounded tsp. curry powder or paste
1 oz. long rice
1 oz. sultanas
1 crushed clove garlic
seasoning

Melt fat and brown onion, curry powder and flour. Blend in stock smoothly and bring to simmering point, stirring continuously. Add plums, garlic, sugar, chili and sultanas. Simmer 45 minutes. Correct seasoning, add rice and cook further 15 minutes.

FLAGEOLET CREAM

6–8 oz. green beans from 'over blown' French bean pods (p. 74)
½ pint stock or salted water
½ pint milk
few tarragon leaves, chopped finely
1 oz. each margarine and flour

minced green tops from 2–3 spring onions or 8–12 chive blades
1 yolk
2 tbs. thin cream or substitutes
seasoning
little fingernail croûtons fried in 1 oz. butter

Simmer beans in stock until tender 12 to 20 minutes. Melt margarine, add flour off heat, blend, add milk and mix smoothly bringing to simmering point. Add to pan of cooked beans stirring to blend both liquids well. Adjust seasoning. Add onion. Mix yolks and cream and pour hot soup on to them. Put a few croûtons in each plate or send to table in separate bowl.

First Courses and Snacks

SPAGHETTI NAPOLITANA AND OTHER PASTA

SAUCE

Serves 6.

12 oz. tomatoes skinned, roughly chopped
2 medium onions sliced
1 clove garlic crushed in 1 level tsp. salt
¼ pint light stock
1 rasher bacon diced
freshly ground black pepper,

salt
1 oz. margarine, lard, good bacon dripping or 1 tbs. oil
bouquet garni including blade of mace and 1 clove
1 tsp. lemon juice
1 dessertsp. chopped marjoram (1 tsp. dried)

Melt fat and soften onion and bacon. Add rest of prepared ingredients except marjoram and simmer together 35 to 40 minutes with lid half off pan, stirring and bruising tomato until pulpy. Then boil fast 3 to 5 minutes to reduce slightly if on the watery side. The sauce should not, however, be thick like apple purée.

While sauce is cooking weigh up pasta, prepare pot for it and grate cheese. The proportions for these are:

For a first course (when quantity of sauce serves 6): ¾ 1 lb. pasta
For light lunch or supper for 4: 1 lb. pasta
For main meal for 4: 1¼–1½ lb. pasta
Allow ½ oz. cheese per head for first course;
1–1½ oz. (according to type of cheese and tastes) for lunch;
1½–2 oz. per head for main meal

There are three main types of pasta commonly available in Britain for this sort of dish: spaghetti, macaroni and tagliatelli (white and green – the latter being particularly attractive for a first course at a dinner-party). Cooking time varies from 7 to 20 minutes after water has come to the boil again after putting in the pasta. Most packeted or branded pasta states the time required. It is important not to overcook pasta to a slimy, slithering slush. 'Al dente' is the Italian expression indicating the right texture for pasta – literally 'to the teeth', that is, just biteable.

There must be enough boiling salted water in the pot for the pasta to absorb some and swell, and then to swim round easily, and finally to float lazily to the surface – a sign that it is done.

Allow 1 level tsp. salt per 1½ pints water. Water must be absolutely boiling before putting in pasta. Gradually insinuate long types into the pot as the part in the water softens, and can be bent round to fit. Bring water to boiling point again but then lower heat to a simmer. Drain well, do *not* rinse, meantime melting a little butter or good oil in the still-warm pan, returning the drained pasta to it, and turning just to coat it all in fat. This stops sticking and makes serving easy.

Dish individually on plates for preference, spooning sauce on top, and dusting with marjoram and a little of the cheese, sending rest to table in a small bowl or dish, to be added as required. Some cooks brown the first cheese topping under the grill before serving. This gives a pleasant flavour, also ensuring that the meal is hot – a useful point when many must be served, as pasta cools quite quickly, so needs to be really hot to begin with.

RISOTTI

Allow 2–4 oz. rice per head according to the meal, the amount of other ingredients, and their food value. Risotti can be very meagrely flavoured and garnished, or can be very rich, with the Spanish dish, Paella, at the lavish end of the scale. These rice dishes have the advantage of being cooked entirely in a single pan and with little preparation other than cutting up the ingredients. The rice is not washed as for curry, for the starch in it makes the thickening of the dish. Given here is an example using autumnal vegetables and a single chicken liver. *Chez moi* the presence of a chicken liver in the larder is invariably the signal for a risotto. The amount would make a good supper for two, a light lunch for three, or a first course for four.

4 oz. Patna rice
  2 oz. margarine (or dripping if very good and tasty) or olive oil
  1 Spanish or 2 medium onions sliced
  1 clove garlic crushed in salt
  2 rashers bacon cut in ¼-inch strips
  1 chicken liver cut in long thin strips
  2 oz. cold chicken cut in ½-inch strips (or meat from cooked chicken neck)

¼ pimento very finely sliced
3 tomatoes concassed
3 'flat' mushrooms very thinly sliced
1 pint stock
¼ pint wine *or*
1¼ pint stock *plus*
½ glass sherry (1½ tbs.)
seasoning
bayleaf
dash tarragon vinegar
1 dessertsp. mild chutney, or very small tsp. hot chutney

The very best pans for risotti are frying pans with lids, approximating to the *sautoir* of France. The bigger sort are particularly useful, allowing food to be stirred, moved about and additions made to the dish as needed. They often have egg-poaching attachments available and, if bought in this form, make a most versatile piece of equipment. Ordinary frying pans can usually be successfully covered by a tin plate.

Melt fat, add onion and pimento at one side of pan, rice at other side, and cook over gentle heat until rice is slightly coloured, onion transparent. Push them together to one side of pan, tipping pan and pressing vegetables to make fat run on to empty half. Add bacon and mushrooms, turn in fat, cook 7 minutes. Add liver, cook ¼ minute. Add tomato and garlic and stir all together. Add stock, wine, chicken meat, bayleaf and vinegar. Mix and bring to boil, lower heat barely to simmer, cover and cook 15 minutes. Use an asbestos mat if necessary. Avoid stirring if possible as this may break up the rice. But about half-time run a spatula under the mixture across centre of pan. If sticking add 3 tbs. stock or water.

After 15 minutes very carefully stir in chutney, taste and add seasoning. Return to heat 5 minutes.

Serve with grated cheese if liked.

SAUSAGE TOAD-IN-THE-HOLE
Serves 2.

¼ pint milk and water	4 sausages
2 oz. flour	½ oz. dripping or lard
1 small egg or ½ large	about ¼ pint good thickened
½ tsp. salt	gravy, or bottled or other
pepper	sauce to choice

This is one of the most useful hot meals for the busy since such minimal preparation as it takes can be done well in advance. It can be left ready (at a pinch) in an automatic oven, by mixing 1 tbs. oil in with batter, instead of cooking by pre-heated dripping. But, even if you start the cooking on arriving home, it will be done as you put things away, lay the table, or whatever.

Make the batter as for Yorkshire pudding p. 98 and leave to 'rest', if possible, for at least 30 minutes. Slit sausage skins and discard (skinless sausages are useful for toad). Set oven at 400° F, gas 6, put fat in small square tin just above centre of oven. When fat is hot, pour in batter and return tin to oven. After 5 minutes, open door gently, pull out shelf, and add sausages with even spaces between each. Batter may sink a little but will re-cover. Alternatively, add sausages at the beginning, but first method ensures some batter beneath them and more even rising. Bake 35 to 40 minutes in all until batter is well risen and brown, and sausages well coloured.

Accompany with freshly-made or ready-made English mustard. A salad is the perfect foil, but green beans are the best hot vegetables. Or none. Gravy if available.

Some recipes are given for liver toad. This is only good if you like hardish liver. Kidneys – 'core' removed without separating halves altogether – stand the long cooking better, and are less dry.

Fish

Eels

Rich and nutritious, eels are rarely seen live in fishmongers in the south of England nowadays. They must be absolutely fresh, and should be sold direct from the tank. Eel recipes in old books take up two or three pages, and I quote one or two interest-ing ones here since those with fishermen in the family may find eel recipes in modern books hard to come by. They include some of the few recipes in this book I have not been able to test per-sonally and this is indicated.

KILLING AND PREPARING. Stun the eel, cut through spine just below head. Split down the belly and clean very thoroughly. Remove skin by incising just to depth of skin in a ring round the back of the gills, raise enough skin to grip with a cloth and rip off towards tail. This is a skilled job and will usually be done by the fishmonger or angler.

JELLIED EELS (not tested)

THE JELLY. Use trimmings from turbot, halibut, mackerel which you may get from fishmonger. Just cover with water, add salt, bouquet garni, ½ teacup cider or herb vinegar, good pinch ginger, blade mace, strips lemon rind, juice of half lemon, 1 carrot cut in quarters, celery (or seed or leaves), sprig tarragon or fennel. Simmer all together for 1½ to 2 hours. Cool. Strain.

MARINADE. 1 clove garlic minced, 1 small onion finely sliced, pepper, parsley stalks, bayleaf, 2 sprigs thyme, chopped fennel or seeds, juice ½ lemon, ½ glass sherry, 2 tbs. salad oil. Whisk all well together before pouring on eel.

EEL. Prepare as directed then cut in 2-inch lengths. Marinate for 1 hour, minimum, turning once at least.

FINISHING. When well-flavoured put marinated eel with its marinade into the jelly stock, boil up and simmer 1 hour. Lift out pieces of eel and arrange in shallow dish. Strain liquor and pour over eel. Leave to set.

Although, before cooking, eel is a poor keeper, jellied eels keep several days in a cold larder.

EEL PIE

Cut prepared eel in 2-inch lengths and put in pie-dish with stock not quite to cover. Season lightly. Scatter in 2 or 3 finely sliced mushrooms, 1 sliced onion, 1 tbs. lemon juice, ½ tsp. finely chopped fennel or tarragon. Cover with flaky or rough puff pastry (p. 132), decorating with leaves and glazing with egg. Bake 20 to 30 minutes at 400° F, gas 7, until crust is risen and brown, then lower heat to 300° F, gas 2, covering crust with a twist of damped tissue paper and continue cooking further 30 minutes.

Best served alone. Follow with salad or vegetable as a separate course.

ELIZA ACTON'S CORNISH RECIPE FOR EELS

Serves 6.

Skin empty and wash as clean as possible, two or three fine eels, cut them into short lengths, and just cover them with cold water; add sufficient salt and cayenne to season them, and stew them very softly indeed from fifteen to twenty minutes, or longer should they require it. When they are nearly done, strew over them a teaspoonful minced parsley, thicken the sauce with a teaspoonful of flour mixed with a slice of butter, and add a quarter of a pint or more of clotted cream. Give the whole a boil, lift the fish into a hot dish, and stir briskly the juice of half a lemon into the sauce; pour it upon the eels, and serve them immediately. Very sweet [fresh] thick cream is, we think, preferable to clotted cream for this dish. The sauce should be of a good consistence, and a dessertspoonful of flour will be needed for a large dish of the stew, and from one and a half to two ounces of butter. The size of the fish must determine the precise quantity of liquid and of seasoning which they will require.

I disagree with E.A. about the cream. Tinned cream would be excellent, however, and cheaper than Cornish or fresh double cream.

EELS EN MATELOTE (not tested)

Mrs Beeton circa 1898. Serves 6.

2lbs eels, 5 or 6 young onions, a few mushrooms, when obtainable; salt, pepper and nutmeg to taste; 1 laurel [bay] leaf, ½ pint port wine, ½ pint of medium stock, butter and flour to thicken. *Average cost*, 3s.

Rub the stewpan with butter, dredge in a little flour, add the onions cut very small, slightly brown them, and put in all the other ingredients. Wash and cut up the eels into pieces 3 inches long; put them in the stewpan and simmer for ½ hour. Make round the dish a border of croûtons; arrange the eels in a pyramid in the centre, and pour over the sauce. Serve very hot.

Time – ¾ *hour.*

Seasonable from August to March

FRIED EEL

Cut prepared eels into 2-inch lengths, egg, crumb and fry in deep fat (p. 103) and serve with Hollandaise or tartare sauce (use the Thick Salad Dressing, p. 251, as base if liked).

RAIE AU BEURRE NOIRE (Skate in black butter)

2 lb. skate in 4 portions

COURT BOUILLON.

½ pint water	sprig tarragon (small) or
5 tbs. white wine or cider	fennel
1 slice onion	pinch cumin seed
bouquet garni	2 oz. butter
6 peppercorns	lemon wedges
1 level tsp. salt	

Put all court bouillon ingredients into a covered pan, boil up, simmer 5 minutes and leave to cool 20 minutes. Arrange fish in shallow oven dish. Pour court bouillon over it and bake, covered, at 325° F, gas 3, for 20 minutes. Or poach on top of stove. Drain fish and keep hot, covered to prevent drying. Cook butter in a small pan until it browns well, and either pour all or part over fish, or send to table in sauce boat. Hand lemon wedges, also brown bread and butter, or serve a very buttery, soft pommes purée.

KIPPER CROQUETTES

½ lb. kipper fillets (or other smoked fish, kippers being cheap in September)	flour, egg, dried crumbs for coating
¼ pint well-flavoured binding sauce (p. 113)	fat for frying

Cook the fish by bringing just to boil in water to cover. Skin and pound it to shreds. Mix with sauce, and spread out to get quite cold. With palette knife divide into eight equal amounts. Form into sausage shapes or balls with floured hands. Have ready a plate of seasoned flour, another of beaten egg, and some dried white crumbs on a sheet of kitchen paper. Croquette mixture is soft to handle so do so as little as possible, using slice or palette knife for lifting and turning, also coat by shaking plate of flour to make croquettes roll. Coat first with flour, then brush with egg, lastly lift on to crumbs and roll in them by lifting alternate ends of the paper one in each hand, finally pressing crumbs lightly over surface with fingers. Fry in deep fat until golden. They will be crisp outside, fluffy inside.

Serve with chips, salad, sharp sauce, grilled tomatoes, etc.

CRUMB STUFFED HADDOCK FILLET

2 lb. haddock (saithe/coley or cod) fillet
2 inch-thick slices brown bread
grated rind and juice of 1 orange

2 oz. margarine
clove or garlic crushed in salt *or* 8–12 chive blades finely minced (or other mild onion)

Skin the fish and divide in four. Rub bread down to crumbs. Melt fat in frying pan, add garlic. (If chive is used do not add until end of this crumb mixture stage.) Add orange rind and cook gently 2 minutes. Add crumbs, and stir until all is evenly mixed and absorbed, and crumbs fall apart again. Put fish in greased oven dish, season well, sprinkle with orange juice and spread each piece thickly with crumb mixture. Bake, uncovered, at 375° F, gas 5, 20 to 30 minutes until skewer thrust through thickest piece of fish leaves it easily.

Serve with plainly boiled potatoes, green salad or peas or beans.

Gas-ring cooks can pot roast this dish, well greasing bottom of pan and slightly browning crumb topping at the frying stage before it goes on. Use asbestos mat for preference.

This simple yet sophisticated recipe is adapted from a leaflet issued by the White Fish Authority's Fish Information Service, whose recipes may be applied for. See p. 557 about 'commercial' recipes generally.

Meat

NOCTON BRAWN

Gertrude Goslin's recipe. Serves 8.

Shop brawn gets nastier year by year. Why, heaven knows, since it is so cheap and easy to make. Why dye it pink? Especially as the dye 'takes' only on the fat and the rest stays the natural greige, making the whole look quite poisonous. As a rule, factory tries to imitate home-made, and no brawn ever known was magenta. Why *not* pepper it enough? Those who appreciate brawn do so because it is spicy.

Half a pig's head will fill a quart mould, so two families of four could well share this amount along with the troublesome bit – picking meat from bones.

½ pig's head	ground white pepper
1 onion	2 cloves
1 level tbs. salt in pot (rock salt preferred); more, to taste, later	small sprig sage
	2 sprigs thyme
12 white peppercorns broken slightly	1 level tsp. each chopped sage and thyme tied in muslin

If the head is large enough the cheek may be roasted for a small family, otherwise include it. But if roasted, cut off only the meat, for all bones are required in the brawn pot. The butcher will have removed eye and prepared ear, snout, etc. Put head in large pot, cover well with cold water, add salt, onion, herbs, etc. in muslin. If available some lean beef may be added. Bring to the boil and simmer 3 to 4 hours until flesh falls from bones as you lift them from water.

Tongue, sweetbread and brains may be served separately after about 2 hours cooking. (Serve with good parsley sauce and mashed potatoes.) Otherwise add to brawn.

Pick meat from bones, and try to remove even the smallest fragments of the latter. But work fairly fast as the jelly is very strong and sets quickly. Take two knives and chop meat down very small with scissor-like action. Turn into warmed mixing bowl and add chopped herbs and at least 1 level tsp. white pepper mixed with the herbs and some salt. Taste and add more salt if necessary. Put into quart mould or basin and fill almost to brim with stock from pot. When cold taste again and if not very spicy and tasty melt down and add more seasoning.

The remaining stock makes first-class soup. When cold remove fat from surface and clarify for lard. (The cost, when my mother wrote out this recipe for me in the late 1940's was 'about 5s.')

ELIZA ACTON'S 'OXFORD BRAWN SAUCE' is the perfect accompaniment:

Mingle thoroughly a tablespoon of brown sugar with a teaspoonful of made mustard, a third as much of salt, some pepper, from three to four tablespoonsful of very fine salad-oil, and two of strong vinegar; or apportion the same ingredients otherwise to the taste.

After brawn it seems only right to turn to brains, and, if lucky, this is a time when you may get calves' brains, as surplus calves are slaughtered about now. But sheeps' brains are only slightly smaller and good. Use brains quickly.

BRAINS

Cheap, but still a gourmet's delight. You either can or cannot face the thought, manage to handle them, and bother with the initial fiddly preparation.

For each average appetite half a set of brains; for hearty appetites one set each.

2 oz. butter per set of brains (not more than 1 oz. margarine if you must economize)	juice ½ lemon to each set – more to taste 1½ oz. well-seasoned flour pommes purée (p. 194)

Rinse brains first under running tap to wash out chips of bone. Working with a bowl of lightly salted water, gently remove as much as possible of the thin veinous membrane covering the brains, trying to break up the tissue as little as possible. This takes time and there is no short cut. Some sets seem to peel easily, others not, but avoid the temptation to keep starting in a new patch. It helps a bit sometimes to part the 'hills' very gently and pull the membrane from the 'valleys'. (Use the brain-wash water on a prized plant in the garden, but dig a little ditch first, covering in afterwards against flies.) Poach cleaned brains in lightly salted water with a dash of lemon juice or vinegar, for 5 minutes. Drain, then leave to get cold beneath a slightly weighted plate to compact and flatten to a good shape for the final cooking. Provided storage is cool, brains are usefully cooked over two days. Until poached, however, brains are highly perishable.

Either leave the brains in two large lobes, or cut them into largish pieces. Coat lightly in seasoned flour, and fry in three-quarters of the butter until evenly golden. Lift on to hot dish, previously bordered with very good pommes purée. Heat rest of butter in pan, add lemon juice and when just bubbling add 1 tbs. water, mix well to deglaze pan somewhat, and pour over brains. Serve hot.

Also try the Béarnaise or Mock Béarnaise on pp. 119, 250.

MINCED LAMB FOR STUFFING A MARROW

½ lb. cooked cold lamb (including a proportion of fat)
1 rasher bacon
1 medium onion
3 ripe tomatoes (or ¼ pint tomato juice)

2 oz. Quick Quaker macaroni (or other small pasta)
1 tsp. chopped mint
pinch ground clove
seasoning
½ oz. margarine

First mince the onion and bacon and put them in small pan with margarine and the skinned, quartered tomatoes to cook down while you mince the lamb, prepare marrow (p. 353), and cook macaroni. If using tomato juice you can cook macaroni in this. Mix all cooked ingredients thoroughly. Season to taste, add mint and ground clove, mix again. Fill marrow and bake at 325° F, gas 3, for 1 to 1½ half hours or until skewer inserted in fleshiest end of marrow will leave it easily.

VEAL PAPRIKA

1½ lb. stewing veal (imported
pie veal is best)
1 small onion
1 level tsp. Hungarian
paprika, or up to 1 tbs. of
other makes

½ oz. each lard and butter
5 tbs.–¼ pint sour cream or
½ carton yoghurt and
2 tbs. top milk
5 tbs. pint red wine (optional)
¼ pint stock or water

TO ACCOMPANY: ½ lb. small pasta – shells, vermicelli etc.,
or rice.

Remove bones, fat and gristle from veal and cut in large squares,
not little lumps. They may be 'shallow' rather than cubes.
Brown briskly in fat (heat lard before adding butter) with the
onion, cut in quarters. Add paprika, lower heat and coat meat in
paprika by stirring about for 3 to 5 minutes. Add stock, bring to
simmering point, add wine and simmer 1½ to 2 hours or until
meat is perfectly tender. Stir in cream over heat for a few
minutes.

Serve with pasta or rice.

PORK AND BEANS OR
BOSTON BAKED BEANS

1½–2 lb. pickled pork (or
pickle a lean cut yourself
p. 547)
½ lb. dried haricot or other
beans (p. 139)
bicarbonate of soda

1 large onion
1 tsp. made mustard
5 tbs. Fowler's treacle
stock, water, tomato juice as liked
or available

Soak beans in double their bulk of water over night. Next day
pour beans and water into saucepan, add large pinch bicarbonate
and bring to the boil, cooking 5 minutes. Rinse in cold water
and drain well. Slice onion. Put pork in bottom of cocotte or large
pan. Mix onion with beans and pour over. Fill with cold liquid to
cover, which may be one or a mixture of all three mentioned, but
avoid salty stock as the pork has enough already. Mix the treacle

and mustard with some of the liquid to pour over last. Cover closely and cook for 8 hours in or on lowest possible heat. Each 3 to 4 hours, inspect the pot, adding water as needed.

Serve with cabbage or spinach.

Vegetables

RATATOUILLE

In those southern departments of France where it originated, ratatouille cooks all day. It may also include meat, often mutton, sometimes goose, and is often eaten at the *vendange* when the tireless grape pickers and important manipulators of the presses take their huge midday meal.

There is no need to have all these ingredients, and certainly substitute marrow in place of aubergine and *courgettes* if it suits you. (Note : If you serve this at any dinner-party expect a clean dish, so if you want some next day reserve it hidden deep in your larder !)

1 medium aubergine	liked)
1 lb. courgettes or young marrow	2 good tbs. olive oil (or 2 oz. butter)
¼ lb. mushrooms	½ oz. goose or duck fat if available
½–¾ lb. tomatoes	
¼–½ green pepper	freshly ground black pepper, salt
2 medium onions	
2 cloves garlic (more if	

Skin the tomatoes. Slice finely mushrooms, pepper, onion. Cut thickly aubergine, courgette (1½-inch lengths) or marrow, tomatoes. Well crush garlic in salt. Heat oil and fat, add green pepper, cook 3 minutes on low heat. Add mushrooms, onion and stir into fat; add courgettes, aubergine and tomato. Cook until tomato softens and juice runs. Add garlic, lower heat still more and cover pan. Cook 30 minutes, stirring occasionally. Taste, season well and continue cooking for 15 to 20 minutes. Remove lid and cook further 15 to 20 minutes or longer. The cooking time may be varied with lid on or off according to how long you wish the ratatouille to take, but in any case 1¼ hours. Raise heat and drive off some of the moisture if at all watery. The ratatouille should never be dry or crumb-like to look at, but should be a thick, coarse purée with the various vegetables just about distinguishable if examined closely.

Some cooks peel and seed the aubergines, but I never feel it necessary beyond scraping out a few of the more obvious seeds. If the courgettes or marrow are old enough to need peeling don't use them, but marrow must be seeded.

Cold ratatouille is delicious but oil for cooking is then essential.

FRIED MARROW

A good way with older fruits

Prepare the marrow in chunks about 2 inches square. Simmer until tender in salted water just to cover, to which you have added 1 slice onion, sprig each sage and parsley, ¼ bayleaf. When just tender, drain and cool. (May be usefully done the day before.) Roll in seasoned flour, egg, crumb and fry in shallow fat, turning once. Cheese or egg sauce or a bacon rasher may be added for a light luncheon snack.

HORSE OR FIELD MUSHROOMS

Still seen in some country shops, horse mushrooms are a rare delicacy. Usually much larger than cultivated sorts they are excellent 'breaded' as an older generation of country people said. For 6 large mushrooms:

2 oz. fresh white or brown
    crumbs
2 tsp. minced onion
1 tsp. each chopped mint and
    parsley

1 egg
3 tbs. milk
2 oz. butter
seasoning

In 1 oz. butter, soften the onion. Add crumbs and stir in well. Add herbs and seasoning, mixing with 1 tbs. milk and the beaten egg. Leave aside for flavours to develop.

Meanwhile cut stalks from mushrooms and carefully peel the caps by turning back the very edge and pulling the strip of peel towards the centre. Inspect top and stalk end. If slightly pitted with holes, drop into lukewarm water slightly salted. This will bring out the grubs of the mushroom fly, and if there are many you may prefer to discard the mushroom, but as a rule a few holes signify only one or, at most, two grubs and if these come out all is well. Mushroom peppered all over with holes should not be used. Put the remaining butter and milk in a shallow oven dish in a low oven to melt. Chop finely the washed mushroom peelings and stalks and add to crumb mixture. Divide into as many portions as there are mushrooms, spread on the underside of caps. Set these in oven dish, cover lightly with foil or greased paper and bake 20 minutes in low oven 325° F, gas 3.

PAPRIKA POTATOES

(PAPRIKA KARTOFFELN – Bohemian)

1 lb. large raw potatoes (best at end of season – or firm French or Dutch salad potatoes will do at any season)
1 onion
2 oz. bacon or good pork dripping
¼ pint stock
¼ pint sour cream or ½ carton yoghurt and 2 tbs. top milk
seasoning
½ tsp. Hungarian paprika – more of other types
parsley

Melt fat, add finely sliced onion, sautée till golden brown. Add thickly sliced potatoes, season lightly, add paprika and stir 1 minute. Add stock. Cover and simmer 1 hour. Ten minutes before serving, add cream and finish cooking. Sprinkle with chopped parsley before sending to table.

Puddings

BLACKBERRY AND APPLE PUDDING, TART AND FLAN

Proportions and method are exactly the same as for Gooseberry and Rhubarb on pp. 294, 256, but care must be taken with the filling. Have as many blackberries as possible up to half quantity with the apples. But they are very liquid so fill pudding well or fruit will go down very much. Some cooks like to cool the filling the day before and then add extra apple purée to make more body. Bramble pips bother some people, when the blackberries may be cooked separately and sieved. This produces a very liquid purée and extra apple should be added.

Serve with extra sugar and plenty of cream.

These notes on the pudding apply equally to blackberry and apple tart.

For Bramble Flan cook about ¼ lb. blackberries with 3 oz. sugar, and sieve. Fill a blind-baked pâte sucrée flan case (p. 129) with lightly rinsed whole raw fruit. Thicken the purée with 1 tsp. cornflower or arrowroot, and pour boiling hot over the raw fruit, brushing a little over the sides of the pastry. Cool and serve with whipped cream and castor sugar.

SWEET-TOOTH'S PUDDING

remains of currant loaf or
    stale buns
2–3 oz. butter (or mixture
    butter and margarine)
½ pint milk
1 egg

vanilla essence (not merely
    something labelled 'Flavour')
brown sugar (soft and/or
    demerara)
golden syrup

Slice loaf just under ¼-inch thick, buttering the slices thickly, and spreading with syrup on which you sprinkle a coating of brown sugar. If you have both kinds, use soft sugar here. With the slices line a 1 pint pie dish. Put 5 drops vanilla essence into a teaspoon (to save accidentally tipping in too much) and beat it into the egg and milk. Pour half this into the lined dish. Float a layer of prepared slices on it, pour on rest and float a final layer thickly coated in sugar – demerara if available. Leave about 30 minutes if possible for bread to absorb liquid. Bake 30 minutes at 325° F, gas 3, above centre of oven, then 10 minutes at 400° F, gas 6, to brown top.

APPLE SNOW

An old, exquisite – and exquisitely simple – favourite.

1 lb. or a little over, cooking apples	grated rind and juice of 1 large lemon
2–3 oz. castor sugar	½ oz. (1 envelope) gelatine

Wipe apples, remove carefully any blemishes but do not peel. Core and quarter, and cook over low heat, without water or sugar to a mush. Sieve into mixing bowl. Dissolve gelatine in 2 tbs. water and stir into still warm purée with rind, sugar and juice. With strong hand whisk, or rotary beater beat constantly until mixture is pale, fluffy and completely cold. If using electric mixer rest it after maximum time stated by manufacturer, between beatings so as not to overheat motor. Beating time will be greatly reduced if bowl is stood on ice. Mixture may be cooled before beating starts, but you will spoil the result if you leave it too long. Do not beat in an aluminium vessel as this may discolour the mousse. Some cooks fold in a stiffly whisked white at the end, but more than one softens the flavour too much. Pile up in serving dish (or glasses where more convenient) and decorate with thin spikes of angelica and almond, or mint leaves thinly coated with egg white, dipped in castor sugar and left to dry out. Hand castor sugar, cream, ratafias as preferred.

When there is a glut of apples from the garden Bramley tree you can make double quantity, put half in a deep jelly mould, cover with foil and keep in cold to produce a trouble-free pudding a couple of days later. A good pudding from many points of view, because vitamin-rich yet easy to digest, attractive to look at, easy and cheap to make.

CHOCOLATE FLAN

Adapted from another family recipe, this may vary in cost as you please. Can be made as tartlets, but is less lush.

6 oz. flaky pastry (p. 130)
2 oz. plain chocolate (unsweetened or bitter is best)
2 oz. sugar (3 for totally unsweetened chocolate)
2 oz. butter/margarine
2 small eggs or 1 large plus 1 tbs. milk (economical, but less good)

4 oz. cake crumbs; or 2 oz. crumbs, 2 oz. ground almonds; or up to 2 oz. fresh white breadcrumbs, the rest cake crumbs or ground almonds
2 or 3 drops vanilla essence

Bake blind a 7 inch flan-case – see sides come well up, and only just allow pastry to set and colour very lightly. Meanwhile cream yolks, sugar and vanilla essence, soften chocolate and butter over very low heat without melting, and beat into yolk mixture. Fold in crumbs. Whisk whites until you can invert basin without their moving, fold into rest, turn into flan-case and bake at 350° F, gas 4, just above centre of oven for 35 to 45 minutes. Serve hot or cold with single cream.

Cocoa and extra butter may be used in place of chocolate, when the amount of butter must be varied according to the crumb mixture: slightly less where more ground almond is used. In this case use 2 eggs, 4 heaped tsp. cocoa, 1–1½ oz. extra butter. Cream cocoa into just-softened butter, do not allow it to melt. This method is to be preferred if good plain chocolate is not available.

Plums

All the recipes for apples, rhubarb and gooseberries may be used for plums. The following recipes are particularly good.

PLUM SPONGE

Halve and stone ½ lb. really ripe good-sized Victoria plums. Crack stones (with sharp blow from hammer or weight, if nutcrackers are not available, the stones folded in paper), skin kernels and put them in each half-plum. Turn the fruit downwards in a sponge sandwich tin which has been thickly buttered and sugared. Make a 1 egg quantity Victoria sponge mixture (pp. 501, 509), *beating very well*. Spread over plums and bake at 375° F, gas 5, until sponge is golden – about 30 minutes. Sugar a round plate, turn out. Serve with sugar and cream, or a boiled egg custard (p. 137) to which, where possible, a dash of wine or liqueur is added.

PLUM OMELETTE

Serves 4.

Make a 4-egg omelette omitting pepper and all but a pinch of salt. Fold into it 3 to 4 tbs. plum purée. Sugar well.

A finish may be given by having ready a fiercely glowing grill. See the omelette has plenty of creamy mixture when cooking stops. Fold omelette over purée, tumble on to a fireproof dish, sugar, and put under grill as near as possible for a few seconds to caramellize sugar. Also, a dash of spirits or liqueur added to the egg mixture is good.

PLUM MERINGUE

Halve and stone 1 lb. plums, add 3–4 oz. sugar and simmer in pan, or bake in foil-covered dish until tender, then leave to cool somewhat. Whisk 2 egg-whites with a pinch of salt until stiff, whisk into them gradually 4 oz. sugar, reserving 1 tsp. Pile over cooked plums, scatter with sugar, set in oven. If to be eaten quickly, cook meringue in moderate oven (375° F, gas 5) about 30 minutes. If to be eaten cold, dry it out in a very low oven (250° F, gas ½) 1 to 1½ hours.

October

Soups
First read soup notes p. 112.

MARROW SOUP

Home grown marrows may by now be somewhat elderly. Useful as bulk in preserves of various kinds, they also make pleasant soup with a delicate nutty taste and thick yet unstodgy texture. Different stocks, milk, herbs, spices, as well as varying the pro- and cream liaison may be used for extra nourishment. Serve with croûtons. Where liked these may be fried in fat in which a crushed clove of garlic has first been lightly fried.

1 marrow	1 good sprig each of any of
2 oz. butter/margarine	the following; parsley, thyme,
1½ pints water or light	basil, celery leaves, dill or
stock	fennel or *small* sprig tarragon
1 small onion	seasoning

Peel, seed and cut marrow into inch pieces. Fry in the butter with the sliced onion until a good golden colour. Finely chop herbs and add, stirring into hot butter 1 minute. Add stock, and simmer 1 hour or until marrow is pulpy. Sieve or beat to purée. Adjust seasoning. Add a little cream or top-milk if liked. A yolk and cream liaison may be used for extra nourishment. Serve with croûtons. Where liked these may be fried in fat in which a crushed clove of garlic has first been lightly fried.

GAME SOUPS

Serves 8.

The price of game birds comes down by October, and there is

game of all kinds and qualities by this time. Housekeepers on budgets may not be able to afford roast grouse, but perhaps a casserole of grouse has been enjoyed, or a hare has been roasted and jugged, leaving behind gravy, carcasses and giblets. Any or all can be made into a game soup of more or less meatiness and flavour, according to the amount of 'remains', but in any event warming and savoury. The method and ingredients given are adaptable.

carcase and gravy from dish
  of game
1 each onion, carrot, stick
  celery – sliced
big faggot of thyme and
  parsley
2 oz. mushrooms or stalks
1 quart brown stock
  if possible, or use beef
  bouillon cubes
6 black peppercorns

salt
½ lemon
1 oz. each margarine or
  bacon dripping, flour
5 tbs. sherry, port or red wine
1 small tbs. rowan jelly or
  sieved dark marmalade
liver of the game if possible,
  a chicken liver, or 1 oz.
  pig's liver can be used.

Melt fat and fry sliced vegetables a good brown. Slice mushrooms thinly and add them, frying 1 minute. Scatter in flour and fry until a good nut brown. Gradually blend in the stock, stirring out all lumps. Add lemon rind in thin parings, the juice, faggot of herbs, peppercorns, and the game carcase but not the gravy. Bring to simmering point and cook 2½ to 3 hours. Strain. Discard herbs and peppercorns, pick over carcase, retaining as much meat as possible and also the vegetables and mushrooms. Put all through Moulin. In a little fat briskly brown the liver, and put this also through the sieve. Return soup to pan, using a tablespoonful or so to thin the jelly or marmalade before adding this also to soup. Lastly add the gravy and wine, and reheat soup to simmering point.

Serve with croûtons and diced frizzled bacon if liked.

If a very thick soup is liked, crumble a ¼-inch thick slice of wholemeal bread and whisk into soup before serving.

TOASTED BARLEY SOUP

STOCK VERSION.

Serves 6.

1–1½ oz. barley	1 oz. good dripping (chicken, bacon, beef)
1 quart chicken stock	seasoning

MILK VERSION

Serves 4.

1 oz. barley	¾ oz. butter/margarine
1–1½ pints milk	seasoning

Fry barley in fat over low heat until it is really well coloured, turning often. It will swell up and may 'jump', so cover hand with oven glove or cloth. Keeping hand covered, off heat add liquid. Season to taste, simmer gently 30 to 45 minutes until barley is tender.

CREAM OF PARSLEY SOUP

½ pint Béchamel sauce (p. 117)	2 oz. parsley
4 oz. potatoes	1 small onion
½ pint light stock or water	seasoning

Scrub and halve the potatoes, peel and quarter the onion. Cook in stock 30 minutes. Skin potatoes, sieve with onion. Blend with sauce and bring to simmering point. Finely chop the parsley, add to soup and simmer 5 minutes.

See also Parsley Consommé (p. 363).

First Courses and Snacks

PÂTÉS AND TERRINES

Call them potted meat if this French name seems too high-falutin' to you. Note also that the French names are nowadays

412

confused: to be absolutely correct a pâté should be called (and cooked) pâté *en croûte* (see raised pie notes, p. 342); while the slice of minced meat we more usually see is cut from a *terrine*, and is cooked in a china dish, being turned out or not as preferred. Pâtés are one of the oldest ways of preserving meat, although they are usually too popular to last long.

Cost varies with local prices and availability, and although needing little skill, they need good arm and wrist muscles if you want to make a quantity, for the mincing can be a longish job, especially if your mincer is the smallest size. But as most men enlist male help if you want to make a lot of pâté in a little time. Some butchers will do the mincing for you, but then you must be willing to fit in with their plans. Most butchers finish mincing and have cleaned the machine before opening their shops, so you would need to order your meats the day before.

However, there is no need to make a minced texture. The meat may be sliced or chopped or diced, though you should allow extra cooking time the more coarsely it is cut.

As with raised pies fat is necessary and this may be distributed through the pâté in several ways. For instance: bacon rashers may line the baking dish, be put in a layer through the meat and as a covering on top; slices of fat pork may be interspersed through slices of meat; fat may be minced in with the rest of the ingredients; softened butter, margarine or lard may be stirred into the mixture.

Marinading adds enormously to flavour and tenderness, but is not necessary with all mixtures.

Seasoning is most important and it is unwise to cut down the amounts stated. Few people care to taste enough of the raw mixture to judge the seasoning, and in any event the taste is quite different after cooking. The high proportion of fat absorbs seasoning, and nothing would be more disappointing than an insipid final result to what had smelt so delicious in the cooking. For pâtés have the same inviting effect that baking bread has, and the temptation to eat them as soon as they come out of the oven is very great. They can be eaten hot, indeed, but will soon disappear if so, and you lose the pleasure of the jelly.

In cooking, the meat shrinks as the juices run from it, but

don't be tempted to cut the cooking time. The shrinkage only goes so far, and unless well cooked, like all meat, the pâté will be hard and rubbery instead of smooth and about the consistency of cheese. Some old recipes for brawn, which is after all a kind of pâté are called *Fromage de Porc*. Keeping the pâté under weights while it cools compacts it to this close, firm texture, making cutting easier; also giving a better shape, and flattening it for turning out.

Turning out is optional. Some people like the look of a lining of bacon rinds when the pâté is turned out, or the pattern of layers, where these exist. Others haven't dishes they think attractive enough to put on the table. As mentioned in the raised pie notes, there are elaborate (and expensive) terrines for pâtés imitating raised pie crusts, and from one of these it would be pointless to turn out the pâté. Less expensive are the many decorated or plain white china soufflé dishes. For my part I see nothing wrong with a pie dish or plain brown cocotte if the whole pâté is appearing on the table. However, it is more prudent for the sake of economy to cut the required number of slices and arrange overlapped, like sliced cake, on the serving dish; or on individual plates. Adorn with fresh green salad leaves if you must, but never slices of tomato.

The invariable accompaniment to pâté is hot toast and a generous dish of butter. Oven-crisped French bread-sticks are equally good, and where good fresh rolls and butter can be bought nearby, a slice of pâté makes a welcome desk lunch. Pâtés are a very rich concentrated form of meat, so if used as a first course, a little goes a long way.

A fairly usual mixture of meats is a smallish proportion of liver, about three times more of fat meat, and twice that of lean meat. But examples of three kinds follow, and quantities may be varied according to season and availability. A softer texture is obtained by adding cream to the mixtures.

PÂTÉ DE CAMPAGNE

2–3 oz. pig's liver
½ lb. belly of pork
1 lb. lean veal, hutch rabbit,
   or slice from leg of pork
1½ level tsp. salt
almost level tsp. freshly
   ground pepper

about ¼ lb. streaky bacon
   rashers (smoked gives
   better flavour)
2 allspice berries
6 juniper berries
1–2 cloves garlic
1 shallot or small onion

MARINADE 5 tbs. each wine and stock

Remove gristle and bone from the meats, and mince them, preferably twice. Use smallest plate of mincer if mincing once only, otherwise use a coarser plate the first time round, changing to the finer one last. Or chop finely.

Liver is elusive stuff to mince, and it is a good plan to start with it so that the rest will force it through. 'Pie veal' may be used if of good quality from a not too gristly part of the animal, imported pie veal being best. However, work will be very easy if your buy a leg of veal or pork for roasting, cutting your own pound of flesh from it. Crush the spice berries coarsely between two old metal spoons. Put garlic and shallot through mincer, or chop very finely. Mix all ingredients except the bacon well together to distribute seasoning and spices evenly. Mix wine and stock and blend well with meat mixture. Leave at least 2 hours; overnight where possible.

Remove rind from rashers, spread and flatten them and line dish, overlapping rashers for complete covering, or arranging them in a regular pattern. Put meat in dish in two portions with layer of rashers through the middle, or in one lot as preferred. Cover top with more rashers if liked, this time cut in thin strips and lay over in lattice.

Cover with foil or buttered greaseproof and bake *au bain marie* at 325° F, gas 3, for 1½ hours. If a very small deep dish is used, or if double quantity is made in a single deep dish, 2 hours may be necessary. Add water to *bain marie* as needed. When done, remove covering, rest fresh buttered paper on top, foil on this, and then weights. For longer keeping seal completely when cold with a ¼-inch layer of melted butter on top.

A GAME PÂTÉ

½ lb. (minimum) raw meat
  from hare, pigeons or
  elderly game birds
½ lb. belly pork
½ lb. Scotch or English skirt
about 3 oz. fat ham or back
  bacon rashers, cut very
  thin
liver from hare or birds, or
  2 oz. pig's liver
1½ tsp. salt
½ tsp. pepper
½ tsp. sugar
5 tbs. sherry or red wine
2–3 tbs. double cream (or
  tinned, or sour)
5 tbs. stock
sprig fresh thyme, or pinch
  dried
grated rind and juice of ½
  orange
clove garlic
1 tsp. minced onion, or
  8–10 chive blades chopped

This pâté is very attractive sliced rather than minced. The slices must be really thin (see raised pie notes pp. 342–4), and if you explain what you want to him, your butcher will probably slice the skirt for you. He might also prepare the pork if not very busy, though being a firmer texture it is not a problem.

Remove skin from birds and carve meat from them in thin slices. Remove rind, gristle and bones from pork, and cut in thin rashers. Cut skirt in broad thin slices. Mince liver.

In a small basin or cup stir together salt, pepper, finely chopped herbs, onion, garlic and orange rind. Mix wine, sugar and warmed orange juice in one cup, cream and stock in another. When sugar is melted mix both liquids.

Cover bottom of dish with ham or bacon slices. Then fill dish with rest of ingredients, except liver, in layers, keeping it to the same rotation, inserting a layer of ham or bacon about half way up, on top of which putting *all* the liver. After each complete round of layers add 2 tbs. liquid, followed by sprinkling of seasonings. When all meats are used up, sprinkle with rest of seasoning, pour on remaining liquid; cover with final layer of bacon in lattice or as liked.

The meat must be well packed into the dish so that it goes to edges, and into corners if square dish is used, and it must be pressed down from time to time.

Tiny, very firm mushroom buttons are a pretty addition if available. A line of them through the centre is enough, so they show when the pâté is sliced. Should you happen to have pistachio nuts you can do the same with these, likewise with blanched almonds.

Cover and leave about 2 hours for flavours to blend. Cook as previous recipe, sealing in the same way if required.

CHICKEN LIVER PÂTÉ

1 lb. chicken livers
1½ oz. best beef dripping (I mean from joints, not the butcher)
a spoonful or two of the jelly gravy coming from roast joint or fowl

4 tbs. thin cream
2 large eggs
1 small clove garlic
seasoning

Rinse livers and remove 'strings'. Crush garlic very well in salt to make it juicy and rub the clove and any salt all over inside of mixing bowl, discarding after this. Warm the bowl and cream the dripping to soften without oiling. Add livers, and chop them a little to mix with dripping. This is the trickiest bit, as the dripping refuses to cling and has to be 'buttered' on to the livers rather. Warm the gravy just to melt it, and mix with cream, add beaten eggs, and stir into livers. Season lightly. Put mixture through Moulin or in blender. If you have neither, chop finely at dripping stage. But don't attempt to put through ordinary sieve. The texture is at its best if Moulin is used. Brush out a small dish or plain mould with salad oil, fill with mixture which must not come completely to top in case pâté rises. Cover with well buttered greaseproof or foil, and steam 1½ to 2 hours. Where a steamer is not used see that water comes only three-quarters way up mould. Can be cooked *au bain-marie*, but water must be boiling to begin with. When quite cold turn out.

SUGGESTED ACCOMPANIMENTS. A very crisp lettuce,

lightly dressed with vinaigrette is excellent with this, as also two 'wedges' or so of hard-boiled egg. See that the toast is thin, but not at all rusk-like, i.e. made at the last minute.

EGGS IN THE NEST

1 lb. well-made purée of
   potatoes
1 tsp. minced onion or fresh
   herbs to choice

4 œufs mollets (p. 148) or
   poached eggs

Pipe half potato in thick border round a circular oven dish. Brown under grill. Fill bottom of dish with rest of potato in which flavouring has been mixed. Put the eggs in the nest. Serve hot with a green vegetable or salad.

GRATED SALAD

3 carrots
2 small crisp apples
1 dozen radishes
8 oz. cheese

juice of ½ lemon
salad oil
seasoning
made mustard

Peel and grate carrots. Wipe apples, quarter, core and grate them, squeezing lemon juice on them immediately. Mix juice well into apple to keep colour, then mix with carrot. Add 2–3 tbs. oil into which you have whisked the seasoning and made mustard. Mix all well, pile in dish. Cut cheese neatly into cigarette-sized sticks. Slightly flatten top of salad and arrange cheese, log-pile wise, on top.

SUGGESTED ACCOMPANIMENT. Hot toast and butter.

BAKED SAVOURY SOUFFLÉS

Quantities given here will serve 6 for a first course, 4 for light luncheon. Increase amount for main course. There is nothing difficult about making a baked soufflé if you follow instructions step by step as numbered, use a proper china soufflé case, and cook as directed.

Some cooks like a fast oven, producing a soufflé crisp outside and almost raw in the centre, others cook more slowly for an almost sponge-cake consistency throughout. There is also a method of folding in whites so little that the result is more like the nursery pudding known as 'floating islands' – blobs of meringue in custard.

As given here the result will be spongy outside, slightly liquid in the centre, and of even texture.

Soufflés deflate very rapidly, particularly in draughts. They also shrink if 'kept hot'. Therefore time them so that they are served as soon as ready. It is always the rule that the diners should be kept waiting for the soufflé rather than the reverse.

Soufflé cases are sold by numbers. The most useful size for a family of 4 to 6 is No. 2. This holds something over a pint of water if filled to the brim. Pyrex-type 'baking dishes' do not exactly correspond, so get one holding more rather than less. Cake tins may be used if of heavy gauge tin, but they tend to overcook the outside. Individual soufflé cases are often called ramekins.

I do not find the traditional paper band tied round the outside of the soufflé case is necessary for baked soufflés of the quantity given here. But if using a cake-tin then use the band, not because the soufflé will flow over the tin's edge, but to prevent over cooking. The band should be of double greaseproof coming 2 to 3 inches above edge of case. It will be needed, whatever the baking vessel, for increased quantity of ingredients. The portion of paper coming above rim must be lightly brushed with melted butter or oil, as must the case or tin itself.

1½ oz. each butter and flour
1½ gills milk
3 large egg yolks ⎫ N.B. In increasing quantities remember that
4 whites ⎭ there should be 1 white more than yolks
3 oz. grated cheese (should include some Parmesan if possible); or pounded meat, fish, fowl etc; or 2–3 tbs. spinach purée; or very finely sliced or chopped mushrooms, asparagus etc. as available
Seasoning: cayenne, Tabasco, mustard as suitable

(1) Prepare soufflé case and stand on baking tray.

(2) Set oven shelf in centre of oven, and pre-heat to 400° F, gas 6.

(3) Melt butter. Stir in flour off heat. Add milk and blend smooth. Return to gentle heat and bring to boiling point stirring rapidly, or whisking, to avoid all lumping. Cool somewhat.

(4) Meanwhile prepare cheese, haddock, or whatever.

(5) Separate eggs, dropping whites into small mixing bowl, but beating each yolk in turn into the cooled panada. Season this. Add cheese or other ingredients. Where coarser ingredients are used, such as mushroom slices, they are better put in bottom of case.

(6) With rotary whisk beat whites, adding good pinch salt, until there is no sliding of contents when bowl is inverted.

(7) Turn yolk mixture on top of whites and, with metal spoon or spatula, rapidly and lightly fold and 'cut' mixture together until no more lumps of solid whites appear. Do not over-fold so that air bubbles are collapsed, and mixture begins to get runny. It should be spongy. (I am indebted to Len Deighton's *Où est le garlic?* for the obvious-seeming tip of adding panada mixture to whites. The opposite is more often taught, when it is easy for the heavier mixture to remain an unblended 'custard', at the bottom of the bowl.) *Do not linger over this operation.*

(8) Turn into prepared soufflé case and bake 30 to 40 minutes until soufflé is well risen, with centre 2 to 3 inches higher than the rim of case, lightly browned, and springy if slightly pressed. *Serve at once.*

Half quantities may need slightly less, larger quantities slightly more baking time, depending on size of baking vessel and depth of mixture.

Quantity will fill 8 to 10 ramekins, taking 10 to 15 minutes to cook.

SUGGESTED ACCOMPANIMENTS. Green salad, vinaigrette dressing; paper-thin brown bread and butter (if suitable – e.g. for shrimp, cheese, crab etc.).

Fish

FISH PLATE-PIE

1 lb. saithe/coley or cod fillet	1 tsp. minced onion
2 oz. mushrooms or stalks	seasoning
1 large or 2 small eggs	8 oz. shortcrust pastry (p.
5 tbs. white wine or cider	127)
5 tbs. stock or water	egg to glaze
large sprig chopped parsley	

Skin fish, pull out stray bones. Thinly slice mushrooms. Cut dough in half, lining shallow pie plate with one half, reserving rest for lid. Put fish, onion, mushrooms, liquids and salt in saucepan, bring to boil and cook briskly 3 minutes stirring well. Cool a little. Add parsley, some pepper, and the beaten egg. Adjust seasoning and allow to cool. Put into lined plate, roll out lid, damp edges and cover down, knocking up edges (see diagram on p. 125) and patterning with fork, adding trimmings as liked. Mix a little egg, salt and water, and brush top. Bake at 375° F, gas 5, for 25 to 30 minutes until pastry is well coloured.

PILCHARD SHELLS

1 small tin pilchards in tomato sauce	1½ oz. grated cheese
	1 oz. dried crumbs
1 lb. pommes duchesse or purée (or packet mashed potato)	pepper
	scallop shells or shallow baking dish

Break up the fish slightly and mix with its sauce. Fill centre of 4 scallop shells with fish and pepper lightly. Pipe a thick border of potato round edge of shells. Mix cheese and crumbs and strew over top of fish. Bake at 400° F, gas 6, 20 to 25 minutes until potato is slightly coloured. Or grill.

SUGGESTED ACCOMPANIMENTS. Sweet corn in melted butter; cauliflowers; baked whole tomatoes.

Good for single-person supper.

SARDINE SALAD

Serves 4 for luncheon or supper main course; 6 to 8 for first course.

2 tins sardine
½ pimento
8 black (or green) olives
3 tomatoes
1 medium onion (optional)

2 large Belgian endives (or
    chicory when in season)
rind of ½ lemon
vinaigrette dressing made with
    juice from the ½ lemon
freshly-ground black pepper

Finely slice pimento. Thinly pare lemon and cut peel in needle shreds. Stone olives and slice or chop coarsely. Concass the tomatoes and cut in strips. Cut onion very finely in rings and separate these. Break endive leaves in two or three pieces, or shred coarsely, and mix with some of vinaigrette. Put pimento, tomato, olive, onion and lemon shreds into a bowl and mix with rest of vinaigrette. In a shallow square or oval serving dish make a bed of the endive. Cover with mixed salad. Put sardines down centre of dish, sprinkle them with a little lemon juice, and pepper well.

SUGGESTED ACCOMPANIMENT. French bread stick; unsalted butter.

Useful addition to slimmer's menu eaten with Cambridge Loaf etc.

SPICED GRILLED FILLET

2 lb. fillet of saithe/coley, cod,
    or haddock *in one piece*
½ tsp. mixed spice
¼ tsp. ground ginger
½ tsp. salt
1 cardamon seed crushed
    (optional) or any other
    less usual flavour available,
    e.g. coriander, dill or
    fennel

cayenne and fresh black
    pepper
pinch caraway seed
 1 dessertsp. brown sugar
grated rind and juice of ½ lemon
1½–2 oz. margarine/butter
1 clove garlic minced
    (optional for those who
    dislike it)

Cream ⅔ of margarine slightly. Add spices, except pepper, seeds, sugar, lemon rind and garlic and cream again. Heat the grill.

Skin the fillet, and spread unflavoured portion of fat thinly on this side. Salt lightly and sprinkle with a little lemon juice. Put on gratin dish and grill 3 minutes. Using two fish slices or similar, turn. Salt uncooked side, sprinkle with juice, and spread with flavoured fat. Grill 5 to 8 minutes until well coloured, basting once with juices in dish. Garnish dish with its accompanying vegetables one down each side of fillet, which is carved into four portions at table.

SUGGESTED ACCOMPANIMENTS. Small boiled potatoes tossed in butter, salt and parsley; cauliflower, in florets with white sauce. Sauté potatoes; fried onion rings. Purée of potatoes; grilled tomatoes.

Vary herbs and spices as liked. Choose accompaniments that are bland, to contrast with spicy flavours, or that compliment taste or texture.

Meat

BOILED LEG OF MUTTON AND CAPER SAUCE

Once almost as often eaten as the Sunday roast, boiled mutton dropped out of fashion with the huge rise in the imports of New Zealand lamb, the quality, quantity and freezing of which made young, roasting animals available cheaply, virtually all the year round. Nevertheless, lamb does become rather less good about now, while home-killed beef is beginning its best, but most expensive season. This is where mutton comes into its own. Instead of a disappointing roast joint, go for a dependable boiled joint that will cost less. Leg is the traditional joint, but there is no reason why the small household should not boil a best end, or, in Scotland, a chump end, to serve with caper sauce. All that needs to be done is to remove as much fat as you conveniently can.

Mutton, being older, is a larger animal, and true mutton joints are better for families of four or more, or for entertaining. However, one of the lower grades of New Zealand lamb makes a good substitute. These lower grades may have a blue ticket marked with a 4 or T, or a red ticket with the letters YL, YM or YH on them. Unfortunately few people are aware of the excellent detailed grading system of New Zealand meat, so the less scrupulous butchers simply remove all tickets. Bargain butchers, however, are likely to have only these less high grades, while the high-class family butcher may never buy below the top two or three grades. For a boiled leg of mutton it may pay for once to patronize a cheap butcher, but don't let him know you intend boiling your joint, or he may dig you out something too tough and elderly to taste of anything. A true mutton joint may have to be ordered from your family butcher in advance. The best quality mutton is usually reserved for large-scale caterers such as hospitals, schools and restaurants who can make use of big joints, and these customers would probably have regular orders with the butcher, so he would have to buy extra for the odd order from a private household.

Very important in shopping for this dish is to make sure of the size of your saucepan. The larger covered roasters might do the job if the joint were not of the largest size, but if any part of the joint were out of the water, it would be necessary to turn it from time to time.

COOKING. Cut the shank bone through, but include it in the pot. Trim off excess fat. Fill a large pot with enough water to cover, adding 1 tsp. salt for each 1 lb. meat. Add:

6 crushed peppercorns	small sprig rosemary or sage
1 onion	(or dried leaves)
1 carrot quartered	1 clove garlic
1 stick celery (or dried	1 pig or calf's foot where
leaves, or seed, in muslin)	possible, bacon or pork
1 clove	rind as available

Bring water to boil, put joint in and boil up. Draw aside for 15 minutes until water cools somewhat. Return to heat and bring slowly up just to simmering point. This method seems to seal the meat without its hardening too much, and without making so much scum. Keep at the simmer for 2 to 3 hours according to size, and the amount of 'doneness' you like. A 5 lb. leg (or half leg, if very big, and the butcher is agreeable) is a smallish mutton joint, a 9 lb. joint would be large. Lamb, of course, is smaller even in the less good grades mentioned. After first 15 minutes of simmering remove any scum that may have risen. Drain before dishing. Serve broth separately.

NOTE: The broth makes excellent soup stock, particularly if foot, rinds etc. are used.

CAPER SAUCE. ½ pint Béchamel (p. 117) very well flavoured or white sauce made with 1 oz. each margarine and flour, and with a generous ½ pint milk so that the sauce is rather on the liquid side. If liked, use ½ pint milk and thin with 3 to 4 tbs. stock from the cooking pot. Chop 1 level tbs. capers, 1 good sprig parsley, add to sauce with dash of lemon juice or tarragon vinegar.

NOTE: Also good with boiled mutton is cherry sauce (p. 351), and pickled damsons (p. 525). Eliza Acton recommends a cucumber sauce, but I consider this too delicate with the already bland meat.

SUGGESTED ACCOMPANIMENTS. Cornish turnips or swede; marrow cooked with tomato; ratatouille; carrots Espagnole; plain potatoes; any tomato dish.

ROAST RABBIT

1 whole young rabbit (hutch is best unless you have a reliable source of supply for wild rabbit)	½ pint milk. 4–6 rashers streaky bacon 4 skinless sausages

STUFFING

2 tbs. fresh white crumbs	1 tsp. minced onion
½ tsp. thyme	1½ oz. fat for frying
1 egg	rabbit offal
seasoning	

Paunch the rabbit, reserving the liver, heart and kidneys (or get this done by the butcher). Remove the head, using it and the heart to make stock for gravy.

Finely chop liver and kidneys, melt fat and fry onion brown, add the chopped offal, and fry briskly 1 minute. Add crumbs, seasoning and ½ tsp. thyme (finely chopped) or, if dried, use good pinch. Beat egg lightly and add this to moisten stuffing. Add 1 tbs. milk if necessary. Season and fill paunch with stuffing and sew up with needle and coarse thread. Truss front legs of rabbit back, back legs bent against body to make a compact shape. Put in roasting tin, season, and pour round half the milk. Cover with bacon. Roast ½ hour at 400° F, gas 6, or 1 hour at 325° F, gas 3. Baste with milk from time to time, adding more in tin as necessary. Half way through add the sausages. 20 minutes before the end, remove bacon, dust with flour, and baste with milk to brown. Dish with bacon and sausages, and keep warm. Add stock to roasting tin, scraping down browned milk and juices, mixing to make gravy.

SUGGESTED ACCOMPANIMENTS. Redcurrant jelly; pommes Sicilienne; Franklin's potatoes; sauté potatoes; cabbage (see recipes); saged onions.

Hare

Even for a family there is plenty of meat on a good young hare, and as the flavour is very distinctive though delicious, one doesn't want more than two meals running of hare. To make still more variation I divide the hare into the saddle – not cut in chunks as butchers are inclined to do – and the four limbs. (The head is included in the pot with the limbs, but I am too squeamish to care to eat it, so I pick meat etc. from bones for puss.) Having divided the hare, I roast the saddle whole, and jug the rest, including, of course, the blood which, correctly, should be given you in a carton, or you may take your own container.

ROAST SADDLE OF HARE

Reserve liver and kidneys.

STUFFING.

3 oz. fresh crumbs
½ tsp. chopped thyme
1 egg
1 tsp. minced onion
1–2 mushrooms (or stalks)
   minced finely

1½ oz. bacon dripping (note
   extra fat to counteract
   dryness of hare meat)
seasoning

Melt fat, brown onion, add mushroom, cook 1 minute. Off heat add crumbs, flavourings and beaten egg.

Season inside of saddle, fill with stuffing and stitch up flaps of skin to make a neat shape. Any spare stuffing is rolled in floured hands into small marbles, and fried, or baked in tin, and either served with the saddle or the jug.

Roast, covered with bacon and basted with milk, as for the rabbit, but omitting sausages. An hour may be necessary if the cushions of meat each side of the backbone are very thick.

SAUCE. Meanwhile scald the liver and kidneys and chop finely. Melt 1½ oz. butter/margarine, add 1 tsp. each minced onion and mixed thyme and parsley and the liver, and fry gently 7 minutes. Strain butter into second small pan, add 1 oz. flour and fry a good nut brown. Add ¼ pint stock and any milk in roasting tin, ½ clove garlic crushed, 5 tbs. wine. Blend smoothly and add liver mixture, mixing over gentle heat. When hare is dished make up any liquid in roasting tin to ½ pint with water. Heat to boiling point, scrape pan down well, deglazing the juices to make a rich gravy. Add enough of this to sauce to make ½ pint, dishing the rest in gravy-boat. Give sauce a final simmer while finishing rest of meal and dish in sauce boat.

SUGGESTED ACCOMPANIMENTS. Redcurrant jelly; plainly boiled small potatoes; sprouts, or cauliflower (butter – no sauce).

JUGGED HARE

Part or whole hare including blood and heart	water or light stock
	salt
2 oz. butter/good dripping	forcemeat as above
1 oz. seasoned flour	bouquet garni
onion stuck with 1 clove, 4–6 peppercorns	½ clove garlic
	1 tbs. redcurrant jelly
¼ pint red wine or 5 tbs. each wine and sherry or port	1–2 tbs. lemon juice, few strips lemon peel

NOTE: The 'jug' was probably once really a jug or jar of sorts. Although any saucepan or cocotte will do, it is best to have something tallish and narrow if possible, for little liquid is used, and a broad pan tends to cook this away, and also prevents it coming up round the meat to impregnate it with the flavours. At present there is a revival of the old 'Nottingham jars' for braising and stewing, and this is an excellent vessel for jugging hare as for many stews. They can be used on top of the stove on an asbestos mat.

Have 'jug' warming in low oven. Wipe hare joints, and cut to size required. Roll in seasoned flour.

Heat 1½ oz. butter in frying pan. Fry hare a good brown and put in jug with onion, enough hot liquid barely to cover, bouquet, garlic, wine, lemon rind and juice. Cook about 3½–4 hours (300° F, gas 2) until tender enough to bone easily at table. Meanwhile, use remaining flour and butter together to make a *beurre manié*. Make and fry the forcemeat balls, or reheat them if left over from roast as above. When hare is done remove it, thicken liquor with *beurre manié*, adjust seasoning, adding a little extra wine if liked. Finally, and when liquor is just off boiling point, whisk in jelly and blood. Either return meat to stewing jar or pour liquor over the meat in a deep dish. Group the forcemeat balls at one end of dish or strew on top of jar or serve in small hot dish separately.

SUGGESTED ACCOMPANIMENTS. Redcurrant jelly; liver
sauce (see roast hare); plain potatoes; sprouts or cabbage.

BOHEMIAN ROAST PIGEON

1 plump young pigeon between each two people may be enough
where birds are boned and appetites on the small side. Draw
the birds carefully yourself, otherwise you must explain to the
poulterer that you will need the giblets, but do not want the
skin too much torn open at the vent. Still better, if you know
how and have time, bone the birds yourself, 'replacing' bone
with the stuffing and sewing up down the backs. The giblets can
then be removed intact from the carcass. This is also easier and
more economical at the table. However boning is by no means
essential.

I came across this dish first in Prague, and its elegance and
the use made of fruit in this context, is a reminder that this most
Mozartian city is half rooted in Western Europe, and was once as
busy a cosmopolitan meeting-place as Vienna, whose intellectual,
academic, artistic and culinary renown it has shared, rivalled
and, sometimes, surpassed.

2 roasting pigeons
fat bacon rashers (or lardons if liked)

FARCE

1 egg	1 oz. chopped mushroom (or
1 oz. margarine	stalks)
finely chopped giblets of	2–3 oz. fresh white crumbs
pigeons	
1 tsp. each chopped onion	
and parsley	

GARNISH. Compôte of any selection of fruits, either smallish
or cut small. For instance, sectioned orange or satsuma, sliced
apple or pear, plums, pipped and skinned grapes, dried apricots,
home-bottled peaches or other summer fruits, or good quality
canned fruits may be used at discretion. The latter will not need
poaching. Allow about 4–6 small fruits, or pieces, per helping.

Poach fruit, by separate kinds, in syrup of ¼ pint water, 2 oz. sugar.

Make farce by softening mushrooms and onions in margarine, then mixing in rest of ingredients, stuff birds, truss to neat shape with thin string, tying thin slices of fat bacon or pork fat over breasts, or, if boned, breasts may be larded with one or two thin lardons and covered with a slice of fat during cooking. Put in roasting tin with a little water poured over the bottom of tin. Twist foil or greaseproof over tin, or roast in covered roaster. Roast at 400° F, gas 6, in middle or just above middle of oven for 20 minutes. Remove cover, continue cooking 10 minutes. Remove rashers, leaving them to crisp at one side of tin if liked. Lightly flour breasts, baste with juices and fat in pan, and cook further 15 minutes to brown breasts. Dish, arranging 2 bouquets of poached fruits at either side of dish. Using ¼ pint stock or water, deglaze the roasting tin, adding 2–3 tbs. fruit syrup, and some dry white or red wine if available, or a dash of liqueur.

SUGGESTED ACCOMPANIMENTS. Sauté potatoes or game chips (packet crisps do very well); Franklin's potatoes.

In Bohemia potatoes are not an all-year-round vegetable for everyone. Instead rice, noodles or tiny pastry dumplings might be served. Also suitable are haricot, butter or similar beans (p. 139) plainly cooked and served in a little butter/margarine. Green flageolets, as on p. 74, would be excellent, but with butter, not sauce; cabbage; sprouts; salad.

PIGEON PIE

3 plump pigeons	light stock
carrots	1 lemon
12 tiny onions *or* quartered medium onions	few mushrooms
	2 tbs. of sherry
1 oz. butter	6 oz. flaky pastry made with
oil	dripping (see p. 130)

Make dripping flaky pastry. Rest this while cooking filling. Brown a layer of thickly-cut carrot rings in a little butter and oil in frying-pan, transferring them to cover bottom of cocotte when coloured. Keep hot. Add onions to pan and brown. Add to cocotte. Add ½ oz. butter to pan, and sear pigeons, adding whole to cocotte with a few bacon rinds. Pour in ½ pint light stock just to cover carrots. Add few strips lemon rind, cover down well and cook in moderate oven 1 hour, then low oven further ¾ hour, or until skewer easily runs through top leg-joint. Add stock as needed. Bone at once by dividing along breast-bone and pulling from carcase with legs and wings. Separate these and slide meat from small bones. Fill 2-pint pie dish with breasts, using scraps from legs etc. to fill gaps, together with a few mushrooms or stalks, cut coarsely. Season layers lightly. Add cocotte vegetables, discarding rinds. Stir in 2 tbs. sherry to liquid and fill pie dish, reserving surplus. Roll out pastry ¼ inch thick. With pastry wheel cut strips from edge of paste sheet to fit flange of dish. Damp flange, press on strips, cut lid slightly larger than outer rim of flange, damp flange, press lid well on, knock up edges, adorn with leaves, etc. as liked, glaze with yolk, salt and water, and bake at 425° F, gas 7, until risen and well-coloured – about 25 minutes. Serve with more carrots or Bohemian cabbage (p. 157).

STEAK AND KIDNEY PUDDING

There are many slight variations of this English classic. Those in this version are my own, based on a family original.

12 oz. each Scotch or English skirt and shin of beef (note that shin is superior to leg; body (or flank) skirt is better for this purpose than rump skirt)	10 oz. suet crust (p. 133) 6 oz. ox or pig kidney 1 heaped tbs. seasoned flour boiling stock or water

Cut kidney in inch strips, cut beef into slices about 3 by 2 by ¼ inches. Tumble beef in flour to coat, roll each strip round a piece of kidney. Line greased 2-pint basin with ⅔ suet crust rolled out fairly thinly. Roll out last ⅓ to fit top. Fill meat into pudding, pour in hot stock to come ¾ way up, or slightly more. Damp lid edges, press well to edges of lining. Cover pudding with greased paper, then damped greaseproof or foil. Allow for pudding to rise by pleating paper. Tie securely. Steam for 3½ to 4 hours.

STEAK AND KIDNEY PIE

Pastry as for Pigeon Pie, filling as for Steak and Kidney Pudding, a little fried onion (optional).

Put the pie to bake as for Pigeon Pie. When the crust is risen and light brown evenly all over – about 25 minutes, take out pie and lower heat to 275° F, gas 1.

Lightly twist tissue paper over crust. Return pie to oven and continue cooking 3 to 3½ hours. Inspect crust about each hour. If darkening appreciably, lower heat to 250° F, gas ½, or put oven shelf down to lower half of oven. Very lightly damp tissue on outside before re-covering pie. This will be found a much superior pie to those in which the meat has first been stewed. Carrots Espagnole (p. 434) are an excellent accompaniment.

Game Accompaniments

The traditional British accompaniments for game birds are : fried crumbs, tiny sausages, bacon rolls, bread sauce, game chips, watercress or green salad, gravy made in roasting tin, croûtes, especially under bird during cooking to catch juices.

Cabbage and sprouts are also excellent done in any of the ways suggested throughout this book, except that any sort of thickened sauces are not desirable, since the other accompaniments are rich enough. Mushrooms, courgettes, marrows, spinach, peas and beans all go well, and there is no need to stick to what is called 'correct', if what you have on hand is good or preferred. As you will see from the pigeon recipe, other countries have very different and equally good ideas.

These days I never make game chips, but buy packet crisps if at all. I don't, in fact, care much for them with meals, they are awkward to eat, they get soggy at once if in contact with gravy, and they get cold in seconds. I would always prefer small ordinary chips or *pommes alumettes* – chips cut square and small, though not quite as small as the matchsticks implied in the name – or sauté potatoes. Otherwise, what with bread sauce, crumbs and croûtes, potatoes can often be omitted altogether.

Bread sauce is very English, but very good also are fruit sauces such as cranberry, plum, or apple; jellies such as rowan, red-currant, raspberry or bramble; orange marmalade, damson cheese or blackcurrant jam, if of good flavour.

Salads such as orange, chicory and mint dressed with lemon vinaigrettes; Waldorf salad; plum, lettuce and a few blanched almonds; cucumber, apple and parsley; all give piquancy to contrast with richness.

Stuffing game birds is quite commonplace on the continent, and these stuffings do not necessarily include breadcrumbs, nor need you follow a recipe, but invent your own. For instance, a purée of spinach and mushroom (or stalks) seasoned and bound with yolk and sour cream or yoghurt is good. Nut meat, bought from a health food store, can be added to mushroom, plus the chopped liver of the bird and a little onion or garlic juice. Pommes duchesse (which, by the way, is another good potato method for game), or purées with herbs, onion, the liver and grated citrus fruit rind, makes a delicious stuffing, in particular for the small birds where one or a half is a portion, and this absolves you from some cooking, for you simply make enough of the potato stuffing to bake a spare dishful for the table, and omit any other potatoes. Another good alternative is Franklin's potatoes (p. 435), combining bread sauce with potatoes.

Vegetables

BAKED CAULIFLOWER

Cut the stem of a cauliflower nice and flat so that it stands well. Cook it in boiling salted water, 20 minutes. Drain and stand in deep oven dish. Cream 1½ oz. margarine/butter, finely chop one rasher bacon, a few leaves tarragon, sprig parsley, 1 tbs. dried crumbs and mix into butter. Cut this in several pieces and dot over cauliflower. Rest a butter paper on top and bake in moderate oven 350° F, gas 4, for 5 minutes. Remove paper, sprinkle all over with 1½ tbs. herb vinegar, white wine or cider. Return to oven for 10 to 15 minutes. Serve in hot shallow dish, pouring butter sauce over top. Big cauliflowers should be simmered 30 to 40 minutes, but baking time is the same.

CARROTS ESPAGNOLE

1 lb. carrots	seasoning
½ pint good stock	1 tsp. tomato purée
½ small onion	1–2 tbs. sherry
bouquet garni	½ oz. each margarine and flour
piece celery (or substitute)	1 crushed clove garlic

Scrape the carrots, cut smaller if large, and cook in stock with onion, celery, bouquet and garlic for 20 to 30 minutes until tender. Remove from stock and keep hot in serving dish. Strain stock, melt margarine in rinsed pan, scatter in flour and cook to a good nut brown. Blend in stock, bringing to the boil without lumps. Add tomato purée and sherry, adjust seasoning and cook 2 minutes. Pour over carrots.

A good dish to show off home-grown carrots. The stock becomes well flavoured with the carrots as they cook, and the resulting sauce has a sweet-and-sour taste of its own. Useful for brightening up end-of-season lamb, and the beef stews, which often have to be the lot of budget cooks at the beginning of the home-killed beef season, when roasts are dear.

SAGED ONIONS

¾ lb. onions	salt
1½ oz. margarine	black pepper
2 level tbs. fresh white crumbs	½ carton yoghurt (optional)
1 level tsp. chopped sage (½ tsp. dried)	

Related to sage and onion stuffing, but in a form suitable to be used as a vegetable.

If very strong flavoured, blanch the whole peeled onions 1 minute. Slice coarsely, sweat in margarine until tender, then add salt and fresh black pepper to taste, stir in the sage and crumbs, turn into oven dish and bake at 400° F, gas 6, until top is lightly coloured, about 20 minutes; or grill. Spoon band of yoghurt down centre, garnishing with black pepper.

FRANKLIN'S POTATOES

½ pint slightly liquid bread sauce (p. 182) – cut bread down slightly
1 lb. potatoes that have been boiled 10–15 minutes according to size

1 tbs. crumbs browned in ½ oz. margarine (optional)

Fill a small gratin dish with alternate layers of bread sauce and potatoes, sliced about ⅛-inch thick, starting and ending with sauce. Top with crumbs and bake at 300° F, gas 2, for 30 minutes.

Puddings

Pears

Cooking pears, in particular those from old trees, can be tasteless. They need baking or stewing in a well-flavoured light syrup, when they usually turn a most beautiful pink, a bonus to reward you for your trouble.

Where there is a glut of eating pears, it is often convenient to poach some of these, rather than having them go 'sad', which they do so abruptly. In this instance, less flavouring is needed, but you must add colour to the syrup.

The preliminary cooking done, there are two flavours particularly sympathetic to pears. Sauces made with either, and served with the pears hot or cold, are equally delicious.

SYRUP FOR STEWING PEARS

½ pint water or ¼ pint
water ¼ pint red wine
½ inch cinnamon stick or
few drops vanilla essence,
especially for dessert pears

4 oz. sugar
strips of lemon rind
little red colouring if liked

Dissolve sugar in water, add cinnamon, rind and boil up. Add wine, where used, and colour. Put peeled, cored pear halves in a cocotte or saucepan and cook either at 275° F, gas 1, or on top of stove at barely simmering point for 1 to 4 hours according to size of fruit and age of tree. Very old trees sometimes produce pears impervious to hours of cooking. An hour in the pressure cooker (add sugar after cooking) will often do better than 3 to 4 hours of ordinary cooking.

Poach dessert pears very gently, turning carefully now and again. Usually 30 minutes will do for unripe specimens, while 10 minutes may do for ripe pears. The pressure cooker may be too fierce for tender fruits.

WINE SAUCE FOR PEARS

1½ gills of syrup in which
pears have cooked, if
cooked without wine
½ gill wine or
scant ½ pint of wine-

flavoured syrup with 1–2
tbs. added to sharpen the taste
½ oz. cornflour or 1 level
dessertsp. arrowroot

Slake cornflour with a little cold syrup. Boil up rest of syrup, pouring a little on cornflour, then pouring this back into pan. Cook only until the sauce clears or it may thin again if arrowroot is used. Stir all the time.

CHOCOLATE SAUCE

4 heaped tsp. cocoa
1 heaped tsp. cornflour
¼ pint milk

5 tbs. water
1½ oz. sugar
3 drops vanilla essence

Mix cocoa and cornflour with water. Dissolve sugar in milk, then bring milk up to boil, pouring on cocoa mixture and stirring very well. Add *three drops only* vanilla. Return to pan and boil up, stirring very rapidly. Cook few minutes whisking all the time. Cool, stirring continuously to prevent skin forming if to be used cold.

NOTE: Cocoa, these days, is often to be preferred to so-called plain chocolate.

Arrange pears in serving dish, and mask with either sauce, hot or cold. (My preference is for cold.) Hand single cream separately.

PEAR FLAN

Blind-bake a flan-case of pâte sucrée (p. 129). Fill with cold cooked pear halves or quarters, arranged daisy-petal fashion with points to centre. Make wine sauce, correcting to a good colour if necessary, pour over pears to fill flan, brushing over edges and sides to glaze. Decorate with large rosettes of whipped cream. Serve slightly chilled.

POIRES EN SURPRISE

Serves 6 to 8.

Peel, core and quarter four pears, cook until tender in wine syrup as above. Cool, draining well on a sieve, and arrange over bottom of No. 2 soufflé case (1½-pint dish). Make half-quantity of chocolate soufflé mixture on p. 460. NOTE: Cook pears day before if convenient, make chocolate mixture to panada stage early in day.) *Preheat* oven to 400° F, gas 6. As soon as egg-whites are folded into mixture, turn on top of pears, and bake for 25 to 30 minutes. Hand chilled single cream separately and/or the wine syrup, thickened to make sauce as described above.

A fine pudding for the Christmas period as a change from the rather similar tastes of cake, pudding and mincemeat, it makes use of home-bottled fruit or late fresh pears, for those blessed with the old-fashioned sort of cooking pears that store (not to mention the loft in which to store them !).

SUDDEN GUEST PUDDING

From a recipe of Madame Rigot.
Serves 6.

3 pears (dessert, cooked,
  tinned, or bottled)
any of the following:
  2 pieces stem, or preserved
  ginger (I have used 4
  'chocolate gingers' on
  occasion)

6–8 glacé cherries, or pieces
  of any candied fruit, or
  pineapple pieces
2 tbs. dried fruit
about 1 oz. almonds or
  walnuts (or other nuts)

SYRUP.

¼ pint water plus 1 tbs.
  ginger syrup where
  available
2 oz. sugar
3 drops vanilla or dash wine,
  brandy, rum or liqueur

squeeze lemon juice or sprig
  mint or syrup in which
  pears were cooked, or
  from tin or bottle, with
  dash of wine etc.

Arrange pear halves, hollow side down, down centre of oblong shallow dish. Blanch almonds, split and sliver them, or chop walnuts coarsely. Heat syrup gently, and poach dried fruit, cherries, halved, and ginger, which has been sliced thinly, 5 minutes. Put each sort separately down dish in lines parallel with pears. Reduce syrup somewhat. Spoon over pears etc. Scatter nuts over pears. Serve as cold as possible. Cream is, as always, desirable when available. It is surprising how pretty this can look, and it has a light, fresh taste unexpected in a dish composed of so many sugared ingredients. Lincoln Cream-type, or ginger biscuits are also good with it if substance is needed.

PUMPKIN PIE (not tested)

Pumpkins may be used much as marrow is used, although the taste is sweeter, and the texture less watery and slightly glutinous. They come into their own, however, for the pudding course.

½ lb. flaky or sweet short-crust pastry (pp. 129 and 130)	2 eggs
	grated rind ½ lemon, 1 tbs. juice
	¼ lb. sugar
1½ lb. pumpkin	2 oz. margarine
2 tbs. black treacle or soft brown sugar	2 tbs. spice (mixed spice or 1 each any sort preferred)
½ pint milk	pinch salt

Simmer pumpkin, which you have pared, seeded and cut in 2-inch pieces, in ¼ inch water over low heat until it is mushy, stirring frequently. Cool, then squeeze pulp in your hands, or an old clean tea-towel until really well drained of moisture. Over gentle heat mix in all ingredients except eggs. Add these off the heat, turn into pie-dish, cover with pastry, and bake until pastry is risen and well coloured. Serve with single cream and sugar, or plain ice cream.

A dash of sherry, brandy or rum is an improvement. Some recipes also advise separating eggs, and folding in stiffly whisked whites last of all after allowing mixture to cool – a sort of soufflé.

November

Whilst hardly anyone I know, including myself, has ever obeyed the sort of advice that would have us defrost our refrigerators each week, clean our ovens after each Sunday's roast, get our early potatoes in by the first week in March, and our bulbs planted before the end of November, most women soon learn to get as much done as possible towards Christmas cookery in November. Quite apart from the cook spending (what should be) a gay holiday in the bosom of the family, rather than an exhausting marathon in solitude in the kitchen, matured cakes, puddings and mincemeat are far better in flavour and texture, doing justice to the hard work that goes into them. Then, if you have children, there is plenty of time to plan the cooking so that they can join in. This is not merely for their amusement. Children do many jobs very neatly and well, and can relieve you of labour. They enjoy, and feel proud of helping, and are truly involved in the family feast, and boys as well as girls these days can only benefit from knowing what goes on in a kitchen.

Christmas Cooking Preliminaries

Cake

If liked use rich fruit cake recipe p. 500, using butter or a 75 per cent butter to 25 per cent margarine proportion for better keeping and flavour; and soft brown sugar and 1 heaped tsp. cocoa for darker colour and richer taste if liked.

or: See recipes in chart on p. 512.

or: If you are not a cake-maker, or are busy, consider buying now a good fruit cake to be decorated later. Some firms (notably Marks & Spencer) have begun to sell their rich fruit cake mixture in several sizes specially for Christmas, with or without almond paste.

Gas-ring cooks may be interested in the steamed method of cooking cakes, p. 491.

CHRISTMAS PUDDING

This is the recipe said to have been made in the Royal kitchens since the reign of George I. It has had deservedly wide circulation, having a beautifully light texture and fine flavour. The quantity given will fill two 1-pint pudding basins.

5 oz. suet	1 oz. citron peel cut thin
¼ lb. each:	(buy citron cap, not
small raisins (i.e. seedless,	chopped peel)
though I prefer the others)	¼ pint milk
fresh plums (i.e. prunes,	¼ tsp. mixed spice
get the best)	⅛ tsp. nutmeg
demerara sugar	½ tsp. salt
stale white crumbs (i.e.	¼ wineglass brandy
white, 2 days old bread)	to this I add: ¾ oz. almonds
2 oz. sifted flour	blanched and shredded
2 eggs	¼ medium carrot grated

'Whip eggs to light froth, add milk and rest of ingredients by degrees, mixing thoroughly. Allow mixture to stand in cool place for 12 hours to ripen. Pour into moulds and boil 8 hours.'

To enlarge on these original directions: sieve spices with flour. Mix all fruit, nuts etc. first in basin with brandy. (Use 5 tbs. strong ale as alternative.) Put butter paper on top loosely, then greaseproof, Cropar cooking parchment (or foil), with pleat across to allow for rising. Tie down well. Remove from pot when cooked and leave in a warm dry atmosphere for 24 hours so that covering papers dry out well.

Some cooks change the covers, but the paper gets a thin coating of melted suet during the cooking, which acts as a seal helping to keep the pudding fresh and moist, and so long as the covers are thoroughly dried out, I favour not changing them. When completely cold store puddings in a cool place wrapped, basin and all, in foil.

However, if you want merely a spoonful or so of pudding on Christmas day, and don't want a pudding for later in the year, buy one of the many excellent shop puddings. (The brand I've found quite excellent, and at a modest price, is 'Sunblest', which is on sale at many bakers in south-east England. Medium sizes are less numerous, so buy in good time.)

Mincemeat

For a very long time the meat in mincemeat has been reduced to a mere small proportion of suet, but in the past a proportion of lean beef featured in most mixtures, whilst Eliza Acton's own recipe includes a pound of ox tongue. Older mincemeat recipes also included a high proportion of lemons, and these and the apples were often cooked. Brandy and sherry, which were not then very dear, were poured in generously. This was not because our forebears hoped to get tight on mince pies, but because alcohol was one of the best preservatives.

There is no particular pattern of proportions for mincemeats so, for interest, I give a *fin-de-siècle* Beeton recipe, and a wartime economy version. If you like, make a cross between the two.

I use something different each year when I make mincemeat – for example, drained pineapple pieces; some chopped preserved ginger and its juice; a few chopped Elvas or Carlsbad plums; a few marrons; some chopped dried or tinned apricots or prunes. Shop mincemeat responds well to a few additions of one's own, and these can of course include a stiff dose of spirits (Vodka-mince would probably have got a nod from 007), or wine. Most shop mincemeat is teetotal, but the *Spectator*, in surveying the field, found some brands quite well laced.

MRS BEETON'S 'EXCELLENT MINCEMEAT'

Ingredients: 3 large lemons, 3 large apples [cookers], 1 lb. each of stoned raisins, currants, suet. 2 lb. moist sugar, 1 oz. each sliced candied citron, orange and lemon peel, 1 teacup brandy, 2 tbs. orange marmalade.

Grate rinds of lemons, squeeze out juice and strain it. Boil remainder of lemons until tender enough to pulp or chop very finely [2 hours at least]. Add to this the apples which have been baked, skinned and cored. Add rest of ingredients by degrees mixing thoroughly. Put into stone jar with closely-fitting lid. Ready for use in a fortnight.

I think you could omit the candied lemon peel if necessary, as there is plenty of lemon flavouring as it is. And I would add ¼ lb. shredded almonds. This amount is suitable only for a large household. Quarter it for the average family of four, who don't wish to have mince pies other than at Christmas, while half quantity will yield plenty for most families.

ECONOMICAL MINCEMEAT

¼ lb. each raisins, currants, sultanas (dates may be used in place of one of these)
½ lb. grated apples
¼ lb. grated carrot

2 oz. sugar (soft brown is best)
¼ lb. suet
1 tsp. mixed spice (or a mixture to choice)
½ tsp. lemon essence
few drops almond essence

Mix all well together and pot. Will keep no longer than 2 weeks in kitchen, 3 weeks in cold larder, 1 month in refrigerator.

This recipe demonstrates the preservative power of alcohol. It is, of course, a relic of a time when all manner of foodstuffs were in short supply or non-existent. But as a basic, very cheap recipe it is of good flavour and texture. With a few additions, or merely an increase of, for instance, the sugar or suet quantities the use of fresh lemon juice and rind (1 lemon), or ¼ lb. candied peel, it becomes quite rich enough. A spoonful or so of cooking sherry will give it the seasonal kick and longer keeping qualities.

With Christmas cooking, shopping and so on, November is a month when quickly-made daily dishes are doubly welcome. Many of them will be found in the 'Convenience Food' section on p. 462, and I have included some among the seasonal dishes that follow.

Soups

BROWN ONION SOUP

Serves 6.

1 lb. onions	1 quart water
6 crushed peppercorns	
1 large bayleaf	tied in muslin
2 cloves	
piece root ginger (if available)	
1 oz. flour	2 slices stale bread spread
1½ oz. good dripping (or	with French mustard (optional)
margarine)	1½ oz. grated cheese
1 rounded tsp. salt	

Peel and slice the onions medium thin. Brown them slowly in fat in thick pan without burning, add flour and continue cooking until a good rich colour. Meanwhile have the water on to boil, and pour when boiling a little at a time on to browned flour and onions, blending carefully. Add salt and spices and leave simmering 1 to 1½ hours. When ready to serve, cut bread into 2-inch squares, strew thickly with cheese, just colour under grill and float on soup before sending to table. Or send bowl of cheese to table to be sprinkled on soup as liked.

QUICK KIDNEY SOUP

¼ lb. each minced beef and	1 tbs. chopped parsley
ox kidney	sprig thyme (or pinch dried)
1 onion	seasoning
1 oz. flour	1½ pints water
¼ oz. margarine	

Put onion through mincer or chop finely. Melt fat, add onion, turning well in fat. Add mince, cook over low heat 2 minutes.

Stir in flour, and continue gentle cooking, stirring occasionally. Meanwhile mince kidney and add to pan when rest of ingredients have turned a good nut brown. Cook 2 minutes. Add water by degrees, stirring out all lumps, and finally bringing to simmering point, adding thyme, and seasoning to taste. Simmer 30 minutes, or longer if preferred. Stir in parsley just before serving.

This soup need take no longer than 50 minutes total time to prepare and cook. But longer cooking will do no harm if it fits your plans better. A quick nourishing luncheon or supper would be a bowl of this soup, followed by cheese and an apple or pickles, or Mock Duck (see next page).

First Course and Snacks

MAÎTRE D'HÔTEL KIDNEYS

(Supper dish for 4. Halve quantities for savoury for 4. Useful single-person household dish.)

5–6 oz. butter/margarine (but proportion of butter is essential)	1 tsp. minced onion
	8 sheep's kidneys (New Zealand are usually cheaper)
2 tbs. chopped fresh herbs with slight preponderance of parsley	4 rounds toast or fried bread (fried in butter)
about 1 tbs. lemon juice or to taste	stock or water
white pepper	1 tbs. sherry, dry white or red wine (optional)

Cream 2 oz. of the butter, gradually working into it the lemon juice, herbs and a good shake of pepper. Divide it into eight neat pieces, using butter pats if available. Set aside in cool place to harden. Meanwhile discard fat from kidney, and skin and split them, but do not cut through completely. Remove fibres.

Make toast, de-crust, butter it with some of the unflavoured butter and put on serving dish to keep warm. Or fry (de-crusted) croûtes in about 1 oz. butter. Heat rest of butter, add onion, and

445

fry kidneys, cut side first, about 2 minutes each side. Put two on each croûte. Boil up ¼ pint water, or light stock, in the pan, mixing butter, onions and juices, and reducing slightly. Season lightly, add wine. Spoon a little over each croûte. Just before serving put a pat of the herb butter on each kidney.

A rasher of crisply grilled bacon may be added. The kidneys may also be served on a bed of rice or in a border of canned peas or mashed potato, though these may take more time. But as given here the dish is both light and rich, and will satisfy most appetites as a main course at the lighter meal of the day. A greater proportion of margarine may be used where the dish is for a savoury.

MOCK DUCK

This was the family name for it, though why, heaven knows, since in any of its many variations it never tastes like duck and certainly doesn't look like duck.

6–8 oz. good quality Cheddar cheese

1 tbs. made mustard (more if liked)

2 tbs. vinegar (maximum), or vinegar and lemon or orange juice

about 2 tbs. milk

1–2 oz. butter

Any of these:

Worcester Sauce;

Tomato ketchup; Yorkshire relish; Horseradish sauce; sweet piccalilli or 'Branston' type pickle; sweet chutney; 1–2 raw eggs well beaten; garlic or onion juice

Grate or chop the cheese and begin working in the butter, mustard, milk and vinegar until you have a thick purée of a taste that satisfies your palate. It should be hot, a little sharp, but also creamy. Then add what you like of the other ingredients - or anything else you fancy, including beer or brandy if you need pepping up. Pile the mixture on broad fingers of generously buttered bread or toast, accompanied by potato crisps, chips, tomatoes, salad, or anything readily eaten in the fingers with the minimum of fuss. About 2 oz. cheese per head will do for an average snack, 1 oz. for an appetizer or savoury. More for the hungry.

GAME OR FISH ÉCLAIRS

1 quantity of choux paste
(omitting sugar) as on p. 133

1 oz. very finely grated
cheese (Parmesan if
possible, but if Cheddar
it must be dry to grate
almost to powder)

¼ pint Spanish sauce, (p. 118)
or white sauce as
appropriate

2 tbs. gravy from the meat
used (or milk, wine etc.)

3 oz. cooked game (or any
sort of fish – white,
smoked, shell), minced or
pounded

1 tsp. minced onion just
softened in ¼ oz. margarine

pinch chopped thyme

Pipe éclairs (p. 536), 2 inch long with ½ inch pipe, bake at 400° F, gas 6, in centre of oven for 25 minutes. Draw out shelf, and sprinkle tops of éclairs lightly with the cheese. This job must be done quickly. Return for 5 to 10 minutes. Remove one of the éclairs and gently press the sides. If not quite crisp and firm return for further 5 minutes at lower heat if necessary.

While baking, make filling by mixing meat, sauce and flavourings to a soft but not runny consistency with the extra liquid (you may not need all 2 tbs.). Fill through slit in sides with ¼ inch pipe or teaspoon. Serve hot or cold with salad. For entertaining make baby éclairs 1¼ inch long with ¼-inch pipe.

EGGLETS

For using up odds and ends.

6 oz.–¼ lb. rich cheese pastry
(p. 183)

5 tbs.–¼ pint mayonnaise or
thick salad dressing (pp.
248 and 250)

2–3 hard-boiled eggs

herbs as available

Line 8 small patty tins (or half-line larger sizes), or barquette moulds if available, with the pastry rolled out thinly. Bake blind (by lining each with tissue paper on which are set a few beans) exactly as you would for a flan case. Meanwhile chop the eggs fairly finely and mix with the mayonnaise and chopped fresh herbs if available. When pastry cases are cool, fill, piling up well. Serve hot or cold with salad if liked. May also be made as a flan but more filling would then be needed.

WALDORF SALAD

An American classic. Delicious at any time, it is a boon in winter when salad ingredients are dear and poor. Accompanies anything, improves lesser fare, adorns feasts.

Exact ingredients can't be given as all depend on the sizes of celery stalks and apples, and one's own taste. Take roughly equal quantities of sharp crisp apple and celery (e.g. one medium Granny Smith or Newton to three medium stalks celery), to 4–6 walnut halves. Chop celery and apple in pieces of about equal weight or size. Core, but do not peel the apple. Finely chop the walnuts. Mix together in mayonnaise or thick dressing to taste. Bramleys are good here, but discolour quickly unless sprinkled well with lemon juice, when the dressing may thin slightly. After salad has been mixed a little time walnut juice may turn it slightly purplish. If this bothers you mix only at last minute, otherwise it is a good item for mass-production if kept covered in cold. Flavour improves, too.

Fish

BISCUIT FISHBALLS

Author's recipe.

The mixture is a form of rough *quenelles*, using raw fish and a panada, but the method is quicker, the texture coarser, while the nutty flavour is unusual and popular. May be adapted for cooked left-overs of poultry, fish, game, ham etc. :

2 oz. 'high-baked' water biscuits (4 oz. if fishballs are to be fried)

½ lb. white fish after bones and skin have been removed

1 tsp. minced onion or 1 clove crushed garlic

seasoning

pinch dill or fennel seed or dried tarragon

pinch nutmeg

2 oz. margarine/butter

1 large or 2 small eggs

¼ pint milk

1 egg (if fishballs are to be fried)

oil or fat for frying

(1) Put water biscuits through mincer, or pound them to crumbs.

(2) Mince the raw prepared fish, or chop or pound it until of purée texture.

(3) Melt fat, and sweat onion or garlic few minutes – do not brown.

(4) Add fish, seasoning, dill and nutmeg.

(5) Heat milk, tip in, *off the heat*, 2 oz. biscuit crumbs. Stir few minutes to allow to swell, and cool a little.

(6) Beat egg and add to crumb mixture.

(7) Combine fish and crumb mixture blending well. Leave 15 to 20 minutes, while making sauce and preparing frying pan, if the fishballs are to be fried. This may be deep fat bath; or shallow pan with good ½ inch fat – preferably oil – for frying.

(8) Form cooled mixture into golf ball sized croquettes in floured hand. Either: (a) egg, roll in rest of crumbs and fry in deep fat until golden about 3 to 4 minutes; or fry in ½-inch shallow fat for 4 to 5 minutes, turning; or (b) poach in barely simmering *court-bouillon* made from fish trimmings, ¾ pint water, lemon, onion, bouquet garni, seasoning.

(9) Serve with tomato sauce (p. 149), tartare sauce (p. 233) or any variety of good white sauce, in that order of preference.

SUGGESTED ACCOMPANIMENTS. Grilled, or whole baked tomatoes; mushrooms; boiled, sauté, or chip potatoes.

NOTE: Slimmers can make them with Bisks, which is how this recipe came into being, but it is then no longer cheap.

COD BRETONNE

(A very quick method of Boulestin's.)

This becomes a favourite of everyone I know who has ever tried it, being as delicious – fresh tasting yet mild – as it is quick, simple and cheap. Saithe (coley), haddock and brill – all good in November, are much nicer than cod, unless you can get the salt cod of Boulestin's original recipe. This is already a Soho rarity since the spread of deep freezing, so that it will not be found easily elsewhere.

1½ lb. white fish fillet after skinning
1½ gills white wine (or cider) and water
1 tbs. olive or good salad oil
1 oz. fat and flour worked into a *beurre manié*

1 level tbs. minced shallot (or ½ tbs. onion)
1 rounded tbs. chopped parsley
salt and pepper
4 croûtes (either fried bread or hot buttered toast)

Cut fish into chunks and put with rest of ingredients, except *beurre manié*, into saucepan over good heat. Cook very fast for 5 minutes, stirring with wooden spoon so that fish breaks up into flakes. Off heat, scatter *beurre manié* over, cut into smallish bits. Give it a stir to melt somewhat. Return to heat, and cook about 2 minutes more to thicken the dish. Pile on to croûtes and serve very hot. A little Anchovy Paste or Gentleman's Relish on the bread is good. As an alternative serve in a rice or potato ring.

Herrings – a reminder

Herrings are abundant and cheap throughout the winter. The chief classic ways of cooking them in the British Isles are noted below.

N.B. Always scale herring before preparing, scraping with a knife from the tail towards the head, or ask fishmonger to do so.

FRIED

IN SALT. Leave heads on, roes in as preferred. Gut and wash out, trim off tails and fins. Heat enough salt to cover the bottom of a *heavy* frying pan. When very hot, but not brown, lay fish on hot salt and continue cooking about 5 minutes until they are brown and crisp. Turn and repeat for other side. Serve with lemon wedges and brown bread and butter.

IN OATMEAL. (A superior method.) For each 4 herrings: 3 tbs. oatmeal or porage oats, 1 tbs. seasoned flour, 5 tbs. milk, 4 rashers bacon or 1½ oz. lard for frying. Behead, scale, clean, split and bone fish (see p. 90). Dip in seasoned flour, brush with milk, roll in oatmeal pressing this well on to fish. Fry the bacon until crisp, tilting pan to collect fat. Keep rashers hot. Or heat lard until smoking. Fry the coated herrings until brown and crisp, turning once. Good with fresh crisp oatcakes and grilled tomatoes.

PLAIN. Prepare as above. Slash sides diagonally about 1 inch apart. Fry in good dripping or, preferably, oil. Serve with lemon wedges and mustard sauce (p. 118).

BAKED. Either whole or boned. Butter inside and out with melted seasoned margarine. If boned, roll up from head to tail. Arrange in baking dish, cover with greased paper. Bake 15 minutes in moderate oven.

BOILED. (See *Herrings Lowestoft*, p. 337), or in *court bouillon*.

GRILLED. Either slash the sides, split, or fillet (pp. 87-90). Grill closed, or flat, until crisp. Serve with mustard sauce, flavoured butters, lemon and, at this time of the year, try cranberry sauce (p. 554).

GREY MULLET

Although not very widely distributed, now is the time of year when these fish are plentiful and good. Any of the methods for Red Mullet (pp. 313-14) are suitable.

Meat

BEEF

Home-killed beef is at its best in autumn and winter. This is
the season of cattle shows, but even farmers who make no claim
to be prize-winning breeders, like to have their neighbours nod-
ding approval over the gate at fine animals, as the year comes up
to Christmas; while those who *do* show will be weeding out
better from best, and this means a general high grade of beef
coming into the slaughter-houses just now; with prices, naturally, to match. However, the high standard means that cheaper
cuts now are as good as dear cuts at other times, so forget about
sirloin and wing ribs and try foreribs and brisket. Top rump,
when of this fine quality, may be substituted for topside, although both should really be pot roasted at other seasons.

To remind yourself of the finer points, turn to the Roasting
Notes on pp. 96–7.

In some parts of Britain carving is traditionally done with the
carver sitting down. Although I learned to carve standing, I find
the sitting method better for most purposes, and recommend
anyone to try it who finds carving difficult. For some reason,
sitting down to carve is considered the more skilled, so you may
gain lustre by adopting a method you really find easier!

A razor-sharp knife is essential. Consult the notes on knives
and knife-sharpening on p. 48.

The best fork is a simple affair with two long prongs and a
brass guard all round as on a fencing foil, to be found in every
chef's equipment, and called a cook's fork. William Page of
Shaftesbury Avenue stock them, as do any ironmongers sup-
plying 'the trade'. That such a fork doesn't match your wedding-
present carving outfit is less important than that it is an efficient
and safe tool for a skilled and important culinary job. Good carving is not only essentially economical, it also helps the texture,
because the cutting across the grain of the meat further breaks
up fibres softened in cooking; and it improves the appearance of
the dish since neat slices are obviously more attractive than ragged lumps.

MIROTON

A good beef rechauffée

Make additions to the following sauce to choice – a dash of wine or good vinegar, a spoonful of tomato purée, a dab or so of mustard.

2 oz. fat (half butter)	½ lb. approx. cold lean beef
¼ pint minimum Sauce	thinly sliced
Espagnole (p. 118), good	2–3 medium onions finely
thickened gravy, or stock	sliced or chopped
thickened with ¾ oz. flour	brown crumbs

Have ready a heated dish. Reserve ½ oz. butter, lightly browning onions in rest. If using thin stock, scatter in flour and brown well. Add liquid and flavourings. Spoon half this sauce into hot dish, overlap beef slices on this, pouring rest of sauce over beef. Sprinkle thickly with crumbs, dot with butter, brown under grill. Serve at once.

If liked, dish with border of pommes purée, tinned pease pudding or creamed carrot, Cornish turnip etc.

GAMMON STEAKS WITH PINEAPPLE

4 gammon slices ½-inch thick	4 dessertsp. demerara sugar
or collar, back, ham (some	1 small can pineapple pieces,
firms packet these 'ham	or fresh pineapple, or
steaks' in varying qualities)	oranges (2 large)
French mustard (for once,	16 cloves
English French mustard is	
better)	

The meat should have a modest proportion of fat. Remove rind and nick all round edge of slices about ½-inch deep at 1-inch intervals. Stick 4 cloves into the fat of each slice. Spread a thin layer of mustard over slices and sprinkle them with sugar. Arrange in a shallow fireproof dish – or two dishes if necessary. Scatter over each about 1 rounded dessertsp. pineapple pieces or segmented orange (p. 104), and sprinkle each with some of the juice. Pour a ½-inch depth of juice over the bottom of the dish, adding about 4 tbs. water. Bake at 375° F, gas 5, for about 35 minutes until surface is brown and meat tender.

SUGGESTED ACCOMPANIMENTS: Spinach in any form; creamed celery (p. 457); plain potatoes or noodles; tinned butter beans.

NOTE: For small appetites ½ a slice of gammon will be enough. If using fresh pineapple, simmer a slice (cut up) in ¼ pint water, 2 oz. sugar for 20 minutes and use the syrup that results. The juice running from the oranges as they are segmented, plus that squeezed from the peelings can be made up to a teacup of syrup with 1 oz. sugar and water.

Liver

The decline in the standard of butchery is nowhere more apparent than in the cutting of liver. Its quality, also, has fallen in proportion as its price has risen, and it is apt to be tough, stale and full of 'pipes' no matter what the price. And see note on calves' liver on pp. 80–81. I am assuming, therefore, that lambs' or perhaps pigs' liver will be bought by most people. The latter, if prepared as I suggest below, can be very good. Bad butchering of liver is more serious than might be thought, for clumsy, tough liver cooks badly, which can put some people, notably children, off eating it altogether, yet it is so rich in iron and the principal vitamins – the B-group especially – that it should figure in everyone's menus at least once each week.

Try to buy the liver in one piece and cut it yourself, otherwise ask the butcher to cut it under your eye. The slices should be a little more than ¼-inch thick, so study the thickness gauge on p. 135 and fix the dimension in your mind's eye before setting off to shop.

A butcher once told me that liver should be cut down the length of the lobe; that cut width-wise it breaks the fibres in such a way as to toughen the meat in cooking. Only stewing it for about 2 hours would then make it tender. Other butchers and chefs disagree, but notice this next time you make a Bolognese Sauce, where cross cutting is necessary. Only the fact that the dice are very small renders their hardness acceptable. Also try cutting lengthwise next time you have fried liver. Cut either way, each slice has an edging of thin membrane, and a 'fair share' of pipes and tender meat.

Nutritionally, as well as gastronomically, the less cooking the better. But like steak, where liver is to be stewed or braised, then long slow cooking is necessary. Fried liver, cut as suggested here little more than $\frac{1}{4}$-inch thick, needs only to be seared on the outside, when the inside will be pink and juicy, but not at all raw-tasting. The cooking is accomplished in a matter of seconds. The fat must be smoking, and butter may form a proportion for flavour. Lightly powder the liver slices with flour and a *little* seasoning. Cook four slices at a time, and when the fourth slice is put in, it will be time to turn the first. When the fourth is turned, the first will be done. Beads of blood should appear on the surface, and when lifted, the slice should be pliable. If pressed with a finger tip it should feel spongy. If hard and rigid it is over-done. Cook liver at 'last minute', and do not keep in oven more than 1 to 2 minutes.

Allow 2 slices per person (about 2 oz.). Most liver dishes, like those given here, include other meats – bacon, sausage etc. and, where economy must be studied, this is necessary. But liver is rich and strong-flavoured, so that the piquancy of bacon, or spici-ness of sausages is also welcome gastronomically. Some recipes recommend soaking liver in milk, or washing it to lessen the strong flavour, but this must cause some loss of nourishment. Otherwise a quick rinse under the tap before cutting will do little harm, and may be desirable where pig's liver is to be quickly cooked.

LIVER PAPRIKA

8 thin slices of liver (about $\frac{3}{4}$ lb.)
1 medium onion
4 rashers of bacon
4 small sausages (skinless) *or* 4 sausagemeat balls
2 oz. mushrooms
$\frac{1}{2}$ tsp. Hungarian paprika, or 1 tsp. other sorts

$\frac{1}{2}$ carton yoghurt or 2–3 tbs. sour cream
$\frac{1}{2}$ oz. each butter and flour
$\frac{1}{2}$ pint light stock or water
1–2 tbs. sherry or wine (optional)
1 dessertsp. chopped parsley
seasoning

455

Pull off surrounding thin membrane from liver slices, and remove thicker segments of pipes where visible. But these operations should not reduce the slices to a mush, better to leave them to the eaters in such a case. Slice the onion and chop the parsley. Have all the ingredients ready to hand. Fry the bacon and sausages, arrange them at either end of a serving dish and keep hot. Fry the onion a good brown, tilt pan to retain fat, pressing it out of onion. Keep onion warm on one side. Cut mushrooms in quarters if large, and fry them, adding a little lard if necessary. Put them with the onions. Add butter to pan and heat until it bubbles. Mix flour, paprika and seasoning, using it to dust liver. Fry liver and rest of paprika mixture briskly, giving liver no more than 30 seconds each side. Let paprika and flour continue cooking as you lift out liver to centre of serving dish. Return dish to oven. Pour stock into pan, stirring well and scraping all juices from bottom and sides to mix with sauce. Boil very fast for 1 minute to reduce. Add yoghurt, sherry, onion, mushrooms and parsley, bring up to boil again, stirring well. Pour over liver and serve at once.

SUGGESTED ACCOMPANIMENTS. Pommes purée, plainly cooked rice or pasta; Carottes au lard (p. 457), mousse of sprouts (p. 458); any green vegetable.

BAKED LIVER

8–12 thin slices good ox or pigs' liver (¾–1 lb.)	seasoning
2 rashers streaky bacon	1–2 oz. margarine/butter
1 tbs. chopped parsley	little white wine (optional)
1 shallot or small onion – minced	5 tbs. stock or water
	flour

Dust liver lightly with flour and seasoning. Heat fat in frying pan, just sear and lightly colour liver, set aside. Dice bacon small, and fry with shallot until lightly coloured. Add parsley and stock and bring just to simmering point. Season very lightly, add wine if used, pour half the mixture over the bottom of a shallow cocotte or oven dish. (If cooking on top of stove frying-pan may be used with some kind of cover. In this instance pour off half of

sauce into a warmed cup.) Lay liver on this and spoon rest of
sauce over liver. Cover closely and cook in low oven for 1 hour.

SUGGESTED ACCOMPANIMENTS: .Pommes purée; Carottes
au lard; spinach, mousse of sprouts.

Vegetables

CAROTTES AU LARD (bacon-fried carrots)

1 lb. carrots	½ oz. butter
1 dessertsp. chopped parsley	2 rashers streaky bacon
1 oz. lard	seasoning

Scrape the carrots and cut into wedges or thick slices. (Baby
carrots should be left whole.) Blanch 1 minute. Heat lard
thoroughly, add butter, and when bubbling add carrots, and
cook over low heat on asbestos mat turning occasionally half
covering pan with lid. When tender (about 30 to 45 minutes)
add bacon cut in very small dice, fry until just beginning to
colour but not at all crisp. Add parsley and seasoning and serve.

CREAMED CELERY

1 lb. outer part of a head of celery	seasoning
½ pint milk	1 egg
1 oz. each margarine and flour	1 tsp. minced onion ⎫ optional pinch thyme ⎭

Scrub the celery and cut into inch pieces. Blanch 1 minute.
Drain. Throw into boiling salted water just to cover, with onion
where used. Simmer 15 minutes. Drain, reserving water. Melt
butter, add celery. Shake in flour off heat, mix well, add milk and
boil up stirring smooth. Add thyme. Simmer in sauce to finish
cooking, stirring from time to time. Correct seasoning. Thin
down slightly with 1 to 2 tbs. of water in which celery was
cooked. Beat egg, stir it in, and serve.

BRUSSELS SPROUTS MOUSSE

1 lb. freshly cooked young sprouts	nutmeg
2 eggs	seasoning
¼ pint binding white sauce	

Sieve the cooked sprouts (or purée with sauce in blender). Mix with the warm sauce, and season with salt, pepper and nutmeg. Separate egg whites and yolks, beat the latter well into mixture. Whisk whites until stiff, fold into mixture, and bake in greased deep pie-dish or soufflé case for 35 minutes at 375° F, gas 5.

Puddings

TRIFLE

The name suggests what the airy reality should be. Trifle is a delicate topping off to a dinner party, or to a party buffet. One of its virtues is that the flavour can be varied to suit the rest of the menu and the time of year. Another is that, although cold, it isn't of the coldness that makes one shudder in winter, perhaps because of the sherry, and also because it should be scarcely colder than room temperature when served. Thirdly it can be made well in advance, and will not spoil, even if made the day before, indeed keeping a day improves the dish. Trifle cannot be made on the cheap, but don't think that by substituting jelly, cans of unsuitable fruits, and a mass of bright decoration for the sherry and cream in this simple recipe, you will save money. You will spend just as much but have a clumsy, sugary pudding in place of a frothy, nutty, exquisite *bonne bouche*.

5 sponge cakes	¼ pint cream
1 oz. blanched shredded almonds	1 egg white
¼ pint sherry	1½ tsp. sugar

CUSTARD

½ pint milk	3 drops vanilla
2 eggs	1 level tsp. cornflour (optional)
½ oz. sugar	

JAM

raspberry, strawberry, or apricot of good quality

FRUIT

raspberries, strawberries –	pears – fresh
fresh, frozen or canned	peaches – fresh or home-
apricots – fresh or canned	bottled, not canned

Drain canned or bottled fruit, skin (p. 328), stone and slice peaches etc. Thaw and drain frozen fruit. Reserve the juice.

Split sponge cakes, and spread with jam, put together spreading tops also, but thinly. Set in a glass serving dish, cutting them to fit. Pour over them all but 2 tbs. of sherry, also a few spoonfuls of fruit juice. Make custard (p. 137) but separate one of the eggs, whipping the white and folding this into the custard after cooling it slightly. Add fruit on top of sponge-cake layer, scatter half almond shreds over fruit, spoon custard over top, and leave until custard is quite cold and set. Meanwhile put cream and 1½ tsp. sugar in small basin and half whip (cream must be absolutely fresh or it may thicken too quickly). Add sherry gradually as whipping proceeds. When it will hold its shape, whip the egg white to a dry stiff snow in another basin, and fold into cream mixture, blending lightly but well. Fill over the set custard, and keep in cold until 1 hour before serving. Toast remaining almond slivers lightly and, just before serving, spike the cream with them.

BITTER CHOCOLATE MOULD

Author's recipe.

2 oz. cocoa	1 pint milk
1 oz. cornflour	1 egg
1 tsp. powdered coffee	½ oz. gelatine dissolved in
3 oz. sugar	½ gill water
5 drops vanilla essence	

Whisk together sugar, egg, cocoa, coffee, cornflour and vanilla. Heat milk to just below boiling point. Pour on to cocoa mixture beating continuously until thoroughly mixed. Return to pan, and bring just to boiling point over low heat, stirring and whisking fast and furiously, removing from heat at each sign of lumps coming up from base of pan, and whisking them out. (You need both a wooden spoon to scrape bottom and sides of pan, and a strong whisk or fork.) When mixture is evenly thickened, and just bursting up through the surface, give final stirring and whisking off heat, before beating in the melted gelatine. Cool somewhat, stirring, to lessen the skin that will form. (Skin can be avoided almost entirely if you have the time to stir until quite cold, but this is unnecessary as the skin is not unpleasant.) Rinse out a pint mould with cold water, pour in mixture and leave to set. Served chilled with cream.

BAKED CHOCOLATE SOUFFLÉ

An absurd mystery is made of soufflés. Read the savoury recipes on p. 418. The procedure for sweet soufflés is the same.

Point to watch in making this one, as with all chocolate mixtures, is to beat out all lumps as you go, removing pan from heat as often as necessary.

Melt ¼ lb. chocolate in ½ pint milk. Melt 1½ oz. margarine, mix in 1½ oz. flour, blending smooth. Add milk mixture, cook to smooth panada. On cooling add 3 yolks. Whisk 4 whites to snow, fold in. Turn into prepared No. 2 size soufflé case (7-inch cake-tin or a 1½ pint dish), bake at 400° F, gas 6, for 45 minutes.

Remember diners must wait for soufflé, not the reverse.

ALL-AT-ONCE PUDDING

In the course of manufacturing margarine and the white cooking fats, sensibly called shortening in America, it has been discovered that the secret of light creaming-method mixtures lies in thorough beating of the fat rather than anything else. From this, the manufacturers' test kitchens have evolved a new and time-saving method of cake and pudding mixing which, if you buy their ready-whipped fats, allows you to mix everything at one go, sometimes in little more than half a minute (Half-a-Mo Pudding?). You can do it slightly less rapidly with an ordinary margarine, shortening, or butter, if you simply cream the fat until it is pale and fluffy – about 4 minutes good beating – and then add everything else and stir. I now use this method a great deal more than the old-fashioned and laborious methods, and over a busy period such as Christmas, you might like to have a go at it via a steamed pudding. This recipe uses a cheap shortening which doesn't state that it is pre-creamed, but works as if it were. Some of the pre-creamed or whipped fats are not so very cheap. Some manufacturers issue recipe leaflets and booklets for this method.

4 oz. each Sainsbury's 'Shorteen', sugar, and *self-raising flour* (N.B.) 2 eggs pinch salt 1 dessertsp. milk if small eggs	any one of the following: 1 tbs. powdered coffee; 1 dessertsp. ginger; rind and juice of ½ large orange or 1 lemon; 2 oz. dried fruit

Put all ingredients into mixing bowl and stir briskly with a wooden spoon until all are smoothly and evenly blended. (About 1 to 2 minutes depending on ingredients and your mixing.) Put into prepared pudding basin, cover in usual way and steam about 1½ hours. Serve with a simple syrup, jam, or cornflour-thickened fruit-juice sauce (p. 120) appropriate to the pudding; custard; Sabayon Sauce (p. 121); or extra sugar.

NOTE: If using plain flour add 1 rounded tsp. baking powder. The texture of puddings and cakes made in this way is a little more open and, sometimes, more crumbly than those made by the traditional method, but they are perfectly light, spongy, risen and even in texture.

December

****

Using Convenience Foods

Because even the best of organizers finds Christmas cooking time-consuming, because the most devoted cook likes a day off from her own food, and finally because most food prices are high during the month anyway. December makes many so-called convenience foods both welcome and comparatively good value for money.

Many of the foods now coming under this new label are old-established, although the purpose behind them was rather to preserve food than to save time preparing it, or to make a profitable business from them. Fish and chips, when good, are one of the best of all convenience foods.

The three chief kinds are: tinned, dried, and frozen. The first two are the most widely useful since they keep perfectly and almost indefinitely without any elaborate storage apparatus. The third keeps foods in a condition little short of perfect freshness and undiminished nutritional value, but requires refrigerated storage, and should be used as quickly as fresh food once out of cold store.

Up to the 1914–18 war a middle-class woman had to be in dire straits indeed to have no servant at all, and very modest households expected to keep at least two servants, one of whom would certainly perform such kitchen duties as preparing vegetables, in the rather rare instances where the housewife herself liked to do the cooking. These days our kitchen maids do their work far removed from the kitchens where their handiwork is used. Instead of the sink, they stand at the conveyor belt or bench of the food factory or processing plant. To feed your family entirely on ready-prepared vegetables would probably add to your food bill the amount that a 1914 kitchen maid cost in what were known as board-wages – the arrangement whereby the resident servants were paid enough money to buy their own food.

Not all convenience foods, however, cost more. One of the oldest is junket which is very cheap. Smoked fish might well be included under this heading, and no one could want a quicker cheap meal than a poached Finnan haddock or a grilled buckling. Eggs must take pride of place among convenience foods. Not only are they cheap and nutritionally A1, but they combine well with other ready-prepared foods. For instance *œufs mollets* dishes can be quickly produced by using one of the packet or tinned sauces.

My chief quarrel with factory foods is misleading labelling, which makes them seem more than they are. Very few of the so-called 'family size' packs of complete meals or dishes would satisfy one hungry schoolboy. Nor am I saying that there aren't ready-prepared foods that I scorn: I have noted my dislike of tinned peas elsewhere in this book, and I can't say I think much of tinned peaches or salmon. Shortcrust pastry is one of the frozen foods I feel really contemptuous about. You could make your own, much nicer, short paste in less time than it takes to thaw out the frozen variety. Puff pastry is another matter; many people cannot master the art, or have neither the time nor conditions allowing them to make puff pastry. But many useful and pleasant dishes require it, and it combines well with other prepared foods to make quick and attractive dishes.

For one category of eaters convenience foods seem the perfect answer: the bedsitter community. These days they can get everything ready-prepared and eminently storable, from sliced onions to crème caramel.

Here then is a quick survey of the field, with suggested uses strictly keeping to a minimum of work and time.

Soups and Stocks (or Bouillon)

PACKETED DRIED. Cheaper than tinned, average 1½ pints per packet, but a little longer and more trouble to prepare. Some can be used as sauces: use half the packet with about quarter the quantity of water recommended for soup, about 6 fluid oz. (that is a generous ¼ pint). Chicken or beef stock cubes may be used for a quick cup of thin broth. (Good value at Sainsbury's and Marks & Spencer.) Oxo is among the oldest bouillons.

PASTE. Bovril and Marmite. Best known as quickly-made invalid broths. Use in weak concentration for stock or sauce base.

TINNED. Dearer than packeted, but ready in seconds. Use concentrated versions for sauces. Most tins give quantity for sauce, otherwise use half amount stated for soup, diluting to taste. Sainsbury's are good, cheap, but limited kinds and, so far, no condensed versions. Heinz are good for the latter.

NOTE: Tomato soups make poor sauce, being too sweet. Use the proper purée. Libby does a tinned sauce, but distribution of this is patchy.

Fish

DRIED, SALTED. Kipper, bloater, buckling, red herring:
Only the last may need introducing, though formerly it was a commonplace. It is preserved in salt and needs soaking out. But some connoisseurs prize it above the rest. Consult Madame Prunier's Fish Cook Book, edited by Ambrose Heath, at your public library, for a red herring recipe.

Put kippers in no more cold water than will just cover them. Bring to the boil. As soon as water boils they are done. Overcooking turns them to mushy rags. Drain well. Put generous pat of butter on top. Kippers in polythene with butter are not worth the extra. They do smell, because in the packing it is unavoidable that much oil gets on outside of bag; and your own butter is no problem. But filleted kippers are useful.

Smoked Haddock, 'golden cutlets', smoked fillet:
As a rule the last only is not haddock, but cod. Golden cutlets are small filleted haddock – sometimes whiting – and useful for children and other bone haters, also for mixing with other ingredients. Cook haddock as kippers; don't waste milk on the cooking, spend the money on extra butter for putting on top. So far, freeze-dried fish seems confined to the few prawns that figure in some of the 'complete meals'.

TINNED. Sardines and tuna are the only satisfactory tinned fish from the gourmet viewpoint. (Bargain-hunt for both in supermarkets.) The rest are a matter of personal preferences. Pilchards are filling and cheap, red salmon absurdly dear, prawns and the like prohibitive. But the small tins or jars of dressed crab make useful titbits, sandwiches or, mixed with Béchamel sauce, fillings for bouchées, tartlets etc. Van Smirren is a good make and cheap.

FROZEN. Little time and trouble are saved by uncooked frozen fish and, indeed, plaice fillets are more trouble and expense than they are worth, since they need thawing in order to skin them and, when skinned, represent precious little food. Cod and haddock steaks are useful and though dearer than fresh fish, are skinless, boneless and solid. Used with a tinned curry sauce they can make a quick main meal. Main point of frozen fish is for those with a bad fishmonger or no fishmonger at all (but probably with a deep-freeze compartment for storing a few packets), e.g. country dwellers who can get fish only on a weekly or monthly shopping expedition, or bedsitter tenants. Fish fingers, subject of jokes, scorn, inverted and plain snobbery, make quite a tasty meal now and again for a change, but you need half-a-dozen to satisfy a healthy appetite, and therefore they are far from a bargain. As for fish-cakes, it is better to make your own. Sainsbury's frozen fish is cheap and good, no money being wasted on technicolour packing. Bird's Eye is easy to find, quality and freshness often outstanding.

Meat

Best-known convenience meats are the products of the pork butcher or cooked-meat shop: ham, brawn, sausages, pressed and corned beef, tongue and pies. All good from good shops and, since the last war, big nationally-known makers have improved products. Also, good cheap sausages now come from Ireland. Sainsbury, Walls, Harris, Purity (Irish), Marks & Spencer, are among the best and cheapest.

TINNED. Beef leads the tinned meats, and there are many versions of stewed and corned beef. Which? reported on the stewed, but by the time you read this their 'Best Buy' may have vanished from the shelves, as has happened with several food items they have put in top place, but which were not among the most heavily advertised brands. A tin of stewed beef and a packet of frozen puff pastry make a quick pie that will yield 4 moderately filling helpings. The original wartime 'Spam', made in America, was excellent. Its imitators since have not come up to the mark, and the 'Spam' made (under licence from the parent company) outside the U.S. is expensive, and for my taste salty. However, a tin of cheap 'chopped luncheon meat' is useful on the tin shelf as a standby if you run out of bacon, and makes quite a good meal fried or grilled, with poached or fried egg, plus tinned broad or baked beans, or spinach, or frozen vegetables.

Just edging their way into this meat section are so-called complete meals rejoicing in names like (or almost like) 'Bangers Bolognese', 'Spaghetti Stroganoff', 'Veal Vesuvius'. They contain tiny amounts of unrecognizable stewed-to-a-rag meat in a sea of pasta and cornfloury gravy, heavily charged with onion essence and monosodium glutamate, that bringer-out of flavour that figures in so many convenience foods. Children love them, and come to no harm from an 'individual portion' tin – so long as you have plenty more for them to fill up on. If you have a scrap of white sauce, a scrap of meat, a spoonful of peas, you could add the lot to one of these tins for a quick late-night snack. Digs dwellers might like a tin for stock against a crisis, but these 'meals' are dear and over-weighted with starch.

Better-value tinned meat meals are steak and kidney pies, but you must have an oven (tin serves as baking vessel), and Polish (and other Iron Curtain) stuffed peppers or cabbage. The latter also come in glass jars. The stuffed peppers are particularly meaty, and the sauce, though lavish, is good. Less good value for money is similar dish of meat balls.

FROZEN. Meat is mostly confined to the hamburger type of meat rissole. Useful and pleasant as a change from sausages, but dearer and no quicker to prepare. Shepherd's Pie is, as far as I know, almost the sole representative of mutton in frozen meats. Their braised beef is tasty but on the dear side.

Vegetables

TINNED. Beans seem to can the most successfully in the vegetable line, broad beans tasting most like the fresh article, but they are, as are most other tinned foods, dear. Baked beans in tomato sauce are the cheapest; if you dislike the flavour of the sauce, tinned butter beans may prove an alternative; the best value in tinned pulses is perhaps pease pudding ('Forge' brand). You can 'curry' it and call it 'dahl', make various vegetarian dishes from it (consult Indian and vegetarian cookery books in your local library); thin it down for soup, add some ready-prepared onions and use it as it is.

I can't say I care much for tinned spinach, and other 'green' vegetables – French beans, celery etc. are too dear for the average purse. Sauerkraut is cheap, particularly Polish in bottles. Add butter/margarine, sugar, pepper, wine, cumin or caraway seed, onion, pineapple or orange juice and so forth to your taste. Excellent with all sorts of sausages. Carrots and tomatoes, however, are good value, the flavour very good. Use tomatoes as you would the fresh variety, as indicated *passim*. Bake, or heat in own tin with two holes pierced in top in boiling water about 5 minutes (water three-quarters way up) rather than frying, as they sputter and break easily. Both carrots and tomatoes are useful allies in winter slimming programmes for bed-sitter dwellers. Supermarkets often have marvellous bargain offers in Italian tinned tomatoes, when it is worth laying in a little stock. Much the same is true of tinned pimentos (peppers) and, although they are not suitable as an accompaniment alone, a little chopped up will greatly improve and help to expand other vegetables. For instance: 1 tiny tin pimento, 1 large tin tomatoes, 1 large tin garden peas, or, a little more expensive, a medium tin of sweetcorn, mixed in small saucepan will provide good, quick and sufficient vegetables for 4. (Add butter or yoghurt as liked.) Put 2 to 3 frankfurters per head on top of the pot for a complete course. See also note on sweet corn at end of this section.

DRIED. Freeze-drying is the latest of the newer methods of preserving food and the results are remarkably good. Flavour and nutritive value are little changed, the vegetables keep possibly as well as tinned food, and without the need for refrigeration. Dehydration also means that the packing is neither bulky nor heavy, so that storage presents no problem and carrying is easy. Peas, beans, onions, mixed vegetables and potato powders or flakes are the most widely distributed vegetables at the present time. The peas are very good, Woolworth's own 'Winfield' brand being cheaper than and as good as most, but a packet will serve two only, not three. The onions are the young-girl-in-digs' dream. No smell in store, or on hands, and 'Swel' brand gives the single person enough in a packet for 6 to 8 dishes.

Dried potato, in powder or flakes, does very well as topping for Shepherd's Pie and, if generously laced with butter/margarine milk, seasoning and other flavourings, and grilled brown, is quite palatable as an accompaniment. But plain with, say, sausages, it does have an offbeat taste – not unpleasant, but not 'natural'. A godsend, however, as a standby for scatter-brains who tend to forget the shopping basics, and incomparably cheaper and nicer-tasting than tinned potatoes. 'Swel' flakes good for taste.

FROZEN. Frozen peas now are, in every respect, as good as fresh peas, sometimes better, and frequently cheaper, as already noted. The best bargains are the plastic bags, since no money is wasted on fancy packaging. This applies to all frozen vegetables. It is sometimes the case that a 'fancy grade' of pea is packed in a technicolour packet, but those in plastic are perfectly tender and of good flavour. Diabetics should note that many frozen peas have sugar added, though this is not always stated on the packet.

The flavour and quality of most frozen uncooked vegetables seems to me impeccable, but those which, from the garden or shop, need sauces and other flavourings, need them just as much when frozen, so the only labour saved is that of preparation. In the case of broccoli, for example, this may merely be washing, and the extra cost of the frozen article gives it no advantage for budget cooks. Broad beans are quite good value, the fresh article so often entailing a great deal of waste, while cut (though not, in my view, sliced) green beans also provide a reasonable amount for the money. At present all these cost less from Sainsbury's self-service shops, where they sell their own brand.

Potatoes come frozen in various guises, cooked or half-cooked. It seems to me better to buy chips from a fish and chip shop if a good one is near at hand, since this saves money and cooking time, the frozen chips being half-cooked and not particularly cheap, though useful in some circumstances. Frood's Potato Puffles are pleasant but dear, Sainsbury's potato croquettes middling in price and taste. Both these, however, can be heated in the oven, which may be useful and means no frying smells. You would certainly need two large packets of either for a family, and I'd still plump for fish-shop chips for value and flavour where available.

NOTE: Having a liking for sweet corn I consider both tinned (though not 'cream-style') and frozen, whole kernel corns compare favourably with fresh cobs, are easier and quicker to cook, and often cheer up other vegetables. Corn seems to have a natural affinity with bacon or pork products, and quick meals from them provide scope for variety with tastiness.

Puddings

The pudding course offers the greatest variety in convenience foods, and is the oldest established. Simple puddings of corn-flour-, or arrowroot-thickened milk, garnished with a spoonful of jam, were quickly run up by Victorian nursery maids for their charges, leading in time to flavoured blancmange powders. Eighteenth-century cooks had to make jellies from scratch with calves' feet, while by the 1890s Crosse and Blackwell and Good-all Backhouse (of Yorkshire Relish fame) were making bottled jellies which the cook melted and poured into moulds of her choice.

Today dozens of quickly-made and completely-made puddings fill the grocers' shelves. There is no need to remind anyone about tinned fruits, rice pudding and steamed puddings of many kinds. I shall merely mention a few lesser known items, or uses of well-known ones. Sainsbury's quite recently introduced excellent tinned raspberries and strawberries. A spoonful of either on ice-cream, mousse, or beaten into yoghurt, is delicious and the small tin used thus goes a long way. Tinned pie fillings vary, but look out for Aylmer's Blueberry – the same thing as wortleberries in Cornwall – which is 'something different' for most of us, though not for Cornishmen and North Country miners. Another excellent Canadian tinned fruit is York black cherries, although not among the cheaper ranges.

ICE-CREAM. If you find ice-cream too sweet, top it with a sharpish fruit – tinned plums, gooseberries, fresh orange, tinned rhubarb, apricots. Also try the hot chocolate sauce, plus a little coffee powder, on p. 436.

Set a blob of ice-cream on a slice of Swiss roll and top with fruit.

Chop up two pieces of stem ginger and press into a block of ice-cream, returning it to freezing compartment of refrigerator to firm up. Serve with banana and ginger juice, cream etc.

Cut a plain ice-cream block into three layers, spread each with good jam – blackcurrant, apricot, marmalade – put together again and firm up. Serve topped with chopped nuts, cream.

Spread each half of a sponge sandwich (shop-made if liked) with jam, grated chocolate, chocolate- or coffee-flavoured butter, cream etc., chill. Meanwhile press an ice-cream block out to fit a (chilled) sponge sandwich tin same size as cake, turn on to one half of cake, top with other half, serve at once, with hot sauce if liked. This is a variation of Baked Alaska (ice-cream block put very hard on top of sponge round, covered in meringue and baked few minutes in very hot oven). Chill utensils when dealing with ice-cream.

Bird's Eye Arctic Roll, and now its imitators – ice-cream rolled in sponge – are good, attractive and versatile.

JELLY. Plain, they are dreary for adult tastes, and why *doesn't* some enterprising manufacturer make them from genuine fruit juice? It takes no longer for them to set, however, if fruit or sponge cake cubes are added (see also, p. 197), and this is a great improvement and very quick, especially if the fruit is chilled while you are making the jelly. Set orange jelly in sponge sandwich tin, and use as filling for sponge sandwich rather as ice-cream above. Top with whipped cream, or ice with orange glacé icing made with real juice – if you have the time. Better tasting, though cloudy, orange or lemon jelly may be made from good fruit squash set with gelatine.

OTHER SET PUDDINGS include Green's 'Carmelle'. I take great pleasure in the carefully arranged faces of some purists when I say that I hardly ever bother with proper crème caramel these days, as I find 'Carmelle' so good. Well, I do and there it is! It sets much sooner than the packet claims, except in summer minus a fridge. Bird's 'Whips' must be the fastest pudding ever; not exactly *nice*, but the chocolate and caramel flavours are passable, and may be a trouble-free method of getting the day's milk dose into a faddy child or milk-hating invalid. Can be used as 'custard' with fruit etc. Quite cheap.

Junket needs a little time to cool off and set, but with a refrigerator this is not a problem. Tablets keep better than liquid but not all chemists or grocers keep rennet tablets. Flavour the milk with chocolate, coffee or liqueur for a change. Don't let directions naming exact temperatures bother you, the milk should be just comfortable to your little finger.

MOUSSE. Bird's Eye and Frood do them in individual and larger sizes. Perfectly fine as they are – thawed out, of course. But you can whip them up with a quantity of yoghurt for economy and add fruits and so on.

NOTE: Recipes are constantly put out by manufacturers for using convenience foods. Bird's Eye, for example, have quite a library. It is worth writing to the big names asking for leaflets, as many have helpful ideas which may well set you off on methods of your own.

Christmas Cooking – Finishing

CHRISTMAS CAKE

The tables on pp. 512–13 indicate quantities of almond and royal icing needed to cover various sized cakes. Consult the general advice on icing for methods of work and timing.

MINCE PIES

Use shortcrust or flaky pastry. For 12 to 16 pies you will need ½ lb. pastry and ½ lb. mincemeat.

Mince pies are another 'proper fiddlin' little job' and the way to get the job done quickly and efficiently is to set up a miniature production line. You need: Rolling pin, flour dredger, 1 pastry cutter same size as diameter of patty tins, 1 pastry cutter one size larger (wine glasses or tumblers may do), dessertspoon, palette knife, pastry-brush, cold water, castor sugar (in dredger if liked). Complete each operation rather than each pie in turn.

(1) Set the oven at 375°F, gas 5, for shortcrust, 400° F, gas 6, for flaky.

(2) Roll out pastry about $\frac{1}{16}$ inch thick. Stamp out 12 to 16 rounds with smaller cutter. (Flour glasses, especially after each cutting to assist in removing pastry since you cannot, in this instance, prod at it from the top). Put these rounds aside for tops of pies.

(3) Re-arrange and re-roll pastry as necessary, cutting bases of pies from this with larger cutter. Line tins with these rounds.

(4) Put a small dessertspoon of mincemeat in each pie. Damp undersides of smaller rounds, cover pies, press down with blunt edge of cutter, or put a clean folded tissue over each pie in turn, to protect pastry where a glass is used. Holding cutter lightly in position cut up (p. 125) edges of pies with side of palette knife to seal.

(5) Brush tops with cold water (brush must not be too wet), dredge lightly with castor sugar. If using sugar-dredger, clean up baking tray from surplus sugar to prevent burning.

(6) If using flaky pastry you may like to line the bottom of the oven with foil to catch any fat that runs out. Bake pies for 20 to 30 minutes until well coloured.

NOTE: Shortcrust pies may be made about five days in advance, flaky pies about one week if storage is cool. Mince pies are at their best served hot. For an extra fillip, prize up tops and insert a teaspoonful of sherry just before serving, hand whipped cream separately, or whisk a couple of tablespoonfuls of sherry into the cream.

DECEMBER

STUFFINGS AND SAUCES

Make stuffings up to three days ahead if you have a refrigerator,
or longer if you put it in the freezing compartment. Recipes for
stuffings are on tables on pp. 483–6. Bread sauce, p. 182, can be
made a day or so ahead if you have a refrigerator. Make stock
from giblets on Christmas Eve, or a little earlier if you have the
bird on hand, but store in refrigerator in this instance. Hard
sauce for the pudding should be made only twenty-four hours
ahead unless you can be sure the container is well sealed, so that
the alcohol and aroma cannot evaporate.

HARD SAUCE

A good quantity for 6 to 8, but if you expect a greedy guest
keep some back in the larder, and divide the amount to be sent
to table into two bowls.

4 oz. unsalted butter	at least 5 tbs. rum, brandy,
4 oz. castor or soft brown	cointreau or other liqueur
sugar	of not too sweet kind

Beat butter until soft, add sugar and beat again until pale, fluffy
and easy to shake from spoon. Beat in the liqueur gradually and
very well to avoid curdling. When the 5 tbs. are in, taste and add
more, by teaspoons, to taste. It is better to have it on the strong
side.

SHERRY CUSTARD

Make 'boiled' egg custard as on p. 137, adding a minimum 3 tbs.
sherry per ½ pint just before serving.

Poultry

Provided there is a cold larder, birds may be stuffed and trussed
during Christmas Eve. Frozen poultry needs at least twenty-four
hours to thaw, while big frozen turkeys or geese may well take
longer. It is therefore best to get the bird home two days before

473

it is to be cooked. Remember that you can only cook what will fit in your oven or oven tins. Disaster will be the thirteenth guest of the girl who invites twelve to Christmas dinner to be cooked in the oven of a bachelor flatlet. Turkeys have not only large knobbly knees but breasts like camel's humps, so when you go shopping take a mental, if not written, note of the dimensions of your oven and meat tin.

Consult the roasting notes and tables for general directions on preparation and timing.

The tables give you other details you need to know according to the size of the bird. From these you should be able to calculate amounts for other stuffings you may prefer.

The ideal way to roast poultry is on a spit, more so when the bird is large for, as you know, temperature varies in different parts of an oven. However this is overcome to a large extent by turning the bird as indicated. Many home cooks roast the Christmas bird very successfully by hanging it from an oven shelf put on the highest rung. If you want to try this method but have no proper hook that can be firmly fixed, choose really thick string, and see that you have loops, or whatever, at each end of the trussed bird, for you will have an almost impossible task on hand if you try to make secure a half-cooked, roasting-hot turkey. Another useful – if slightly messy – method of getting a large bird into a smallish oven is to stand it directly on the bars of the oven shelf, putting a drip tin on the shelf below.

You will have a far more restful day if you make out for yourself a written timetable for cooking the meal. Do this by working it out backwards from the time you intend to dish up. It may sound tiresome, and just one more chore on top of all the rest, but it pays dividends. A model follows on p. 480.

CHOICE OF CHRISTMAS ROAST. The tables that follow include information on duck and goose, but it must be said that neither are economical. Not only is there a good layer of fat on a worthwhile duck or goose – especially over the breast – but the bone amount is greater, while they can never reach the size of turkey. What's more, the breeding of geese is of a low standard in this country whilst, at the same time, our present veterinary regulations prevent the import of the best of all geese – Polish.

(At the time of writing there is hope that any anomalies will be ironed out, and the status quo restored. We used to import Polish geese.) Having said all this, I must emphasize that, for the gourmet, goose or duck will always be preferred to turkey – a dry tasteless bird – for their superb flavour and succulence.

For quantity with cheapness :	frozen turkey
Small amount but cheap :	frozen chicken
Medium amount, medium cost :	capons and free-range chickens
Varied amounts, medium cost :	pork
Varied amounts, dearer cost :	beef
Small to medium amounts, dearer cost :	ducks, geese, pheasants

(A few frozen Danish geese may be available in some shops. They are slightly cheaper than the home-reared birds and of very good quality. Frozen ducks are sometimes cheaper than fresh, but usually small and suitable for only two people.

A REMINDER. Put a piece of fat under the skin of the breast when roasting turkey, chicken, guinea fowl, pheasant etc. See p. 85.

Throughout this book you will find recipes using cooked meats and poultry which should help in making varied dishes to get the most from the Christmas roast. The chapter includes some vegetable recipes suited to the Christmas dinner as well as to the season, an Eliza Acton mincemeat idea, and two puddings, festive and seasonable, but quite out of the dried-fruit-and-suet taste-band of Christmas.

Vegetables

CHESTNUTS WITH SPROUTS OR CABBAGE

Serves 6 to 8.

½–¾ lb. chestnuts	1½ oz. margarine/butter
1–2 lb. sprouts or firm cabbage heart	milk or stock
1 tsp. minced onion	seasoning
1 rasher bacon finely diced (optional)	

475

Make a cut in the base of each nut, then cover well with water and bring to the boil. Using a perforated spoon or tongs and a cloth, pick out the nuts one at a time and strip off shell and inner skin, using a small pointed knife and trying not to break them up too much. If the nuts begin to be difficult to peel, bring to the boil again. Halve them. Melt ½ oz. of the butter, add onion and bacon and soften 3 minutes. Add chestnuts and enough stock or milk just to cover. Season lightly and simmer until tender (20 to 30 minutes). Meanwhile prepare sprouts, or chop cabbage. Boil sprouts 12 minutes in salted water or stock. Cook sprouts and finish cooking in butter. Lastly mix sprouts or cabbage and chestnuts with their flavourings, but if much liquid is left, either pour some off for gravy or thicken with a teaspoon of cornflour. Or dish the two vegetables with the chestnuts piled in the centre of the dish and the green vegetables in a ring round them.

CELERY WITH MUSHROOMS

Serves 6 to 8.

1–2 lb. celery	seasoning
4 oz. mushrooms	1½ oz. margarine/butter
1 oz. flour	½ pint milk
1 tsp. minced onions	1 tsp. chopped parsley
½ tsp. chopped thyme or winter savory (pinch dried)	

Scrub celery, cut in inch lengths and blanch in salted water 5 minutes, drain. Melt fat and soften onion. Wipe mushrooms and slice very thinly. Add to fat and turn well to mix. Add celery and mix again. Blend in flour off heat, season, add herbs, then stir in milk and bring to simmering point stirring out lumps. Simmer about 20 minutes or until celery is tender.

NOTE: Alternatively, cook sprouts as in preceding recipe, mushrooms as above and blend them in milk as above. All these recipes are most suited to turkey or chicken. Other vegetable recipes *passim* should be consulted for original accompaniments for duck, goose or pork. Creamy or sweetish finishes are too bland with these meats unless sharpened, as the following potato recipe, with a distinctive ingredient. Such recipes as leeks baked in tomato sauce, broccoli with egg and lemon sauce, Bohemian cabbage, cabbage with bacon, sprouts with butter and lemon, glazed onions, and obviously many salads make a more original and certainly a more festive contribution than the now humdrum green peas. And for potatoes with rich Christmas meats, for those who enjoy their garlic, *pommes-de-terre à l'ail* are hard to beat.

POMMES SICILIENNE

Serves 6 to 8.

1½ lb. potato quantity of
   Pommes Duchesses (p. 194)
grated rind and juice of 1
   large orange

1 medium onion
½ oz. bacon dripping or lard

Chop onion very finely and brown in fat. Mix, with orange, into duchesse mixture. Use only enough juice to give flavour without making potato too liquid. Pipe through a coarse pipe in large rosettes or pile into dish and brown in hot oven or under grill.

Puddings

PALEY PUDDING

Mrs E. C. Tetley's recipe
6–8 helpings.

This family recipe is a rare combination of richness with a light subtle flavour. Very much an Arabian Nights dish. The mould has a very soft texture and does not stand long after turning out. A sturdier mould results from using cornflour, and how sturdy depends on varying slightly the amounts of cornflour in the tablespoon.

MOULD:

2 tbs. arrowroot	½-inch stick cinnamon
2 pints milk	2 tbs. castor sugar
13 sweet almonds	3 eggs
3 tbs. rose water	1 oz. butter

SAUCE

2½ glasses sherry (¼ pint approx.)	1 oz. butter
	3 oz. sifted icing sugar

Blend arrowroot in a quarter of the cold milk. Add butter cut small. Blanch the almonds and pound them to paste (start them off through mouli-grater if available). Add rose water to almond paste, stir into arrowroot mixture, beating eggs and adding them, also sugar; boil rest of milk with cinnamon and, as it is coming to boil, stir in mixed ingredients. Continue this thorough stirring until mixture is very thick and perfectly smooth. Turn into mould or glass serving dish and chill. If set in mould, turn out only at the last minute, leaving mould over the top to help keep the shape. Keep cold while making sauce just before serving. For this beat butter to a cream, add sherry and sugar beating well. Heat in a small pan.

Serve pudding cold on hot plates with hot sauce.

ORANGES REINE ELIZABETH

Author's recipe.

Seedless satsuma or mandarin oranges are essential to the success of this dish, otherwise it will be bitter.

For each 4–6 oranges : ½ pint water

For each ¼ pint liquid used for the syrup : ¼ lb. sugar

For each 6 oranges : ¼ pint double cream.

(1) Set oven at 275° F, gas 1.

(2) Remove 'eyes' and cover fruit with cold water, bring just to boiling point, rinse in cold water.

(3) Stand, eye-side up, in straight-sided small cocotte. Pour measured water in. Cover and cook in oven 1 hour. Very carefully turn fruit over and cook second hour. (N.B. Oven is essential. Even lowest setting on top may result in fruit splitting.)

(4) Lift fruit carefully on to plate. Measure liquid and sugar

478

for syrup as above. Heat in cocotte without boiling until sugar dissolves. Return fruit carefully to cocotte and replace in oven for ½ hour, turn fruit and continue second ½ hour. Lift fruit out. Boil liquid until syrupy (a little, cooled, will feel slimy if rubbed between finger and thumb, and will turn sticky as it is rubbed). Set fruit and liquid aside separately until cool. Half an hour before serving chill fruit. Dish on serving platter. Spoon syrup, cold but not chilled, over fruit. Pipe a large spiral of whipped cream, or pile a large blob on each orange and spike with two chocolate leaves. (Angelica may be used, but chocolate gives the final flavour.)

CHOCOLATE LEAVES. Method of making these explained to me by Mrs G. Dietsch, chef to Mrs E. C. Tetley. Mrs Dietsch warns that they are difficult to make unless you melt quite a lot more chocolate than you use. On no account dilute the chocolate with even a teaspoon of water, for it will not set. Chocolate discolours and dulls easily, but this does not really notice on the finished dish. Cooking or couverture chocolate behaves better, but costs more and is not universally available. Artificial leaves can be cut from thick waxed paper (e.g. from cereal packet), though less effective.

Pick required number of small leaves (rose, or mint in season). Wash and dry. Melt chocolate in a bowl or better still, on a plate over hot water. On no account overheat. Draw one side of leaf through chocolate, covering completely and quite thickly, but allow surplus to drip off. Rest uncovered side on plate. Chill well until chocolate is set hard again. Carefully peel leaf off chocolate. Keep chocolate leaves in cool between wax paper until required for use. You might be able to use less chocolate by spreading it on leaves, but I found this too long-winded and needing very flat large leaves. The surplus melted chocolate makes excellent soufflés (p. 460), butter-cream and chocolate cake, etc.

MINCEMEAT FRITTERS

From Eliza Acton's *Modern Cookery*.

With half a pound of mincemeat mix two ounces of fine breadcrumbs (or a tablespoonful of flour), two eggs well beaten, and the strained juice of half a small lemon. Mix these well, and drip the fritters from a dessertspoon into plenty of very pure lard or fresh butter; fry them from seven to eight minutes, drain them on a napkin or on white blotting paper, and send them very hot to table : they should be quite small.

I would use oil to fry, kitchen paper to drain, and 6 minutes frying would be enough on average. Protect hand from sputtering.

Christmas Dinner – A model timetable

The model is based on a 'free-range' 12 lb. turkey. A frozen bird of this weight would have to be brought out of the butcher's deep-freeze a full 48 hours in advance. To plan your own timetable start by calculating the time needed for the longest-cooked item – usually the pudding – and fit the other items round it. For example, if you like to work at leisure you will naturally make mince pie pastry two days ahead, the pies themselves the day before. But those who enjoy a bustle can manage everything on the day, although they cannot expect to have much more than a snatched drink with arriving dinner-guests.

48 hours before – make flaky pastry, store in polythene or foil in cold.

24 hours before – make stock for gravy or soup from giblets; mince-pies; stuffings, sauces, garnishes such as sausage or forcemeat balls, bacon rolls (hard sauces should not be made unless they can be stored in sealed containers, otherwise the alcohol may evaporate, with great loss of bite and flavour, especially if a refrigerator is not available); wash vegetables and, where suitable, leave in a little water to give crispness, but do not cut them up or peel, unless refrigerator is available; prepare potatoes for roasting to the parboiled and 'roughed-up' stage, puréed mixtures may be completed to the point where they are ready for piping (they will need re-heating before putting into piping bag).

4 hours before – put on steamer, and when boiling put in the pudding; stuff and truss bird.

3 hours before – put bird in oven (breast down to start, turn after 1½ hours).

2 *hours before* – check water in steamer; if not made in advance, make hard sauce and prepare potatoes and vegetables; assemble dishes and plates to be warmed; lay table. (Bird should be turned about now.)

1 *hour before* – add sausage, forcemeat, bacon rolls etc. to bird.

¾ *hour before* – put potatoes into oven (they should be turned once); flour and baste breast of bird; put vegetable water on.

½ *hour before* – put in vegetables to cook; on very low heat begin re-heating soup, bread sauce etc.

¼ *hour before* – dish bird and garnish, returning to very low oven position; make gravy; dish everything else, potatoes last: pudding may be dished now or just before serving (remember to allow brandy for flaming to take warmth from heat of serving dish before putting match to it); before sitting down put mince-pies in oven, turning to low setting.

CHRISTMAS COOKING CHARTS

(Weight after drawing, but before stuffing)

TURKEY
GOOSE
DUCK
CAPON

} Start at 425° F, gas 7, reduce after ½ hour to 400° F, gas 6; after further ¼ to ½ hour to 350° F, gas 4, until ¼ to ½ hour before the end, when raise to 400° F, gas 6 to brown breast. Do this by lightly dredging with flour and basting with fat and juices in pan. Turn bird as follows: ⅓ total time one side of breast down, ⅓ other side breast down, last ⅓ breast up.

TIME IN THE OVEN

TURKEY	8 lb. (6 to 8 helpings) 2 hours	12 lb. (9 to 12 helpings) 3 hours	16 lb. (12 to 16 helpings) 4 hours	20 lb. (16 to 20 helpings) 4½ to 5 hours
GOOSE	8 lb. (6 to 8 helpings) 2¼ hours	Up to 12 lb. (8 to 10 helpings) 3 to 3¾ hours	Unlikely to find an eviscerated goose weighing more than 12 lb.	
DUCK	3 to 4 lb. (2 to 4 helpings) 1½ to 2 hours	Up to 6 lb. (4 to 6 helpings) 2 to 3 hours		
CAPON	Up to 8 lb. (6 to 8 helpings) 1½ to 2½ hours			

Remember to allow 30 minutes for making gravy, dishing up, tidying yourself. For at least 15 minutes rest the roast in very low heat, when it will compact and be much easier to carve.

STUFFINGS FOR TURKEY OR CAPON

(Weight after drawing)

TRADITIONAL PARSLEY STUFFING

	8 lb.	12 lb.	16 lb.	20 lb.
white breadcrumbs, fresh	1 lb.	1¼ lb.	1½ lb.	1¾ lb.
parsley, chopped	6 level tbs.	8 level tbs.	10 level tbs.	12 level tbs.
thyme, dried	1 level tbs.	1½ level tbs.	2 level tbs.	2½ level tbs.
lemons	1 large, or 2 small	2	2 large	3
salt	2 tsp.	2½ tsp.	3 tsp.	3½ tsp.
pepper	¼ tsp.	½ tsp.	¾ tsp.	1 tsp.
eggs	2	3	4	5
butter, melted	2 oz.	3 oz.	4 oz.	5 oz.

Grate lemon rind and squeeze juice. Mix together breadcrumbs, thyme, lemon rind, salt and pepper. Bind together with lemon juice, beaten eggs and melted butter. Add a little stock or water if stuffing is too stiff.

483

SAUSAGE AND CELERY STUFFING

	8 lb.	12 lb.	16 lb.	20 lb.
white bread, ½-inch thick slices	6	8	10	12
milk	¼ pint	¼ pint	½ pint, bare	½ pint
sausagemeat	12 oz.	1 lb.	1¼ lb.	1½ lb.
celery, chopped	2 tbs.	4 tbs.	6 tbs.	8 tbs.
onion, chopped	1 tbs.	2 tbs.	3 tbs.	4 tbs.
parsley, chopped	1 tbs.	2 tbs.	3 tbs.	4 tbs.
thyme, dried	1 tsp.	1 tsp.	1½ tsp.	2 tsp.
salt	1½ tsp.	2 tsp.	2½ tsp.	3 tsp.
pepper	¼ tsp.	¼ tsp.	½ tsp.	½ tsp.
eggs	1	1	2	3

Cut bread slices into small cubes. Soak in milk for 30 minutes. Mix together sausagemeat, celery, onion, parsley, thyme, salt, pepper, soaked bread cubes, and bind well together with beaten egg.

STUFFING FOR GOOSE OR DUCK

(Weight after drawing)

TRADITIONAL SAGE AND ONION

	3 to 4 lb.	Up to 6 lb.	8 lb.	Up to 12 lb.
onions	2 good size	3 good size	4 good size	6 good size
sage	smallish sprig; good teaspoon dried	medium sprig; 1½ tsp. dried.	large sprig; 1 dessertsp. dried.	2 sprigs. 1 tbs. dried.
breadcrumbs (stale loaf)	2 oz.	3 oz.	4 oz.	6 oz.
margarine	1 oz.	1½ oz.	2 oz.	3 oz.
grated lemon rind (add liver of bird if liked)	½ lemon	1 small	1	2
seasoning				

Method as for saged onions on p. 434. Moisten with a little milk if necessary.

485

STUFFING FOR TURKEY OR GOOSE

(Weight after drawing)

CHESTNUT AND ORANGE STUFFING

	8 lb.	12 lb.	16 lb.	20 lb.
chestnuts*	1 lb.	1½ lb.	2 lb.	2½ lb.
stock or water	bare ½ pint	½ pint	bare ¾ pint	¾ pint
breadcrumbs, fresh	8 oz.	12 oz.	1 lb.	1¼ lb.
suet, finely shredded	4 oz.	6 oz.	8 oz.	12 oz.
salt	¼ tsp., bare	2 tsp.	3 tsp.	3½ tsp.
cayenne pepper	⅛ tsp.	¼ tsp. bare	¼ tsp.	¼ tsp.
oranges	2	3	4	5
eggs, beaten	1	2	2	3
add liver of bird if liked				

Wash chestnuts and make a small slit in each. Cover with cold water and bring to the boil. Boil for 5 minutes, strain and remove shells while hot. Return chestnuts to pan, cover with stock or water. Simmer gently until tender, when liquid should be absorbed. Sieve chestnuts. Grate rind and squeeze juice from oranges. Mix all ingredients together, add, if necessary, a little extra stock to bind.

*Canned chestnut purée may be used.

486

SAUCES

TURKEY	CHICKEN OR CAPON	GOOSE, DUCK, PORK
Bread Sauce, p. 182 (½ pint milk quantity for each 4 to 6 persons)	Bread Sauce	Orange Sauce, Espagnole Sauce, p. 118 (½ pint for each 6 to 8 persons) plus: grated rind and juice of 1 orange; 1 dessertsp. rowan or other jelly, per ½ pint
Cranberry Jelly, p. 554 (½ lb. for each 6 to 8 people)	Cherry Sauce, p. 351 (½ pint per 6 to 8 persons)	Cranberry Jelly
		Rowan Jelly, p. 554 (½ lb. per 6 to 8 persons)
Christmas Cake – see p. 512		Cherry Sauce

487

Cakes, Bread and Icing

◆◆

Cakes

The British housewife dearly loves a cake, so much so that when one firm of advertising agents carried out market research on using recipes in the British Isles, they found that for many women the word cooking *meant* cake-making.

In a general cookery book a section on cakes and bread must necessarily be limited, and in this book in particular must concentrate on being down-to-earth. But there is no doubt that cake-making can be a fascinating hobby. For instance, for the inventive young mother, rather more tied to the house than she would like for the moment, it can provide an outlet for manual skill, imagination and taste, with a nutritious as well as attractive result. The usual drawback to cookery – the ephemeral nature of the end product – is here an advantage: another marvellous cake is always in demand and, unlike a new painting, or piece of sculpture, the problem of where to put it will never arise !

Many 'manufactured' plainer cakes, these days, are excellent, but they lack individuality, while home-made cake is different each time. As for icing, from the simplest swirl of butter-cream to the elaborate Georgian swags, garlands and lattices of royal-iced celebration cakes the field is wide open for the craftswoman. Icing seems to have been uninfluenced by modernism, yet the apparatus of turn-table, many-shaped pipes, confectioners' comb; the plastic nature of the material, and the quite wide range of confectionery colouring and variety of ready-made decorative additions – coffee-bean sweets, sugar mimosa, chocolate dots, silver balls, to mention only the most common – would seem irresistible to the plastically gifted. There is room here for only the sketchiest outline of cake decoration, as of the whole sub-

ject of baking. For a full treatment there are two fine books for
your consideration : *Cake Making in Pictures* by Muriel Downes
(Odhams) which has dozens of step-by-step photographs of
every sort of process, exact description and recipes and inspiring
ideas for decorating; and *Concerning Cake Making* by Helen
Jerome (Pitman) a great classic on the subject, which is specially
strong on traditional British cakes and breads.

When I proposed a cake section to the publisher, my editor asked
if I could suggest, perhaps, a cheap Christmas cake. I could, but
I think few would want to make it. All celebration cakes are
willingly made rich by most families, whatever else they must
forgo, and this not only seems right to me personally, but is
hallowed by tradition of the most ancient and widespread sort.
Anyone old enough to remember the last war can tell tales of
cake ingredients assembled egg by borrowed egg, cadged sugar,
by begged rum and smuggled lemon; for a cake is not merely a
centrepiece on a buffet table, but is a potent piece of magic at
the feast.

As well as such special cakes it is always cheaper to make
rather than buy cakes ready-made, and very decidedly more
nutritious. Cakes can be manufactured almost wholly from
'chemicals'. True they seldom are quite so bad as that sounds,
and the homely baking-powder on your shelf is composed of
chemicals, still the home-made cake is a sound block of concentrated natural foods.

The section is chiefly devoted to the 'Ready-Reckoner', a table
of popular cakes divided according to the method by which they
are made and the mixture that is the basis of the method. In
addition there are one or two atypical recipes for less-known cakes.
Bread is severely practical, being intended for those who find they
must, and those who like to make bread on occasion. In addition
there are a very few yeast-raised classics for fun.

Varieties of Cakes
The chief kinds of cake and their consistencies are :
   Rubbed in mixtures (plainer cakes, economical); spoon should
just stand up in middle of mixture.

Creamed mixtures (rich sponges, fruit and fancy cakes); mixture should fall from spoon when lightly shaken.

Warmed mixtures (high proportion of sugar); soft, or thick pouring batter.

Whisked mixtures (fatless, high proportion of egg); frothy sponge, will pour but does not run and spread readily.

Scones; soft, but not tacky dough.

Making Cakes

For the novice, here are a few golden rules:

(1) *Read all the rules before reading the recipe.*

(2) *Read the recipe, the whole recipe, and stick to the recipe.*

(3) Before assembling ingredients prepare tins, baking sheets etc. Light oven at correct setting, and arrange shelves.

(4) Weigh and measure all ingredients and assemble them where you will mix the cake. (When a vital ingredient gets left out of a cake, usually it is because this was not done!) Assemble all utensils.

(5) Mix and sieve dry ingredients as far as possible, in accordance with recipe.

(6) Chop, clean or otherwise prepare fruit, nuts etc. Clean fruit by rubbing it in a little flour in a bowl-strainer.

(7) Once liquid is added to cake mixtures they should be baked as soon as possible.

TO WEIGH SYRUP. (1) Flour scale-pan before pouring on syrup, or (2) Weigh a cup or basin, then add weights to total of cup + syrup required and pour in syrup.

Baking Cakes

Depending a little on size, the pastry rule is reversed for cakes: the richer the cake the lower the oven. (Some cooks steam large fruit cakes.)

When baking more than one trayful of buns or two sandwich cakes: reverse them on the shelves, once risen and colouring; turn trays or tins round if one side is more coloured; lift out individual buns cooked before the rest.

Once risen and well browned prevent cake top overcooking by: putting lower down in oven, lowering heat, or covering top lightly with damped greaseproof, (cut so as not to overhang gas flame), or butter-paper.

A cake is done when: risen and brown, it also has shrunk from sides a little, springs up again when very lightly pressed with fingertips (not prodded with one sharp finger), and has stopped 'singing'. The last is often difficult. If all other conditions are met but this one, close oven, turn off heat and leave cake to cool in residual heat which will be enough to finish the cooking.

Those who 'cannot resist' opening the oven, must expect failed cakes or bread. Open the oven door only: 8 minutes after putting in most small cakes, rolls or buns; 20 minutes after putting in Victoria sandwich; 30 minutes after putting in fruit cakes or loaves; just far enough to see. Raise the heat slightly while door is open any longer than for a quick look; don't forget to lower heat again. Open and close the door slowly and gently – draughts are enemies to baking.

Steaming Cakes

Rich fruit cakes may be successfully steamed like puddings, provided that they are well covered down, and that the coverings are removed at once when the cake is taken out, so that the top will 'dry out'. Some cooks believe in finishing off the cake for about the last half hour in a very low oven. A 7 to 9 inch cake will take from 3 to 4 hours according to ingredients. The steady heat often results in more even rising and a good flat top for icing. Rubbed-in mixtures will often steam, but Victoria sponge types will be on the heavy side. Use self-raising flour. The method is well worth knowing for use in difficult conditions.

Some Faults in Cake Making

Too much liquid (including eggs) causes cakes to be hard outside, sad (and collapsed) in the middle; fruit to sink.

Too much raising agent (including egg white stiffly whisked), too much beating by electric mixer, especially of flour, too hot an oven causes cakes: a) to rise too high at first and thus collapse finally; b) to rise and expand leaving a hole in the centre or just below top; c) to rise too much and so go dry.

Too little raising agent, too little beating or too cool an oven causes cakes to be damp, heavy and pallid.

Too much beating in of flour can make texture too close.

Wrong shelf positions are the same as wrong oven temperatures.

Sugary mixtures or long baking times are a cause of burnt crusts to cakes. It is worth taking the trouble to band the outsides of tins with thick brown paper.

Lining Tins

Fully-lined means sides and bottom lined with greaseproof paper which is then brushed over thinly with lard or oil. 'Bakewell' (siliconed) paper does not need greasing, may be wiped clean and re-used several times. Siliconed or P.F.T.E.-d tins need not be greased or lined, but I advise very light larding and bottom-lining the first time of use at least.

Bottom-lined means sides greased direct on to metal, bottom covered with greased greaseproof.

Greased or oiled means metal lightly brushed over.

Well greased or oiled means metal thickly brushed over.

For some cakes add a dusting of flour and castor sugar.

ROUND TIN LINING

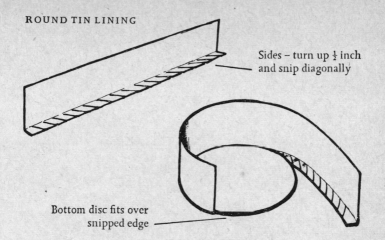

Sides – turn up ½ inch and snip diagonally

Bottom disc fits over snipped edge

SQUARE OR OBLONG TIN LINING

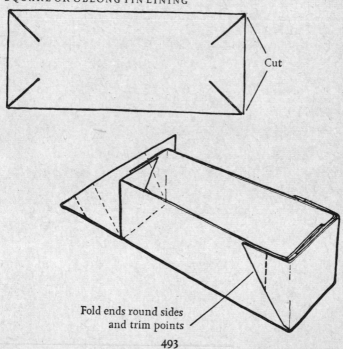

Cut

Fold ends round sides and trim points

A CAKE-MAKING READY RECKONER

Mixture, basic ingredients and preparation	Size and preparation of tin or number of small cakes	Oven heat, time for baking, shelf position	Changes in basic ingredients or method	Finishing, icing quantities
RUBBED-IN MIXTURE				
½ lb. plain flour; 2 level tsp. baking powder; pinch salt; 4 fluid oz. milk; 1 large egg; 3–4 oz. each margarine and sugar.	LARGE CAKE 6–7 inch round tin 8 by 4 inch loaf tin lightly greased with greased paper in bottom of tin.	375° F, gas, centre for 15 minutes 350° F, gas 4, for 1 hour		
Sieve dry ingredients, except sugar, into mixing bowl. Rub fat into flour till crumb-like. Add sugar and any fruit, etc. Add milk, mix in, add well-beaten egg and mix well. Mixture should fall from spoon only if shaken hard. Bake.	SMALL CAKES About 16 buns	400° F, gas 6, 15 to 20 minutes; centre or just above		

LARGE CAKES

Farmhouse	7 by 7 inch square tin prepared as basic recipe	375° F, gas 5, centre; 1 hour	Use only 1 tsp. baking powder plus 1 level tsp. bicarbonate of soda, 1 tsp. mixed spice; replace milk with 3 fluid oz. cold tea plus 1 tbs. black treacle stirred together; ¼ lb. dried fruit including some peel.	Dust with demerara or icing sugar. Cut in squares.
Ginger Spice	As Farmhouse	As Farmhouse	Add 1 heaped tsp. mixed spice; 2 oz. stem or crystallized ginger chopped small. Use larger quantity fat and sugar. Or 3 oz. sugar, 1 tbs. black treacle.	Dust with icing sugar or ice with ¼ lb. white glacé icing. Cut in squares.
Date and Walnut Loaf	Loaf tin, as basic recipe.	As basic recipe, 1½ hours total.	Add 2 oz. each chopped dates and walnuts.	
Plum cake	Round tin, as basic recipe.	As basic recipe, 1¼ to 1½ hours total.	Add 3–4 oz. sultanas, raisins or currants.	

Mixture, basic ingredients and preparation	Size and preparation of tin or number of small cakes	Oven heat, time for baking, shelf position	Changes in basic ingredients or method	Finishing, icing quantities
RUBBED-IN MIXTURE (*continued*)				
SMALL CAKES Rock buns	12 to 14. Mixture is spooned into rough heaps on greased baking sheet.	400° F, gas 6; centre; 15 to 20 minutes.	Add pinch spice sieved with flour; 3 oz. any dried fruit; add egg first then only enough milk to make very stiff mixture.	
Coconut buns	14 to 16 in bun tray or patty tins	As Rock buns	3–4 oz. desiccated coconut added with sugar. 2–3 drops vanilla with egg.	Brush tops with apricot glazé Sprinkle with more coconut, or leave plain.
Lemon or orange cakes	As Coconut buns	As Rock buns	Grated rind of fruit added with sugar, 1 tsp. lemon juice, 2 tsp. orange juice added after egg.	Make simple icing from ¼ lb. icing sugar and juice of fruit, smooth a spoonful on each cake.

Peel cakes	As Coconut buns	As Rock buns	Add 2–3 oz. chopped candied peel with sugar. Pinch spice optional	If available top each with thin sliver of peel from peel cap.
Raspberry or Strawberry buns	As Coconut buns	As Rock buns	Use 1–2 tbs. less milk. Make small cavity in top of each cake and fill with ¼ level tsp. good raspberry or strawberry jam.	Dust with icing sugar.
SCONES ½ lb. plain flour; ¼ tsp. salt; 1 level tsp. bicarbonate of soda; 2 level tsp. cream of tartar; 1 rounded tsp. castor sugar; 2 oz. margarine; ¼ pint milk; or milk with a little water; or sour milk and reduce raising powders by half.	12 2-inch round scones; or divide dough in half and roll 2 rounds, scoring each deeply into 6 triangles. Use sharp knife.	450° F, gas 8, 10 to 20 minutes according to whether individual or large rounds; centre, or just above.	Use half wholemeal flour for brown scones. Add 2–3 oz. grated cheese for savoury, 2oz. dried fruit for tea scones. Half dry sieved potato, 1 chopped bacon rasher for supper scones.	Brush tops with milk or egg before baking.

(NOTE: Scones never rise as well when baking powder is used.) Make as pastry. Roll ¾ inches thick.

CREAMED OR EQUAL WEIGHT MIXTURE

Mixture, basic ingredients and preparations	Size and preparation of tin or number of small cakes	Oven heat, time for baking, shelf position	Changes in basic ingredients or method	Finishing, icing quantities
6–8 oz. self-raising flour; 3 eggs; 6 oz. each margarine and castor sugar	LARGE CAKE 7–8 inch round tin 8½ by 4½ inch loaf tin, fully lined.	325° F, gas 3; centre if plain, below if fruit; 1½ hours.		
Cream fat until broken down evenly (about 2 minutes). Add sugar and any grated peel in recipe, and cream until fluffy and pale. (10 minutes in warm atmosphere.) Add	SMALL CAKES About 20 small cakes in bun trays, paper cases, fancy patty tins and heart-shaped queen-cake tins.	375° F, gas 5; centre or above, 20 to 25 minutes		

beaten eggs by degrees beating well. If mixture begins to curdle add flour and rest of egg alternately. Otherwise fold in flour at end, ⅓ at a time with any fruit added to second ⅓ flour, any extra liquid with final ⅓. Spices etc. to be sieved with flour as usual. The 8 oz. quantity of flour gives a slightly less rich and larger cake, which may take about 15 minutes extra to cook through. Make a hollow in centre of large cakes when in tins.

498

Variations
LARGE CAKE

Madeira	As above, round tin	As above	Add grated rind of 1 lemon. Hollow centre when in tin. When this has filled after about 45 minutes baking, place 2 thin slivers of citron cap to form circle on top. Raise heat while doing this *out of all draught.*	
Cherry	As Madeira	As Madeira	Add 3–4 oz. glacé cherries cut in half, floured with part of recipe flour.	
Chocolate	As Madeira, but clip double brown paper round outside of tin. or Divide between two 7-inch sandwich tins greased bottom-lined	As Madeira, but allow for up to 15 minutes extra baking or in sandwich tins, 375° F, gas 5; centre or just above; 20 to 25 minutes	Use 6 oz. self-raising flour, 2 oz. cocoa, 1 level tsp. coffee powder sieved together. Add 2 tbs. milk. Reserve 1 egg white and add, whipped to snow, after final 1/3 flour is folded in.	Split in half and fill with 2 oz. quantity chocolate buttercream. Pipe rosettes from further 2 oz. or ice top with 1/4 lb. chocolate glacé icing. Decorate with coffee bean sweets, or walnut halves. Or cover top with lace paper mat and dust pattern with icing sugar

Mixture, basic ingredients and preparations	Size and preparation of tin or number of small cakes	Oven heat, time for baking, shelf position	Changes in basic ingredients or method	Finishing, icing quantities
CREAMED MIXTURE (continued)				
Coffee	As Chocolate	As Chocolate	Add 3 level tsp. coffee powder. Melt in 1 dessertsp. milk if liked, to avoid speckles.	As for chocolate, but with coffee flavouring. Icing-sugar decoration less suitable.
Rich Fruit suitable for Christmas or birthday cakes.	As Madeira	350° F, gas 4, 20 minutes, then 325° F, gas 3, 1½ hours then 300° F, gas 2, until 'singing' stops, or skewer is clean; centre or just below; or move to lower position after 1¼ hours to prevent over-browning	Add ¼ lb. each raisins, currants and sultanas; 2 oz. chopped peel; 2 oz. halved cherries; 2 oz. blanched almond slivers; rind of half orange and half lemon; ½ tsp. each cinnamon and ginger; 2–3 tbs. rum, brandy or sherry.	Cover with ¾–1 lb. almond icing. Wrap and store until 1 week before needed. Coat with 1 lb. royal icing. Decorate (see p. 535), or cover top with blanched split almonds before baking for Dundee finish. (Cherries should not be used in Dundee cake.)

500

Victoria Sandwich	Divide between two 7-inch sandwich tins, greased and bottom-lined.	375° F, gas 5; centre or just above; 20 to 25 minutes.	Use only 6 oz. flour	Turn out on sugared paper. Sandwich with raspberry jam. Dust with castor sugar.
SMALL CAKES				
All above, except rich fruit, can be used for small cakes.	20 to 24	As basic instruction.	Omit extra milk to keep mixture rather firm.	Ice to match flavour with glacé icing, or top each bun with suitable fruit.
Lemon cakes	20	As basic instruction.	Madeira mixture.	¼ lb. lemon glacé icing.
Genoese cakes	12 by 8 inch oblong tin, greased and bottom lined for 12 to 16 cakes.	As Victoria Sandwich.	6 oz. flour only	Cut in various shapes, sandwich with butter-cream. Cover with various glacé icings. Decorate with violets, nuts etc.

Mixture, basic ingredients and preparations	Size and preparation of tin or number of small cakes	Oven heat, time for baking, shelf position	Changes in basic ingredients or method	Finishing, icing quantities
WHISKED OR FATLESS SPONGE MIXTURE				
2 oz. each plain flour and castor sugar; 2 eggs.	12 by 7 inch swiss roll tin fully lined, greased and dusted with castor sugar. 2 6-inch sandwich tins lined, greased, sugared. 8-inch round cake-tin greased, bottom-lined greased and sugared.			
Into a saucepan on which mixing bowl stands comfortably put enough water just to avoid touching bottom of bowl. Bring water to boil. Meanwhile away from heat, mix sugar and eggs lightly. Remove pan from heat, stand bowl on it and whisk egg mixture until light in colour and thick enough to 'write initial' before lines vanish. Remove from heat and continue whisking to cool slightly. Fold in flour thoroughly. Turn into prepared tin.				

502

Variations

Swiss Roll	Swiss roll tin as above, omit sugar	425° F, gas 7; above centre; 7 to 8 minutes.	Add 1 tsp. glycerine, spread evenly into corners. 2 tbs. jam for filling.	Turn on sugared paper. Trim hard edges to regular oblong, cut narrow groove 1 inch from one short side. Spread with warmed jam, turn over groove and roll up with help of paper. Stand on 'raw edge' on cooling rack. Work quickly.
Chocolate Swiss Roll	As above	As above	Add 1 tsp. glycerine. Replace 1 level tsp. flour with cocoa. 2 oz. butter cream filling.	As above, but spread with plain or chocolate butter-cream.
Sponge Sandwich	2 6-inch sandwich tins or 1 8-inch cake tin as basic instructions	350° F, gas 4; centre; 20 minutes or 30 to 35 minutes for 8-inch tin.	Divide into two for sandwich tins, spread evenly. Flatten well in single tin, but do not hollow. 2 tbs. jam for filling.	Turn out on sugared paper on cooling rack. Spread with jam when cool. Dust with castor or icing sugar.

Mixture, basic ingredients and preparations	Size and preparation of tin or number of small cakes	Oven heat, time for baking, shelf position	Changes in basic ingredients or method	Finishing, icing quantities
WHISKED MIXTURE (continued)				
Savoy (Sponge) Fingers	Baking sheet, lined with greased and sugared paper. Or grease and sugar sponge-finger tin. 12 fingers.	400° F, gas 7; centre or just above; 8 minutes.	Separate white and yolks. Whisk yolks till creamy. Whip whites to snow. Add sugar to whites by teaspoons, whisking in well. Fold in yolks, then flour thoroughly. Pipe through plain ½-inch meringue pipe in 4-inch lengths on to paper. Dredge with castor sugar to prevent spreading.	Invert paper on to second, sugared sheet and cover with damp cloth to steam off paper from fingers. Peel back carefully. Work quickly, but re-steam as needed. Turn out of sponge-finger tin with palette knife.

504

WARMED MIXTURES

No basic mixture. It is the method that is similar for some mixtures with a high proportion of sugary ingredients.

RICH GINGERBREAD

4 oz. each wholemeal and self-raising flour; 4 oz. margarine; ¼ lb. each golden syrup and black treacle (or all one or other or part dark honey); 2 small eggs; 3 oz. soft brown sugar; 2 level tsp. each ground ginger and mixed spice; ¼ tsp. bicarbonate soda; ¼ tsp. cayenne pepper; 1 tsp. Worcester sauce; scant ¼ pint milk.

8-inch square tin, fully lined and greased.

325° F, gas 3; centre 1½ hours.

2 oz. chopped stem or crystallized ginger and 1 oz. almond slivers may be added for variety, but these may detract from the lightness of the texture.

Halved blanched almonds may be added on top half-way through cooking so that, when cut into squares, each square has an almond in the centre.

Warm fat, sugar, syrup gently until sugar dissolves. Do not overheat. Cool. Sift self-raising flour with spices and bicarbonate of soda. Stir wholemeal flour into dry ingredients. Beat eggs and milk together, pour into dry ingredients. Lastly pour in syrup mixture. Beat batter smooth. Bake.

Mixture, basic ingredients and preparations	Size and preparation of tin or number of small cakes	Oven heat, time for baking, shelf position	Changes in basic ingredients or method	Finishing, icing quantities
WARMED MIXTURES (continued)				
BRANDY SNAPS (Jumbles)				
2 oz. each of: golden syrup, margarine, soft brown sugar, plain flour; ½ tsp. grated lemon rind; 1 tsp. juice; ½ tsp. ground ginger; 1 dessertsp. brandy or rum.	1–2 baking sheets (or use clean back of meat tin – adjust shelf position if necessary to allow for depth). Oil lightly or well grease with lard.	325° F, gas 3; centre or just below; 8 to 10 minutes.	Use honey, orange rind and juice, and cointreau or orange curacao (if available!) in place of lemon and brandy for *Tuiles*	Pipe whipped cream down each end of tube when cold.
	12 snaps.		Use honey and omit brandy, adding total of 4 oz. chopped dried fruit, peel and nuts (leave *uncurled*) for *Florentines*	Melt 2 oz. bitter chocolate. Spread undersides with this, draw fork prongs across chocolate before it sets to make pattern. Cool.

Warm fat, syrup, sugar, rind and juice gently to melt sugar. Sift flour and ginger. Pour cooled syrup mixture into flour adding brandy. Mix to stiff batter. Put out by teaspoonfuls on prepared baking sheet, leaving about 2-inch space all round each for spreading (about 4 per small baking sheet). Have ready oiled wooden spoon handle. When baked immediately 'carve off' sheet and bend round spoon handle to make tubes. Work quickly, re-heating tray in oven if biscuits harden.

(and see p. 461)

FLAPJACKS

4 oz. each porage oats and syrup; 2 oz. each margarine and soft brown sugar.

8 by 8 inch square or 8 by 9 inch oblong approx. Well greased or lightly oiled.

325° F, gas 4–5; centre or just below; 20 to 30 minutes.

While warm score deeply with sharp knife into squares or fingers.

Mix as above, oatmeal replacing flour. Mixture should be stiff. Press evenly into shallow square tin.

507

STIRRED (ALL-AT-ONCE) MIXTURE (and see p. 461)

This method depends on the fat being light and soft. Chambré in temperature of 60° F. Lard and some margarines are not suited to the job. Those that are include:

MARGARINES
Blue Band, Stork, Sainsbury's 10% butter

Mixture, basic ingredients and preparations	Size and preparation of tin or number of small cakes	Oven heat, time for baking, shelf position	Changes in basic ingredients or method	Finishing, icing quantities
STIRRED MIXTURE (*continued*)				
WHITE SHORTENINGS				
Sainsbury's Shorteen Spry Trex (In this order of preference.)				
Less water is needed in pastry. Baking powder is necessary even where self-raising flour is used. Oven temperatures for cakes are somewhat lower than for comparable mixtures made by traditional methods.				

508

VICTORIA SPONGE

6 oz. each fat, sugar and flour (to self-raising flour add 1½ level tsp. baking powder; to plain flour add 3½ level tsp.).

3 standard eggs

Sift flour and baking-powder, put with rest of ingredients (eggs unbeaten) in mixing bowl. Stir and beat 1 minute with wooden spoon. Turn into prepared tins and bake.

Two 7-inch sandwich tins greased bottom-lined. Or one 8-inch cake tin. Lightly greased bun trays or patty pans, or in paper cases. About 18 to 20.

325° F, gas 3; centre or just below; 25 to 35 minutes. As above for 35 to 45 minutes. 400° F, gas 6; centre or just above; 15 to 20 minutes.

Chocolate: add 2 heaped tbs. cocoa blended with 2 tbs. hot water. Cool. Lemon or orange rind of whole fruit, 1 to 2 tbs. juice.

Finish as for cream-ing method sandwich cakes.

509

Mixture, basic ingredients and preparations	Size and preparation of tin or number of small cakes	Oven heat, time for baking, shelf position	Changes in basic ingredients or method	Finishing, icing quantities
FRUIT CAKE				
Fat, sugar, flour and eggs as for Victoria. (To self-raising flour add 1 level tsp. baking-powder; to plain flour 2 level tsp.). Up to 8 oz. mixed dried fruits, nuts, peel, glacé cherries to choice. 1 level tsp. each ginger and mixed spice. Grated rind of 1 orange or lemon. 2 tbs. rum or sherry if available.	One 8-inch cake tin fully lined	325° F, gas 3; centre or below; about 2 hours.	Stir and beat 2–3 minutes.	Cool in tin 15 minutes. Finish as for creaming method fruit cakes.

510

TEA LOAF

4 oz. fat; 8 oz. flour (1 level tsp. baking powder for self-raising, 2 for plain); 1 tbs. treacle, syrup or honey; 2 oz. each walnuts and sultanas; grated rind 1 orange, 1 tbs. juice; 1 large egg.

8 by 4 inch loaf tin fully lined.

350° F, gas 4; centre; about 1½ hours.

Stir and beat 2 to 3 minutes.

Dust with icing sugar. (Should be eaten fairly quickly as tea loaves tend to go dry.)

SHORT PASTRY

4 oz. fat; 8 oz. plain flour; ½ tsp. salt; 3 tbs. cold water.

Use as required. Will line two 7-inch flan rings, rolled ⅛-inch thick.

As for shortcrust.

Stir with fork ½ minute.

SCONES

2 oz. fat; 8 oz. self-raising flour; 1 rounded tsp. cream of tartar. 1 level tsp. bicarbonate of soda; pinch salt; ½ oz. sugar; ¼ pt. milk (scant), less 1 tbs. for glazing.

Baking sheet. 12 scones (2-inch cutter)

425° F, gas 7; above centre; 12 to 15 minutes.

Stir with wooden spoon to form scone dough. Knead gently. Roll out good ½ inch thick. Cut as traditional scones.

Brush tops with milk to glaze.

CHRISTMAS OR CELEBRATION CAKE GUIDE TO TIN SIZE AND RECIPE QUANTITIES

Note that less rich mixtures would need about the same size tins, but baking time would probably be a little shorter.

Ingredients	Tin Size						
	Round tin: 6 inch Square tin: 5 inch	7 inch 6 inch	8 inch 7 inch	9 inch 8 inch	10 inch 9 inch	11 inch 10 inch	12 inch 11 inch
BASIC RICH CAKE MIXTURE							
butter/margarine	4 oz.	6 oz.	8 oz.	10 oz.	12 oz.	14 oz.	1 lb.
soft brown sugar	4 oz.	6 oz.	8 oz.	10 oz.	12 oz.	14 oz.	1 lb.
eggs	2	3	4	5	6	7	8
plain flour	5 oz.	7 oz.	9 oz.	11 oz.	13 oz.	15 oz.	1 lb. 1 oz.
salt	pinch	pinch	¼ level tsp.	¼ level tsp.	½ level tsp.	½ level tsp.	¾ level tsp.
black treacle	½ tbs.	1 tbs.	1½ tbs.	2 tbs.	2½ tbs.	3 tbs.	3½ tbs.
mixed dried fruit	1 lb.	1½ lb.	2 lb.	2½ lb.	3 lb.	3½ lb.	4 lb.
glacé, pineapple, cherries (all optional)	2 oz.	3 oz.	4 oz.	5 oz.	6 oz.	7 oz.	8 oz.
chopped almonds	½ oz.	1 oz.	2 oz.	3 oz.	4 oz.	5 oz.	6 oz.
mixed spice	½ level tsp.	½ level tsp.	1 level tsp.	1½ level tsp.	2 level tsp.	2½ level tsp.	3 level tsp.
vanilla essence	few drops	few drops	½ tsp.	½ tsp.	½ tsp.	1 tsp.	1 tsp.
brandy or rum	2 tbs.	2 tbs.	2 tbs.	3 tbs.	3 tbs.	4 tbs.	4 tbs.
Baking time (at 300° F, gas 2, centre oven)	3 hours	3½ hours	4 hours	4½ hours	4½ hours	5 hours	5 hours

512

Ingredients	Tin Size						
	Round tin: 6 inch Square tin: 5 inch	7 inch 6 inch	8 inch 7 inch	9 inch 8 inch	10 inch 9 inch	11 inch 10 inch	12 inch 11 inch

ALMOND PASTE – SUFFICIENT FOR TOP AND SIDES

ground almonds	8 oz.	10 oz.	12 oz.	12 oz.	14 oz.	14 oz.	1 lb.
castor sugar	4 oz.	5 oz.	6 oz.	6 oz.	7 oz.	7 oz.	8 oz.
icing sugar	4 oz.	5 oz.	6 oz.	6 oz.	7 oz.	7 oz.	8 oz.
almond essence	few drops	few drops	¼ tsp.	¼ tsp.	½ tsp.	½ tsp.	¾ tsp.
egg yolks	2	3	4	4	5	5	6
lemon juice	1 tbs.	2 tbs.	3 tbs.	3 tbs.	4 tbs.	4 tbs.	5 tbs.

ROYAL ICING

icing sugar	1 lb.	1 lb.	1½ lb.	1½ lb.	2 lb.	2 lb.	2½ lb.
egg whites	2	2	3	3	4	4	5
lemon juice (for piping and hard finish)	½ tsp.	½ tsp.	1 tsp.	1 tsp.	1½ tsp.	1½ tsp.	2 tsp.
glycerine (for forked-oven finish, no piping)	1 tsp.	1 tsp.	1½ tsp.	1½ tsp.	2 tsp.	2 tsp.	2½ tsp.

Atypical Cakes

All these three are what may be called dessert cakes: for formal eating, not schoolchildren's teas, for which they are far too dear. But children will appreciate them for a treat in place of a pudding.

STUFFED MONKEY

(Some claim originally Dutch, others originally South African. The name suggests the latter, the petit-four-like result suggests something European.)

PASTRY. You will need only about half this quantity for the monkey, but it is a very popular pastry once tried, and very adaptable, so you may like to wrap the other half in waxed paper, foil or polythene to use for a shallow plate pie, or biscuits. Will keep 2 to 3 days in cold weather in larder; 1 week to 10 days in main refrigerator; 10 days to 3 weeks in 2 and 3 star freezers.

8 oz. plain flour	6 oz. margarine/butter
1 egg	6 oz. demerara sugar
½ tsp. cinnamon	

FILLING.

1½ oz. ground almonds	½ egg
1 oz. butter/margarine	1 drop (!) vanilla
1½ oz. candied peel	1 tsp. sugar

Peel may be any sort, though real citron makes a Rolls-Royce version. After Christmas use up ends of mincemeat, ginger and dates, but peel must dominate.

Make pastry as for pâte sucrée or Lintzer Torte (p. 359). Using about half the given quantity, cut off two thirds of this to line a flan ring (⅛ inch thick maximum); roll out remaining one third for lid.. Mix all filling ingredients thoroughly, press lightly into case, cover with lid, pinching edges to seal. Bake at

375° F, gas 5, for 30 minutes. Carefully remove flan-ring and return to residual heat to harden sides.

Serve cut in *small* wedges – it is very rich – hot with cream; cold with morning or after-dinner coffee. When used in the latter way you may omit the pudding course at a dinner-party.

A GERMAN CHEESECAKE

3 eggs
¾–1 lb. curd cheese (but not
   the sort called Philadelphia)
1½ tbs. raisins
1 oz. blanched slivered
   almonds

3 oz. butter
4–5 oz. castor sugar
1 level tbs. cornflour
large pinch salt
grated rind of 1 lemon

Beat butter with rind and sugar until like clotted cream. Separate the eggs. Add yolks one at a time, beating very well, then curd, cornflour, almonds, raisins and salt, mixing by folding and 'cutting' with palette knife, metal spoon or rubber spatula. Lastly add whites whipped to snow (so bowl can be inverted without white moving). Use Yorkshire pudding tin about 12 by 8 inches. Too wide a tin cooks edges, leaving centre half-raw. Fully line tin. Bake at 375° F, gas 5, centre shelf or just below, for 20 minutes. Lower heat to 350° F, gas 4, for 10 minutes, then to 325° F, gas 3, for 15 minutes, then to 300° F, gas 2 until done. (About 1¼ hours in all.) When done cake will be springy, brown and shrunk from sides of tin. When cold cut in fingers 1½ by 3 inches.

May be made by stirred method (see p. 507) except for egg whites which should be added as above. If using Spry/Shorteen you may omit cornflour as these fats have no water in them, so mixture will be slightly drier.

Cheese cakes should be eaten in 2 or 3 days.

CARIBBEAN CAKE

.(Adapted from cake in Kenwood Chefette booklet. Excellent.)

4 oz. each margarine and
castor sugar
5 oz. self-raising flour or plain
flour mixed with 1 level
tsp. bicarbonate of soda
2 eggs
2 oz. each chopped bitter
chocolate and walnuts
('polka dots' may be used,
though flavour less good)
2 tbs. orange juice
grated rind of whole orange
(brush out grater to get all
of it)

BY TRADITIONAL CREAMING METHOD. Cream fat, sugar and rind. Add eggs by degrees. Fold in sifted flour, chocolate, walnuts and juice.

In loaf tin : bake 45 to 55 minutes, middle shelf, 350° F, gas 4. In 2 sandwich tins : bake at 375° F, gas 5 for about 25 minutes.

BY ELECTRIC BLENDER/MIXER. Pare rind very thinly from orange, spin in blender at full speed 1 minute. Add nuts, and chocolate broken in small pieces. Spin few seconds at full speed. Inspect. These ingredients should not be spun to powder. Quite a lot of coarse little lumps should remain. Change to mixer and cream fat and sugar starting at medium speed, then increasing to full speed (approx. 3 minutes). Add eggs one at a time, beating on full speed 30 seconds per egg. Fold in sifted flour by hand, with nuts, chocolate and juice. Bake as above.

RATAFIAS

(True ratafias now hard to find. Recipe given for that reason.)

2 oz. sweet or ground
almonds
3 oz. castor sugar
1 egg white
1 oz. bitter almonds
Baking sheet lined Bakewell
paper

Blanch and pound almonds then mix both sorts with egg white, slightly beaten. Beat well to a stiffish, sticky paste. Use $\frac{3}{16}$ inch vegetable pipe, and pipe fat blobs about the size of a sixpence, leaving space for spreading. Bake at 375° F, gas 5–6, centre, 10 to 12 minutes. About 30 biscuits. Store in polythene.

NOTE: Macaroons are not the same. Try ratafias with mousses, in trifle.

Bread and Yeast Cakes

I like to bake because ... to do so gives me a feeling of unity with women of other lands and other times.... This, ... is something basic – after the bearing of children perhaps the fundamental female activity.... Yeast ... the fragrant, creamy clay that works its secret magic in the warm bowl ... raising the spongy mass ... inexorably as the rising tide or the waxing moon.... Kneading ... – a hypnotic ritual ... wherein the celebrant ... retains ... the constant satisfying awareness of muscles at work, and the living dough, like potter's clay, beneath the fingers.... it is a noble pursuit, enhancing the corporate dignity of womankind.

From an anonymous (perhaps mercifully?) newspaper article of about a decade ago. Contrast it with the following:

... I made bread regularly – over sixty years ago – and I still remember the backache – and the leathery crusts we had to eat from about Tuesday to the next baking-day.... From the time I was ten, I had to make the bread every time I was at home on a Friday.... I was tall for my age but I couldn't cope with bread-making on the table so a large bread-pan was set on the floor. Into this I put one stone of flour.... When all was ready I ... got down on my knees by the bread-pan.... It was the kneading that decided the texture of the bread.... My hands became a sticky mess.... My back was breaking by the time I turned the whole lot over – all twenty odd pounds of it.... It was a long job.... During the waiting periods ... sometimes I kept back part of the dough ... and made teacakes I liked doing that. It was easy. When the loaves were actually crisping the smell was delicious but you can't live on a smell. Nor can you tear the crust off every loaf to enjoy them while they're crisp. By Sunday they no longer crackled: by Monday they were flabby: by Tuesday they were downright leathery. From then till Friday we ate toast more often than not.... I wouldn't resort to Grandma's way of making bread for all the crusts in Christendom.

Eunice Spencer, Woman's Hour talk, 1966.

To be able to make bread is the same useful sort of accomplishment in the modern world as being able to mend a fuse or change a tyre. There are also women who make their own bread most of the time because they dislike the local bakers' bread. The scent of bread baking is certainly delicious as is the taste and texture of bread straight from the oven. Bread is simple to make and does not need your physical presence for long, but time is essential for the rising. If you want to make bread regularly the secret is to slot the time needed into the pattern of your working day

Bread is usually made in a warm, moist, draught-free atmosphere so the yeast will grow quickly. Exception: If dough is wanted for baking first thing in the morning, put in refrigerator overnight. Kneading spreads the yeast and, at the second kneading, air evenly through the dough. Quite good bread can be made without two kneadings, but is likely to be of less even texture as a result. Baking takes place at a very high temperature to kill the yeast, and so stop the bread rising more than is required, and to make it light and crisp It is nowadays said that creaming yeast with sugar and so on is not necessary to start it into growth, but the sugar adds to the flavour of bread and this is as convenient a way of adding it to the dough as any other. An excellent, full account of the background to bread-making will be found in *Better Cookery* by Aileen King (Mills & Boon), as well as good recipes and information on all the finer points.

Strong flour is seldom found in the grocer's. Buy it from a baker along with the yeast. Dried yeast from chemists does a good job, and should be in airtight storage in the refrigerator for emergencies, but fresh yeast just has the edge on it.

Some Faults in Bread Making

Yeast is killed at a temperature of 140° F. Too great heat during proving will kill the yeast and prevent the dough rising, so bread will be heavy.

Stale yeast, dry mixture or cold atmosphere retard the rising of dough.

Over-proving of dough causes bread to collapse when baked.

Too cool an oven causes holes, heaviness and a thick crust.

Too much yeast gives bread a bitter taste – and does not speed the process.

STANDARD WHITE BREAD

(two small or one large loaf)

1½ lb. strong or bread flour	¾ pint mixed milk and water
1 oz. yeast	1 oz. lard (or good cleared
2 level tsp. salt	beef dripping) *to grease bowl*
1 level tsp. sugar	

Although all must be warm, bowls etc. should not be made hot.

Work in this order :

(1) Boil ¼ pint of the liquid and pour into rest. This gives correct warmth.

(2) Sieve flour and salt into warm mixing bowl, cover with warm cloth.

(3) Cream sugar and yeast, add to liquid, pour into well made in sieved flour. Sprinkle surface with some flour from sides of well. Cover and leave in warm until surface breaks showing bubbles (about 12 to 15 minutes). This is called 'sponging'.

(4) Mix with wooden spoon or one hand to form soft dough. Resist all urges to use both hands.

(5) With sticky hand pull outer diameter of dough down into centre of bowl, turning bowl with clean hand. This makes the hand and arm ache very much until one is in practice. When you begin, take your time and don't think you have to thump the dough or work fast. Gradually the dough draws together, grows elastic and smooth, and comes away from fingers and sides of bowl. Cover bowl with warm damp cloth or polythene and set aside ½ to ¾ hour, in a warm atmosphere : airing cupboard; sunny greenhouse, porch or window (but for these three see top of bowl is shaded from direct sun); on rack over cooker but not over intense heat – a pan of barely simmering water below the rack is enough. If preferred, leave 1 to 2 hours in colder atmosphere. Inspect from time to time, but keep from currents of air or patchy heat, which would cause dough to rise unevenly. Meanwhile lightly grease tins.

(6) When doubled in size, and spongy and airy to the touch,

turn, with floured fingers, on to floured board, knead lightly and fill into greased loaf tin(s). This kneading should be done with the knuckles, but still pulling outer edges of dough to centre. Fold the slab(s) of dough into three and put the raw edge to the bottom of the tin(s) as diagram. Press well into corners of tin. Slash top of loaf if liked.

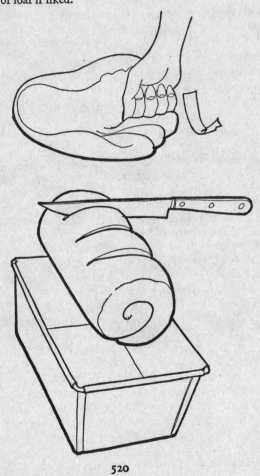

(7) Again put in warm place to rise to top of tin. Cover. Before baking, brush, if liked, with egg and salt to glaze.

(8) Bake at 450° F, gas 8, 45 to 60 minutes. For all-round crisp crust, turn out of tin after 35 minutes, and finish upside-down on baking sheet, or clean bars of shelf.

(9) When ready, the loaf sounds hollow when knocked lightly with knuckles.

(10) Cool on rack for crisp bread; wrap in cloth for soft crust.

NOTE: 12 oz. flour makes 1 lb. loaf. Allow ½ oz. yeast for up to 1 lb. flour, 1 oz. up to 3 lb., 2 oz. up to 7 lb. Allow ½ pint water, 1 good tsp. salt per lb. flour.

BROWN BREAD

Use ½ strong white, ½ wholemeal flour, otherwise make as white bread.

WHOLEMEAL BREAD

Use all wholemeal flour. Omit second rising.

QUICK WHITE BREAD

As the standard recipe, but omit sponging and second rising.

MADAME RIGOT'S BRIOCHE EXPRESS PARISIENNE

8 oz. strong flour
3 eggs
1½ oz. sugar
½ oz. yeast

5 oz. butter softened but
not oiled
large pinch salt

Dissolve sugar, yeast, salt in 2 to 3 tbs. warm water. Add well-beaten eggs, butter, flour, and beat with wooden spoon or hand at least ¼ hour. Turn into well-greased tube-tin and leave to rise (about 1½ hours) until just below top of tin. Bake at 325° F, gas 3, for 20 minutes. Turn out to cool on cake-rack. This quantity fills an 8-inch angel-cake tin. Half-quantity for smaller households.

NOTE: The mixture becomes very light indeed and rises very much. It is as well therefore, to begin with, to use a larger tin than you might expect necessary. Tube tins are best for such light mixtures as they ensure that the centre of the cake cooks through. Remember to grease the tube itself; also to loosen round it before turning out the cake.

DINNER ROLL OR BUN MIXTURE

8 oz. strong flour
½ level tsp. each salt and
    sugar; *for buns* add
    up to 1 oz. sugar

½ oz. yeast
1 oz. margarine
¼ pint milk (scant)
1 small egg (½ large)

Make as white bread dividing dough into 8 to 12 even pieces after first rising. Roll each quite round on board with flat of hand. Prove on baking sheet 15 minutes, until doubled in size. Bake at 450° F, gas 8, 15 minutes. Glaze with beaten egg slightly diluted with water and return to oven 1 minute in residual heat.

CURRANT BUNS

(Makes 8 buns.)

As above, adding 1 oz. currants etc., glaze with hot stock syrup (2 oz. sugar to ¼ pint water). Add 1 oz. extra margarine for richer mixture.

CHELSEA BUNS

As for currant buns, plus 1 oz. extra margarine; 2 oz. dried fruit; ½ oz. peel; 1 oz. brown sugar; 1 oz. melted margarine; ½ tsp. mixed spice. After first rising, knead lightly, roll into rectangle ½ inch thick. Mix fruits, sugar and spice. Soften margarine to cream and spread lightly over dough except for 1-inch margin on one long side. Sprinkle fruit mixture on top not too close to edges. Damp the long side and roll firmly towards it pressing well to keep roll together. Cut into ½-inch slices (8 to 10), set close together in greased square tin, slightly opening out cut edges where stuck. Put to prove until doubled in bulk. Bake at 450° F, gas 8, 10 to 15 minutes. Dredge thickly with castor sugar before separating the buns.

SAVARIN AUX FRUITS

A luxury dish, but too good to omit, because of course far cheaper and better than 'bought'.

CAKE.

4 oz. strong flour	2 oz. butter
¼ oz. yeast	2 eggs
¼ oz. castor sugar	7½ tbs. milk

FILLING:

about 2 heaped tbs. chopped fruit (raspberries, strawberries, peaches, pineapple, fresh or well-drained canned)	¼ pint double cream

SYRUP.

4 oz. granulated sugar	rind and juice of ½ lemon
¼ pint water	2–3 tbs. rum, brandy, sherry (in that order of preference)

Apricot glaze, nuts, fruit, to decorate.

Sieve flour into warmed bowl. Cream yeast with sugar. Gently warm milk to blood heat. Beat eggs well and add to the first the yeast, then the warm milk. Mix and pour into flour. Beat with the hand 5 minutes at least until batter thickens and tends to leave the fingers. Gently warm the butter by putting it in a basin or small pan in water only just above hand-heat, so that it softens to a pouring consistency, but remains opaque and creamy, not clear and oily. Tip it on top of batter, tilting bowl so that it forms a film over the batter. Cover bowl and put in warm to rise – about 40 minutes. Meanwhile butter an 8-inch savarin ring, and put on oven at 450° F, gas 8, shelf in centre. Make syrup (see below). When batter is doubled in bulk beat in the film of butter with the hand, and turn into mould. Leave again covered in warm place until batter reaches top of mould. *Do not overprove.* Bake 25 to 30 minutes until light, crisp and golden brown on top.

SYRUP. Dissolve sugar in water completely without boiling. Add rest of ingredients. Keep warm.

Turn savarin on to cake rack. From now on it remains upside down. Prick all round with skewer and, while still warm, stand rack over large bowl and ladle hot syrup all over it. Then stand the cake in the remaining syrup until shortly before it is to be eaten, so that it is thoroughly soaked in the syrup.

FILLING. Whip the cream until it just holds its shape. Fold in the fruit, chopped small except for about a dozen berries or pieces for decorating. Brush cake over with warm apricot glaze (p. 526) and fill centre with cream mixture, piling up 'Turkish hat' fashion. Decorate with fruit, nuts, angelica as liked. Spike sides of cake with slivers of toasted almond.

The same amount of mixture, syrup and cream will make 8 individual savarins, or babas. For classic babas add 2 oz. currants and bake in dariole moulds. Proving for either: 10–15 minutes; baking: 20 minutes at 400° F, gas 6.

Icing

Good icing needs:
  Orderly working and preparation
  Correct ingredients
  A few basic tools
  Modest aims to start with
  Practice

Preparation

Clear the decks. Set out the equipment and the cake itself so that you can reach everything without having to put down the cake, should you have it on one hand (q.v.).

The equipment must include something on which to stand the cake. This will be a 'turn-table' on cake-rack if you are coating with a runny icing; a turn-table alone if with royal icing, and for piping. There are proper turn-tables of several kinds and prices, or use an inverted cake tin. This will need to be smaller than the cake if you need to catch and re-use surplus soft icing, and for this purpose you will also need a plate under the rack to catch the surplus. You will need a palette knife, preferably of non-stain metal. There must be room to put down the icing itself in its bowl or pan; and for plates or saucers holding icing tubes and prepared decorations. You will need a damp cloth.

Ingredients

Apart from the ingredients for making the icings themselves, you may need jam glaze, extra sieved icing sugar and stock syrup. If using such decorative finishings as chocolate vermicelli, toasted chopped nuts, angelica peel, glacé cherries and edible colouring, have them absolutely ready to use, and set out so that you can pick them up easily. Icing at best is a sticky business, but a well set-out table makes for the speed which produces the best results.

In making up icings follow the recipes and methods faithfully. For instance, the extra trouble of jam-glazing before glacé icing helps make the icing flow evenly and rapidly and prevents crumbs pulling away and mingling into the surplus icing as it runs off, making it unpleasant for re-use. The difference in the two sorts of royal icing may seem trifling, and certainly you can pipe with the softer version, but the decorations are likely to collapse or crack after a short time, so that the time spent on them will have been wasted.

NOTE: Icings needing a sugar thermometer, or that are difficult to make are not included.

Icing Recipes

JAM GLAZES

The most usual and useful is apricot marmalade. The flavour seems to heighten the flavour of the food on which it is used, and the colour blends with most others. Red glaze, however, is necessary when using red fruits. Jam glaze is used as part of many cake-making operations, as well as being a finish in its own right.

Very roughly the proportions are:

Thin glaze – ¼ quantity *by bulk* water to 1 quantity jam.
Standard glaze – ⅛ quantity *by bulk* water to 1 quantity jam.

Thin glaze should be made only in small amounts as it will not keep. Standard glaze is like a rather thin jam and should keep well for some weeks if covered well and stored in the cool.

Glaze is almost always used warm. An ordinary small painter's brush is the best applicator.

STANDARD APRICOT MARMALADE

½ lb. apricot jam; 5 dessertsp. boiling water.

Press the jam through a bowl-strainer into a small saucepan. Spoon the boiling water through the sieve to help clear it, and blend thoroughly over very low heat. Allow just to come to boil. Pot and use as required.

STANDARD RED JAM GLAZE

Either sieve raspberry jam, or whisk redcurrant jelly. Add water and proceed as for apricot.

USES. As under- or crumb-coating beneath soft and almond icings. As 'adhesive' for finishes such as coconut and chopped nuts. As finish for small buns and flans. To flavour sweet dishes and cakes.

HEAVY STOCK SYRUP	LIGHT STOCK SYRUP
½ lb. sugar	½ lb. sugar
8 fl. oz. water	¾ pint water

Melt the sugar in the water without allowing to boil until bottom of pan is free of crystals. Bring to boil and allow to bubble steadily but not turbulently for 2 minutes. Cool and store in clean, dry bottle well corked, in cold place.

NOTE ON OTHER USES: This amount will last well in the average family and may be used for other purposes such as poaching fruits. Both syrups may be tinted, flavoured and thinned somewhat if needed.

Quantities given for the sugar icings that follow are for 7 to 8 inch round cakes, 7 inch square cakes, to avoid waste. Very small quantities of left-over icing are best added to the sweetening for puddings.

SIMPLE BUTTER CREAM

To fill one layer only:

1 oz. margarine or butter *at room temperature*
2 oz. sieved icing sugar
1 tbs. juice/liqueur/strong coffee (for chocolate blend 1 dessertsp. cocoa with 1–2 dessertsp. hot water)

To fill and flat-ice top: Double above
To fill, ice over completely and pipe simple decoration: 4 times above

Beat all ingredients to consistency of whipped cream and use as required.

For piping butter-cream leave it about one hour after mixing in a cool but not chilled atmosphere. If using a piping bag, cool the hands if necessary by running cold water over wrists; and pipe away from heat. In a very hot atmosphere the fat may oil when piping would be hopeless.

NOTE: Some palates prefer a 'gritty' textured butter cream, so use half castor sugar. Granulated sugar spoils both appearance and texture and flavours do not blend satisfactorily. It is also difficult to pipe.

STANDARD GLACÉ ICING

8 oz. sieved icing sugar
3 dessertsp. warm water or
   stock syrup

1 scant tbs. lemon juice,
   strong coffee etc.

Beat together about 5 minutes until glossy, keeping the mixture just warm by standing mixing bowl or basin in a pan of hot water. This may be drawn from the hot tap, but must not be hotter than the hand can bear. Use wooden spoon to beat.

THIN GLACÉ ICING

As above but use two full tbs. liquid. The quantity will coat completely.

CHOCOLATE GLACÉ ICING

(for complete coating of top and sides.)

8 oz. icing sugar	2 heaped tbs. cocoa
3 tbs. hot water or warmed stock syrup	¼ oz. margarine, white shortening; or ½ tsp. salad oil

As above.

FOR PIPING GLACÉ ICING

Add extra sieved icing sugar until icing is just stiff enough for a piped line to hold its shape. (Test by putting a teaspoon of icing into a No. 2 icing tube and pressing it through with the ball of the thumb on to a slab or paper.)

This thicker icing is also useful for covering a cake top only where it is essential not to risk any runs down the sides. Spread quickly while still warm.

ALMOND PASTE

8 oz. ground almonds	½ beaten egg
4 oz. each icing and castor sugar *or*	1 dessertsp. lemon juice
2 oz. icing sugar, 6 oz. castor sugar	3 drops each vanilla and (optional) almond essence

NOTE: It is an improvement if about 1 oz. bitter almonds are included in the mixture. They must be blanched, chopped and pounded well.

Mix sugars and almonds. Add half the quantity of egg and the flavourings and begin kneading the paste. Add only as much egg as will just hold the paste together as a stiff dough. It is easy to get too much egg mixed in, when the paste is sticky, and extra sugar must be added to 'dry' it, thus spoiling the flavour.

For alternative almond paste recipe see chart p. 513.

ROYAL ICING

see chart p. 513.

NOTE: Acetic acid is the professional substance used to harden royal icing for piping. 2 to 3 drops per egg-white is the usual dose. Where a white-iced cake is to be kept some time lemon juice is thought to yellow the icing, hence the acid. However, lemon juice is perfectly acceptable for most purposes and has the advantage of offsetting the sweetness of the sugar.

Outline of Simple Icing Techniques

Foundations

SPONGES AND LIGHT CAKES (butter-cream or glacé icing). These should be brushed over with thin jam glaze. For top and sides of a 7 to 8 inch filled sponge, thin and warm 2 tbs. of standard glaze with ½ tsp. water. If making up specially, sieve 1 heaped tbs. jam into 1 dessertsp. hot water. Blend over low heat. Brush glaze on to cake while warm.

FRUIT CAKES (royal icing). Make or buy almond paste as the quantities in the table on p. 513. Then work as follows:

(1) Cut ball of paste in half and knead one half into a round, the other into a cylinder.

(2) Dust rolling area with icing sugar.

(3) Using the tin in which the cake was baked for a size

gauge, roll out the ball of paste to fit base of tin exactly (this will make it slightly larger than the top of cake). If cake is slightly domed in centre, make edge of circle thicker than centre to help level the top. If highly domed, shave off enough so that cake will stand well turned upside down.

(4) Brush top of cake with warmed standard glaze, then place cake, glaze downwards, on to circle of paste. Turn over and press paste gently on to cake, working it to a level top. Take care not to get crumbs on the paste as these can discolour royal icing.

(5) Roll, and work cylinder of paste with the hands, to a long strip almost the depth of the cake by almost the length of its circumference. This strip may be thinner than the paste on top.

(6) Brush sides of cake with glaze, stand it on its side on one end of the strip, gently turning it so that it 'picks up' the strip by means of the sticky glaze. The weight of the cake will act as rolling-pin to make the strip wider and longer to fit.

(7) Stand it on an upturned smaller tin or turn-table and, with hands cleaned of crumbs, press top and sides together all round to make a neat squared-off finish; and press with palms all round sides to mould paste well to cake. Finish by rolling a rolling-pin over top and round sides.

NOTE: If you are making an elaborate celebration cake well in advance of the date on which it is to be eaten, leave the almond-pasted cake for about a week, wrapped in greaseproof paper in a tin, not in polythene or plastic box, to harden and dry out a little. Fresh almond paste often exudes almond oil which can soak through icing and discolour it.

The foundations laid, you are now ready to ice and decorate.

Start Simply

One's first efforts at icing often take ages and fail to reach the standard one has hoped for. But remember that your own eye is drawn to the faults which seem to you glaring, whereas others see the general effect which seems to them charming. A plaster-like symmetry is not desirable in a home-made cake. Most icing faults are made worse by attempts at improvement, so leave well enough alone. You will soon get the knack, and each cake you make will improve.

BUTTER-CREAM ICING. This is the simplest to make and handle. Very pretty finishes and piping can be achieved with it, as well as good flavour since it will take quite a lot of liquid or dry flavouring without spoiling the texture.

Butter cream is, of course, the most widely-used filling for sandwich and layer cakes, and one of its great virtues is its adaptability. It can be made smoother or rougher by varying the proportion and type of sugars used; whipped cream or white of egg can be incorporated to give extra richness or lightness. Butter cream combines well with other sorts of finishes. For instance the top of a cake may be glacé iced, the sides jam-glazed and coated with toasted chopped nuts, while butter cream is used as a filling and a piped decoration.

As a rule piping in butter-cream is better for being simple and bold.

A very quick elegant finish may be applied to a plain single Victoria sponge by a topping of well-flavoured butter-cream marked into a pattern with a knife point or spoon-handle.

GLACÉ ICING. Sometimes called water icing, it takes a little experience to get the consistency just right for the work in hand. For complete coating I advise practising by using the thinner glacé icing, since it is easy then to see how it behaves when poured. This thin coating will be slightly transparent but, as there will be plenty of run-off, you can give a second coat when the first has had a short time to set.

Standard glacé icing gives a good opaque covering, and should be used for most purposes.

Points to watch with glacé icing are :

thorough sieving of icing-sugar,

temperature of water never to exceed what can be comfortably borne by the hand;

thorough beating to give gloss.

Some cooks add a few drops of salad oil to glacé icing to help gloss and spreading. Oil or other fat is usually added to chocolate glacé icing.

A 'skin' soon forms on glacé icing, so that if you need to

delay using it, store it in a completely airtight container such as a screwcap jar or plastic snap-cover vessel, and keep it in a warm atmosphere. Where only a slight skin forms this is easily beaten out. A wooden spoon is the best implement for beating glacé icing.

Where a cake top is not level it may be necessary to tilt the turn-table to make the icing flow, or use a palette knife to spread it. If the latter, use a dry knife and work quickly. Knife marks will soon vanish. Unless you have a great excess of icing, it is usually necessary to 'help' the icing cover the sides of a cake with a palette knife.

Avoid using fluted tins for cakes you intend to glacé ice, as the icing gets channelled into the grooves, and much knife work is needed to cover the flutes.

It is *essential*, to ensure a good finish, to jam-glaze a cake when the whole is to be coated with glacé icing.

Simple line and dot piping decorations can be done by using the standard proportions slightly thickened with a teaspoon or so of sieved icing sugar well beaten in.

Move glacé-iced cakes to their serving plates or cake-boards as soon as possible, for glacé icing cracks easily once set. For this reason, nuts or similar decorations should also be pressed into the coating quickly.

To cover sides of cake with chopped nuts, crushed caramel and similar finishes, jam glaze them rather thickly. Have the prepared nuts on a sheet of paper. Balance the cake on the palm of the hand and scoop up nuts on palette knife pressing them into sides, turning cake as needed. Surplus nuts fall back on to paper.

To cover tops of small cakes, glaze, and dip into nuts.

ROYAL ICING. For a quick single coating and simple finish use the quantities given in the table. Put almost all the icing on the top of the cake, spread it quickly with bold sweeps of a small palette knife until the top is completely covered by a thick even amount, then take the icing down the sides. Work with the cake on something that you can turn round easily.

If you are to pipe a decoration, get as smooth a finish as you can without fiddling.

For a fork finish see that coverage is even and thick, adding all the icing as you work.

For simple piping reserve about 2 to 4 good tablespoons according to size. For the filigree type of piping you will have to make up a quantity of the harder variety of icing – ¼ lb. (icing sugar) for light decoration; ½ lb. for 'encrusted' work. When royal icing has to be used in stages, keep it well covered with damp cloths or in airtight containers. You will do very well at a first attempt if you simply get your cake or cake-top covered with an even thickness of icing at the right consistency and clear of crumbs. If using royal icing, content yourself either with pulling up the coating all over in peaks with a fork, or piping a single edging of rosettes round the top and base, where cake and board join. With the aid of tweezers add, if you like, a silver ball in the centre of each rosette; a short candle tied with bow and sprig of holly for Christmas; a key – real or artificial – for a twenty-first birthday. A miniature posy of fresh flowers in a liqueur glass; a china black cat; 'boughten' candle holders; all are perfectly creditable ways of finishing celebration cakes.

Do a 'practice write' in icing first on paper cut to the same size and shape as the cake; or mark in a name, a date or wording, faintly with pencil (on hard-set icing), or skewer (on soft icing) and then outline it in silver balls or other edible decoration.

Basic Equipment for Piping

The novice will be able to pipe quite an array of patterns and decorations with merely five icing tubes:

A fine or medium writing tube (Nos. 1 or 2) – fine butter, glacé, royal.

A medium or small rope tube (Nos. 5 or 20) – fine butter, royal.

A wide-ribbed band tube (No. 34) or shell tube (No. 12) – fine butter, royal.

An 8- or 12-star tube (Nos. 8 or 21) – fine butter, royal.

A large petal tube (No. 11) or rose tube (No. 18) – royal.

(The full confectioners' set has thirty-seven varieties. The numbers are different.)

Also: an 8-star meringue (or vegetable) tube – butter, meringue.

Icing tubes are made to fit four sorts of icing holder these days: metal syringe, icing bag with screw fitting, icing bag with plain end; or home-made paper icing bags. The latter are useful where one is decorating in very small amounts of several colours, but they must be very precisely made or they fall apart (see diagram p. 535).

It is impossible to advise anyone that a metal syringe or a bag will suit them best. It is what you get used to with a vengeance. Some cooks say they have more control of the flow of icing from a bag, others think the warmth of the hand through a bag varies the consistency of the icing disconcertingly.

A bag with screw fitting is a good idea, since one can change the tube easily, but many professional confectioners favour the delicate narrowness of paper bags with plain tubes. Paper bags may be bought, but only by the gross and as part of a big trade order. But you might persuade a local baker who specializes in wedding cakes to sell you a small quantity. Make up enough home-made bags before beginning work.

For most amateurs, however, there can be no question that seamless nylon bags are a boon. You will probably need a couple of 9-inch and a 12-inch, the latter for handling the larger amounts of meringue or butter cream.

The ambitious will also need one or two flower nails and a net nail for piping roses and other filigree decorations. However, before buying icing equipment it would be wise to write to the Tala people (address on p. 556), for leaflets on icing. These give a good indication of the range of equipment and what it will accomplish; or they will be able to tell you where their nearest icing centre is, so that you can inspect equipment on the spot. In writing indicate briefly the extent of your ambition – for example, if you are proposing to ice a wedding cake or intend only to pipe children's names on a simple background.

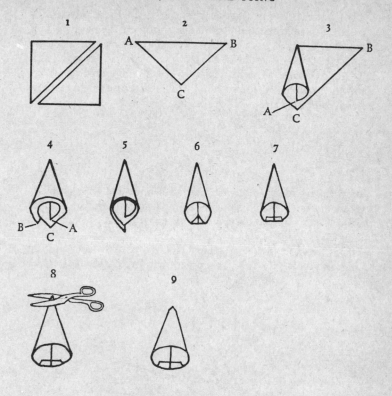

MAKING A PAPER PIPING BAG

Steps 1 to 7. Cut 8 to 10 inch square of thick greaseproof or tracing paper. Halve it crosswise to make two triangles. (Thin paper may be used doubled; will not last well). In turn, draw up points A and B to C to overlap exactly, and meet in straight line down centre of cone formed. Bag may unwind if not done neatly. Double over three-ply point outwards to secure for strongest finish. Cut straight across point about ¼ inch from end to use with metal icing tubes. Cut as in diags. 8 and 9 to make writing and leaf or petal 'nozzles'. Merest fraction usually enough for writing; fine-texture icings only.

ICING SYRINGES. Whether plastic or metal, these are operated by pressure from the thumb through a ring on the plunger, first and second fingers going either through two rings each side on top, or resting on the side of the narrower syringes. As with bags, the ends of tubes must be kept moist, and where different tubes are being alternated, those not in immediate use must be completely kept from air.

How to Pipe

As with any other handcraft, there is a right and wrong way to go about handling the tools and material for piping. For practice use mashed potato or *beurre manié*. (That'll make you get the lumps out)

Bags, whether nylon or paper, must be pressed from the top only. In guiding the tube, if squeezed midway down, or clutched

Correct handhold for small bag

above the metal end, the icing will be forced up out of the top. As the icing is used, the emptied part of the bag must be twisted or folded down close to the filled part. The right hand (in right-handed people) controls the pressure, which makes the designs. The left is merely used as a rest or a guide, as in the diagram on p. 536. You should never let the fingers of the left hand touch any part of the icing bag except where it covers the metal tube. This way you avoid the trouble caused when the right hand doesn't know what the left is doing! A few simple things may be piped entirely from paper (see 8 and 9 in diagram on p. 535).

To pipe a rosette keep star tube vertical and a little above surface. For big rosettes raise tube fractionally as you apply pressure, but keep over same spot. (For fine butter; royal.)

To make a shell border, shell tube must be at angle close to surface. Press and pull sharply away, pressure off, to make point of shell. Overlap each single shell. (For fine butter and royal icing.)

To pipe scrolls, hold star tube at angle, close to surface, keep pressure and movement even until scroll is complete. Take pressure off and pull tube quickly up to leave only tiny point – removable if liked later. (Fine butter; royal.)

To pipe a simple heavy border use star, rope or ribbon tube and double up as you go round. (For fine butter and royal icing.)

To lay on straight lines – as for lattice or basket – hold plain tub or paper bag at angle, touch down end of icing thread to anchor, then, well raised from surface, press steadily, moving bag or syringe towards you above where line is to go. When desired length of thread is reached, relax pressure as you slightly lower bag or syringe, when thread will drop on to surface. (For fine butter, royal and glacé for decoration flat on surface; royal only for filigree work.)

MARBLING. Usually for royal or glacé icings, method can be used to pattern surface of butter-cream. Also, though pattern will blur somewhat, adapt for marbling cream on to surface of soups, fools etc. (see diagram on next page).

1. Put on base coat in first colour; if glacé allow to drip first to avoid 'pulling' pattern

2. Pipe second colour in thin parallel lines across top (or in a spiral from centre to circumference)

3. Draw point of knife at right angles lightly through the lines first one way, then the other, at equidistances (or for spiral from centre outwards, then circumference inwards), pulling lines into points, making feather pattern. Variations may be tried.

WARNING: Never leave icing uncovered in piping tubes. Should it dry out completely, soak ½ hour in warm water before trying to clean tube or you may damage the tube in trying to get it off. When working with several tubes and colours have a folded damp cloth to hand and insert the tubes between the layers. If working in this way you would probably be using small quantities with paper icing bags, when the entire bag and tube should be kept in a bowl or on a plate covered with a damp cloth.

Preserves

••

Jams and pickles are among the oldest preserved foods. That fruit conserved by boiling in heavy syrup must be spread on bread or cooked in pastry before eating, while fruit preserved by scalding in medium syrup may be eaten alone, is a British oddity; made still odder by the further gloss that if the conserved fruits are oranges they should be consumed only at breakfast. In other countries jams are eaten as puddings or sweetmeats. But one English refinement deserves praise: the serving of jam with whipped and clotted cream must be counted a gastronomic triumph.

This section makes no attempt to be exhaustive. The Ready Reckoner tables on pp. 549–55 cover the most popular jams made from fruits grown in the average kitchen garden and found in most shops, or available growing wild; with the addition of marmalade and a few less-known but interesting recipes for pickles and sauces. Those with large kitchen gardens or access to cheap abundance of crops should get the Ministry of Agriculture booklet on domestic preservation for a comprehensive account of bottling, canning and freezing as well.

General Information

To be used in conjunction with the Ready Reckoner table as well as the other recipes.

(1) If you have to buy your raw materials, do a costing first. Where a very good kind of jam or pickle is on sale in the locality at an average price, it may not pay you to give the time or money to home preservation. In costing the job charge your own labour at – to say the least – the current local rate per hour for domestic help. You may find your time would be better spent on something else – dressmaking, house-painting and so on.

At the time of writing, for instance, one can buy first-class South African apricot jam in 2 lb. tins for much less and better than you can make it. There are Polish, Hungarian and Yugoslav jams of several kinds hardly less good than home-made, and several pence a pound cheaper than the cost of the ingredients alone, without counting labour or fuel.

Tomato ketchup is worth making only if you grow the tomatoes.

(2) The recipes given here are based on the scientific facts of sugar-boiling. Correct weighing or proportions are essential. (For the science-mad : jam sets only when the sugar has reached a concentration of 65 per cent.)

You do not make more jam or pickles by adding extra liquid or sugar. Add the first, and you merely stand about waiting until it has evaporated by boiling. Or, if it is not evaporated you will have a runny mouldy preserve. Add extra sugar, and you will have hard, crystallized jam, the fruit flavour of which will be spoiled. Add the correct combination of extra sugar *and* liquid and you may get fractionally more volume of the preserve, but it will be sweeter and runnier than when in perfection.

(3) Barely ripe fruit is best. Over-ripe fruit should be avoided. 1 tbs. lemon juice per lb. of fruit helps the set if fruit is fully ripe.

(4) Timings are given for preserves made in a wide preserving pan. Where a saucepan is used 5 to 10 minutes longer fast boiling may be needed.

(5) Thick pans are essential for making preserves. Where large amounts are to be made in saucepans they may need to be made in two lots otherwise boiling over is likely.

(6) Fast boiling should be maintained, but all the same the heat should not be kept up at the maximum.

(7) Once the preserve has come to boil stir only very slowly with a wooden spoon in a figure of eight, always scraping the spoon well over bottom of pan. This method ensures that the whole surface of the pan is stirred, and any sticking soon detected.

(8) Testing – For those who own a sugar thermometer : jam sets at a temperature of 220° F while on the boil.

Otherwise, in my experience, the 'wrinkle' test is the most satis-factory. Drop a little of the syrupy part of the jam on to a cold thick saucer; stand in cold air about 30 seconds, push with little finger nail; if wrinkles form the jam is done. But they must be wrinkles, not figments of hope or imagination born of a (natural) wish to clear up and go to bed. Nothing is more depressing, not to say wasteful of time, work and materials, than having to de-pot and re-boil preserves that have been undercooked.

(9) Potting needs orderly arrangement to be done neatly, quickly and with the minimum of clearing up afterwards. Pots or bottles must be thoroughly clean and dry. They need not be heated, but should be in the warmth of the kitchen beforehand. You need a filling area covered with clean newspaper on which 4 to 6 pots can be stood, with the other pots to hand; space next to filling area where preserving pan can be placed without risk of tipping or of damaging the surface; a smallish jug or cup for filling; waxed circles for top of jam; a damp cloth.

NOTE: Cellophane or similar outer coverings should either be put on jam at once when it is almost boiling, or next day when it is completely cold.

(10) Store all jams in a dry and, as far as possible, cool atmo-sphere.

Fast, Foolproof Marmalade

(Four varieties.)

These marmalades are not designed for winning prizes at the local flower show, where appearance seems to be rated higher than taste and keeping quality. (I once came out 'top' at a show with a lemon jelly marmalade, recipe supplied by sponsors. On the day there it stood, clear as champagne, a perfect set, with its needle shreds floating elegantly. It was so sweet we couldn't bear it for breakfast, and I decided to reserve it for puddings or tea. A week later it had turned to London fog, and deliquesced. It ended on the compost heap.) This basic recipe produces a thick marmalade of truly orange flavour, with the tangerine note in No. 2 distinct, *plus a good tang*. It will keep certainly for two years in perfect condition if correctly made and stored. The names given to these marmalades are partly family jokes, but make them easier to distinguish in the store cupboard. Make up your own names.

Quantities given here are for those who want to try several at once. To make 12 to 14 lb. of one kind treble the quantity and be prepared to fast-boil for 25 to 30 minutes. In making several kinds do the preliminary cooking of fruit in separate pans so that the cooking liquids receive only the flavours intended. The longest and most tedious job is picking out the pips. Even so, making the basic amount of each of the three kinds, or a large quantity of one kind, can be completed, from wiping fruit to clearing up, in four hours. Yield: about 1 lb. marmalade per orange or lemon, depending on size, type (thick or thin skin) and condition; 2 large tangerines will replace 1 orange, but you cannot make a satisfactory marmalade if you overdo the tangerine amount.

NOTE: Most marmalade oranges on sale these days are very spongy. If possible buy from a greengrocer who will let you pick out your own, when prefer a smaller hard orange to a giant spongy orange. Not all so-called Sevilles are genuine, but this can't be helped. Often the second shiploads, arriving towards the end of January, are better. But don't wait to make marmalade until mid-February when the oranges on sale may well have been in the shop for two or three weeks and are going off.

1. ORANGE MARMALADE – Basic Recipe

4 Seville oranges
1 lemon
2 lb. granulated or preserving
   sugar
1 pint liquid in which fruit has boiled
about 1 lb. sugar in reserve
   in case needed

     } Approx. – see directions

(1) Wipe fruit and put whole into large saucepan. Hold down and add water well to cover.

(2) Bring just to boiling point and simmer very gently 2 hours – *not less*, or shreds will harden when sugar is added.

(3) Lift fruit from liquid on draining spoon and weigh.

(4) In preserving or thick pan put 2 lb. sugar for each 1 lb. fruit. To this add 1 pint of liquid in which fruit was boiled for each lb. fruit. If there is not enough liquid, make up amount with water. Put on *very low* heat to dissolve sugar while you prepare fruit. From time to time scrape over bottom of pan with wooden spoon to find unmelted sugar When found stir very gently. When no more grittiness is felt sugar will have melted, when you can add the prepared fruit.

(5) Cut the fruit into quarters and remove pips. (These may be tied in muslin and added to pan if liked.) Scrape pulp off peel on to a plate or bowl. Either put peel through coarsest plate of mincer, or chop or slice to size preferred. Add all to pan when sugar is melted.

(6) Boil up, stirring slowly and continue boiling briskly, though not furiously, 15 minutes. Remove pan from heat and test. If not set continue boiling 1 minute at a time until test is satisfactory. While testing keep pan off heat or marmalade may overcook. The wastage at this stage can be surprising. There is also a risk of it burning.

2. SUMMER MARMALADE

For the idea of the tangerine peel I am indebted to Mrs Joan Hornsey who also first pointed out to me the common sense of putting the peel through the mincer – a great time-saver. This is often advised now, but was not when she and I began marmalading.

Ingredients as 1. except for the replacement of one orange by 2 to 3 tangerines or satsumas etc. or the peel of about 4, plus juice of 1 medium-sized sweet orange. Peel from Christmas tangerines will keep about two weeks in polythene in a refrigerator, but tangerines are usually still in the shops in January.

Method as for above, but add tangerines (or peel) ½ hour later than rest of fruit, as they can cook to a mush.

3. WINTER MARMALADE

5 Seville oranges
2 lb. demerara sugar $\left.\vphantom{\begin{matrix}a\\b\\c\end{matrix}}\right\}$ approx.,
¾ pint of liquid in which fruit has boiled $\qquad$ see Basic Recipe

As for 1. At fast-boiling stage 2 to 3 minutes longer may be needed, and yield may be slightly less than 1. and 2., owing to setting qualities of sugar.

4. HANGOVER MARMALADE

4 Seville oranges
juice and pips of 1 lemon
1 lb. 14 oz. demerara sugar
2 oz. soft brown or 'pieces' sugar $\left.\vphantom{\begin{matrix}a\\b\\c\\d\end{matrix}}\right\}$ approx.,
¾ pint liquid in which fruit has boiled $\qquad$ see Basic Recipe

Method and yield as 3.

Covering Pickles

Porosan film is useful if bottle tops or vinegar disks for jars are lacking. The newer type of commercial pickle jars and tops, if unbattered, can be used several times over for pickles and sauces if carefully washed, dried and stored after use.

TOMATO KETCHUP

Yield about 4 pints.

4 lb. tomatoes
½ pint vinegar
scant ½ oz. chillies
1 tsp. crushed allspice
1 tsp. cloves or
3 drops clove oil

½ lb. onions
6–8 oz. sugar
1 dessertsp. salt
½ tsp. paprika
½ oz. garlic

Slice tomatoes and start their juice running in thick pan over very low heat. Add peeled garlic and peeled, quartered onions, and simmer until onion is tender – about 2½ hours. Sieve. Return to pan, add vinegar, powdered spices and salt, whole spices tied in muslin. Cook rapidly 35 minutes, stirring occasionally, until thick. Add sugar, turning down heat until it is dissolved. Boil rapidly 10 to 15 minutes. If clove oil is used, add now. Pour into warmed, sterilized bottles or jars and cork, tie down or cover at once.

PICKLED DAMSONS

2 lb. damsons	3 blades mace
2 lb. sugar	1-inch stick cinnamon
¼ pint cider, white or wine vinegar (elderflower vinegar is delicious if available)	½ tsp. allspice berries crushed slightly between 2 old metal spoons

Pierce damsons with needle. Put them in china or enamel vessel with the sugar, spices and vinegar, and leave 2 days. Bring very gently just to simmering point and leave with water *barely moving*, 10 to 15 minutes. Asbestos mat advised. Can be put in Low oven. Put into pickle jars while hot and seal at once. Do not eat for 1 month, however tempted. Always serve sparingly – a great delicacy and not for the unappreciative. Excellent with roast game, grilled or boiled gammon. After a few months the liquid becomes jellied and the pickle still better.

PLUM CHUTNEY

You are warned that this is a very hot number indeed, even if not positively up to Bombay standards. It will delight anyone who mourns the faded glories of Worcester Sauce. The recipe comes from the first cookery book I owned, the imprint page and part of the index of which are now missing. (On two occasions, about a week or so after I passed on the recipe I have seen it in print in the local paper of the district in question so evidently those who try it think highly of it.) This is a chutney that seems to go with the most unexpected dishes – for instance grilled fish, kedgeree, corned beef hash, some kinds of risotti. Best eaten in small dabs, its bite seems to enhance rather than drown subtle flavours. As a situation-saver for devils or curries that haven't quite struck your usual high note you will find it invaluable. (Stir a spoonful in before dishing.)

2 lb. plums	½ oz. garlic
½ lb. apples	½ oz. ground ginger
¾ lb. brown sugar	¼ oz. dried small chillies
1 lb. seedless raisins or sultanas	1 pint brown malt vinegar

Halve and stone plums, pare core and chop apples roughly. Peel garlic and chop coarsely. Chop chillies. Mix all ingredients in large thick pan or preserving pan, bring to boil and cook briskly until thick – about 25 to 35 minutes. Put into jars and cover down when cold.

SPICED VINEGAR FOR PICKLING ONIONS, GREEN BEANS ETC.

1 pint white or cider vinegar	1 level tsp. salt
2 cloves garlic	1 level dessertsp. brown sugar (optional)
1 oz. pickling spices (from Boots, or good grocers)	

Peel and coarsely chop garlic. Add with all other ingredients to vinegar in pan. Barely simmer on whisper of heat, covered, for 1½ to 2 hours. Leave, to mature the flavour, from 24 hours to 1 week, sealed in jar in cool place.

Prepare:
onions by scalding and peeling.
beans by topping, tailing and cutting into inch lengths.
beetroot by cooking (if bought raw) ½ to 2 hours according

to size, then peeling and cubing, slicing or leaving whole, also according to size and preference.

cabbage or cauliflower by shredding or separating florets, soaking 2 days in brine (½ lb. salt to 2 quarts water).

cucumber and onion by slicing thinly.

Bring spiced vinegar to boil. Pack vegetable chosen into jars, and pour hot liquid over to fill jar to brim. Cover when cold.

ELIZA ACTON'S HAMBURGH PICKLE FOR PORK, TONGUE, HAM, BEEF

Boil together for 20 minutes 2 quarts water, ¾ lb. sea salt (for preference), ½ lb. sugar, ½ oz. each saltpetre and crushed black peppercorns, latter tied in muslin; clear scum as it rises, remove muslin, pour pickle into deep earthen crock, and when cold lay in meat, which must be completely immersed. Turn meat occasionally. Tongue, and belly of pork need only up to three days according to thickness. Rounds of beef between 5 days and a fortnight, according to size, but approximately 1 day per lb. (More pickle would be needed for large joints or hams.) Re-use the pickle for up to 3 months, then add half quantity of ingredients to liquid and re-boil. (E.A.'s original quantity was for 2 gallons.)

Pickling Eggs

When plentiful prices drop, making pickling eggs profitable, as well as handy since they can be used for all cooking except boiling. As they get older they are less acceptable fried, because they can 'taste' though not in cakes or other dishes. Whites, which sometimes thicken or go watery, will whip, but need care when separating.

Water glass is a powder mixed as directed, bought from chemist. Needs larder floor space, but is cheap. Mix in a pail into which eggs are lowered until full – several dozen per 2-gallon pail. Re-usable.

Oteg is a patent liquid paraffin wax, sold with its own dipper. Pour some into tea-cup, dip and drain each egg on cake-rack, store in ordinary egg-cartons in cool cupboard or larder. 1 tin does dozens, as surplus is poured back. The liquid keeps, if tin is well closed and stored, for years.

A JAM-MAKING READY RECKONER

Ingredients and Yield	Preparation	Cooking time before sugar boils	Fast boils after sugar has melted
APPLE AND BLACKBERRY			
Yield around 10 lb.	Peel, core, cut apples in thick pieces, and simmer to pulp in half the water.		
4 lb. blackberries	Add blackberries and rest of water and simmer until fruits are completely blended.	30 minutes	
2 lb. sour apples (windfalls)			
½ pint water		20 minutes	
1–2 tbs. lemon juice (according to sourness of apples)	Add sugar, stir in and keep below simmering point until melted, stirring occasionally very gently. Fast boil, test and pot as general notes.	20 to 30 minutes	20 to 25 minutes
6 lb. sugar			
DRIED APRICOT			
Yield around 5 lb.	Wash fruit in cold water to remove grit. Soak in measured water 24 hours. Add juice and simmer till tender.		
1 lb. dried apricots			
3 pints water		35 to 45 minutes	
3 lb. sugar	Add sugar, and dissolve and finish as above.	20 to 30 minutes	15 to 20 minutes
juice 1 lemon			
1 oz. almonds (bitter are good if liked)			

Ingredients and Yield	Preparation	Cooking time before sugar boils	Fast boils after sugar has melted
BLACKCURRANT Yield around 10 lb. 4 lb. blackcurrants 2 pints water for best flavour 3 pints for greater bulk. 6 lb. sugar	Stalk fruit and simmer in measured water until tender. Add sugar and proceed as for apple and blackberry.	45 minutes 20 to 30 minutes	2 to 5 minutes according to ripeness
GOOSEBERRY Yield around 7 lb. 3 lb. green gooseberries 1½ pints water 4 lb. sugar	Top, tail and wash fruit. Simmer in measured water until fruit splits. Mash fruit somewhat, add sugar and proceed as apple and blackberry.	35 to 45 minutes 20 to 30 minutes	5 to 10 minutes according to ripeness

GREENGAGE – *see* PLUM

LOGANBERRY – *see* RASPBERRY

MARROW

Yield around 7 lb.
4 lb. fully ripened marrow weighed after paring and seeding
grated rind and juice of 3 lemons
4 lb. sugar
2 oz. root ginger
2 oz. preserved ginger

Simmer peel and seeds of marrow in water just to cover (about 25 minutes).

Cut marrow into ½-inch cubes. Chop the preserved ginger. Put marrow in large bowl in layers with sugar, ginger, grated rind and lemon juice. Strain liquid from peel and allow ¼ pint to each 1 lb. marrow. Add to basin. Leave 24 hours. Turn all into preserving pan, adding stem ginger, crushed and tied in muslin. Heat to melt sugar.

Simmer until marrow becomes transparent and the liquid becomes a thick syrup. — 20 minutes

Remove ginger. Finish as usual. — 40 to 45 minutes — no fast boil

PLUM

Yield around 7 lb.
4 lb. plums
½ pint water
4 lb. sugar

Wash, halve and stone fruit. (Crack stones, skin and add kernels with sugar.) Simmer fruit till tender. — 20 minutes

Add sugar, and proceed as blackberry and apple. — 20 to 30 minutes — 10 to 15 minutes

RASPBERRY

Yield around 7 lb.
4 lb. raspberries
4 lb. sugar

Simmer fruit till tender. — 15 minutes

Add sugar and melt as for apple and blackberry.
Fast boil — 20 to 30 minutes — 7 to 10 minutes

Ingredients and Yield	Preparation	Cooking time before sugar boils	Fast boils after sugar has melted
RHUBARB Yield around 7 lb. 4 lb. rhubarb (prepared) grated rind and juice of 2 lemons, 2 oranges 4 lb. sugar 2 oz. stem ginger	Cut fruit into 1-inch lengths. Put in bowl in layers with sugar, rind and juice. Leave 24 hours. Turn into preserving pan, adding ginger crushed and tied in muslin. Melt sugar. Boil fast till liquid forms thick syrup.	20 minutes	15 to 20 minutes
STRAWBERRY Yield about 5½ lb. 4 lb. small strawberries juice of 1 lemon 3 lb. sugar	Rinse fruit by putting in colander and running cold tap through it gently. Spread on plates to dry out somewhat before hulling. Put into preserving pan with juice and sugar and heat very gently to melt sugar. Fast boil.	About 30 minutes to melt sugar, which is added with fruit to harden it, and this keeps strawberries whole.	10 to 15 minutes
APPLE JELLY – *see* GOOSEBERRY JELLY			
	Cut out bad patches, cut in halves if using windfalls. Simmer to pulp. Proceed as Bramble.	30 minutes	10 minutes

552

BRAMBLE JELLY

Yield around 4–5 lb.

4 lb. brambles
4 tbs. lemon juice
pared rind of 2 lemons
1 tsp. crushed allspice berries or
1 inch stick cinnamon
1 lb. sugar per pint of strained juice

Put unwashed brambles in pan with water barely to cover. Add juice, rind and spice. Simmer to pulp. Strain through jelly bag, measure juice and put into preserving pan with sugar. Heat only enough to melt sugar.

45 minutes

Fast boil, skim and pot quickly.

20 minutes

10 to 15 minutes

GOOSEBERRY JELLY

Yield around 4½ lb.

2 lb. green gooseberries
1½ pints water
1 lb. sugar per pint of strained juice

Wash fruit, but do not stalk etc. Simmer to pulp.
Strain through jelly bag, allow 1 lb. sugar per pint of juice.

45 minutes

Finish as Bramble.

20 minutes

5 minutes

MINT JELLY (for meat)

Yield as Gooseberry Jelly
Apple or Gooseberry Jelly
1 tbs. lemon juice or
white cider, or wine vinegar and
1 tbs. finely chopped mint per lb.
of sugar used.

Make apple or gooseberry jelly near to setting point, throw in mint and lemon juice, and complete as bramble.

Time as for apple or gooseberry

Time as for apple or gooseberry

553

Ingredients and Yield	Preparation	Cooking time before sugar boils	Fast boils after sugar has melted
REDCURRANT JELLY (for meat or game) Yield around 2½ lb. 3 lb. currants 1 lb. sugar per pint of juice	Pick over and rinse fruit. Do not stalk. Barely cover in cold water and simmer to pulp. Proceed as Bramble.	35 to 40 minutes	3 to 5 minutes (approx.)
ROWAN JELLY (Mountain Ash berries) (for meat or game) Yield around 6 small pots. 3 lb. berries just beyond orange stage 1 lb. sugar per pint juice	Wash and pick over berries. Simmer till tender. Proceed as Bramble.	40 minutes	10 minutes
CRANBERRY JELLY (for meat or poultry) *American recipe, more akin to cheese. Not clear.* Yield around 4 small pots. 2 cups each cranberries, sugar, boiling water	Pick over and wash fruit. Add water and simmer, sieve the whole to make a soft purée. Heat 3 minutes. Add sugar, dissolve it completely. Boil up 2 minutes. Pot in small pots. For immediate use may be set in egg cups (allowing 1 per person) or similar and turned out for serving.	20 minutes 7 minutes	2 minutes

DAMSON CHEESE

Yield around 3 lb.

2 lb. damsons
1 pint water
3 lb. sugar
kernels of fruit or ½ oz. bitter
almonds blanched and split
(optional)

(This method avoids the waste, mess and difficulty of trying to sieve pulp from stones.)

555

Put damsons in cocotte in oven set at 275° F, gas 1. Leave until skins split and juice runs a little.   1 hour

Cool overnight. Next day put water and sugar in preserving pan on very low heat, pouring in any juice from damsons. Stir occasionally while stoning fruit, (use small knife and fork to stone). Sieve stoned pulp and add to pan when sugar is melted.   30 to 45 minutes

Heat to fast boil and cook until jam is very thick and hisses when spoon is drawn across bottom of pan. Care not to burn.   15 minutes

ADDRESS BOOK

General Equipment

William Page & Co. Ltd, Shaftesbury Avenue, London W1.

Leon Jaeggi & Sons Ltd, 232 Tottenham Court Road, London W1.

Both above have catalogues although chiefly for caterers.

Tala Kitchen and Housewares, Taylor Law & Co. Ltd, Tala Works, Stourbridge, Worcs.

This firm issues a special booklet for the domestic market, very fully illustrated, of most of their goods. Send s.a. envelope 4½" x 6½", with request if needed, for local stockists, as Tala will not sell direct to you. For icing queries special section – Anne Anson Advisory Service, same address. Ask stockist for items not listed in booklet, as the firm does hundreds.

Kitchen Scales

H. Fereday & Sons Ltd, Shafesbury Works, 45 Holloway Road, London N7.

For stockists of Weylux domestic scales. Leaflets available.

French Kitchenware

Londoners can find plenty of choice in the big stores, and shops like Habitat; the latter issues attractive mail-order lists. Messrs. Clarbat will also supply names of stockists for Le Creuset, Mijoska simmerers and other items.

Habitat, 77 Fulham Road, SW3. Clarbat, 302 Barrington Road, SW9.

Extractor fan advice

Vent-Axia, 60 Rochester Row, SW1.

Ask for stockists, but in doubtful cases for representative to call and advise.

Garden Seeds

Samuel Dobie & Son Ltd, 11 Grosvenor Street, Chester.

Huge list of familiar vegetables, special varieties, rarities; herbs; also Bunyards specialities, for which ask specially.

Thompson & Morgan, Ipswich.

Familiar and rarer vegetables, herbs.

Most big food manufacturers, many British organizations and foreign trading organizations have useful leaflets about their products, with cooking advice and recipes. Their leaflets, with addresses, are sometimes to be found on the counter at your local shops. For example, British (P.I.D.A.) Danish and Polish pork and bacon producers have literature of this kind. Stork Margarine's almost constitute a miniature library. Watch for offers of this sort of literature in advertisements.

INDEX

558